Methodism and Society
in the
Twentieth Century

METHODISM AND SOCIETY

Volume II

Methodism and Society in the Twentieth Century

Walter G. Muelder

Edited by the Board of Social and Economic Relations
of The Methodist Church and Published by

Abingdon Press

NEW YORK   •   NASHVILLE

METHODISM AND SOCIETY IN THE TWENTIETH CENTURY

SET UP, PRINTED, AND BOUND BY THE
PARTHENON PRESS, AT NASHVILLE,
TENNESSEE, UNITED STATES OF AMERICA

Introduction

IN THE CONCLUSION OF HIS CLASSICAL STUDY OF *The Social Teaching of the Christian Churches,* Ernst Troeltsch made the remark: "Faith is the source of energy in the struggle of life, but life still remains a battle which is continually renewed upon ever new fronts." If Troeltsch were alive today, he would find ample confirmation of this statement in the upheavals of the twentieth century. The arena of the social struggle has become global. Myriads of human beings in Asia, Africa, and Latin America have seen a glimpse of a better life and are rising to claim their share in the resources of the earth. Revolutions in expectations are breeding revolutions of the social order. Changes which once took centuries are now telescoped into decades. Modern science and technology are providing unprecedented opportunities for the enhancement of life or for totalitarian regimentation of human ants. The entire globe is an explosive "area of rapid social change" from which no country is exempt. In an interdependent world, the battle for freedom from hunger and misery, from diseases and illiteracy, from injustice and tyranny, from the threat of atomic annihilation, is everybody's concern and everybody's responsibility.

Does the Christian faith furnish a "source of energy" and a sense of urgency and direction in this new battle for the dignity and welfare, no longer of particular groups of underprivileged alone, but of every member of the human race? It must frankly be acknowledged that the churches, as often in the past, are disappointingly slow in their response to swiftly changing situations and weak and divided in their social witness. For many Christians, the world-transforming power of the gospel is reduced to the virtue of social respectability.

Yet, in the longer perspectives of history, it must also gratefully be recognized that this century has witnessed an almost miraculous

5

upsurge of social concern in widening Christian circles. The labors
of the pioneers of the American social gospel movement and related
endeavors in Europe, though often decried by advocates of a theological and economic status quo, have not been without fruit. From an
irritant, the movement has turned into a ferment. From an act of
prophetic revolt, it has developed into an impressive range of official
and unofficial program activities of the churches—largely reformist
and educational, it is true, yet not insensitive to the urgings of the
prophets to translate "social creeds" into bolder and more costly
deeds.

Acceptance of social responsibility on the part of the churches,
however variously conceived, has to such an extent become a part of
American culture that it is easy to overlook its comparative novelty.
A glance at the international scene furnishes an even more telling
indication of the truly amazing growth of social awareness within
the short span of a few decades. When the Methodist Episcopal
Church and the Federal Council of the Churches of Christ in America in 1908 adopted the "Social Creed," such a step would have been
unacceptable to most Protestant and Eastern Orthodox bodies on
other continents. The first ecumenical world conference on Practical
Christianity, held in Stockholm in 1925, was above all a stirring con-
fession of the failure of the Christian churches to live up to their
mission in society. But one needs to have only the slightest acquaintance with the program of the World Council of Churches, a generation later, to become aware of the extent to which the struggle for
a responsible society has become a commonly accepted obligation.
The huge project currently undertaken by the World Council on
"The Common Christian Responsibility Toward Areas of Rapid Social Change" is a very instructive illustration of this change of
mind.

The progressive leavening of the life of the denominations and the
growth in sensitivity and professional expertness, which characterize the movement of social Christianity at home and abroad today,
are doubtless in part a response to the pervasive pressures of history. But they also reflect profound changes in the Church's
understanding of its own life and mission. A few of these changing
emphases may be listed in summary fashion:

(1) There is a new emphasis on the Church—the people of God,
the body of Christ—as a corporate agent of social criticism and redemption. Its primary impact on society does not reside in its social
teachings and program activities. Its impact derives above all from
its very existence in the world as a community of believers and from

the redemptive radiance of their life in prayer and worship, in Christian self-discipline, and in care for the neighbor near and afar. (2) The gospel of salvation is the opposite of religious individualism; it is social because it is personal. Its concern is not with disembodied souls nor with material progress without soul, but with the wholeness of man-in-community. (3) The Christian social witness becomes relevant and effective in the myriads of decisions and actions of laymen and lay women as they seek to live out their faith in the rough-and-tumble of everyday life. The Evanston Assembly of the World Council of Churches in 1954 offered a pointed formulation of this view: "The real battles of the faith today are being fought in factories, shops, offices, and farms, in political parties and government agencies, in countless homes, in the press, radio and television, in the relationship of nations." (4) There is also a growing recognition that social prophecy, in order not to remain a pious but ineffectual gesture, must be instrumented by social and political realism and translated into strategic planning. In the complexities of an increasingly organized and technicized society, the scattered efforts of individuals and small groups in immediate situations do not suffice. Christian efforts need to be co-ordinated in an all-inclusive strategy—a strategy which rests on an incisive diagnosis of national values and evils, which projects Christian imperatives into captivating and realizable goals, and which knows how to utilize the decision-making processes in an organized society.

The last point is worth stressing. Despite its flourishing busyness, the Christian social witness is caught up in a grave though mostly unavowed crisis. The root cause of the crisis lies, no doubt, in the fact that the "source of energy in the struggle of life" (to quote again Troeltsch's phrase) for many Christians has lost its transforming dynamism. But there is also a disturbing feeling that much of the Christian social witness is "beating the air"—not only because it is often hesitant and weak but because it has become uncertain of its target. Hampered by social and ethical myopia, Christian groups are slow to recognize that the battlefield of social responsibility has become vastly expanded and more complex. A missionary strategist once remarked: "The devil never laughs so heartily as when he succeeds in luring devout Christians to concentrate their efforts on secondary fronts. For then he has the central front, unguarded, all to himself." Though some may take exception to the language, no one can deny the pertinency of this observation in a time when the configuration of the battle is under-going such swift and extraordinary changes.

It is not without reason, therefore, that Christian leaders are pay-ing increasing attention to broader questions of aims and goals and the attendant problems of long-range planning. What are the pur-poses of this nation? What are the purposes of the Christian Church in and beyond the nation? To be sure, there is a legitimate place for particular "causes" and "emphases." But, in the opinion of many, the present situation calls for an imaginative attempt to rethink larger priorities. To take an illustration, are those right who sug-gest that the overriding Christian social concerns in the years ahead should be world peace under law, a more equitable partnership in utilizing the abundant material and technological resources of the earth, and the population explosion?

It is in this world context that the project on *Methodism and Society* is set. Like other Christian bodies, Methodism is challenged to ponder the lessons of its heritage, to redefine its social motiva-tions and ideals, to assess its present activities and resources, and to project adequate strategies for more vigorous advance. The MESTA[1] study is an exploratory contribution to this task. Although it is chiefly concerned with the interaction of Methodism and Ameri-can society, its broad Protestant approach, it is hoped, will commend it to the attention of social-minded Christians in other denominations as well.

Following the invitation from the Board of Social and Economic Relations, the committee appointed by the Boston University School of Theology faculty prepared a prospectus which was approved by the Board in September 1957. The committee has worked as a team in the general planning and in the definition and constant review of scope and research procedures. While the designated authors have carried primary responsibility for the writing of the individual volumes, these also include, in varying degrees, contributions of other members.

The preliminary survey of source materials indicated that such a study, to fulfill its purpose, would require a far greater amount of primary research than had been originally anticipated. Hence the committee carried out a series of specialized projects covering such sources as Annual Conference Journals and regional periodicals, files of boards and agencies of The Methodist Church, educational curriculum materials, and personal records. Limitations of time and

---

[1] The term "MESTA," frequently used in these volumes, is an abbreviation of the original working title, "Methodist Social Thought and Action."

resources have prevented more than a sampling of representative periods, regions, and types of data. The largest single project (designated MR [2]) was a nation-wide inquiry into the religious and social beliefs of Methodists. A full account of this particular inquiry is given in a mimeographed monograph by Herbert E. Stotts.

The findings of the whole project have been condensed in a series of four volumes appearing under the general title of *Methodism and Society*.

Volume I, *Methodism and Society in Historical Perspective*, traces the social history of Methodism up to 1908, when the adoption of the "Social Creed" by the Methodist Episcopal Church and subsequently by the Federal Council of Churches of Christ in America opened up a new period. Beginning with a consideration of British Methodism from John Wesley to 1850, it recounts the checkered history of Methodism's interaction with the American environment.

Volume II, *Methodism and Society in the Twentieth Century*, brings the story up to the present time, correlating the growth of social concerns with major developments in national life. In further parts, the volume examines the contributions of specific agencies and groups, both official and unofficial, and gives a topical presentation of Methodism's stand on major issues.

Volume III, *Methodism and Society in Theological Perspective*, pursues a two-fold aim. After analyzing the social implications of John Wesley's thought, it discusses major trends and emphases in relating religious convictions and social conduct as they appear in twentieth-century Methodism in the United States. The constructive part suggests in broad outline a theology of society which is both rooted in the truths of the Christian faith and relevant to the contemporary social scene.

Volume IV, *Methodism and Society: Guidelines for Strategy*, relates the findings of the preceding studies to the insights of social science into the processes of decision-making and planning. Against this background it seeks to develop a framework of principles and considerations which may serve as guidelines for a realistic strategy of social education, leadership, and action.

Some of the general features, and limitations, of the project should be pointed out. As the reader of the volumes will notice, the study pays major attention to the institutional manifestations of Methodist social concern. Such an approach may tend to create the one-sided impression that the social witness of Methodism is to be seen chiefly in its institutional activities and in deliberate efforts of clergy and lay professionals to promote social change. The committee was, of course, aware of the fact that the social radiation of a church is an expression of its total life as it interacts with the environing culture, and especially of the countless decisions of individual Christians in the run of everyday life. It has therefore sought to probe also these elusive realities at certain points—particularly through the inquiry into the actual religious beliefs and social attitudes of Methodists, referred to above as MR [2].

The fact is often overlooked that The Methodist Church as a denomination is not limited to America alone. It is world-wide in structure and polity, as evidenced by the composition of its top legislative and executive organs, the General Conference and the Council of Bishops. A study of the varied relations existing between Methodism and society around the globe would be of great benefit in fostering a deeper sense of fellowship and a mutual understanding of the widely differing conditions under which Methodists are called to bear their social witness. The present volumes, however, are focused on the religious and social scene of the United States, with some notable exceptions. Thus Volume I includes an account of the social history of British Methodism from Wesley to 1850. The narrative of twentieth century developments in Volume II suggests the influence of international perspectives on General Conference resolutions and Board actions. The deliberative parts of Volumes III and IV possess, in the nature of the case, a transcultural reference.

The ecumenical aspirations and affiliations of Methodism pose a somewhat similar problem, especially with respect to Volumes III and IV. It would have been theoretically possible to attempt to define a distinctive Methodist theology of society and a corresponding social strategy. Both theological and pragmatic reasons led the committee to adopt a different course. Methodism is officially committed to the cause of Christian unity. Methodist pronouncements and attitudes today are more expressive of the common outlook of social-minded Protestantism than of a separate tradition. Moreover, in the realm of strategy and action, it would clearly be self-defeating to seek to do in isolation what can be accomplished more effectively by a pooling of resources. Guided by such considerations, the committee has deliberately chosen to place its discussion of Methodist social responsibility in the broader framework of co-operative Christianity. Especially in the constructive parts, emphases of the Methodist heritage have been freely combined with the experiences and insights of the ecumenical community. It is hoped that this approach not only will be recognized as congenial to Methodism, but also will enhance the contribution of the project to a common task.

As previously indicated, the research phase of the project has been a co-operative venture of high order. It has benefited from the assistance of hundreds of correspondents, collaborators, and advisers across the country—denominational and interdenominational executives, liaison persons with the boards of The Methodist Church, ministers and laymen engaged in social work, academic scholars, social researchers, theological students, and so forth. Altogether over six thousand persons participated in the inquiry on "The Beliefs of Methodists." Drafts of the manuscripts were reviewed by members of the subcommittee of the Board of Social and Economic Relations as well as by outside experts.

Substantial reviews of the manuscript of the present volume on *Methodism and Society in the Twentieth Century* were contributed by James Luther Adams, Paul A. Carter, Georgia Harkness, Robert M. Miller, Bishop G. Bromley Oxnam, Frank Templin, Luther Tyson, and Bishop Lloyd C. Wicke.

Of the faculty members of the Boston University School of Theology, William C. Moore did substantial research on church school materials, and Donald T. Rowlingson assisted in the reading of Southern periodicals. Members of the committee have used the opportunity of exploring aspects of the project in seminars. The following students of the School furnished resource materials in the form of term papers, research memoranda, and, in a few instances, doctoral dissertations on related topics: Donald W. Anderson, C. Phillip Bosserman, John C. Campbell, John H. Cartwright, Lloyd E. Chorpenning, Ivan N. Clark, John T. Dahlquist, James B. Darcy, Richard L. Deats, Dewey R. Findley, Harold W. Garman, Ronald H. Goetz, John H. Graham, Hugh E. Haggard, Richard L. Hamilton, Donald H. James, Pierre M. Kempf, C. Travis Kendall, C. Eric Lincoln, Robert Paul Lisensky, Robert C. Mezoff, Leslie H. McKeown, Orloff W. Miller, Ralph T. Mirse, Charles H. Moore, Robert W. Musil, Joseph A. Perez, Charles M. Prestwood, F. Warren Rempel, C. Allyn Russell, Robert L. Shelton, John J. Shephard, James A. Smith, Robert E. Snyder, Henry J. Stonie, Duane F. Stroman, Harry G. Swanhart, Alfred H. Tracy, Mark C. Trotter, John G. Wall, Douglas E. Wingeier, and J. Philip Wogaman.

The voluminous material thus assembled is deposited in the library of Boston University School of Theology, which has established a repository of documents and publications on Methodism and society. A portion of the data has also been transcribed and coded in a punched-card file.

The committee wishes to express its deep gratitude to all those, named and unnamed, who in various ways so generously contributed to this undertaking.

Special thanks are due to the librarian of Boston University School of Theology, Jannette E. Newhall, who, with her staff, not only unsparingly assisted the committee in its researches but also provided office space in a congenial atmosphere.

NILS EHRENSTROM
PROJECT DIRECTOR

Foreword

THIS VOLUME IS PART OF A LARGER STUDY OF "METHODISM and Society" undertaken by the Board of Social and Economic Relations of The Methodist Church in co-operation with the faculty of the Boston University School of Theology.

It is the hope of the Board that the four volumes of the project will serve as a foundation for study and action in the church, with the aid of forthcoming study guides and interpretive materials, and that it will be used extensively by professors and students in colleges, universities, and seminaries, and by scholars doing independent study. The volumes should find their place as a significant contribution to ecumenical interests and research in the broader reaches of the total Christian impact upon society.

The interest of The Methodist Church in social matters goes back to its founder, John Wesley. It was an integral part of the thought, life, and activity of early Methodism. This interest in the welfare of people and the direction which society takes has been of increasing concern to The Methodist Church in the United States of America.

"The Social Creed" of the Methodist Church was adopted by the General Conference of the Methodist Episcopal Church in 1908. This was a turning point in the life of Methodism and for all the churches associated together in the Federal Council of the Churches of Christ in America. For it was the "Social Creed" of The Methodist Church which was adopted with little change as the social ideals of the Federal Council of Churches in 1908.

The Board of Social and Economic Relations was established by the General Conference of The Methodist Church in 1952 and received as its mandate the implementation of the "Social Creed."

As the new board began its work in race relations, economic life, and social and civic welfare, it soon became apparent that there was no systematic, objective survey and evaluation of the historical in-

13

volvement of Methodism in the United States in social issues and the realization of social justice by the society.

Such questions as the following seemed to require answers:

Has The Methodist Church actually been a determining factor in the achievement of social justice in the United States?

Has The Methodist Church largely reflected advances made by secular and political institutions or has it actually been a pioneer for social justice which is the assumption that most Methodists make?

What has been the relationship of Methodist social action to Methodist theological beliefs?

Is there a well-defined Methodist theology for social action?

What has been the relationship of Methodist social action to that of other churches?

What have been the special social action emphases characteristic of Methodism in the United States?

What should Methodist social action be and do in the future?

The board decided to undertake a study of Methodism and the social scene in the United States of America and applied to the Fund for the Republic for a grant to undertake the project. The fund made a grant which has been supplemented by the board's own funds and by a research grant from Boston University to bring the project to conclusion. We are grateful to the fund for its support.

The board consulted with various educational institutions of our connection and decided that the project would be well done at the Boston University School of Theology. We are especially glad that Nils Ehrenstrom, professor of ecumenics at Boston, and for many years the director of studies for the World Council of Churches, consented to become the chairman of the committee and project director. The other members, appointed by the faculty, were Dean Walter G. Muelder; Paul Deats, Jr., associate professor of social ethics (secretary of the committee) Richard M. Cameron, professor of church history; Allan K. Chalmers, professor of preaching and applied Christianity; S. Paul Schilling, professor of systematic theology; and Herbert E. Stotts, professor of church and community. They have discharged their responsibilities with imagination and diligence and have worked in the closest co-operation with the board and its sub-committee for the project.

The board's own committee consisted of:

MR. SAMUEL W. WITWER, CHAIRMAN
MRS. T. J. COTTINGHAM, SECRETARY
BISHOP LLOYD C. WICKE

BISHOP WILLIS J. KING
DR. GEORGIA HARKNESS
THE REVEREND FRANK M. TEMPLIN

They were the responsible representatives of the board in the formulation, organization, and carrying out the undertaking.

The board extends its deepest thanks to each member of the committee for doing so well a task which consumed many hours of detailed and hard work. We are especially grateful for the work of Mr. Witwer who spent many days with the faculty committee to bring the project into formulation and fruition.

The books were written by members of the faculty committee as follows:

Volume I *Methodism and Society in Historical Perspective*—
Richard M. Cameron
Volume II *Methodism and Society in the Twentieth Century*—
Walter G. Muelder
Volume III *Methodism and Society in Theological Perspective*—
S. Paul Schilling
Volume IV *Methodism and Society: Guidelines for Strategy*—
Herbert E. Stotts and Paul Deats, Jr.

To these authors we express our thanks and commend their work to the church.

Another group of persons actively participated in the undertaking. These were the expert critics who reviewed the books. At least four critics were chosen for each book (including one non-Methodist). These critics examined and evaluated the books carefully from the vantage point of their own specialized technical skills. To these critics we are indebted for incisive, objective, and constructive suggestions which improved the early drafts of the manuscripts greatly.

We are especially happy to acknowledge the work of Charles H. Seaver of White Plains, New York, who for many years has worked in similar projects and who in this connection edited for style and content and prepared the indexes.

All concerned with the project are conscious of the special responsibility which the office staff, both in Boston and in Chicago, assumed in bringing the entire undertaking to completion

The board and the faculty of Boston join in hoping that this project will be a forerunner of other larger and more penetrating analyses of the total social scene and the part of Methodism in it.

Above all, it is the earnest desire of all those who participated in any way in the project that the work will be an honor to the Lord whom we serve and be one of his instruments to sharpen the social witness of his Church in the world.

The project has been a co-operative one. The gathering and selection of the material, the interpretations and evaluations, and the method of presentation have been the primary responsibility of the faculty committee and the individual authors to whom the board extended great freedom. In no sense, therefore, can or should any statement in the books of this project (except direct quotations from official actions) be regarded as an official declaration of The Methodist Church or of the Board of Social and Economic Relations.

ALFRED DUDLEY WARD
GENERAL SECRETARY
BOARD OF SOCIAL & ECONOMIC RELATIONS
AND GENERAL EDITOR OF THE PROJECT

Contents

17

PART TWO: THE STRUCTURE OF THE METHODIST RESPONSE

PART THREE: MAJOR AREAS OF METHODIST CONCERN AND ACTION

PART FOUR: ISSUES FOR THE FUTURE

PART ONE

The Development
of the Methodist Response

CHAPTER ONE

The Social Gospel as Response

THIS BOOK IS THE STORY OF METHODIST SOCIAL THOUGHT and action in the twentieth century. It relates the development of the "social gospel" within one of America's great Protestant denominations. The story is told in three ways: first as a running account of the Methodist response to the major social, economic, and political events of the twentieth century; second as an exposition of the structure of the Methodist response, paying attention to the various aspects of its polity, its educational system, and the various boards and agencies which have a special responsibility in the fields under study; and third as a systematic interpretation of the church's position on major problems such as temperance, race, industrial relations, world peace, and others. Finally, there is a brief evaluative chapter some of whose topics will be anticipated in this introductory discussion.

To begin anywhere in history is an arbitrary action; so too with this volume which is one of four studies planned as a comprehensive whole. The reader must not expect a full treatment here of matters planned for the other books in this series. The first volume also is historical and surveys developments down to 1908. It was in 1908 that the General Conference of the Methodist Episcopal Church adopted a "Social Creed" which had been prepared by leaders in the newly organized Methodist Federation for Social Service. That year marks also the birth of the Federal Council of Churches of Christ in America, which took over substantially the statement of social ideals as they had been formulated in the "Social Creed" of Methodism.

The present volume covers principally the next fifty years, stressing not theological doctrines but social norms, ideals, pronouncements, programs, and types of action. Theological foundations for social thought and action are the primary concern of the third volume. The fourth volume deals with method and strategy. It brings to bear on the present and future planning of social education and action the significance of the first three volumes along with the results of contemporary sociological theory and the comparative thinking of other church bodies concerned with sound strategy.

Methodism has developed its social ideals and pronouncements as an integral movement and institution in American social and cultural life. The reader is asked not to suppose that Methodism is unique. In many ways it is characteristically American, though its scope is world-wide. The course of American democratic thought is a mighty stream into which many tributaries of doctrine, opinion, attitude, and conviction have poured their treasures. It will not be possible in so short a compass to acknowledge at many points the similarities and dependence of Methodism on other streams in the great river system into which flows a continent of religious idealism and which empties into the sea of mankind's moral and spiritual deeps. More references are made to the Federal Council and the National Council of Churches than to other religious institutions, but even here the allusions are only a token of scores that ideally should be made.

How are we to approach the "social gospel" in Methodism? Its influence must not be overrated and its role can easily be exaggerated. A concentrated treatment like this one can easily create the impression that this is the Methodist story of the twentieth century. This story, however, is limited to the development of the Methodist social conscience. For the temptation to regard this as the whole there are two good correctives. One needs only to remember that some Methodists in local churches still believed in 1959 that the Commission on Christian Social Relations had to do with church suppers and other fellowship responsibilities, whereas it actually existed to implement the leadership offered by the Board of Temperance, the Board of World Peace, and the Board of Social and Economic Relations, and to stir interest and action in these areas in the local church. Moreover, there have always been aggressive groups in Methodism who have combated any social gospel orientation. It is well to remember also that the social-economic leadership in the Methodist Episcopal Church was largely provided between 1908 and 1939 by the unofficial Methodist Federation for Social Service, and that an official Board of Social and Economic Relations was not established until 1952. A Temperance Society had been organized in the Methodist Episcopal Church in 1904; a Board of Temperance and Social Service in the Methodist Episcopal Church, South, in 1918; and the Commission on World Peace in 1924.

In the other branches of Methodism covered by this present account there was no organization that corresponded to that on World Peace or the Methodist Federation for Social Service. In the Methodist Episcopal Church, South, there existed from 1935 to 1939 the Council on a Christian Social Order. Another reminder of the relative position of the "Social Creed" or the "social gospel" in any branch of Methodism is that it does not as yet belong to the official pattern of every local church. In the mentality of Methodism a Commission of Christian Social Relations is at present optional. Its mandatory location along with Membership, Missions, Evangelism, and Finance has been provided by the General Conference of 1960. Even though the General Conference makes it a mandatory part of the work of every local church, much prayer and education will be necessary before the clergy and the laity fully support it. In June 1959 ten thousand local Methodist churches had formed Commissions of Christian Social Relations. By June 1960, this number had grown to sixteen thousand and the name changed to Christian Social Concerns.

An important aspect of social education and action in the major branches of Methodism has been the work of the women's groups. There has been a tendency to neglect the history of concern for social questions in fields like race relations, temperance, international relations, economic issues, citizenship, family and community relations, as found in all the societies which merged in the present Department of Christian Social Relations of the Woman's Division. The Ladies Aid grew steadily in its concerns as did the various Methodist women's associations. Christian Social Relations were a notable part of the Woman's Missionary Council of the Methodist Episcopal Church, South, between 1910 and 1940. Christian Citizenship and Personal Service formed a full-fledged department in the later development of the Wesleyan Service Guild before unification. There was close co-operation with the Woman's Home Missionary Society and eventually an emphasis on the importance and necessity of social reform emerged. In the Woman's Foreign Missionary Society after 1925 there was a committee on World Fellowship which in 1931 became the Committee on World Citizenship with an active educational program. These last three groups were parts of the Methodist Episcopal Church before unification in 1939. Beginning in 1928 the woman's program of the Methodist Protestant Church also included a Department of Christian Citizenship.

These considerations and others have led certain scholars to hold that the social gospel in American Protestantism is by no means a radical or frontier position taken by the churches on social issues.

25

They assert, on the contrary, that it is a part of the customary accommodation of denominations in order not to lose contact with those liberal social forces which are already taking more advanced social positions in American life and doing so with power. This type of observation cannot be lightly dismissed. The term "social gospel" represents a broad movement rather than a school of thought. It is used here as a familiar short-cut for social thought and action, roughly equivalent to "the responsible society" in current diction. Four sociological observations are considered which have tried to show that the social gospel is adaptive and accommodative rather than a radical initiation by the churches into our national civilization. These we should briefly consider.[1]

A first thesis is that the problems with which the social gospel dealt had been urgent for more than a generation and had been recognized by secular organizations for several decades. There can be no doubt that the urban and industrial revolution in the nineteenth century caught the churches unprepared to deal specifically with the many needs and crises of the economic order. Naturally, the demands for social betterment were most acutely felt in those parts of America's pluralistic culture where exploitation was the keenest. The nation has developed unevenly; national strategies in church social programs have been difficult to achieve; and denominational groups have proliferated without let or hindrance.

Recent studies like that of Timothy Smith have shown a close relationship between revivalism and social reform in the North,[2] and even the secular movements whose social platforms anticipated the social creed by several decades fed on the "American Creed" which was strongly influenced by Protestant ideals. R. H. Gabriel asserts that the foundation of the American democratic faith was a frank supernaturalism derived from Christianity.

[1] See J. Milton Yinger, *Religion in the Struggle for Power* (Duke University Press, 1946), pp. 130-42. See also his *Religion, Society, and the Individual*, where this analysis is given a wider sociological setting. Henry F. May, *Protestant Churches and Industrial America* (Harper, 1949), and Paul Carter, *The Decline and Revival of the Social Gospel* (Cornell, 1954), describe this situation pointedly. See also for this section such books as Carl L. Becker, *Freedom and Responsibility in the American Way of Life* (Vintage Book, 1945); Richard Hofstadter, *The American Political Tradition* (Alfred A. Knopf, 1949); F. Ernest Johnson (ed.), *Wellsprings of the American Spirit* (Harper, 1948); James Dombrowski, *The Early Days of Christian Socialism in America* (Columbia, 1936); C. H. Hopkins, *The Rise of the Social Gospel in American Protestantism* (Yale, 1940); Richard Hofstadter, *Social Darwinism in American Thought, 1860-1915* (Univ. of Pa. Press, 1944); Thorsten Veblen, *Theory of the Leisure Class* (Macmillan, 1899); Frederick L. Allen, *The Big Change* (Harper, 1952).

[2] Timothy Smith, *Revivalism and Social Reform* (New York: Abingdon Press, 1958).

26

The twentieth-century student is often astonished at the extent to which supernaturalism permeated American thought of the nineteenth century. The basic postulate of the democratic faith affirmed that God, the creator of man, has also created a moral law for his government and has endowed him with a conscience with which to apprehend it. Underneath and supporting human society, as the basic rock supports the hills, is a moral order which is the abiding place of the eternal principles of truth and righteousness.[3]

In times of national crisis such as in World War I and World War II there could not have been so powerful a social fusion in national ideals had they not already been rooted in the American conscience. They have at times been the sources of patriotic idolatry. From its inception the national democratic ideals have been a secular religion for the masses. Both secular and religious movements drew heavily upon them. Gunnar Myrdal, in his survey of the unity of American ideals amid the diversity of American backgrounds and the conflicts of interests, classes, and races, noted that "there is evidently a strong unity in this nation and a basic homogeneity and stability in its valuations." [4] Compared to every other country in Western civilization, the United States "has the *most explicitly expressed* system of general ideals in reference to human interrelations." [5] E. S. Bates says, "Democracy was envisaged in religious terms long before it assumed a political terminology." [6]

There was, perhaps, not quite the degree of unity with respect to these norms at the turn of the present century that prevailed during the second World War when Myrdal made his observations. In the meantime the public schools and the churches played a very significant part. As this unity pervaded the nation the American creed received innumerable formulations and adaptations in clubs, courts, unions, business associations, and newspapers as well as in the schools, colleges, and churches. They were variations on the ultimately religious themes of the essential dignity of man, the fundamental equality of all men, their inalienable rights of freedom, justice, opportunity, and self-development. The American creed became a faith in democracy, where democracy expressed an affirmation of an unlimited right of personality to develop a social order for its own realization. Various facets of the creed often conflicted

[3] R. H. Gabriel, *The Course of American Democratic Thought* (New York: The Ronald Press, 1940), p. 14.
[4] Gunnar Myrdal, *An American Dilemma* (New York: Harper and Brothers, 1944), I, 3.
[5] *Loc. cit.*
[6] E. S. Bates, *American Faith* (New York: W. W. Norton & Co., 1940), p. 9.

with other affirmations, and special interests pressed their claims under the guise of approved ideals. The humanitarian drive created a persistent admiration for leaders who embodied these goals. Myrdal noted, significantly, that "America has had gifted conservative statesmen and national leaders, and they have often determined the course of public affairs. But, with few exceptions, only liberals have gone down in history as national heroes." [7]

The thesis that the churches as organized bodies developed their "social creeds" as a pattern of accommodation is partially correct, but the other side of the case points to the pervasive influence of the Christian ethic in creating the democratic faith.

Gaius Glenn Atkins reminds us that there was much evangelical zeal behind the social ferment of the first two decades of the twentieth century. He says:

"The first fifteen years of the twentieth century may sometime be remembered in America as the Age of Crusades. There were a superabundance of zeal, a sufficiency of good causes, unusual moral idealism, excessive confidence in mass movements, and leaders with rare gifts of popular appeal. . . . Twentieth-century church crusades were also a continuation, in social, moral, and even political realms, of nineteenth-century evangelism." [8]

A second thesis is that the churches as a whole accepted the sufferings of the masses as inevitable and that they did not make a place for common laborers until the latter had taken steps to rectify their own situations. It is pointed out that in the field of race relations organizations for self-help of minority groups anticipated by several years the organized efforts of the denominations either individually or co-operatively. As the workingmen and the racial minorities gradually won a measure of economic and political power, "social Christianity" adjusted to this emergent fact in order not to lose what influence it yet maintained over a large group of people.

There is much evidence to sustain this thesis which is closely related to the one previously discussed. The Grange and the trade unions are two examples which can be supplemented by the phenomenal growth of fraternal orders in the late nineteenth century. Co-operation became a watchword among farmers and workers alike and they banded together for mutual help and protection. Such

[7] Myrdal, *op. cit.*, p. 7.
[8] Quoted in R. T. Handy, "The Protestant Quest for a Christian America," *Church History*, 22 (1953), 16.

co-operation dated from frontier days. The Grange was the first nation-wide organization of farmers, called at first the Patrons of Husbandry. Beginning as a social and educational order, its members were inevitably involved in business politics. Trade unionism antedated the Civil War as did a great many of the socialist or communistic experiments which were widely scattered in the country in small communities.

Co-operative developments of both a local and wider membership type became self-conscious when the farmers and the workers began to see the banker and money lender as a dangerous enemy. Suffice it to say that by 1880 "Wall Street" was a name that described an ogre whom organized religion was not driving out. The churches were not meeting adequately the needs of the new day as reflected in the quasi-religious fraternal orders which had their golden age from 1865 to 1910. The Knights of Labor, for example, active from 1869 to 1885, (1) organized themselves on fraternal order lines; (2) had a quasi-religious ritual; (3) had as first president a man trained for the Baptist ministry, Uriah Stephens; and (4) dropped some of their secret fraternalism to avoid Roman Catholic official censure.

In this rapidly changing era multitudes of individuals sensed and experienced the fact of insecurity. The fraternal orders mentioned above offered a limited protection of their members in the form of insurance or mutual aid of other kinds. Many of these were due to crises of an economic character, but many were also due to the desire to achieve a fuller life. Among the members of the colored minority the development of secret orders suggests the importance of fraternity as compensation for the inferior station in life which they were compelled by many forces to accept. In the case of immigrant groups the fraternal orders provided comfort in a strange land and assisted individuals to hold fast to their native culture. To the low-paid white-collar class arising in the new cities secret societies offered escape from the drabness of life in the routines of offices and agencies. Thus in the heyday of these grass-roots groups many needs were fulfilled which fed on the American dream and challenged the churches. Gabriel points out that between 1870 and 1910 some thirty-five hundred mutual assessment associations came into being. Of these perhaps three thousand failed. The average life of those that failed was about fifteen years.[9] Thus the fraternal orders like the trade unions were based on the idea that their welfare depended on their own initiative.

[9] R. H. Gabriel, *op. cit.*, p. 190.

Ten years before the adoption of the "Social Creed" by churches Samuel Gompers saw in the labor movement the ideals of the democratic faith at work. He said in 1898:

> The trade unions are the legitimate outgrowth of modern society and industrial conditions. . . . They were born of the necessity of the workers to protect and defend themselves from encroachment, injustice and wrong. . . . To protect the workers in their inalienable rights to a higher and better life; to protect them, not only as equals before the law, but also in their rights to the product of their labor; to protect their lives, their limbs, their health, their homes, their firesides, their liberties as men, as workers, and as citizens; to overcome and conquer prejudice and antagonism; to secure to them the right to life, and the opportunity to maintain that life; the right to be full sharers in the abundance which is the result of their brain and brawn, and the civilization of which they are the founders and the mainstay; to this the workers are entitled. . . . The attainment of these is the glorious mission of the trade unions.[10]

On the other hand, there is evidence that concern for workers' movements was marked as much by the fear of their ideology as by desire to keep them related to the church. An editorial in *Zion's Herald* in 1895 dealing with a book, *What Is the Meaning of Christian Socialism,* written by a German pastor, stated:

> The churches which are hanging back do so from fear of a one-sided Socialism which is Christian neither in spirit nor endeavor. The Christianity of Jesus Christ is complete in its range; it makes provision for both soul and body. Followers of the Lord Jesus Christ do not realize as they ought the misery, suffering, and injustices of the world they live in. . . . Thousands of their brothers and sisters are huddled in haunts of misery and shame. . . . Fathers are driven to the devil by the merciless Moloch of poverty. . . . The dawning of the new epoch of social service in the spirit of Jesus Christ means the dawning of the new epoch of social redemption for millions of downcast and downtrodden men and women.[11]

In the turmoil of social life at the turn of the century not only Protestant but also Roman Catholic clergy became sensitive to the forces demanding change. Like most Americans, the progressive conservatives in both groups, or liberals as they may be called, regarded the social problems as essentially soluble. They moved forward as participants in a broad movement which endorsed social reform somewhat tentatively.

[10] Samuel Gompers, *Labor and the Common Welfare,* pp. 6-9.
[11] *Zion's Herald,* 73 (1895), 72.

Though the transition was particularly difficult for a Catholic priest, under the guidance of certain strong liberal leaders like Gibbons, Ireland, Spalding, Keane, McGlynn, and Hecker, a liberal social development entered the church. The greatest incubus to Catholic reform was not the organizational resistance, though this was often strong in cities where immigrant populations were presided over by conservative bishops, but the widespread religious belief that human enterprise was presumptuous.[12]

To the conservatives the proper response to social problems was devout passivity. One Roman Catholic Archbishop advised his people that God permits poverty as "the most efficient means of practising some of the most necessary Christian virtues of charity and alms-giving on the part of the rich, and patience and resignation to His holy will on the part of the poor." [13] But Gibbons was to defend the Knights of Labor along with Keane and Ireland; McGlynn was to become a champion of the views of Henry George; Ireland and Keane were to support new approaches to charity and alms-giving; Ireland was to be a strong advocate of temperance; and all these liberals were to be known as friendly to the public-school system.

Leaders like Walter Rauschenbusch, who had a hunger for evangelizing the worker, rejected, as did Leo XIII,[14] both an unchristian socialism and unsocial Christianity. The coming of the social gospel movement was not basically a strategem to gain the assent of the trade unions, but a demand to express in theology and action the whole gospel of salvation. For example, in 1890 Walter Rauschenbusch and Ira D. Sankey selected and edited a German translation of gospel hymns entitled *Evangeliums-Lieder*. It followed in the main the central message of evangelical Protestantism of that period. This book was widely used among German Methodists. In the same year Rauschenbusch wrote an article on society and the individual in which he expressed the integral wholeness of individual and social salvation. His classic formulation stated a conviction which was to characterize not only his ministry but that of social evangelism generally:

Most people look only to the renewal of the individual. Most reformers look only to the renewal of society. We believe that two factors make up the man, the inward and the outward, and so we work for the renewal and Christianization of the individual *and* of society.

[12] Robert D. Cross, *The Emergence of Liberal Catholicism in America* (Cambridge: Harvard University Press, 1958), p. 107.
[13] *Ibid.*, p. 107.
[14] Pope Leo XII was, of course, opposed to all forms of socialism.

31

Most Christians demand the private life for God and leave business to the devil. Most social reformers demand justice for business life, in order that private life may be given to pleasure. We plead for self-sacrifice in private life, in order to achieve justice in business life that purity in private life may become possible.

Most Christians say: "Wait till all men are converted, then a perfect social order will be possible." Most social reformers say: "Wait till we have a perfect social order, then all men will be good." We say: Go at both simultaneously; neither is possible without the other.

They all say: "Wait!" We say: "Repent, for the kingdom of God is at hand." [15]

A third thesis states that the agencies of the "social gospel" in the various denominations that developed in the early twentieth century were not making radical challenges to the existing power structure. The "social creeds," notes Yinger, demonstrated that the churches were "for labor" by echoing some of labor's milder demands. "These demands were put in somewhat ambiguous language, however, and their realization by conciliation, cooperation, and the development of character was emphasized." [16] Some of the employers and other leaders were already perceiving that their best interests were not being undercut by the demands of the workers for social betterment. These representatives of the middle and upper classes, who were often generous, supported and attended the churches. In this situation "social Christianity" illustrated the dilemma of religious leadership whereby the church accommodates in order to have leverage on the society it serves.

Although this thesis has much to commend it, the record of social concern includes some vigorous, though small, radical protests. Socialism provides a case in point. Though the Christians in socialism were not large in number, they formed a significant, well coordinated, and aggressive minority. In 1903 the Reverend Edward Ellis Carr, a Methodist who had withdrawn from his denomination to form a "People's Church" and had joined the Socialist Party, began the publication of *The Christian Socialist*. Then, stimulated by frequent suggestions in this little journal, the Christian Socialist Fellowship was organized in 1906. The avowed objectives of the Fellowship included the following: "Its object shall be to permeate the churches, denominations, and other religious institutions with the social message of Jesus; to show that Socialism is the necessary

---

[15] Quoted in Dores Sharpe, *Walter Rauschenbusch* (New York: The Macmillan Co., 1942), pp. 82-83.

[16] J. Milton Yinger, *Religion in the Struggle for Power* (Durham: Duke University Press, 1946), p. 140.

economic expression of the Christian life; to end the class struggles by establishing industrial democracy and to hasten the reign of justice and brotherhood on earth." [17]

Eugene V. Debs was invited to address the Fellowship in 1908. It grew to a considerable size and had a wide interdenominational following in terms of subscribers to the journal; there were more than 300,000 in 1909. Leaders like Walter Rauschenbusch also addressed the group, though he refused to identify the kingdom of God with any historical form of socialism. He never joined the Socialist Party. During World War I many of the Fellowship members left the party and eschewed socialism. The magazine changed its name to *Real Democracy*. It turned against the Socialist Party which it labeled "a bigoted, bitter, unscientific, foolish, anti-religious sect." Debs went to prison for speeches delivered in Ohio and Indiana against our entry into the war, though he was supported politically by many workers.

The trade union movement, as represented by the American Federation of Labor under the leadership of Samuel Gompers, was itself far from being a radical enterprise. Indeed craft unionism had become business unionism, eschewing revolutionary political goals, and seeking to achieve its ends primarily through collective bargaining. There were vigorous socialist leaders like Eugene Debs who had a substantial following, but their popularity rested on the effectiveness with which they organized workers, the personal quality of their leadership (including in Debs' case both warmth and charm), their ability to win strikes, and their success at the bargaining table. Some leaders in the social gospel movement, like the Congregationalist George D. Herron, were closely associated with Debs and the founding of the Socialist Party of America; but in most Methodist circles in 1900 and 1908 the social leadership had more moderate goals. Not until the era from 1929 to 1936 were many religious leaders to challenge seriously the predominance of the profit motive and the capitalist system. Even then the socialist alternative was not championed by the majority who attacked the "system." As we shall see below, the most extreme position which Methodism was ever to take on the economic system as a whole was in 1932. Since 1936 its economic pronouncements have declined in their militancy, as have those in other major denominations, along with the majority of secular leaders.

The social gospel movement, then, has not been on the whole a radical movement. It was developed and carried along, as C. H.

---

[17] *The Christian Socialist*, May 15, 1909, quoted in R. T. Handy, "Christianity and Socialism in America," *Church History*, 21 (1952), pp. 39-53.

Hopkins says, by progressive orthodoxy.[18] This means that it was conservative with a creative impulsion. In the form in which it was expressed in official Methodism it did not explicitly threaten the foundations of the American business system. However, because it included both an implicit and an explicit critique of capitalism and sought to bring the principles of Christianity to bear against a materialistic social order that seemed exclusively devoted to profit, it reproved the majority of the Methodist church members rather than reflecting their economic opinions. Methodism has as explicitly defended the kernel of private property as ever Leo XIII did in his rejection of socialism. Throughout the whole subsequent discussion this fact must be kept in mind.

The fourth and final thesis holds that the "social gospel" movement's expression of intense social criticism and action was never a popular movement. Only a minority in the denominations identified themselves with it, and many of these were related to theological seminaries, to boards and agencies, or to councils somewhat remote from the power tensions of local churches. This point must be granted. The way in which the social conscience of The Methodist Church has developed and become active in the church program of the twentieth century is the burden of this volume. We shall note in the course of the exposition how Methodism's response to the major problems has varied from region to region. Even at the present time there are significant differences on some of these issues among the five regional jurisdictions of the church.

The problems which the Methodist conscience confronted, we may note in summary, were not entirely new; the churches were not always the first to grapple with them; the major institutions and agencies of the social gospel movement did not radically challenge basic power structures; and when it was prophetically critical the movement was never a popular movement.

The story of Methodist social thought and action in the twentieth century may reinforce certain critical judgments on the social gospel movement. Many readers may agree with Henry F. May's evaluation of the early period of moderate social Christianity and feel that it holds for the period under consideration as well. He says:

The progressive writers in the early period were over-optimistic facile and vague. They were uncertain as to their precise social role and

[18] C. H. Hopkins, *The Rise of the Social Gospel in American Protestantism* (New Haven: Yale University Press, 1940), pp. 55, 61, *passim.* Some of the early church-school literature of Methodism stated that its social point of view was that of progressive conservatism.

unable to solve the problem of ends and means. They failed to achieve their hope of overcoming the hostility that had long existed between Protestantism and organized labor. These shortcomings persisted into the twentieth century at least sufficiently to produce a reaction from the Social Gospel in recent times. From its religious background, middle-class American progressivism may have inherited some of its weaknesses: its lack of thoroughness; its substitution of enthusiasm for economic analysis; its tendency to underestimate its opponents, to believe with every victory that the war is over.[19]

Along with such an appraisal the reader may also agree that "without the support of religious argument, bringing to bear the most deeply-rooted beliefs and appealing to the most powerful human motives, the up-hill fight of the progressives might have been far more difficult." Social thought and action involves the interplay of liberal, progressive, and conservative forces, with radicals and reactionaries at the extremes. The story of developing social conscience inevitably emphasizes liberals and protagonists of change. Such an emphasis does not impugn the motives of the conservatives in the church or their role in society.

Before proceeding to the narrative account of the development of Methodist thought and action, it may be helpful to add two additional introductory comments: one dealing with the chronologies employed and one for non-Methodist readers. The accent of this interpretive history is on Methodism as a response to the major events of the twentieth century as they affected the denomination in the U.S.A. To conserve space and the time of the reader, the different periods of this history are introduced by a chronological table. It is against the background of these recorded events that Methodism has developed. There are many items on which the church took no specific position. Nevertheless, they may serve as a reminder of the multitudinous forces at work in its historical environment. The selection of events grows out of a comparison of several standard chronologies and major social histories of the past fifty years. The chronologies are not definitive, and the reader will doubtless miss some items and wonder at the inclusion of others. At best they are guideposts to chart the course of remembered action.

For some non-Methodist readers who may inspect this volume before they have examined Volume One of this series, it will be useful to add a brief note about the three branches of Methodism which in 1939 united to form The Methodist Church. These are the Methodist

[19] *Protestant Churches and Industrial America* (New York: Harper and Brothers, 1949), pp. 264-65.

Episcopal Church; the Methodist Episcopal Church, South; and the Methodist Protestant Church.

In 1938, at the threshold of union, Methodism had nineteen divisions in the U.S.A. Ten of these were entirely Negro. Of Negro Methodists 85 per cent were in Negro divisions, and fifteen per cent (about 350,000) were in the white or mixed divisions. Methodist union brought into one church an estimated 99 per cent of all white Methodists in the United States. The large number of Negro Methodists still in separated bodies constitutes an important historical and sociological factor in the present race relations within The Methodist Church.

The Methodist Episcopal Church was organized at Christmas 1784. In the course of time there were numerous splits in American Methodism. The Methodist Protestant Church came into separate existence in 1830 on the issue of administration and polity. This denomination arose in protest against the continued exclusion of all laymen from the legislative, executive, and judicial bodies of the mother Methodist Episcopal Church. There was also opposition to the episcopacy and the presiding eldership.

The Methodist Episcopal Church, South, arose from different grounds of division and was organized in 1844. The issue was not primarily ecclesiastical but social, and involved the entire nation. There was an impasse over the question of slavery. As the ministers of the Northern states became more and more severe in their condemnation of slavery, their censure fell heavily on those who upheld and defended slavery. Before the controversy ended, the question of authority and power of the General Conference of the church became involved along with the definition of the status and power of bishops. Finally a Plan of Separation was adopted and the Methodist Episcopal Church, South, came into existence.[20]

In the plan of union which created The Methodist Church in 1939 provision was made for five jurisdictions based on geographical divisions and one jurisdiction based on race. This jurisdictional system is currently under serious review by the General Conference and the annual conferences which comprise the basic units of the church's polity.

The social witness of Methodism is full of lights and shadows. Its history is a fluctuating and pulsating movement determined by its own growing understanding of its gospel and mission and by the tempestuous events of America's developing civilization. Its tempo varies from region to region and from one annual conference to

[20] Volume I of this series deals fully with this question.

another. Sometimes its action has ridden the crest of military patriotism and nationalism, and sometimes it has mobilized its sprawling strength in behalf of sharing American sovereignty with international bodies like the United Nations. Methodists have been pioneers for social justice and witnesses at the trial of civil liberties, and they have been captives of regional mores and industrial indifference. All in all, as the succeeding pages will show, The Methodist Church has struggled to save the world beyond its doors and the worldliness which occupies its pews and sometimes designs its policies. This book tells the story of Christian social conscience in the present century.

CHAPTER TWO

Prelude to the Social Creed

Chronological Outline of
Major Events in American Social, Economic, and
Political History: 1900 to 1908

MCKINLEY AND ROOSEVELT ADMINISTRATIONS: 1901-08

1900—In the fall election imperialism is the main issue. It dies down soon after election is over and new administration takes over (1901). Philippine insurrection (1899-1902).

North Carolina amends constitution on suffrage with "grandfather clause" (1900). Alabama follows suit (1901). The U. S. Supreme Court found these clauses unconstitutional under the Fifteenth Amendment. (Guinn vs. United States, 238 U.S. 347; *1915*).

The most efficient device to keep Negroes from voting was the "white primary." The Democratic party prohibited Negroes from participating in primary by means of state-wide rule (by 1940) in nine Southern states: Mississippi, Alabama, Georgia, Florida, South Carolina, Louisiana, Arkansas, Virginia, and Texas.

"Open-Door" Policy for China announced.

1901—McKinley shot and Roosevelt made president.

Boxer Indemnity.

U. S. Steel Corporation organized.

150,000 steel workers strike for union recognition and fail.

Immigration from Europe (1901-10) is 8,136,-000.

1902—Chinese Exclusion Act.

Anthracite miners strike, involving 145,000 men.

1903—Roosevelt seizes Panama Canal.

Department of Commerce and Labor authorized.

Wright brothers invent the flying machine.

1904—Roosevelt re-elected.

1905—Race Riot in Atlanta.

Investigation of Life Insurance Companies.

First motion picture theater opened, in Pittsburgh.

1906—Roosevelt offers to help in Russo-Japanese War. He receives Nobel Peace Prize.

Bureau of Immigration and Naturalization established.

Meat Inspection and Pure Food laws.

President orders eight-hour labor law applied to all governmental work.

Elkins Act asserts federal control over interstate railroads.

1907—Standard Oil found guilty of accepting rebates.

John D. Rockefeller gives $32,000,000 to General Education Board.

Act prohibiting political contributions by corporations.

1908—Danbury Hatters' case, Sherman Act used against general boycotts by unions.

Strike of 250,000 coal miners.

Conservation Commission appointed by President Roosevelt.

Roman Catholic Church in the United States removed from the supervision of the Congregation of the Propaganda and given full ecclesiastical status.

Ne Ternere manifesto of the Roman Catholic Church makes marriages between Catholics and non-Catholics invalid unless performed in the presence of a priest and two witnesses.

Establishment of the Federal Council of the Churches of Christ in America.

THE EPISCOPAL LEADERSHIP OF THE METHODIST CHURCH entered the twentieth century with a clear sense of the close relationship of religion and political responsibility. What this relationship would entail they could not of course foresee. But neither could they repudiate the inseparability of political and Christian stewardship. In 1900 they declared: The church

"must insist that [its children] hold their political franchise as a chief part of their stewardship for Christianity. Upon particular secular questions the church . . . delivers no judgment. Even as to the particular legal methods by which moral evils . . . shall be repressed, the church is not an authoritative teacher . . . but the Christian cannot . . . separate [his political function] from his religion." [1]

What would the agenda of Methodism be? In 1903 in New York City, at a celebration of the two hundredth anniversary of John Wesley's birth, Bishop Andrews proclaimed a revived Christianity which taught a higher appreciation of man, of his rights, his interests, his possibilities.[2] Justice and pity are expressed in more equitable governments, more humane laws, abolition of slavery, prison reform, education; in efforts to bring rich and poor, laborer and capitalist, to a common understanding of their mutual brotherhood; in private and public charities for the relief of suffering such as hospitals, asylums, and homes. "Christianity," said Bishop Andrews, "has become sociological, and its spirit of love influences many who do not openly acknowledge its claim. . . . The church has something more to do now than to teach men to get to heaven; it must teach them how to behave on the way." [3]

Zion's Herald editorialized on an Epworth League convention in 1900: "The Epworthian was taught to be a Christian of the largest and truest type. . . . He is to recognize God's ownership in his property and in himself. . . . He must be a public spirited patriot, interesting himself in everything that concerns the welfare of his nation and his race." [4]

These themes were to be deepened in seriousness and spelled out in conflict in the ensuing decades. More conservative Methodists, however, were to fear the growing "social gospel" which these themes expressed. So, for example, the "Pastoral" of the Wesleyan Methodists urged them to be zealous lest they should be found more humanitarian than religious, more ethical than theological, more aesthetic in their worship than contrite and adoring.[5]

---

[1] Episcopal Address on the Church and Citizenship, *Zion's Herald*, 78 (1900), 588. On the specific question of Prohibition, Methodism was later to defend and advocate a particular legal method.
[2] *Western Christian Advocate* (March 4, 1903), p. 7.
[3] *Ibid.*, pp. 7, 8.
[4] 78 (1900), 903.
[5] *Ibid.*, p. 1159.

In the first decade of the present century Methodism suffered from the lack of development in social doctrines such as had been put forward by Congregational and Episcopal leaders in the two preceding decades. Though Methodists had always prided themselves on being a church of the poor and lowly, they were not as yet in a cultural position to give the quality of witness which later became characteristic of a portion of the denomination. They had, to be sure, passed resolutions on Reconstruction, the Mormon question, narcotics, and temperance, but not on the ethics of business. At the turn of the century Methodism's strength lay in the rural area rather than in the great industrial cities.

In 1900, in the northeastern portion of the United States, 43 per cent of the people lived in towns and villages under ten thousand population. In the South 87 per cent and in the North Central portions 76 per cent lived in similar situations. In the West about 70 per cent lived in places under ten thousand. At that time the total Methodist membership was 4,226,327, which was 5.6 per cent of the nation's population. Rural Methodism may have accounted for 90 per cent of the denomination's total.[6] Accordingly, its annual conferences and the General Conference were bound to be less impressed by the labor question in the cities than were denominations having more central ecclesiastical leadership in industrial centers.

When social conflicts involving questions of monopoly and impoverishment were discussed by the bishops in addresses to the General Conferences, they emphasized preaching to the rich their perils and responsibilities and to the poor the familiar doctrine of patience. In 1896 the address to the Methodist Episcopal General Conference added endorsements of arbitration and profit-sharing. The new winds of social thought were felt first among intellectuals and certain industrial workers, but neither of these was strongly represented in Methodism.

Certain emphases in Methodist theology also contributed to its relatively late start in the "social gospel" movement. The economic virtues of Puritanism—frugality, thrift, hard work, sobriety, temperance—were prominent. In its evangelical zeal Methodism was deeply impressed with revivalism and its late-nineteenth-century stress on sin as the sufficient explanation of all social evil, and with individual redemption as the only remedy. Revivalism was less socially productive than it had been at mid-century. Indeed, in 1882, the *Christian Advocate* pointed with fear and warning toward the growing influence of "Bushnellism" and cited men like Gladden and

---

[6] This percentage is only a rough estimate.

Munger as promoters of dangerous theological tendencies. In short it was their theology, more than their social liberalism, that bothered the *Advocate*. Bushnell was not particularly liberal in the social-political sense.

A. International Affairs

Methodism was concerned in only a passing way with the new international situation in which the United States was involved. Methodism's official concern with policy on such matters as the "open door" policy, the "Boxer Uprising," the "Boxer Indemnity," Japan's ambitions in China and Manchuria, American interests in Caribbean waters, the Panama Canal, the "Big Stick" policy, "dollar diplomacy," and the like was relatively small. Nor did it evince much interest in the First Hague Conference (1899) or its successor (1907). Sustained interest in these matters was to come retrospectively. There was, of course, missionary concern for China and popular interest in Panama.

The First Hague Conference recommended three means for settling disputes without resort to war: (1) through good offices and mediation, which, when offered by a third party to powers at war or about to go to war, must not be considered an unfriendly act; (2) through international commissions of inquiry, for which so many precedents existed, particularly in the relations between Great Britain and the United States; and (3) through submission to a new court of arbitration to be established at The Hague.

At the Second Hague Conference the United States began a persistent campaign to commit the nations of the world to the settlement of their disputes by peaceful means. The American delegation worked strenuously, although unavailingly, for the creation of an international court of justice, comparable to the United States Supreme Court, to which cases could be referred for adjudication.

One of the consequences of the Second Hague Conference was a model arbitration treaty, which all the nations of the world were urged to follow in negotiating treaties with each other. Under the administrations of Roosevelt, Taft, and Wilson the United States worked diligently for arbitration and by 1914 had obtained arbitration treaties of one kind or another with every one of the European nations eventually allied against Germany in the first World War. Perhaps significantly the nations that became allied with Germany persistently rejected the American proposals.

Methodism in the Episcopal Address of 1908 noted with gratification the advance made in the previous quadrennium toward methods of peaceful settlements of disputes. Tribute was paid to President Roosevelt, and to Mr. Carnegie who devoted a portion of his fortune to the cause of peace. The Bishops expressed regret, however, that "Questions of National Honor" were still withheld from the jurisdiction of the Hague tribunal.

B. Race Relations

R. M. Miller notes that it is one of the ironies of American history that the Progressive Era witnessed a retrogression in the area of race relations. As the churches advanced the social gospel idea, the lines of segregation within and around the denominations hardened.[7] In the South race prejudice prevented any effective union of agrarian reformers and the Negroes in behalf of improving their lot, while in the North the trade-conscious or craft-conscious character of the unions inhibited their organization of Negroes, who thus continued to be part of the mass of unskilled labor.

Other methods of disfranchising Negroes included educational requirements. These were applied usually only to Negroes. Property requirements for voting were employed throughout the first half of the twentieth century by Alabama, Georgia, and South Carolina. A "character" requirement operated also in Louisiana and Georgia. Between 1898 and 1908 ten southern states (Alabama, Arkansas, Florida, Louisiana, Mississippi, North Carolina, South Carolina, Tennessee, Texas, and Virginia), through constitutional provision or statutory law, adopted a poll tax requirement for voting. Simpson and Yinger note graphically the effect of these constitutional provisions in a state like Louisiana:

The number of registered Negro voters in 1896 was 130,344; in 1900 it was 5,320. For one reason or another, the number of Negro registrants had dropped to 1,772 in 1916. The following figures refer to (1) the twenty-one-year-old and literate Negro populations in certain states in 1920 and (2) the Negro voters at any time, 1920-30, in those states: Alabama 269,847 and 3,500; Georgia 369,511 and 10,000 at most; Mississippi 290,792 and 850; Virginia 248,347 and 12,000 to 18,000.[8]

There was a race riot in Atlanta in 1905. The following year the Bishops of Southern Methodism spoke of race problems only in terms of mission to Negroes which was individualistically evangelical. Even Negro education was a mildly controversial issue.

[7] *American Protestantism and Social Issues, 1919-1939* (Chapel Hill: University of North Carolina Press, 1958), p. 10.

[8] G. E. Simpson and J. Milton Yinger, *Racial and Cultural Minorities* (New York: Harper and Brothers, 1953), p. 418. See C. Vann Woodward, *The Strange Career of Jim Crow.*

"They (the Negroes at our doors) need and must have the pure gospel, and our Christian sympathy. Nothing else will redeem and elevate them. Not by statutes and constitutions—not by legislation, state or national—not by politicians, national or ecclesiastical—but by the Bible and the spelling book are these people to be saved, and thus every other social problem to be satisfactorily and finally solved." [9]

General, indefinite, and passive statements have often characterized the Church's position on race. Aggressive, specific, and action-laden pronouncements have been rare. Challenges put to the Church have often evoked vague responses or none at all. In the 1906 General Conference of the Methodist Episcopal Church, South, there was a stirring address by the Reverend G. C. Rawlston of the Colored Methodist Episcopal Church. Among other things he pleaded for a change in the separate-car law so as to give equal conditions to the races in all points of convenience.

It is a great sin, and a sin under God, to abandon the Negro to the tender mercies of corporations. . . . Why should the white men of this country enact a law to put me into the hands of a railroad corporation, compel me to pay twenty-five or thirty dollars from here to the Far West, and I then be hauled with less consideration than the ox to the slaughter? [10]

This statement was applauded, but there is no evidence that any General Conference in the South until unification ever called upon the corporations or the state governments to equalize the racial accommodations in Southern transportation. The Northern church was quite silent until the twenties.

C. The Industrial Order

The financial, industrial, and commercial aspects of capitalistic development precipitated a series of challenges and crises. "Big business" was a frightening reality. "Rugged individualism" had run riot. One corporation after another, successfully claiming the legal rights of persons, had grown to monopolistic proportions. In 1897 the total capital of million-dollar corporations stood at $170,-

[9] Episcopal Address, Methodist Episcopal Church, South, 1906. The Episcopal Address is delivered at the General Conference and is printed in the *Journal*. For economy in footnoting the reader is referred in the context to the year in which the Episcopal Address is given. Before 1939 the quadrennial General Conference of the Methodist Episcopal Church met in the twentieth century in 1900, 1904, etc., and the Methodist Episcopal Church, South, met in 1902, 1906, etc. When official statements of the bishops are referred to, the utterance is the Episcopal Address, unless explicitly noted otherwise.

[10] *Journal*, General Conference of The Methodist Episcopal Church, South, 1906, p. 318.

000,000; in 1900 it stood at $5,000,000,000; and in 1904 at $20,-500,000,000. Mergers, horizontal and vertical combinations, and giant corporations became the order of the day. In 1901 J. P. Morgan helped organize the first of America's billion-dollar companies, the United States Steel Corporation. Similar trends were at work in tobacco, petroleum, sugar, copper, beef, starch, flour, whiskey, and so on. The monopolistic trends were a threat to adherents of old-fashioned *laissez-faire*, to farmers, and to frontiersmen as well as to labor leaders and socialists.

America was aroused to the crisis in the social relations of business and its significance for the common people by many men and events, including a group of energetic journalists called by Roosevelt the "muckrakers." They exploited the seamy side of business endeavor [11] in popular magazines like *McClure's*, the *Cosmopolitan*, *Everybody's*, the *American*, *Pearson's*, *Munsey's*, and the *Arena*. Ida M. Tarbell exposed the "History of the Standard Oil Company"; Lincoln Steffens described "The Shame of the Cities"; Thomas Lawson dealt with "Frenzied Finance"; Charles Edward Russell attacked "The Beef Trust"; Ray Stannard Baker wrote "The Railroads on Trial"; and many other trusts were analyzed. Through his *The Theory of the Leisure Class* (1899) and *The Theory of Business Enterprise* (1904), Thorstein Veblen provided reformers of the following generation with many telling arguments against "predatory wealth."

Space does not permit a detailed description of the social excitement and litigation that attended the action of Theodore Roosevelt as "trust-buster," but as a context for the emergence of the Social Creed first formulated by the Methodist Federation for Social Service [12] and then adopted by the Methodist Episcopal Church and the Federal Council of Churches of Christ in America, mention of a few governmental actions is especially relevant.

There were many prosecutions under the Sherman Anti-trust Act. A number of regulatory laws were passed by Congress, notably with reference to the railroads. For example, the evil of rebates was curbed by the Elkins Act of 1903. In 1906 the Hepburn Act added power and prestige to the Interstate Commerce Commission and extended its jurisdiction significantly. That same year a Pure Food and Drug Act was passed. In 1911 under President Taft Congress

[11] See C. C. Regier, *The Era of the Muckrakers* (1932); *The Autobiography of Lincoln Steffens* (2 vols., 1931), and F. C. Howe, *The Confessions of a Reformer* (1925).

[12] This organization changed its name in the forties to The Methodist Federation for Social Action. It will be referred to generally in this text as the Federation whenever the full title is not used.

passed an act prohibiting the use of misleading labels, though the evil of fraudulent advertising escaped unscathed.

President Roosevelt pressed a "square deal" policy in industrial relations. During the anthracite coal strike of 1902 he intervened, and a commission of seven was appointed and made a decision which favored the miners' cause. In this industrial conflict the characteristic religious attitude of the operators was expressed by George F. Baer, president of the Philadelphia and Reading Coal and Iron Company, in a letter which found its way into the press. He wrote: "The rights and interests of the laboring man will be protected and cared for—not by the labor agitators, but by the Christian men to whom God in His infinite wisdom has given the control of the property interests of the country." [13] This philosophy was to be for many years a source of resistance to the application of the Social Creed of the churches.

Another area of major concern was the conservation of the nation's natural resources. Most of the public lands that were arable had been sold or given away. Millions of acres of good land had been ruined. Four-fifths of the nation's forests had been chopped down and not replaced. A few large lumber companies had gobbled up most of the rest. Mineral resources in the form of metals, coal, gas, or oil had been exploited with tragic wastefulness. Water-power sites were turned into profit-making utilities without consideration of beauty or flood-prevention. The outlook for conservation was pessimistic. The federal administration, however, put forth great energy in achieving the Reclamation Act of 1902, the Inland Waterways Commission of 1907, and the Commission on Country Life in the same year.

D. Emergence of the Social Creed

Methodism's own formulations of social doctrines and resolutions, though later in some respect than those formulated by others, benefited from the developments in the "Progressive Era from 1890 to 1910." For more than a decade prior to 1908, the year of the Social Creed, a campaign for social democracy had been under way. William Jennings Bryan had called his history of the campaign of 1896 *The First Battle*. This title was prophetic of the next two decades. There was revolt or reform in almost every department of American life as old political leaders were defeated and new ones established; as political machinery was reconstructed and political

---

[13] Quoted in John D. Hicks, *A Short History of American Democracy* (Boston: Houghton-Mifflin Co., 1949), p. 636.

practices were given critical scrutiny; as economic institutions were requested to justify themselves or mend their ways; and as innumerable social problems were avidly studied.

Historians have pointed out that "almost every notable figure in this period, whether in politics, philosophy, scholarship, or literature, derived his fame in part from his connection with the reform movement." [14] In the political arena were Weaver, Bryan, LaFollette, Roosevelt, and Wilson. In philosophy there were Borden P. Bowne, William James, Josiah Royce, and John Dewey. In economics and history were Thorstein Veblen, Richard Ely, and Frederick J. Turner. In literature there were William Dean Howells, Frank Norris, and Hamlin Garland. "The heroes of the day were all reformers." [15]

The greatest figure of the social gospel was Walter Rauschenbusch. His first great classic, *Christianity and the Social Crisis*, appeared in 1907. Before that year had ended, five socially minded ministers, Elbert R. Zering, Herbert Welch, Frank Mason North, Harry F. Ward, and Worth Tippy, organized the Methodist Federation for Social Service. Like the Church Association for the Advancement of the Interests of Labor in the Protestant Episcopal Church, this voluntary society pushed the claims of social Christianity within Methodism. The five leaders proposed "the formation of a society to stimulate a wide study of social questions by the Church, side by side with practical social service, and to bring the Church into touch with neglected social groups." As expressed in the constitution, the Federation's purpose was "to deepen within the Church the sense of social obligation and opportunity, to study social problems from the Christian point of view, and to promote social service in the spirit of Jesus Christ." Study, action, and service marked the emphasis of an early pamphlet entitled *What Is It?*

At the Baltimore General Conference of 1908 four memorials were presented and acted upon requesting (1) the formation of a Department of Church and Labor, (2) a special Secretary of Immigration, (3) a Commission to investigate the relation of the Church to social problems, and (4) recognition of the Federation for Social Service. It is significant that one third of the Episcopal Address that year was devoted to social questions. The General Conference adopted the famous "Social Creed of Methodism," and not only recognized the Federation but commissioned it to study four phases

[14] Allan Nevins and Henry Steele Commager, *A Short History of the United States* (New York: The Modern Library, 1945), p. 387.
[15] *Ibid.*, p. 388.

of the relationship of Methodism to social action. These four questions were: What specific principles and measures of social reform demand the approval of the Church? How can the agencies of this Church best be utilized or altered so as best to promote those principles? How may we best co-operate with other denominations to this end? How can theological school curricula and Conference studies best be modified to better prepare our preachers for efficiency in social reform? [16]

The General Conference of 1908 summoned the Church to continue and increase its social service in both study and preaching. Its Men's Brotherhoods, Sunday schools, and Epworth Leagues were commissioned to awaken and direct the spirit of social responsibility; and every Methodist was called upon to seek that "kingdom in which God's will shall be done on earth as it is in heaven." At the next General Conference (1912) the report prepared by the Federation was adopted and the Federation was declared to be "the executive agency of the Church to rally the forces of the Church to the support of the principles and measures thus approved."

The formulation of the statement on the Church and Social Problems was destined to be called the Social Creed.

THE SOCIAL CREED

The Methodist Episcopal Church stands—

For equal rights and complete justice for all men in all stations of life.

For the principle of conciliation and arbitration in industrial dissensions.

For the protection of the worker from dangerous machinery, occupational diseases, injuries, and mortality.

For the abolition of child labor.

For such regulation of the conditions of labor for women as shall safeguard the physical and moral health of the community.

For the suppression of the "sweating system."

For the gradual and reasonable reduction of the hours of labor to the lowest practical point, with work for all; and for the degree of leisure for all which is the condition of the highest human life.

For a release from employment one day in seven.

For a living wage in every industry.

For the highest wage that each industry can afford, and for the most equitable division of the products of industry that can ultimately be devised.

[16] Worth M. Tippy, (ed.), *The Socialized Church* (New York: Eaton & Mains, 1909), p. 281. See also the unpublished doctoral dissertation by Milton Huber, "The History of the Methodist Federation for Social Action" (Boston University, 1949).

For the recognition of the Golden Rule and the mind of Christ as the supreme law of society and the sure remedy of all social ills.[17]

In 1912 this statement on "The Church and Social Problems" was revised. Three bishops were appointed to the Federation's executive council and the Reverend Harry F. Ward was called to be its secretary. The following year he began his career as a theological professor at Boston University School of Theology while continuing as the executive officer of the Federation. With the backing of the General Conference the Federation was able to expand its program. It was again approved by the General Conferences of 1916 and 1924. It received no financial support from the Church, but served in those years as the "authorized agency of the Methodist Episcopal Church for the purpose of raising before the Church the question of the social implications of the gospel of Jesus." [18]

The Social Creed of Methodism has, as is well known, a significant relationship to the founding of the Federal Council of Churches of Christ in America. Social problems had been one of the moving forces behind the organization of the Council. Between the time of the holding of the "Inter-Church Conference on Federation" in New York in 1905 and the first meeting of the Federal Council in December 1908, the continuing committee responsible for the "plan of federation" maintained an active interest in social issues. In both its 1906 and 1907 reports attention was given to organized labor, temperance, immigration, international arbitration, and child labor. When the Federal Council convened in Philadelphia, a special theater meeting was held in the interests of the Church and labor at which D. A. Hayes, fifth vice-president of the American Federation of Labor, Bishop E. R. Hendrix (M.E., South), president of the Federal Council, and Charles Stelzle "spoke to an audience that Hayes described as the largest gathering of workingmen he had ever seen in Philadelphia." [19]

One of the important actions of the Council was the adoption of the committee report on "The Church and Modern Industry" which was presented and largely prepared by the Reverend Frank Mason North.[20] This was an epochal eighteen-page statement which related

---

[17] *Discipline*, Methodist Episcopal Church, 1908, pp. 479-81.

[18] See the *Discipline*, Methodist Episcopal Church, 1912, pp. 512-14.

[19] C. H. Hopkins, *The Rise of the Social Gospel in American Protestantism*, p. 306.

[20] Elias B. Sanford (ed.), *Report of the First Meeting of the Federal Council of the Churches of Christ in America, Philadelphia, 1908*. (New York: 1909). See *Frank Mason North, December 3, 1850-December 17, 1935*, a memorial prepared and published by Friends of Frank Mason North (New York: 1936), p. 6.

the headship of Christ to social reform and personal redemption. Paragraph nine of the report contained the formulation of social principles known as the "Social Creed of the Churches" as it first appeared. It was taken almost verbatim from the Methodist pronouncement on "The Church and Social Problems"—also largely written by Frank Mason North—except two paragraphs. The "creed" was considerably modified by the Council in 1912 and then stood in that form until 1932. Both the Federal Council reformulation and that of the Methodist Episcopal Church in 1932 reflected the new situation created by the Great Depression, which we shall note in due course below.

The Methodist Episcopal Church, South, was not stimulated to respond as strongly to urban industrial problems by 1908 as her Northern sister had been. Not until 1914 did she adopt the Social Creed. Yet in 1906 the Episcopal Address delivered at the Southern General Conference noted that "the star of a new industrialism has turned Southward and lingers in the skies that bend over the lower Mississippi Valley. . . . This amazing industrialism has developed a materialistic spirit, hitherto unknown among us, that menaces the very kingdom of Christ." The bishops also called attention to the tremendous significance of the city in modern life. "The real rulers of the nation are the men of the city." Not only do they control the prices of the stock market, but they also "establish the ethical standards of the nation and determine its political destiny."

The city is the place where the immigrants concentrated. Immigration was challenging the South as well as the North. In 1906 the Southern bishops declared, "Already in some of our states there are large foreign communities, as yet ignorant of our language and unacquainted with our national genius. To meet these coming thousands with the educative and redemptive agencies of the gospel is the urgent duty of the Christian churches in these Southern States." Two years later the Northern bishops expressed "profound regret that so many of the immigrants stay in the greater ports." This means a slower assimilation of American ideals. "It means also the continuance of imported anarchistic and communistic ideals, as property in land is impossible for most who remain in the cities. Property in land is a chief solvent of anarchistic ideas."

In 1908 the *Methodist Protestant* editorialized on the widespread unemployment, noting that "there is plenty of labor for every man who is willing to work." It held that the Salvation Army had the solution in its program. Contrariwise, "in our judgment the problem of labor will not be solved by labor unions, by legislative enactments, or by political gerrymandering." [21] Before the Great Depression the only reference to economic questions found in the minutes of the Baltimore Conference of the Methodist Protestant Church was in 1914 on the occasion of a visit by Harry F. Ward in the cause of social evangelism. It passed a vigorous statement on the industrial message of the Church and suggested the formation of a larger, stronger committee to study what each church should know about the community.

On the question of world peace one finds that in 1911 there was support for the position taken by the Federal Council of Churches in favor of obligatory arbitration in settling international differences. The war, of course, aroused the Methodist Protestants, as it did the other branches of Methodism. They said in 1919: "A united church must take a firm and final stand for world peace on the highest principles of justice and righteousness. . . . War must be rendered impossible in any future time of the world's history." [22] Comments on the peace question in the other branches will be presented in connection with the period of the first World War.

In summary we may note that of the major types of social problems the race question received the least attention in the awakening of Methodism's social conscience in the early years of the twentieth century. The emergent social creed was clearly oriented to the new situation in urban industrial America. Methodism's official step in formulating a creed on social issues was closely linked in time and spirit to the founding of the Federal Council of Churches of Christ in America. This intimate relationship was to mark the witness of both these bodies from 1908 forward.

[21] The *Methodist Protestant*, 78 (1908), 3. This magazine was published by the Methodist Protestant Church.
[22] John Bayley Jones, "The Approach of Baltimore Methodism to Social Problems" (unpublished S.T.M. thesis, Wesley Theological Seminary, Washington, D.C., 1942), p. 28.

CHAPTER THREE

The Social Creed Before World War I

Chronological Outline of
Major Events in American Social, Economic, and
Political History: 1909 to 1916

TAFT AND WILSON ADMINISTRATIONS: 1909-16

1909—William Howard Taft is inaugurated as twenty-sixth president.

Homestead Act is enlarged. That year sees the founding also of *America,* a leading Catholic (Jesuit) magazine deeply interested in church-state problems.

The Sixteenth Amendment (income tax) is submitted to the states.

First prominent use of the political "recall" in Los Angeles.

1910—Act requiring publicity of political contributions.

Immigration in 1910 is 1,041,570; in 1913 it is 1,197,892. The total from Europe (1911-20) is 4,376,564.

Organization of the National Association for the Advancement of Colored People.

Great forest fires raged in the Northwest, showing reckless waste in natural resources. In 1912 great floods damage property in the Mississippi Valley. In 1913 was the dedication of the Keokuk Dam, then the world's largest power dam.

Communications are brought under the Interstate Commerce Commission. The I.C.C. prosecutes many companies.

1911—The Supreme Court sustains the decree dissolving the Standard Oil Company of New Jersey for violating the Sherman Antitrust Law. Action taken also against the American Tobacco Company.

McNamara brothers are convicted of dynamiting the Los Angeles *Times* building.

1912—A major textile strike in Lawrence, Massachusetts. The nation agitated also over the I.W.W. (International Workers of the World). Massachusetts passes a Minimum Wage Act, one of the first. Congress passes the eight-hour day provision in all federal contracts.

Congress establishes the Federal Children's Bureau "to investigate and report on all matters pertaining to the welfare of children and child life." Congress also initiates an experimental parcel post; prohibits the use of false assertions and labels on drugs; submits to the states the Seventeenth Amendment providing for the popular election of Senators; and legally discontinues the appointment of missionaries in government Indian schools.

The Progressive Party emerges and nominates Theodore Roosevelt. During the general campaign women are conspicuously active and agitated for national suffrage. Six Western states have already granted it. Four more follow by 1914.

1913—The inauguration of Woodrow Wilson and the triumph of the Democratic Party. The states ratify the Sixteenth Amendment.

Increasing and severe labor unrest. Congress establishes the Department of Labor.

Widespread interest expressed in "widowed mothers" and "pension" laws.

In California the legislature passes the anti-alien land ownership act and Japan lodges a formal protest.

1914—The first World War breaks out, coinciding with the founding of the Church Peace Union and the World Alliance for Peace through the Churches.

The public schools of Gary (Indiana) adopt the

plan of excusing pupils at certain hours for religious instruction in the churches.

Birth control movement launched by Mrs. Margaret Sanger, and later vigorously opposed by the Roman Catholic Church.

Industrial relations and business life reflected conflict and tension. In South-central Colorado in 1914 there was industrial war. Congress passed the Clayton Act, sometimes called the Magna Carta of Labor.

Congress establishes the Federal Reserve System.

The International Harvester Corporation found guilty of restraint of trade.

Trouble arises from a deep-running social revolution in Mexico, and Congress authorized the use of force.

Opening of the Panama Canal and the establishment of a permanent government in the Canal Zone.

1915—The United States becomes increasingly involved in the European War, especially after the sinking of the *Lusitania*. Though Wilson holds to the slogan, "Too proud to fight," and officially adopts a policy of neutrality, the U.S.A. becomes the arsenal and the chief storehouse for the Allies.

"Open door" policy reaffirmed.

Domestically, the cost of living rises higher than ever before in the nation's history.

The "grandfather" clause in the Oklahoma constitution declared unconstitutional.

Nineteen states have adopted prohibition.

Twenty-eight states have welfare laws for widows and dependent children.

Pope Benedict XV welds "Catholic Action" into an effective unified force for Catholic influence on the social order.

1916—During the war immigration declines, in 1916 being down to 298,826.

Income tax declared constitutional.

Demand for an eight-hour day and time and a half for overtime by 400,000 employees of 452 railroads.

A Child-Labor Act passed.

Adamson Act establishes the eight-hour day for railroad operators.

A military expedition enters Mexico under Pershing. Carranza protests. Carranza's demands rejected.

America protests submarine warfare; also protests mail seizures by the Allies. Indebtedness of foreign countries to U.S. amounted to nearly $2 billion.

Despite labor troubles economic development is unprecedented. Steep rise in prices.

During a San Francisco preparedness parade a bomb explodes, killing a number of people. Thomas J. Mooney and Warren K. Billings found guilty, thus setting off a *cause celebre* in civil liberties.

SOME OF THE "MUCKRAKERS" HAD CHAMpioned the cause of social justice for the Negro and exposed the general disenfranchisement of the Southern Negro. 1910 saw the organization of the National Association for the Advancement of Colored People by a group of militantly concerned whites and Negroes. Roosevelt's Progressive Party advocated Negro suffrage, but had, in any case, little support from the "solid" democratic South, which meant also that it took little political risk in advocating it. Bryan and later Wilson were dependent on Southern support and hesitated to demand the extension of political democracy through Negro enfranchisement. Wilson was believed by Negroes to be too "Southern." The Negroes in 1912 stuck with Taft.

The area which saw the development of much reform agitation and legislation paid increasing attention to the question of woman suffrage. Labor and the temperance forces had consistently favored the vote for women because they were convinced that the vote would promote social legislation. The democratically minded Populists had favored it earlier. Women suffragists also kept the campaign alive. They identified their campaign with the movement to restore natural rights to all individuals, to provide equality of opportunity, to abolish political corruption, and to defeat the powerful money or monopoly interests. The movement made headway in Europe and in a number of states.

In 1912 Theodore Roosevelt's campaign included a
woman suffrage amendment to the Constitution, but
it was the First World War with its need for full
mobilization of woman's support that put the program
across (1920). It should be added that the suffrage
movement was closely connected with the antisaloon
campaign. The Prohibition Amendment was ratified
in 1920. Both Prohibition and Woman's Suffrage were
heralded as victories for purer politics, a cleaner national life, and an effective public control of political
life. They were thus not isolated issues, but integral
parts of the inclusive reform programs of the Progressive Era.

A. The Message of the Methodist Federation

In 1910 the Methodist Federation for Social Service under its
editorial secretary, Harry F. Ward, brought out an introduction
to the study and practice of social service entitled *Social Ministry*.[1]
It was a symposium of twelve essays giving a synoptic challenge,
beginning with "The Social Message of the Prophets," "The Social
Ministry of Jesus," and "The Social Activities of John Wesley,"
and then covering such topics as "The Industrial Revolution," "The
Labor Movement," "The Salvation of the Vagrant," "The Organization of a Church for Social Ministry," "Social Service in the
Rural Church," and "The City and the Kingdom." There are nu-
merous references to contemporary writers like Francis Peabody,
Shailer Mathews, Walter Rauschenbusch, L. Brace, Richard T.
Ely, J. Hobson, Washington Gladden, L. T. Hobhouse, Edith Abott,
C. R. Henderson, and Josiah Strong. Like other writings of these
men, this book reflected a strong evangelical spirit. Its social passion was firmly grounded in scriptural and Methodist foundations.

Harris Franklin Rall, then President of Iliff School of Theology,
in writing on the new political, economic, and social democracy,
said:

If it shall come, this spirit of Jesus must lead us. He must give the true
foundation for government, which shall make God and his righteousness
the seat of authority, and the task of the majority not to make right but
to find that right and express it. He must give a new basis for its
democracy. . . . The truer foundation will be his [Jesus'] conception of
man. Men are not equal, but all are of God and all belong to him. The
poorest is beyond the measure of material values.[2]

[1] Harry F. Ward (ed.), *Social Ministry* (New York: Eaton and Mains,
1910).
[2] *Ibid.*, pp. 54-55.

The President of Garrett Biblical Institute, Charles J. Little, put the challenge arising from the social activities of John Wesley squarely before Methodists and answered thereby the cries to preach "the simple gospel." Said President Little:

> In America especially the social problem has developed with amazing suddenness and in startling complexity. If Wesley scorned to solve it in the England of his day by such platitudes as, "The simple gospel is all that people need," it is mere sloth on our part to be repeating the chatter that he derided. He combined the finest qualities of the great preacher with the ceaseless efficiency of the practical philanthropist; and it is indolent mockery of the real Wesley to worship the revivalist and to deny the friend of the prisoner and the helper of the poor; to praise his linguistic powers, yet to forget that every modern language acquired by him was acquired to help him reach the hearts and minds of those that spoke a different tongue.[3]

Harry F. Ward, then pastor of the Euclid Avenue Methodist Church in Oak Park, Illinois, analyzed the various elements and viewpoints in world labor movements and pleaded for a right relationship in the United States between organized labor and the churches. He saw in the churches an opportunity and obligation to clarify the latent ideals of the labor movement in terms of the kingdom of God. Ward concluded,

> Whether or not this will be realized as also whether or not the movement will pass beyond class boundaries, develop a universal social consciousness, and recognize itself as part of the larger movement for industrial democracy, depends largely upon the relations between it and organized religion. Indeed, the future of both depends in a very large degree upon the establishment of sympathetic, cooperative relationships between them.[4]

At the moment when Ward was making his appeal for a *rapprochement* between organized religion and organized labor, there were estimated 500,000 homeless, shiftless, unproductive vagrants in the United States. Their support involved a tax of $100,000,000 on the public. Railroads believed that they suffered $25,000,000 a year from their depredations. The Reverend Edgar J. Helms of Morgan Memorial Church in Boston set himself to do something practical in this area. His genius was the beginning of the Goodwill Industries which have blessed tens of thousands in scores of cities in the past half-century.

[3] *Ibid.*, pp. 72-73.
[4] *Ibid.*, pp. 130-31.

In the symposium already cited Helms wrote:

The writer has had many years of experience in gospel work for the vagrant. He has studied this work in most of the great cities in our land and in Europe. He is fully persuaded that any material relief offered without an opportunity to earn it, or any relief that is not clean and wholesome and sanitary, is worse than a mistake. Until the state and municipality can be induced to provide for all needing industrial relief, the writer believes the church would do well to provide industrial institutions in which an opportunity will be afforded all unfortunate persons to earn the supply of their physical needs.[5]

At this time Worth M. Tippy was pastor of Epworth Memorial Church in Cleveland. He held that every church should be a socialized church. "It is erroneous to consider that only institutional churches are truly socialized. Every church should look upon the creation of just and happy social conditions as one of the prime objects of the institutions of religion." [6] He was realistically aware, of course, that most churches had little understanding of the social problem in all of its terrible significance and possessed little of the true social spirit. He undertook to show how a local church should be organized to perform its social mission.

The pastor will have to lead and must become a student of social questions, including practical experience in scientific methods of charity and in constructive reform.[7] Therefore he must become involved in all facets of social welfare by direct personal involvement. "No pastor," he argued, "is ready to lead a church into a larger social program until he has proven to his people and to the people of his neighborhood, by such service, that he knows what to do, and that he is activated by compassion and not by motives that are primarily ambitious and intellectual." [8]

Dr. Tippy advised the creation of a social service committee, drawing on a recommendation to that affect in the encyclical of the Lambeth Conference of 1908. This committee was to have general supervision of the charitable and social service work of the church and its various auxiliary organizations. "The committee shall keep in view the correlation of the church with the Federation for Social Service and other connectional movements of the Methodist Episcopal churches of Cleveland, the Associated Charities, and such other

---

[5] *Ibid.*, pp. 200-201.
[6] *Ibid.*, p. 231. By "socialized" he meant a church intelligently concerned for social need.
[7] *Ibid.*, p. 233.
[8] *Ibid.*, pp. 233-34.

charities and movements for social betterment and social reform as the Official Board may authorize upon its recommendation." [9]

Such a committee would probably suffice in most situations, but for larger churches he proposed a Charities Council, with a salaried staff. Tippy was an earnest proponent of close co-operation with and referrals to organized charity on a wide service area basis, as well as with the Juvenile Court. He stressed the idea of the church as a neighborhood center and decried the exclusive and nonsocial character of some urban churches. He anticipated many principles later accepted elsewhere, if not generally practiced. In 1960 they seem almost commonplace.

"The first is that every church should determine, as the first obligation, to minister to the people of its immediate parish." [10]

"The second principle is that the character of the work which is to be undertaken should be determined by a study of the needs of the parish and of the membership of the church." [11]

He was painfully aware that Protestant churches in America were neglecting industrial neighborhoods.

They tend to seek self-support, and turn naturally to residence suburbs, or to sections of cities where better paid workingmen have their homes. There is urgent need of a new policy, in which strong churches and city missionary unions shall systematically plant highly socialized churches, with properly trained and sympathetic pastors, in crowded sections of cities, or provide better facilities for churches already existing. This is the most effective way for the churches to keep near to the masses of the people.[12]

If Methodism had earnestly followed this program and been faithful to the principles cited above, the inner city perhaps would not today be the dilemma for churches which it has become.

Cities in 1910 were already in a critical condition. Thirty years earlier their corrupt municipal governments had been analyzed by Lord Bryce. Frank Mason North, Secretary of the New York City Church Extension and Missionary Society, saw the great distance that separated them from the kingdom of God. He saw also that the cities were crucial to winning America for Christ. "Tens of thousands, yes, hundreds of thousands, of the boys and girls of our cities are growing up into citizenship and home-making, with no spiritual sanction for conduct, no conception of God, no knowl-

[9] *Ibid.*, p. 235.
[10] *Ibid.*, p. 242.
[11] *Ibid.*, p. 243.
[12] *Ibid.*, p. 244.

edge of the Bible, no reverence for essential truths, and with an atrophied moral sense." [13]

Few Northern leaders were keenly aware of the Negro's problem in the city. North's was one of the few voices who heralded the founding of the N.A.A.C.P. Here as elsewhere the Methodist Federation for Social Service showed the way. Dr. North wrote:

Instance [sic] a specific racial problem, that of the American Negro. The amazing progress of forty years must not betray us into a denial of present facts. Too much cannot be said in praise of the enterprise which, in school and shop and farm, is opening life and opportunity to the vast multitudes. But the Negro will not be a successful factor in our modern civilization unless he can survive the test of the city. On the streets of our cities, not upon the plantations of the Southland, will he find his birthright. Unless a character be developed which shall emerge from the complex conditions of our civic life unsullied, the citizenship of the future is not his. The shame of the labor caste which denies him the rights of organized industry, of the social feeling that makes him not workman but servant, of the civic and religious indifference which drives him to conditions of living which are the sure degradation of the white race which so frankly asserts its superiority, is a part of the current chronicle of our American life. Through sea and desert he may be led, but he comes to the Kingdom only through the conquest of the high-walled cities.[14]

Dr. North recognized that the crisis of the Negro's future was located not only in the agricultural South but even more in many industrial Northern cities. Fifty years after North wrote his analysis thousands of Negroes had achieved full-fledged citizenship, with many economic, social, and cultural opportunities. For many more thousands the critical years are today and tomorrow.

B. Industrial Criticism

When the General Conference of the Methodist Episcopal Church met in 1912, the Episcopal Address made a significant general indictment of evils in the present working of the capitalist system:

Organized capital stands indicted at the bar of public judgment for the gravest crimes against the public welfare. Among the counts are: (1) conspiring to advance prices on staple commodities indispensable to life, (2) resorting to adulteration of foods, fabrics, and materials in order to increase profits already excessive, (3) destroying competition, (4) suborning legislation and robbing the people of the first orderly recourse of the weak against the strong.

[13] Ibid., pp. 310-11.
[14] Ibid., pp. 311-12.

These indictments were common to the social gospel witness of the time as evidenced by such writings as those of Walter Rauschenbusch.

In the industrial field the General Conference noted in 1912 and repeated in 1916 a call for the eight-hour day and for laws forbidding the employment of workers for seven days continuously. Wages should be calculated on a six-day basis.

The outstanding infamy of the current labor situation was the chaining of little children to the wheels of trade. On this subject of child labor the two sections of Methodism spoke with the same protesting voice.

The bishops in the North in 1908 said: "While in many states the law now protects children from severe and continued labor, at the expense of health, growth, and education, it is yet true that in some states the legislation is inadequate in that the age at which the child may be employed in mines, mills, factories, stores, and other places is too low and the penalty on parents for misrepresentation as to age is too slight."

When industrial plants have invaded the mountain regions, or have come near them, it is not uncommon to see the father and mother in middle life supported entirely by the labor of their children in the mills. Any change from these conditions is resisted, not only by those whose children are thus employed, but by owners who often reside in states where the laws against child labor are ample. In the name of Jesus Christ we protest against the sacrifice of childhood on the altar of mammon, whether it be by the sloth of parents or the greed of proprietors.

The bishops were equally concerned in 1912 and 1916: "Neither Milton's nor Goethe's devil could have devised a plot against humankind more demoniacal in torture or in destructive consequences than this outrage upon helpless childhood by commercial greed."

The two major branches of Methodism also affirmed the principle of industrial democracy as expressed in the rights of workers to organize and to bargain collectively. In the South the affirmation was still on the level of Episcopal admonition, but in the North the General Conference spoke in official legislation as well. When the Church spoke, it linked rights with duties and protested against any partisan spirit. The Episcopal Address of 1912 stated: "We therefore declare our approval of labor organizations and other defensive alliances of all whose interests are threatened or invaded. Such united and unified action is their only recourse under present conditions. At the same time we cannot ignore the fact that organized labor also faces public judgment on the charge of lawless rioting, violence, and even murder, in its efforts to enforce its decree." The bishops stressed a continuing concern in 1916.

We call upon our members as employers, investors, or wage earners to do everything in their power to further measures such as trade agreements between employers and organized workers, minimum wage adjustments, profit-sharing cooperative plans, which look toward the maintenance of a living wage, the correction of unjust inequalities in the distribution of wealth, the increasing democratization of industry, and the Christianization of the world's work in the name of that abundant life which our Master came to promote.

The Northern bishops were especially emphatic in 1912 against the use of lawless rioting and violence to gain union objectives. "Our people who are members of labor unions must recognize that no circumstances short of personal peril under dangerous assault can justify violent or lawless methods in seeking relief from hard conditions." This rejection of violence was part of a clear recognition of the need for collective bargaining. Following the lead of the Methodist Federation for Social Service, the General Conference took a position which was reaffirmed in principle in 1916 and 1924 as follows: "The immediate application in every industry of the principle of collective bargaining is not only essential to the protection of the modern industrial worker, but it is the first step toward the cooperative control of both the process and the proceeds of industry which will be the ultimate expression of Christianity in industrial relationships." [15]

It is significant that collective bargaining should have been recognized as having a function in industrial democracy beyond that of ordinary business unionism. In this respect the Church's position in 1912 was clearly in advance of the two major political parties of that day, though not taking the positions of the Socialist Party. The platform of the Progressive Party would have found the above sentiment supportable.

Significantly, when the Church spoke on questions of wages, it related them to the whole question of social justice and the distribution of wealth. It saw that the worker's dependence on employment raised questions of society's obligation to provide employment in an industrial society, and that employment and human dignity were closely related. "Above all," said the General

[15] *Discipline*, Methodist Episcopal Church, 1912.

Conference of 1916, "it is necessary for the Church to proclaim to the nation until it is embodied in law and custom that the right to work (the only property right which many of the workers have) is a spiritual necessity, that the exercise of this right makes for spiritual development and the denial of it entails spiritual disaster." [16] The General Conference consistently called for a living wage in every industry and the highest wage that each industry can afford." [17] It noted, further, that out of some of the very industries that pay inadequate wages great fortunes were being built. "Against such inequalities the Christian conscience must protest, and they must be removed." Members of the church were called upon as employers, investors, and wage earners to do everything that lies in their power to further the most equitable division of the product of industry that can ultimately be devised.[18]

Agitation for and the growth of trade unions aroused much debate on the various forms of collective bargaining and hence of the types of shops where unions were effective. As a consequence the General Conference was called upon to declare itself on this issue in 1916 and again in later periods when the union shop was under discussion.

There are two methods of collective bargaining now in use, one requiring the employment of only union men, the other providing that a preference shall be shown, both in hiring and dismissal, to union men. To those employers and workers who reject both, the Church must point out that they are under moral obligation to discover some other form of collective bargaining that will make more for the good of the industry and of society at large. It would follow that the Church as a larger employer of labor must in some way realize collective bargaining, either in one of the existing forms or some other yet to be devised, and every possible effort should be made to work with organized labor in so far as its methods are just and the rights of the unorganized are not infringed upon.[19]

As an employer of labor in the field of publications, the church's policies were subject to persistent and often acrimonious debate for many years. The question of the union shop became an acute issue in the twenties and again in the decade following the passage of the Taft-Hartley law in 1947, especially in the two quadrennia following 1952. "Right-to-work" laws were then passed in almost all the states of the Southeast Jurisdiction and in several others.

[16] *Discipline*, Methodist Episcopal Church, 1916. "Right to work" had a different significance here from the present Right-to-Work movement.
[17] 1908, 1916, 1924.
[18] 1916.
[19] *Discipline*, Methodist Episcopal Church, 1916.

Methodist opinion and influence on these laws will be discussed at an appropriate place below.

Returning now to the response of Methodism to the industrial situation in 1912, we may note its attention to such matters as the "black lists" and questions of community, health, and social insurance. The bishops stated that the use of the "black list" and the "boycott" is in the nature of "conspiracy against the rights of individual judgment and conscience, and un-American in principle and dangerous in tendency." The General Conference called also for the prevention of preventable diseases by spreading the knowledge of sanitation and by enforcing individual responsibility for the health of the community.[20] On the question of social insurance it said: "The entire force of the churches should be thrown into the nation-wide campaign by investigation and legislative enactment to protect the workers from industrial diseases, and to provide swift and sure compensation for the sufferers from such accidents and diseases."[21] In the same spirit the church demanded the enactment and enforcement of proper building codes, for it held that the relation between bad housing and sickness of the body and the soul was established beyond question.[22]

In 1914 the Methodist Episcopal Church, South, adopted the Social Creed in the same form as the North. The Bishops' position on labor carefully avoided espousing or attacking the cause of the workers, as witness the Episcopal Address:

> The Church, however, no more than her Divine Lord, will consent to be used as a judge and divider in the distribution of earthly goods among rival claimants and contending classes. While sympathizing with the poor, dwelling with them amid their hardships, espousing their interests, and relieving their distresses, she cannot serve as the partisan of a class, whether rich or poor.

C. Temperance and Prohibition

The General Conference of the Methodist Episcopal Church established The Board of Temperance in 1912, the Temperance Society having existed since 1904. Its first headquarters were in Wichita, Kansas. In 1916, during the great campaign which wrote into law the Eighteenth Amendment, the offices were moved to Washington, D. C. Clarence True Wilson was the first secretary of the organization. He was a noted figure in the temperance cause

---

[20] *Discipline*, Methodist Episcopal Church, 1912.
[21] *Ibid.*, 1912.
[22] *Discipline*, Methodist Episcopal Church, 1916.

from 1910 to his retirement in 1936. His successor, Ernest H. Cherrington, was for many years a leader in the Anti-Saloon League and editor of the Anti-Saloon League's *American Issue.*

During the long crusade leading up to the era of Prohibition, Methodists were strong supporters of the nondenominational Anti-Saloon League, and its representatives made systematic presentations in local churches and at Annual Conferences. The national Anti-Saloon League was organized in the Calvary Baptist Church in Washington, D.C., in December 1895. At the height of its power it had the support of as many as sixty thousand agencies and a budget of $2,500,000.00. It achieved unprecedented political power. It was founded for action and took an uncompromising position aimed at nothing less than the destruction of the entire traffic in alcoholic liquor.

At first, the churches' traditions of nonintervention in politics produced doubts and resistance, but as hope for success grew in local, state, and finally national legislation the churches rallied to its program of political action. The League was often confronted with the charge that it was a political machine, and answered: "The church is a machine and the League is a machine within a machine." [23] The satire of this sentence was, of course, unintentional.

The League established a large publishing plant in 1909 and by 1912 issued more than forty tons of temperance literature each month, including thirty-one state editions of *The American Issue.* This was only the beginning. Between 1909 and 1923 the American Issue Company produced 157,314,642 copies of temperance papers, 2,000,000 books, 5,000,000 pamphlets, 115,000,000 leaflets, 2,000,-000 window cards, and more than 18,000,000 other cards. One writer, Odegard, states: "One might almost say that the liquor business was drowned in a deluge of temperance literature." [24]

Control over elections was the strongest weapon of the Anti-Saloon League. It was nonpartisan and became a single-cause agency, supporting those candidates in the major parties who were favorable to its policies. Their voting records on other issues were of little consequence. Nominations were watched carefully and the League was prepared to deliver or withhold a large bloc of votes, a power feared by the major parties. After establishing its legis-

[23] Luke Ebersole, *Church Lobbying in the Nation's Capitol* (New York: The Macmillan Co., 1951), p. 10.
[24] Peter Odegard, *Pressure Politics,* pp. 74, 75. Quoted in Ebersole, *Ibid.,* p. 10.

lative office in Washington (1899), it developed a very impressive lobby. It drafted and introduced bills, watched bills after introduction, lobbied among Congressmen, arranged for hearings, created public opinion, arranged for the filing of petitions, and directed temperance legislation in general.[25]

Few of the Anti-Saloon League leaders were interested in general "social gospel" activities. Indeed, many who developed an all-out interest in political action leading to Prohibition were opposed to political action in the field of industrial relations. No "social gospel" group ever approached the degree of political action which characterized the work of the Anti-Saloon League and the Methodist Board which worked with it in Washington. In politics its strategy was impressive. Much of its power and effectiveness came from the support of groups like the Methodists.

At this point something more must be said about the relation of Prohibition to the "social gospel" movement which had already borne fruit in the Social Creed in 1908 and 1912, as we have seen. "Our mental image of Prohibition," says Paul A. Carter, "comes down to us from the 'roaring 'twenties,' and is colored by the notion that Prohibition was exclusively the work of moralizing Puritans compensating for the repressions of their own harsh code in a spurious indignation at the pleasure of their neighbors."[26] It is easy to forget the multitude of earnest men and women who fought liquor not because it made men happy, but because they knew it made them defeated and unhappy. Prior to the Volstead Act the dry crusade spoke the language of a social and humanitarian reform which had a deep kinship with the social gospel.

Social reform with the anti-liquor crusade goes back clearly to the age of Jackson and had along with prison reform a long and honorable record of humanitarian concern. Carter points out, for example, that the Prohibition Party developed platforms from 1872 onward which did not confine themselves to the liquor issue. These platforms were, indeed, usually far in advance of the regular Republican and Democratic platforms, seeking such reforms as the direct election of Senators, the abolition of the electoral college, woman suffrage, and "the separation of the money of government from all banking institutions" thirty-seven years before the Federal Reserve Act was passed. In the period of Theodore Roosevelt and

[25] Ebersole, *Ibid.*, p. 11.
[26] Paul A. Carter, *The Decline and Revival of the Social Gospel* (Ithaca: Cornell University Press, 1954), p. 32.

Woodrow Wilson it stood for employers' liability legislation and the abolition of child labor.[27]

The development of the Anti-Saloon League tended to change the concern of the "dry" forces to a single focus, but one must not forget that the temperance cause was against an entrenched, well-organized, wealthy industrial empire. This "demon Rum" engaged in political corruption of the kind earlier fought with eagerness by the Populist and Progressive crusaders. The attack was in part like that on the trusts. The Presbyterian weekly, *The Continent,* noted this in an editorial in 1920:

> In a time when the social conscience of America was aroused as never before to condemn grafters who stole from the people profits for which they rendered no tangible return, the distilling and brewing businesses loomed up as the grossest of all such offenders. For they were fleecing the poorest classes of millions upon millions of hard-earned cash without ever returning to them a pennyworth of any kind of value, economic, physical, or social.[28]

The temperance movement involved not only the propriety of a personal act but also the legitimacy of a business. Dabney says that the Methodist Episcopal Church, South, "was the most militantly aggressive of all the large American churches in its hostility to the saloon"; and yet their "vigorous excoriation of lynching and their exhortations to employers to grant their employees a living wage stamped them as the Southern denomination that . . . probably did most to further social well-being" in that period.[29] Temperance, however, was the bridge over which the Southern Church in Methodism walked into the political arena.

What brought the Methodist Episcopal Church, South, into political social action was, then, neither the industrial question of labor and capital nor the question of the Negro within its gates, but the question of temperance and Prohibition. During the twenties this issue was to dominate social action in the South and to raise fundamental questions of the church's role in politics. Prior to the rise of Prohibition Southern Methodism had taken a political action position symbolized by statements in the Episcopal addresses of 1865 and 1894. During the Civil War the bishops had said:

"Know your high calling. Preach Christ and Him crucified. Do

[27] Carter, *Ibid.,* pp. 32-33.
[28] See Carter, *Ibid.,* p. 33.
[29] V. Dabney, *Dry Messiah* (New York: Knopf, 1948), p. 43, cited in Carter, *Ibid.,* pp. 33-34. Dabney, it should be noted, was very critical of Bishop Cannon, thus making this evaluation especially noteworthy.

not preach politics. You have no commission to preach politics. The divinity of the Church is never more strikingly displayed than when it holds on its ever straightforward way in the midst of worldly commotions." This admonition did not, of course, keep Methodist preachers from preaching politics during the war.

In 1894 the Episcopal Address stated:

It is not amiss to repeat what has often been repeated—that our Church is strictly a religious and in no wise a political body. Our sole business is to preach and serve the kingdom of God. There are many questions— economical, social, and in part ethical—of burning interest in this day which our pulpit and Churches may be tempted to substitute for the simple gospel. . . . The more deeply we keep ourselves to the one work of testifying to all men, the better shall we promote the highest good of our country and race. As a Church we are not related by affiliation or antagonism to any political party. As a citizen every man should carry his judgment and conscience into politics and all other spheres of life.

About 1907 a wave of prohibitory legislation against the saloon had begun to sweep over the nation. By 1919 thirty-three states had by statute or constitutional provisions prohibited the liquor traffic. The movement had the backing of many educational, medical, industrial, and social welfare agencies, but the energy and political drive was in large measure supplied by the Methodist Episcopal Board of Temperance, Prohibition, and Public Morals which was organized in 1916. Prohibition was supported by many resolutions in the Methodist Episcopal Church, South. Its General Conference in 1910 adopted the following:

Whereas, the Methodist Episcopal Church, South, has ever gone before the world as the unalterable foe of the liquor traffic, and is a prohibition church, which will never consider a compromise with this heinous sin; and whereas greater strides have been made in temperance in the home of Southern Methodism—in the South—than in any other part of our union in recent years, to the furtherance of which our Church has been one of the principal factors:

Resolved, that we hereby appeal to the President and Congress of the United States to take immediate action and pass this bill (regulating interstate shipments of liquor) for the protection of the people from this great curse.[30]

The commitment and approval of the bishops were indicated in their address of 1926 when they stated that "The National Prohibition Law promulgated in 1920 is the most remarkable social enact-

[30] *Ibid.*, II, 330.

ment by any great nation to promote the general welfare by the restriction of the activity of the individual."

The political and social effectiveness of these Methodist efforts were apparent before World War I, which served to stimulate the cause. In 1914 the secretary of the Liquor Dealers Association said:

"It is only necessary to read the list of those preachers who are active in the present propaganda for legislative prohibition to realize that it is the Methodist Church which is obsessed with the ambition to gain control of the government." [31]

While the extremity of this statement must be corrected by more prudent historical judgments, it remains a fact that Methodism was a controlling power in the movement for prohibition on both the state and the national level. During the period between the passing of the Eighteenth Amendment in 1920 until its repeal in 1933 the primary public interest of the Methodist Church, particularly in the South, was for and in defense of Prohibition.

The organized temperance movement had a powerful ally in the church-school literature. The *Adult Student* will serve as an example. From its beginning in 1908 through 1917 the *Adult Student* had a temperance lesson each quarter. In 1918 these were discontinued and temperance was dealt with only incidentally as a factor in lessons dealing with social conditions. Occasional lessons and articles on temperance began appearing again in 1929. In 1932 the emphasis again became pronounced.

In the Berean Graded Lessons there were constant references to the liquor problem from 1910 to 1915.

The Women's Christian Temperance Union and the Anti-Saloon League were described as allies of the church in the campaign against the liquor traffic. "All the enemies of the liquor traffic center about the Church." When the agents of the liquor industry attacked what was being said, the writers of the church-school literature regarded this as evidence that they were making themselves felt. This response to criticism, we may add, has not always been the pattern on other social issues. Both South and North the educational impact for temperance and later for Prohibition was persistent and unrelenting. In 1919 an elective course in the Sunday-school curriculum was authorized and the statement made: "Notwithstanding the adoption of the Prohibition Amendment, it is felt that such a course as is proposed is still greatly needed as a means of creating intelligent public opinion as a basis for the effective enforcement of the measure." The *Adult Student* took the same line in 1920.

[31] *Ibid.*, II, 333. See H. U. Faulkner, *The Quest for Social Justice, 1898-1914* (*History of American Life, vol, XI*), p. 224.

D. Expressions on Race Relations

The Bishop's Address of the Methodist Episcopal Church, South, in 1910 took pride in its ministry to the Negro, pointing out that the Colored Methodist Church had grown from 20,000 members in 1870 to 233,000 in 1910, with more than $3,000,000 in church property, aside from schools and colleges. The address called for continued missionary activity and rejoiced at the close relationships which obtained between the two churches. At this General Conference a speaker from the African Methodist Episcopal Church made a plea for help on two or three burning problems of Negroes.

The first was for a closer fellowship of Methodists across racial lines. "No co-religionists in the Southland are more widely separated, it has been remarked, than are the Methodist ministers of the two great races." He pleaded, next, for better homes built in sanitary districts for Negro tenants. "One should not be alarmed," he said, "at the fearful death rate of the city Negroes of the laboring class, in view of the unsanitary and unhealthy condition of the houses in which they are forced to live. . . . The marvel is not that so many of the occupants of these dwellings die, but that so many of them live at all."

The speaker recognized that the power to change these conditions was in the hands of the parishioners of the ministers to whom he was speaking. He concluded: "The Negro Church pledges itself to teach cleanliness and sobriety, and asks that you meet us a little way by providing for those of our people who are daily in your employ such places of abode as will conduce to their health and happiness." [32] In the next twenty years no General Conference of the denomination took any specific action on any of these points, though there were many references to the making of zealous efforts for the salvation of their souls.

About this time serious efforts were undertaken to reunite divided Methodism. It is instructive that the jurisdictional conception was a continuing part of the Southern plan from the beginning of unification efforts and that one of the provisions in it was the continued segregation of most Negroes and most Negro churches. For example, in 1914 the Report on Church Relations proposed that the colored membership of various Methodist groups should be included and recognized as one of the "Quadrennial or Jurisdictional Conferences of the proposed reorganization." [33] The idea of Jurisdic-

[32] *Journal*, General Conference of the Methodist Episcopal Church, South, 1910, pp. 380 ff.
[33] *Journal*, General Conference of the Methodist Episcopal Church, South, 1914, p. 261.

tional Conferences is ambiguous and paradoxical because it refers, on the one hand, to five regional divisions of American Methodism based on geography and, on the other hand, to the bulk of Negro Methodists and Negro churches which overlap the geographical jurisdictions. There were also some Southerners who did not wish Negroes in the reunited church at all.

Both the North and the South had a philosophy of "separate but equal," but the North wanted a relationship which was less separate and more than that desired by the South. As John M. Moore has said,

The South and the Southern Commissioners were all but unanimous in the opinion that a united Negro Methodist Church in the United States, embracing the Negro constituency in the Methodist Episcopal Church, the Colored Methodist Episcopal Church, and the two African Methodist Episcopal Churches, should be the goal in the union movement. To that end they held that the Negro membership of 315,000 in the Methodist Episcopal Church could best be served, and could best serve the cause of union, through an independent organization of their own. The Northern Commissioners held that their Negro constituents could not be set up into an independent organization except by their own will and action and that they were unwilling to inaugurate such a movement. . . . Separation of the races in the South had become a well-established custom. The Southern people were fully convinced that this state of things was best for both races, and best for Southern civilization, and that it should continue. Any movement or trend that might change this condition was disturbing and was regarded with suspicion and opposition. This philosophy of race relations was deep-seated and stronger even than any church affiliations.[34]

It is fair to say that this philosophy was held by Bishop Moore himself and controlled the racial aspects of the jurisdictional idea of union.

When in 1928 the General Conference of the Northern branch of Methodism passed a resolution that the General Conference meet only in those cities where Negro delegates could be entertained on the same basis as white delegates, there was a strong reaction in the Southern branch. Some feared that the resolution would prove to be a roadblock on the road to reunion of the churches.[35] This position did not finally prove to be an insuperable obstacle. It came up and had to be voted again in 1944 in a different form to assure suitable

[34] John M. Moore, *The Long Road to Methodist Union* (Nashville: Abingdon Press; 1943), p. 137.
[35] D. W. Culver, *Negro Segregation in the Methodist Church* (New Haven: Yale University Press, 1953), p. 68; John M. Moore, *Ibid.*, p. 183.

and adequate accommodations. However, the question of local community relations among Methodists has been a heartache until the present time. In large sections of the deep South today there is virtually no communication among Negro and white Methodists living in the same local community. White pastors sometimes do not know that there is a Negro church of their denomination in the same town. This problem will be discussed more fully in a later section.

Thus far we have had little occasion to note any well-developed position on questions of social education and action of the Methodist Protestant Church. Its expressions followed along the lines of individual piety and puritan morals. The General Conferences of that branch of Methodism from 1900 to 1916 passed strong resolutions on Sabbath observance and opposed such matters as Sunday trains, the delivery of Sunday mail, and Sunday transactions of business. They opposed also bathing, boat, buggy and bicycle riding, ball playing, letter writing, novel reading, and social visiting on the Lord's Day. They attacked all Sunday employments which "cannot be undertaken in the name of the Lord and do not minister to His glory." The resolutions admonished, in behalf of family and public worship, the reading and study of God's word, the ministrations to sick and distressed persons, self-denying missionary labors, and "similar sacred engagements."

A *Methodist Protestant* editorial [36] in 1916 lamented a measure enacted by the Baltimore City Council permitting Sunday baseball in the parks.

It is a dash in the face of the moral and religious sentiment of the community and it proves how much we are under the domination of the Roman Catholic Church and the foreign elements. . . . A voting contest carried on by one of our debauched newspapers showed a great majority in favor of Sunday games. Nine-tenths of the votes were Catholics and foreigners and the Church people simply refused to be drawn into such a contest.

It is significant that this same journal ran no editorials on more basic issues of social Christianity, though they were being discussed in the other branches of Methodism in conjunction with meetings of their General Conferences, especially in the Northern Church.

There were, to be sure, many vigorous resolutions on temperance in the General Conferences from 1900 to 1916. They attacked not only the sale and use of alcoholic beverages but also the sale and

[36] June 28, 1916.

use of opium and tobacco. They were opposed to the institution of the saloon. Ministers who used tobacco were earnestly requested to cease doing so.

The Methodist Protestant Church revealed its first official concern for widespread social reform beyond the realms of temperance and Sabbath observance when its General Conference in 1916 endorsed the Social Creed. It stated:

> Because the Methodist Protestant Church is vitally and sympathetically interested in every social and philanthropic movement that makes for human welfare, and we have a league offensive and defensive with all who labor for the establishment of the Kingdom of God on earth, we heartily and in the spirit of fraternity concur in the comprehensive and un-equivocal declaration promulgated by the General Conference of the Methodist Episcopal Church and adopted by the Federal Council of Churches.[37]

This conference appointed a special Commission on Christianity and Social Service.

In 1920 the Quadrennial Conference noted the need for reform in the relations of capital and labor. It was concerned over the strain between the two groups, their striving to control government for their own purposes, and urged that they apply the Golden Rule to their problems to serve the common good.[38] This was the last time that a statement of a Social Creed or solicitous concern for indus-trial relations ever appeared in the *Disciplines* or General Confer-ence *Journals* of the Methodist Protestant Church. The Commission continued to exist but addressed itself to other questions.

The social conscience of Methodism in the period from 1908 to 1916 developed both education and action instrumentalities. It began to formulate its social gospel in books, episcopal addresses, and church-school literature; it sharpened its criticism of the industrial order and understood more clearly the problems of factory workers; it entered actively into the field of temperance and looked toward Prohibition; and it took its first steps towards expressing the Social Creed in both the Methodist Protestant Church and the Methodist Episcopal Church, South.

[37] *Journal of the Methodist Protestant Church*, 1916, p. 138.
[38] *Ibid.*, 1920, p. 106.

CHAPTER FOUR

World War I and the Turbulent Twenties

Chronological Outline of
Major Events in American Social, Economic, and
Political History: 1917 to 1929

1917—America entered World War I
Woodrow Wilson returned to White House,
1916.
The Prohibition Amendment was offered to the
states by Congress, and, having been ratified
by two-thirds of the states, was duly promulgated in 1920. Repealed in 1933.
Imprisonment of many political offenders under
wartime legislation.
Conscientious objectors generally court-mar-
tialed.
The new constitution of Mexico, attempting to
curb the power of U.S.A. in Mexico.
Congress passed an Immigration Act over the
president's veto.
Congress also had its first woman member, Miss
Jeanette Rankin of Montana.
The Russian Revolution took place. Soviet government established.

1918—Wilson announced his "Fourteen Points."
Armistice signed.
The life of the people was significantly reor-
ganized during the war under war commissions: food, manufacturing, fuel, labor,
finance, science. Labor showed continued improvement in hours and conditions. Federal
Child Labor Law of 1916 was declared unconstitutional.

1919—The Treaty of Versailles. Adoption by Paris conference of provisional covenant of League of Nations, for which Wilson was responsible.

Woman Suffrage constitutional amendment submitted to states.

General industrial unrest due to high cost of living and belief in profiteering.

Strike of police in Boston. Strikers all discharged.

Long debate on Peace Treaty and League of Nations. Ratification refused.

Strike of the Steel Corporation employees in September. Martial law in Gary. Strike called off January 1920. Interchurch World movement report on the strike sides with labor and helps lead to eight-hour day in steel industry. President Wilson stricken.

Demobilization virtually completed.

Passage of Volstead Act to enforce Prohibition Amendment.

Strike of 600,000 soft-coal miners.

"Red Scare." Deportation of alien anarchists.

Last great "Wobbly" agitations, most notably around Seattle.

The National Catholic Social Welfare Conference organized.

American Communist Party organized.

1920—Immigration down to 43,001. Population reached 105,700,000.

Eighteenth Amendment (Prohibition) went into operation under the Volstead Act.

Nineteenth Amendment (Woman Suffrage) proclaimed.

Senate again rejected peace treaty.

Eugene V. Debs nominated for president by the Socialist Party while serving a sentence in jail as World War I political offender.

New York-San Francisco Air Mail Route opened. Government subsidizes air mail.

United Mine Workers strike in anthracite fields.

Fall in price of wheat caused some banks to close.

First radio broadcasting takes place.

The American Civil Liberties Union organized. The National Defense Act provides for office of Chief of Chaplains.

1921—President Harding inaugurated. Hughes appointed secretary of state.

Census report shows that more than 51 per cent of the population of the U.S.A. live in cities and towns of more than 2,500. Foreign-born population is 13,920,000.

Supreme Court sustains convictions of William D. Haywood and 75 other members of I.W.W.

Harding speaks against League of Nations and for a peace by resolution.

Conference on limitation of armaments. Some reduction of armaments agreed on.

Labor unrest expecially in mining.

1922—Widespread strikes in the textile industries of Rhode Island, Massachusetts, and New Hampshire. Severe Lawrence strike.

600,000 coal miners strike.

Senate ratified the treaties for limitation of naval armaments.

Child Labor Law of 1919 held unconstitutional.

Post Office Department adopts eight-hour day.

Supreme Court holds that labor unions are liable to suit for damages arising from a strike.

Ninety per cent of the railway shopmen strike because of the reduction in wages ordered by the Labor Board. The Railroad Labor Board, by resolution, outlawed the shopmen who abandoned their work.

Harding appoints special Commission to Study the Coal Industry. It recommends in 1923 government regulation intervention, and operation of coal mines in emergency.

Supreme Court upholds rights of parochial schools.

1923—Immigration rises to 522,919.

Harding advocates U.S. adherence to Permanent Court of International Justice.

Harding dies; Coolidge becomes president.

Coolidge advocates a reduction in taxes, opposes the soldiers' bonus, advocates adherence to

World Court with reservations, but repeating President Harding's attitude in refusing to consider adherence to League of Nations, pledging enforcement of the prohibition laws, urging legislation to ensure continuous and adequate coal supply, but not favoring federal legislation on financial relief for farmers.

Coolidge and Hughes reject plea of Russia to resume negotiations for recognition.

1924—Immigration 706,896.

Oil scandal charges. Teapot Dome Oil Reserves lease. Albert B. Fall refuses to testify before Senate Committee.

Other frauds and scandals in the Federal government. Indictments against Fall, Sinclair, and Doheny. Senate eventually condemns the actions of Fall and Doheny.

Senate refuses to amend Immigration Bill to include the "gentleman's agreement" with Japan. Quota fixed at 2 per cent of nationals in the U.S. in 1890 and excludes immigrants not eligible to citizenship.

Bonus Bill for veterans passed over Coolidge's veto.

Socialists endorse La Follette's candidacy for President.

Klan active at Democratic national convention.

Samuel Gompers dies; William Green elected president of A.F. of L.

1925—Mrs. Nellie T. Ross, first woman to become governor, takes oath in Wyoming.

U. S. Supreme Court declares the California Alien Land Law violates neither the U. S. Constitution nor the Japanese-American Treaty of 1911.

U. S. Supreme Court declares the Oregon school law requiring the attendance of all children at public schools unconstitutional.

John Thomas Scopes is found guilty by a Tennessee Court of teaching the theory of evolution in violation of the law of Tennessee.

Stockholm: Universal Christian Council on Life and Work.

1926—Senate resolves in favor of adherence to the World Court.

Strike of 156,000 anthracite miners settled. Provision for annual revision of contract and mediation.

Textile strike in Passaic, New Jersey.

1927—Regular radiophone service is initiated between New York and London.

Radio Control Bill, providing for licensing all broadcasting first by commission of five and later by Secretary of Commerce, passes Senate.

Coolidge vetoes the Farm Relief Bill.

Supreme Court declares that the Doheny leases of oil land are voided because of fraud.

Supreme Court declares unconstitutional the Texas statute barring Negroes from voting at the Democratic primary.

Sacco and Vanzetti sentenced to die. Executed August 23, 1927.

Charles A. Lindbergh flies non-stop to Paris.

1928—Kellogg-Briand Pact on outlawing of war.

Severe New Bedford textile strike.

Alfred E. Smith (N.Y.) nominated Democratic candidate for President.

State Department announces recognition of the Nationalist government of China.

The Foreign Missionary Conference of North America (Protestant) declared: "Force for the protection of missionaries is in general a serious hindrance to missionary work."

1929—Senate ratifies the Kellogg Anti-war Pact.

Hoover inaugurated thirty-first President of the United States.

House and Senate pass the Farm Relief Bill, providing for the creation of a Federal Farm Board of six members, with a revolving fund of $500,000,000. President signs the bill.

Thirty-eight nations protest against proposed high rates in tariff bill.

Rapid decline of prices in Wall Street. "The Crash."

A. Methodist Responses in World War I

1. FROM PEACE TO WAR

The first decade of the present century saw a rapid development of peace societies. A year like 1905 experienced a host of peace sermons preached. The National Department of Peace and Arbitration of the Women's Christian Temperance Union published a course in World Peace for Sunday schools. In 1910 Andrew Carnegie devoted part of his fortune to the promotion of international peace. Optimism for peace abounded. William W. Sweet has observed: "It was now the height of respectability to condemn war as barbaric and to advocate peace as an enduring ideal, and great and good citizens all over the land came to believe that humanity was finally nearing the goal of universal peace." [1] The Methodists, however, were slow to develop their pronouncements on international affairs and war. When they did, they followed the ideals and hopes of the democratic movement of the times.

Arbitration was one of the watchwords of the era. In their Address to the General Conference of 1912 the Bishops said:

The people are praying for an end of war and pleading for international arbitration. . . . Save in wars of the people for freedom, the thrones and honors have gone to the few, and thorns to the many. . . . Law is better than force, and patience is a wiser diplomat than threat and bluster. . . . The people can and must assert their nobler love of country by demanding that no American battleship shall disgrace its colors in a war for trade, or any war, until every peaceful resort has been thoroughly tried. . . . Let every Methodist pulpit ring out clearly and insistently for peace by arbitration. [2]

The General Conference, however, took no legislative action on peace or international relations, except the following brief comment: "It (the General Conference) does not recognize that any differences can arise between nations that may not be submitted honorably to an impartial tribunal for settlement and adjudication; and it extends to President Taft profound thanks for his persistent efforts to establish the principles of international arbitration." [3] Little more was said in the General Conference of 1916. Methodists were "reminded that the Methodist Episcopal Church, in all lands

---

[1] W. W. Sweet, *Methodism in American History* (Nashville: Abingdon Press, 1933), p. 370.
[2] *Journal of the General Conference of the Methodist Church*, 1912, pp. 216-17.
[3] *Ibid.*, p. 377.

and under all flags, stands for world righteousness and world peace, the ultimate disarmament of all nations, the social redemption of all peoples." [4] The belief was expressed that the United States might well take the lead in establishing a league or federation of nations, a concept which President Wilson was to father at war's end.

Churches with British origins, such as the Scotch Presbyterians, Wesleyan Methodists, Congregationalists, Baptists, and Universalists, strongly favored the mother country even before the United States entered the First World War. The transformation from peace sentiment to war as a holy crusade happened overnight. In January 1915, a questionnaire sent to ten thousand clergymen by the Church Peace Union showed that 95 per cent were opposed to an increase in armaments. But by March 11, 1917, 158 out of 210 New York clergymen who answered an inquiry from the Federation of Churches favored going to war. [5] A Methodist bishop in Detroit guaranteed either to regenerate or to eliminate all recalcitrant ministers from his conference. [6]

The First World War was a crude mixture of idealism and crass nationalism, of a holy crusade for international democracy and a stifling of freedom at home. In the fever of war freedom of expression was often repressed, as when Eugene Debs, the popular socialist leader who had received a million votes in 1912, was sentenced to a ten-year imprisonment for having denounced the Administration's prosecution of men charged with sedition. Many gifted critics, like Randolph S. Bourne, [7] found no vehicle for publishing their denunciations of the compulsive power of the state in wartime.

Academic freedom suffered also. Columbia University asked for the resignation of two men who criticized America's entrance into the war. At the University of Nebraska a dozen professors were tried, the objects of lamentable hysteria. Professional patriots took the occasion to ferret out socialists, liberals, and German-language teachers. It was a hysteria that did not spare the church or culture in its passionate and unreasoning hatred of everything German, including literature, philosophy, and music—a wild and fearful

---

[4] *Journal*, 1916, p. 719.

[5] R. H. Abrams, *Preachers Present Arms* (Philadelphia: Round Table Press, Inc., 1933), p. 26. See also Merle Curti, *Peace or War: The American Struggle, 1636-1936* (New York: W. W. Norton & Co., 1936) ; Norman Thomas, *The Conscientious Objector in America* (New York: B. W. Huebsch, 1923).

[6] See the running account of such utterances in Abrams, *op. cit.*

[7] Bourne was a literary critic who trenchantly expressed the opposition of the "suppressed minority" to the war. See his *Untimely Papers* (New York: B. W. Huebsch, 1919).

hatred of the "Hun," the German beast, the murderous Kaiser. German Methodist churches had their cornerstones painted yellow; their pastors were threatened; and the members were taunted with scorn and insults.

One of the effects of the war was to divert a good deal of the moral idealism that had been going into movements for social justice into new channels marked out by the vigorous leadership of President Wilson. The peace movement was, of course, thoroughly disrupted. Critics of war paid a heavy price. Socialism was split wide open by the question of patriotism. The majority of the party who remained loyal to international proletarian ideals suffered from the sudden raging of the "holy crusaders." Even the enthusiastic supporters of the New Freedom lost their zeal in the fury and destruction of the war "to make the world safe for democracy."

2. ESPOUSAL OF WAR

With the coming of war in Europe and its expansion to include America, church sentiment changed from efforts to support neutrality to enthusiastic espousal of America's participation. The case of a Methodist minister, E. P. Ryland, while not typical, shows how difficult it was for conscientious objectors during the war. Pacifism was as suspect as treason. The *California Christian Advocate* stated: "It is a little difficult to understand the mental operations of certain persons who pride themselves as being conscientious objectors to war." [8]

Ryland was district superintendent in Los Angeles under Bishop Adna W. Leonard and refused to co-operate in a series of patriotic services and rallies proposed by Bishop Leonard. The clash was dramatic. Bishop Leonard expressed his sentiments openly:

I intend that the world shall know the position of the Methodist Church in the World War. This is a war for human liberty. It is a war for Christian principles. The Methodist Church is four-square with President Wilson. We will bring to the flag every atom of strength—we will fight as individuals and as a church. The Methodist Church will allow no other organization in the land to outdo it in demonstration of loyalty and patriotism. [9]

[8] "Conscientious Objectors to War," *California Christian Advocate*, 66 (Sept. 27, 1917). Quoted in S. Raynor Smith, "The Attitudes and Practices of the Methodist Church in California with Reference to Certain Significant Social Crises" (unpublished dissertation, University of Southern California, 1955), p. 268.
[9] "A Change in the Los Angeles District Superintendency," *Ibid.*, 66 (Dec. 20, 1917), 4. In Smith, *Ibid.*, p. 269.

Ryland persisted in his conscientious objection, saying: "I have tried in this very trying ordeal to be true to my Lord . . . I cannot consent to the right of war. To me it is utterly wrong . . . I could not become a part of an active war movement in the Church. To have to leave the Church is distressing to me, but I am trying to maintain a white inner life." [10] Ryland was deposed from his office because of his pacifist views and the Annual Conference went on with the war. He left the ministry of the Methodist Church.

Within a decade the pendulum of sentiment swung a full arc and the church learned to separate patriotism and militarism and to develop some spiritual objectivity to nationalistic fervor. By 1931 the Southern California Annual Conference resolved: "We affirm the right of our members to refuse, on the basis of conscience, to support any war." [11] Dr. Ryland was invited to seek admission to the Conference, and he was readmitted with full recognition of the years of service that had intervened. California Methodism reaffirmed the stand on conscience in 1936, declaring: "We hold freedom of conscience to be so precious a heritage that it must never be surrendered." [12] California's role in defending conscientious objectors in the thirties will be noted below.

Leaders who had been prominent in the desire to awaken Methodism and the churches to their responsibility in industrial relations were no less active in supporting World War I. One of the major differences between social liberals in World War I and World War II was their lack of restraint in support of the war effort of the nation in the first conflict and the absence of concern for conscientious objectors. The influence of Worth M. Tippy was no less great in the Federal Council than in Methodism.

In *The Church and the Great War*, Tippy exclaimed: "The churches are in the thick of the greatest opportunity that this generation will ever see. . . . The churches seem to be on the threshold of a new era of high social consciousness as well as spiritual." "The spirit that moves the nation is the spirit of God." "The church is to express the spirit which moves the nation. It is to sustain the conviction that the issues are moral." [13] Such words did little to support the claims of conscientious objectors or to give them a recognized place in wartime society, but did much to give the war the character of a holy crusade for democracy. "Conscientious ob-

[10] Edwin P. Ryland (Personal Diary), Smith, *Loc. cit.*
[11] *Journal, Southern California Conference*, 1931, p. 104, quoted in Smith, *Ibid.*, p. 387.
[12] *Journal, California Conference*, 1936, p. 56, Smith, *Ibid.*, p. 388.
[13] Quoted in J. A. Hutchinson, *We Are Not Divided*, p. 179.

jectors" were, of course, difficult to separate from nonconscientious objectors who wanted to escape service and let others respond to the nation's call.

In support of the war the Southern branch of Methodism was as vocal as the North. Addressing the church in 1918, the bishops said that in their judgment President Wilson "was fully warranted in taking this extreme step (drawing the sword), and we should be less than patriotic and courageous Americans if we failed to give him our cordial support in every way. . . . We protest against the utterance of any word that would either weaken his hand or give the slightest encouragement or comfort to our national foes."

One of the speakers at the General Conference in Atlanta was Mayor Charles W. Gordon, a Canadian chaplain, whose pen name was Ralph Connor. His speech was a major event causing the Conference to burst spontaneously into cheers and prolonged applause. "My business as Chaplain," he said, "was to help make a man a better fighter. To put into his heart the thing that would take his fears away."

The Canadian command wants the chaplain "to tone up his men." The Methodists, he insisted, must prepare a nation for sacrifice "so that the women will keep sending their sons away willingly and not break them down with lamentations and tears. You are going to teach all men the old, old doctrine that the pathway to glory is the path of the Cross." "When the war is over, and I will tell you when it is going to be over, too, if you like." The delegates cried, "Tell us, tell us." "The war will be over when two million Americans get over there and give us an exhibition of the real American punch. Then, when that American punch is gotten in upon the wicked, dark-hearted Germany, the war will be over. And, brethren, that heart is darker than you know, and more wicked than you know, and more irreligious than you know; and all its wickedness is a part of its system. Do not discount any atrocity, for they are all true." [14] The ministers responded eagerly and much more. They once again led their people under the signs of Constantine, Charlemagne, and the Crusader against the infidels.

3. THE CASE OF MOONEY AND BILLINGS

Although the main wartime concern of the Methodist Church in social issues concentrated on patriotic and industrial problems, it did not entirely overlook the question of prisons and the penal system. Nowhere else is there a severer test of the loyalty of the

[14] *Journal of the Eighteenth General Conference of the Methodist Episcopal Church, South,* 1918. pp. 401-2.

church to Christ than in the earnestness with which it gives itself to the outcast and criminal classes. The community must be taught to seek not the punishment but the reformation of offenders, and experiments must be tried until the community learns how to reclaim the criminal and prevent crime.[15]

When the United States entered World War I, however, many political offenders were imprisoned following the enactment of wartime legislation. In the heat of patriotic passion some began long periods of incarceration. Not until 1933 were some of them freed in a general Christmas amnesty. This situation stimulated certain Annual Conferences, such as the Rock River, Colorado, and Puget Sound conferences, to call for the release of prisoners. The Methodist Federation for Social Service joined in the quest for release.[16]

A special case in point was that of Thomas J. Mooney and Warren K. Billings, who were tried and convicted as guilty in connection with a bomb explosion which killed a number of people during a 1916 San Francisco preparedness parade. R. M. Miller has traced the role of Methodists in the efforts to bring justice to these two men whose guilt many felt had not been proved. For years there was little action at the national denominational level. In 1929 the New York East Conference pledged itself to work for the release of Mooney and Billings. The Federation and the California Conference asked for the pardon of the prisoners. In Los Angeles and in the California State Federation of Churches Methodists were prominent in interdenominational efforts on their behalf. Then in 1931 the National Church Committee on Mooney and Billings was organized, with Bishop F. J. McConnell serving as chairman and Stanley High and Paul Hutchinson associated with him. They wrote to the Governor of California: "It is too late for either mercy or justice to Mooney and Billings. You cannot take fourteen of the best years of a man's life and still do justice. It is not too late to retrieve some shattered remnants of self-respect of the American people." [17]

A special committee of the Fresno District Council of the Methodist Episcopal Church issued a statement that the men should long since have been pardoned. On the Interreligious Committee for Justice for Thomas J. Mooney, A. A. Heist served as chairman and other Methodists included L. O. Hartman, L. H. Hough, F. J. McConnell, and H. F. Ward. The committee published *Our American Dreyfus Case: A Challenge to California Justice*. This pamphlet was

---

[15] See *Discipline*, Methodist Episcopal Church, 1916.
[16] R. M. Miller, *op. cit.*, p. 182.
[17] *Christian Century* (February 25, 1931), quoted in Miller, *op. cit.*, p. 277.

circulated widely in California and elsewhere in the nation. It said in part: "If the three former governors were not sycophants of such subversive (i.e. vested) interests, then they were amazingly and criminally ignorant, totally unworthy of the high office entrusted to them by the people of the state. We are forced to one conclusion or another." [18] The Southern California Annual Conference branded the trial a miscarriage of justice and a "frame-up." *Zion's Herald* believed the very foundation of the Republic was imperiled by the situation in California, and the *Northwestern Christian Advocate* came to the defense of the prisoners. The *Epworth Herald* called upon its readers to right this wrong.[19]

Mooney was pardoned unconditionally January 7, 1939 by Governor Culvert L. Olson, who, in his campaign for election, had announced his intention to that effect. Billings' sentence was commuted October 16, 1939, and he was set free.

4. THE CRISIS OF GERMAN-SPEAKING METHODISM

Methodism's response to the American scene cannot be adequately stated without taking account of its foreign-language work and its mission to national minorities, such as Germans, Scandinavians, Filipinos, Chinese, and Japanese. The story of German-speaking Methodism may be used as a paradigm for the other groups. The most suitable place to insert a brief account of the relation of German-speaking Methodism to the social development of the United States is the period of World War I. Numerically speaking, German-speaking Methodism was not a large body. In 1915, at the height of its development, it numbered ten Annual Conferences with 644 preachers and 63,260 church members. (When the European membership is added, it numbered at that time about 1,200 preachers and 120,000 laity.)

In evaluating its cultural significance Bishop Nuelsen says:

The future Church historian analyzing the various elements in the complex picture of American Protestantism will recognize in German Methodism a force that has done a twofold work: First, *it has introduced into American Church life some of the finest traits of German Christianity, and secondly it has been one of the most efficient agencies for Americanization that America has produced.* It has become one of the most valuable training schools for Christian citizenship. The German Methodists have never been an isolated block in the life of the nation. They have never

[18] *Our American Dreyfus Case* (1935), pp. 39-40.
[19] These sources are cited in R. M. Miller, *op. cit.*, p. 177. See also Arthur Garfield Hays, *Trial by Prejudice* (1933).

been a reactionary group hankering back to Old World social customs and political loyalties.[20]

He goes on to state: "It is not a vain boasting but stating a historic fact when I maintain that no other German-speaking Church has in the last hundred years done so much to introduce immigrants from the Old World into the spirit of American evangelical Christianity and make them staunch supporters or promoters of the ideals of Protestant Americanism as did the German-speaking Methodists." [21]

Like almost all Americans these Methodists were surprised and shocked by the outbreak of war in 1914. They were for the most part modest people, concerned with their own neighborhoods, farms, churches, small trades, and shops. A few were rising to national prominence in business, politics, and education.

The war placed the German-speaking Methodists in America in a difficult and often cruelly distressing situation. Their ties to the national fatherland were natural, but the propaganda of the Allies whipped up hatred of everything German to a white heat. The American propensity to respond to atrocity stories wiped out the virtue of thinking and developed the intensity of war feelings. British clergymen in American pulpits portrayed the barbaric cruelty of the Huns. In many towns and villages people of German extraction felt the full brunt of George Creel's propaganda efforts. For example, the imprint of a bloody hand stared down at tens of millions of Americans from a poster bearing the legend: "The Hun, His Mark. Blot it out with Liberty Bonds."

In this heat of hate every German-American was made to feel that the burden of proof was on him to demonstrate that he was not a secret agent of the Kaiser. To allay suspicion many Methodists were made to feel that they should not preach or pray in German. The *Christian Apologist* was forced to file translations of articles with postal authorities and for safety's sake preferred to publish war and political news in English.[22]

Two or three illustrations will suffice to disclose the temper of the times.

At Baldwin-Wallace College, students petitioned for the removal of the president on the alleged ground that he failed to denounce

[20] Paul F. Douglass, *The Story of German Methodism. Biography of an Immigrant Soul*. With an Introduction by Bishop John L. Nuelsen. (New York: The Methodist Book Concern, 1939), p. xvi.
[21] *Ibid.*, p. xvii.
[22] *Ibid.*, p. 189. The German title of this chief organ of German-speaking Methodism was *Der Christliche Apologete*.

"German crimes and atrocities," and had avoided mention of the war. While nine bishops conducted an investigation, the students staged a spectacular parade outside the conference room and sought the removal of the college executive.[23]

For their part the bishops, assembled in semiannual session at Grand Rapids, Michigan, in April 1917, proclaimed:

God himself makes peace. . . . There can and there ought to be no peace, until it stands squarely based upon righteousness. . . . We urge that your patriotism take on sacrificial forms and without delay of an hour. . . . We stand with the President in his message to Congress where he said: "The right is more precious than peace. . . . The wrongs against which we array ourselves are not common wrongs, they cut to the roots of human life. The world must be made safe for democracy. Its peace must be planted upon the trusted foundations of political liberty. . . . We fight for such a concert of free peoples as shall bring peace and safety to all nations and make the world itself at last free." [24]

German Methodists responded to such sentiments of patriotism and sent about five thousand soldiers, a twelfth of the membership of their churches. With their patriotism questioned by their own episcopacy in many instances, they went to great lengths to prove their thoroughgoing Americanism.

Despite the terrible strains of the war, Methodism in Germany did not separate from American Methodism in the United States. There was, of course, some demand for separation, but under the wise leadership of Bishop Nuelsen division was avoided. In his report to the General Conference of 1920 he spoke of this problem and the threat of resurgent nationalism in a prophetic way:

While the war was raging it seemed almost inevitable that Methodism in Germany would be compelled to sever its organic connection with an organization that emphasized so markedly its Americanism. I counseled moderation and delaying decisive steps until passion should cool down, judgments could be clarified, and the whole situation be normal again. . . . To my mind, it would have been a great pity if any branch of the Church of Jesus Christ, especially a Church that places the emphasis not upon externals but upon the spiritual message, should separate on national lines—while other agencies, some of them indifferent, even hostile to Christianity, strain every effort to extol the ideal of universal brotherhood above national issues.[25]

[23] *Ibid.,* p. 191.
[24] *Ibid.,* pp. 191-92.
[25] *Ibid.,* p. 194. See *Journal of the General Conference of the Methodist Episcopal Church,* 1920.

In *Der Methodismus in Deutschland nach dem Krieg*[26] he voiced the authentic message of Methodism as a supranational fellowship at work for peace. He said:

There is no German Christendom, no German faith, any more than there is an English or an American. Christianity is supranational. In the kingdom of Christ there are no trenches and no customs boundaries. Human beings are the same everywhere. They must be brought under the power of the spirit, purified and consecrated as human instruments to the service of God—not by isolation but by contact. It would be as much a tragedy for our German peoples as well as for Christendom if the many-sided and mutual relationships built up over so many years should be broken. I hold it as one of the most important tasks of peace to build the bridges again, to tie together the broken cords, so that Christians of different lands can learn to understand one another again, to win each other's confidence, to enrich our mutual contact. The separation from America just at this time would have the effect of accelerating the divisions of Christendom.[27]

In many states the passions of war led to anticultural excesses, to disillusionment with ecclesiastical leadership, and to support of vengeful guilt clauses in the peace treaty. The Ohio legislature passed a bill outlawing the teaching of German below the eighth grade. Governor James M. Cox (1917-21) in supporting the bill said that teaching German to American children was "not only a distinct menace to Americanism, but it is part of a conspiracy formed long ago by the German Government in Berlin." [28] Even colleges suspended the teaching of German and did not revive German courses for a decade. Some continued it, assuming its usefulness for a presumable army of occupation. German Methodist pastors were disillusioned.

One leader commented after the war: "Our preachers lost faith in our leaders. Many of them were so utterly disappointed that they would have left the ministry but for the fact that that would have meant intolerable privations for their families. The war experiences reduced them to become bread servants; men who formerly were most loyal and enthusiastic ministers of the gospel and patriotic citizens." [29] Such disillusionments were only confirmed at the international level by Article 231 of the Treaty of Versailles which placed on Germany "the entire responsibility . . . of Germany and

[26] Bremen: Buchhandlung und Verlag der Traktathauses (n.d.).
[27] Quoted in Douglass, *op. cit.*, p. 196.
[28] Douglass, *op. cit.*, p. 194.
[29] *Ibid.*, p. 199.

her allies for causing all the loss and damage to which the allied and associated governments and their nationals have been subjected as a consequence of the war imposed upon them by the aggression of Germany and her allies."

Such is the context of the years of crisis through which German-speaking Methodism in America passed just prior to its liquidation in the merger movement. We shall have to consider that phase of its history when we analyze the social response of Methodism in the mid-twenties. Meanwhile the impossibility of paying a reparations bill of 132 billion gold marks, the great inflation in Germany, and the world-wide revulsions to war made eventually for a radical reappraisal. The Archbishop of York, preaching in Cathedral Church of Saint Pierre, Geneva, on January 31, 1932, at the opening of the Conference for the Reduction and Limitation of Armaments, declared: "If the spirit that guides us is to be the Gospel, the War Guilt Clause must go—struck out by those who framed it." [30] On May 24, 1932, the General Conference of the Methodist Episcopal Church (Atlantic City) adopted the following resolution: "We believe that the time has come for the world to acknowledge the fact that the sole guilt of the German nation for the World War cannot in justice be maintained." By 1932 Hitler was knocking at the door of supreme power in Germany and the name of German Methodism in America had been virtually erased as a symbol of a living ministry.

B. The Social Gospel in the Twenties

Some have characterized the twenties as the era of the decline of the social gospel. So far as the Methodist Church is concerned this characterization must be treated with some caution. There are, perhaps, seven factors which can be listed on the side of a slump in enthusiasm for social Christianity.

(1) There were important sectors of the church in which an effective movement for the social gospel had not existed. (2) The twenties reflected a shift in American social balance of power between rural and urban life when for the first time the population was weighted on the side of the cities. (3) Despite echoes of revivalism, there was a declining interest in sin among many intellectuals and in many liberals' pulpits. (4) The Prohibition crusade became a single cause focused on legality rather than maintaining its earlier pristine motivation. (5) Much energy went into the fundamentalist-modernist controversy and the discussions of

[30] *Ibid.*, p. 207.

the relations of science and religion. (6) Some of the earlier social gospel leaders had died and a weariness set in on the part of others in a period of social distress and rising prosperity. (7) The conservative and reactionary forces of social life were aggressively at work. In the period of growing isolationism nationalistic complacency became the order of the day. The debunking of the World War played into the hands of proponents of a smug satisfaction with American life.

Postwar nationalism created acute problems and tended to reinforce the reactionary group attitudes of those who attacked civil liberties, internationalism, and the rights of labor. While these trends were marked, it would be an error to overlook the development of social concern and action in the decade from 1920 to 1930. Pacifism was in the ascendancy. Social prophets like Sherwood Eddy, Kirby Page, and Reinhold Niebuhr were eagerly received in many colleges, seminaries, and conferences. For the South this development included the controversy over biblical criticism through which the church was preparing itself for social action. Twenty-five years earlier corresponding controversy could be found in the seminaries and Annual Conferences in the North.

The professional patriots were not pacified by the Armistice or the efforts to devise peace treaties and a League of Nations. They were joined by a host of Americans who toasted on every occasion the obvious superiority of the United States to Europe. On every side the sensitive social conscience was sickened by the inverted idealism of "100 per cent Americans." There was a close connection between patriotism and the property interest, between blindness to the nation's diversities and the repression of minorities of all kinds.

Merle Curti writes:

During the struggle unity had been artificially imposed by the exigencies of war. Once the crisis was over, the disunity of American society was evident. The I.W.W. reappeared, and strikes began again. The possibility that the old program of reform might be resumed alarmed many men and women of position and substance. Such signs of disunity led to legal efforts to compel Americans to be patriotic and above all to identify patriotism with the security and sanctity of private property. There followed the Lusk Laws requiring New York teachers to take oaths of loyalty and, in effect, of conformity; attacks on social studies textbooks deemed either too internationalistic or too socialistic; and the circulation of black lists stigmatizing even the mildest liberals as "subversive" and "un-American." In addition, constitution worship became an almost religious cult in certain quarters. Thus the effort was made, in the name

90

of patriotism, to conceal divisions within American life and to maintain the social and economic *status quo.*[31]

The "constitution worship" was often less than real. In fact, the constitution was being flouted by the "100 per cent Americans" and self-appointed superpatriots.

The nationalistic patriots and superpatriots did not go unchallenged. Many scholars and cosmopolitan men of letters deplored the anti-internationalism of the Harding-Coolidge era.

The churches played a part in pointing out the necessity of American co-operation with other nations if war and the breakdown of civilization were to be avoided. Religious leaders persistently stimulated church opinion and sentiment for international co-operation. The appeals were far-reaching and realistic. The peace movement developed to a more significant level of idea and action than ever before. The psychology of repudiating war underwent a phenomenal rise, especially among ministers, including many Methodists. Its pacifism was not isolationist but positively internationalist. The demand that the government do something to reduce armaments and promote financial stability in Europe had a broad base in church assemblies.

1. METHODISM AND CIVIL LIBERTIES

"America in 1919 and 1920 resembled a gigantic Salem," says R. M. Miller, "in which some preachers, as in the days of the witches, led the hunt for the enemies of the Lord." [32] But the church was not to be muzzled by the "Red" scare. The Methodist Federation for Social Service devoted several issues of its *Bulletin* to the "Red" scare and upheld the cause of civil liberties. *Zion's Herald* maintained an independent position and the *Nashville Christian Advocate* was an outspoken organ in the South. There were other expressions of a sober defense of liberty. In July 1919 a number of New York church leaders, among them Ralph W. Sockman and Frank Mason North, issued a stirring plea for free speech, free discussion, fair trials, due process of law, and open-mindedness. They said: "A common resolve to abide by our time-honored principles of free discussion and the regular processes of constitutional government is the need of the hour. Unhappily, violence, recently employed in the name of patriotism, has been allowed to go un-

[31] Merle Curti, *The Growth of American Thought* (New York: Harper and Brothers 1943), p. 690.
[32] Miller, *op. cit.*, p. 188.

punished by the authorities, and has even been praised by leaders in government and in the press." [33]

A Methodist bishop protested with others the action of the New York legislature in refusing to seat five duly elected Socialists. This protesting group, called together by the Federal Council of Churches, said: "We have long been saying that constitutional changes can be effected without violence in America because of our right to free expression of opinion by voice and ballot. We cannot now deny this American substitute for violence without directly encouraging resort to revolution." [34]

The Lusk bills in the New York legislature, designed to curb radical thought but endangering civil liberties for all, were fought by men like F. Ernest Johnson, G. A. Coe, R. W. Sockman, Worth M. Tippy, and Charles E. Jefferson. Harry F. Ward preached the need for sanity.

Bishop Williams branded the raids by Attorney General Palmer as the foulest page in American history.[35] The New York East Conference went literally to the rescue of immigrants seized in the Palmer raids for deportation and held without trial.[36]

When the Y.W.C.A. adopted the Social Creed, already made famous in denominational and interdenominational circles, that society was vigorously attacked by the Employers' Association of Pittsburgh and incurred financial loss because of the assault. The challenge was answered by a number of Methodist journals.

The *New York Christian Advocate* observed that the attack on the Y.W.C.A. was only a preliminary to a full-scale onslaught against social Christianity, for these businessmen "can hardly be so unchivalrous as to wage war only upon women." [37]

It is impressive to note in some Methodist journals the consistency of fearless objectivity and sober perspective on the Communist threat in America. The threat from domestic Communists seemed very slight to some. For example, the *Northwest Christian Advocate* noted in 1927 that "the proportion of Communists to the population of the United States is about the same as the proportion of baldheaded bachelors to the entire membership of the House of Representatives." [38] Three years later it noted that the threat of internal

[33] *Ibid.*, p. 189.
[34] *Christian Register* (Feb. 5, 1920), p. 131. Quoted in Miller, *Ibid.*, p. 190.
[35] *Ibid.*, pp. 191-92.
[36] Carter, *op. cit.*, pp. 26-27.
[37] *New York Christian Advocate* (Feb. 10, 1921), p. 172. Quoted in Miller, *op. cit.* p. 32.
[38] *Northwest Christian Advocate* (July 21, 1927), p. 675. Quoted in Miller, *Ibid.*, p. 194.

Communism as a menace was hardly a fact and the talk of millions of "Reds" pure moonshine. The *Nashville Christian Advocate* maintained in 1930 that "Communism in these United States does not seem . . . in any slightest degree a menace. The theory is utterly alien to the genius of our people. In their zeal to suppress every manifestation of it, even in a purely theoretical form, our police authorities seem . . . more likely to do harm than good." [39] That same month *Zion's Herald* editorialized: "What a sad and depressing situation! The monster Communism is gnawing at the very vitals of American institutions while the poor American capitalist goes blithely on his unsuspecting way! Nonsense!" [40]

Individual Methodists could, of course, be found on several sides of an issue such as the "Red" scare of 1919.

Bishop Richard J. Cooke believed the government was too soft on the "Reds," and asserted that no methods were too severe to destroy the enemies of the country. He asked: "Shall the snake warm himself under the wings of the Constitution?" [41] The Reverend George Albert Simons argued that deportation was the most merciful of all penalties that could be imposed upon Bolsheviks.

This excitement over Communism was part of the drive to "return to normalcy." Once the Germans had been subdued, a series of chain reactions was set off in the form of negative responses in economics, immigration policies, and civil liberties. There were scandals and corruption in high places. There were also widespread and violent strikes, a resurgent Ku Klux Klan movement, a wave of anti-Semitism, and a discordant Congress in conflict with the President.

2. LABOR AND INDUSTRY

In the 1920's American economic reform sentiment had a long dry spell. A book on this period by John Chamberlain was entitled *Farewell to Reform.* Lincoln Steffens, spectacular muckraker of the Progressive Era, expressed disillusionment with reform, and suggested that America would achieve socialist goals within the context of a beneficent capitalism. The mood was quite unlike that in Upton Sinclair's *The Jungle,* or Jack London's *Martin Eden,* or the essays of Randolph Bourne. No book in the still pulsating Protestant social gospel had the vogue of Charles Sheldon's earlier *In His Steps.*

[39] *Nashville Christian Advocate* (July 8, 1930), p. 1029. Quoted *loc. cit.*
[40] *Zion's Herald* (July 23, 1930), p. 933. Quoted *loc. cit.*
[41] *Zion's Herald* (June 18, 1919), p. 778. Quoted in Miller, *op. cit.*, p. 187.

METHODISM AND SOCIETY IN THE TWENTIETH CENTURY

On the contrary, the most popular book on a religious subject was Bruce Barton's *The Man Nobody Knows*. In it Jesus is identified as the prototype of the modern businessman. It was for two years a "best seller." There was a prevailing mood that the government should let business alone and that, as President Coolidge said, "the business of America is business."

The ruling idea of prosperity was linked to such other dominant themes as mass production, high wages, high-pressure selling, installment buying, service, and "bigger and betterism." Popular sentiment became indulgent to the scandalous behavior of certain public utilities and the blatant corruption of public officials. Prosperity propaganda and lush incomes in certain quarters could not fully hide the fact that real wages of unskilled labor did not improve and that the income of the lowest tenth of American farmers actually decreased. Some industrial labor did fairly well and the Model "T" Ford became popular, but the bottom stratum of labor and the unemployed had it very hard.

At the close of the war both labor and management were released from most of the restraints of the government on industrial relations. Thanks to Chief Justice Taft, the government got some new injunctive power which caused some resentment in the labor movement when used in industrial disputes. Business expanded and living costs rose 27 per cent during the eighteen months following the Armistice. Workers continued to join unions and in 1919 and 1920 added a half million to their ranks, bringing the total to over five million, the highest peak to be reached until 1937 during the "New Deal." Almost every union gained during this brief period.

Union efforts to expand collective bargaining conditions led to many bitter disputes. In 1919 over four million workers were involved in strikes, the greatest number in any year in United States history.[42]

A number of these strikes were for improved working conditions in already organized trades and industries, but many were efforts to obtain recognition or to strengthen a tottering collective bargaining arrangement. The cost of living was twice as high in 1919 as in 1914.

The largest strikes occurred in steel and bituminous coal mining. The steel strike involved 367,000 workers and was primarily for union recognition. Though the strike was lost, the publicity given to the working conditions in the industry caused the eight-hour day to be substituted for the twelve-hour day thereafter. Methodist par-

[42] Florence Peterson, *American Labor Unions* (New York: Harper and Brothers, 1945), p. 14.

ticipation in this investigation will be noted below. While the controversy was still in progress a strike of 425,000 miners was called in the bituminous coal industry. Despite two federal injunctions and citations of numerous union officials for contempt of the Lever Act (passed during the war but not used until after the Armistice), the miners stayed out for three months and returned to work only after President Wilson secured a compromise wage settlement.[43]

In an effort to get industry back on a peacetime basis President Wilson convened in October 1919 a conference of representatives of employers, labor, and the public to "discover such methods as had not already been tried out of bringing capital and labor into close co-operation." Interestingly among the twenty-two "public" representatives appointed by the President were J. D. Rockefeller, Jr., Bernard Baruch of the Stock Exchange, Elbert H. Gary, chairman of the U. S. Steel Corporation, and a half a dozen other manufacturers. The conference split on the question of collective bargaining and trade unions. Gompers presented an eleven-point resolution, including the right of wage earners to organize into unions and to bargain collectively.

By way of contrast the employer group resolved for "the right of employers to deal or not to deal with men or groups of men who are not his employees," stating further that the arbitrary use of collective bargaining "was a menace to the institution of free people." The representatives of the public indorsed the principle of collective bargaining, but insisted that employee representation plans be included as proper collective bargaining agencies. In these circumstances the conference broke up in a few days.[44]

For fifteen years following the great steel strike there was no serious effort to organize the industry. But the success of the employers encouraged the movement to destroy unionism throughout all industry. This open-shop movement had the support of manufacturers' associations, boards of trade, chambers of commerce, builders' associations, bankers' associations, so-called "citizens' associations," and even farmers' organizations. This was the so-called "American Plan" to save workers, as the policy statement of the American Bankers' Association put it, "from the shackles of organization to their own detriment." [45]

Organizations for promoting the "open shop" existed in virtually every industrial center in the nation, those in California, Illinois,

[43] *Ibid.*, p. 213.
[44] *Ibid.*, p. 15.
[45] *Ibid.*, p. 16. Quoted from *Industry* (January 1, 1921).

and Michigan being especially active. These organizations conducted "patronize the open shop" campaigns, and some extended such direct aid to employers as maintaining blacklists of union members and furnishing money, spies, and strikebreakers to employers involved in strikes. In some of the industrial disputes that characterized the twenties the unions made slight gains or held their own.

On the whole, however, the open-shop drives and the postwar depression resulted in major losses to organized labor. Union membership dropped from a peak of 5,000,000 in 1920 to 3,500,000 in 1924 and continued to decline even after the return of business prosperity. Some large corporations adopted programs which many employers felt made unions unnecessary. These programs included welfare activities, employees' pension plans, group life insurance, and medical services; also professional management services to handle grievances; and support of plant baseball teams, glee clubs, dances, and other recreation when off the job.

The over-all result was a bitter stalemate in industrial relations continued through the twenties. Then, when the depression of 1929 came, union membership fell to less than three million, harassed by injunctions and "yellow-dog contracts."

3. THE STEEL STRIKE REPORT

In the judgment of Anson Phelps Stokes, "probably no single industrial dispute in the history of the United States will show more clearly the attitude of Churches, both locally and nationally, than the steel strike of 1919." [46] As represented in the Inter-Church World Movement and the Federal Council of Churches, this attitude is expressed in two important volumes, *Report on the Steel Strike of 1919* and *Public Opinion in the Steel Strike*. These reports were the product of an investigation by the Inter-Church World Movement, a rather grandiose venture in co-operative Protestanism. The chairman of the General Committee was Robert Lansing (1864-1928), formerly Secretary of State; the chairman of the Executive Committee was John R. Mott (1865-1955); and the commission that made the investigation included Bishop Francis J. McConnell (1871-1953). McConnell's moral leadership in the investigation has made him a major hero of it. Bishop James M. Cannon also belonged to the commission. The investigation began three weeks after the opening of the strike and transmitted its report to President Wilson on January 27, 1920.

There was much to investigate. Besides the twelve-hour day and

[46] Anson Phelps Stokes, *Church and State in the United States*, II, 346.

the long shift, there was the horrible conduct of the strike, especially in western Pennsylvania. Louis Adamic describes how freedom of speech and assembly was utterly abolished, with mounted police galloping through the streets, beating up men and women, shooting at them, barring them from grocery stores to starve them out, dragging them off to jail and keeping them there without bail, breaking into workers' houses and forcing men back to work at gunpoint, and conducting other acts of terrorism.[47] During the steel strike of 1919, however, the churches by and large were hardly labor's friend. In the South especially church interference favoring union labor was resented. "Its revolutionary aim," believed the *Arkansas Methodist,* "was to seize control of government as well as industry." One church leader cited the strike as an example of "bolshevism," while the *Nashville Christian Advocate* painted a glowing picture of the happy conditions that prevailed in the mills, concluding that the strike was a grab for power on the part of "Reds." [48] Of course, the church was divided. Some Protestant and Catholic ministers who had large numbers of the corporation's officers in their parishes opposed it at first. Others with large numbers of workers' families favored it.

The *Report of the Steel Strike of 1919* [49] was to show that 69,000 men were working a 12-hour day and 70,000 were getting the lowest rate of pay. The Report said: "This means approximately 350,000 men, women, and children are directly affected by the longest hours or the smallest pay in that part of the industry owned by the United States Steel Corporation, which fixes pay and hours without conference with the labor force." Among the recommendations made by the report were the adoption of the eight-hour shift on all continuous processes, limiting a day to not more than ten hours on duty, limiting the week to six days or fifty-four hours, recognition of the right to join regular craft unions, and a union share in the responsibility for production and in the control of production processes. There was also expressed a concern for labor union democracy, avoidance of violence, promotion of Americanization, and the like.[50]

It must not be forgotten that a large number of the workers in the steel industry were persons of foreign extraction. The attitude of the churches was important for this reason as well as for their

[47] Louis Adamic, *Dynamite: The Story of Class Violence in America* (New York: Viking Press, 1934), pp. 288-90.
[48] Miller, *op. cit.,* p. 257.
[49] Inter-church World Movement, *Report of the Steel Strike of 1919* (New York: Harcourt, Brace, and Howe, Inc., 1920), p. 5.
[50] *Ibid.,* pp. 248 ff.

lives as wage earners in a major American industry. Bishop F. J. McConnell was resident bishop in Pittsburgh. On November 28, 1919, the Pittsburgh Council of Churches addressed an "Appeal to Americans" at a time when the strike was two months old. The opening and closing paragraphs of the "Appeal" state views which illuminate the crisis of that era in industrial relations and attitudes toward foreigners at the conclusion of World War I.

We appeal to you in behalf of our neighbors of foreign birth.

They are among us in large numbers. Thoughtless and mistaken policies toward them at this time will bring grave consequences, both for them and for us. Unfortunately the evidence is unmistakable that some erroneous policies are being followed.

These people in the main are open-minded, honest, industrious, peaceloving. They are mostly from the peasantry of Europe, a stock possible of development into excellent citizenship. . . .

We recognize the presence of some aliens in our midst who have come wholly for selfish purposes and as enemies of our American institutions, and we would have no one misconstrue this statement in such a way as to soften our utter condemnation of their treasonable and insidious attacks upon that which we hold most dear.

Yet the church would be derelict and censurable if it were to remain silent at a time like this, making no protest against these errors so fraught with potencies of evil. We therefore appeal to our fellow Americans for a different course and for prompt and earnest efforts to correct the evil already done.

We appeal to civil officers to be exceedingly careful not to be unjust.

We appeal to employers to give to their employees time and encouragement for cultured life.

We appeal to the public to treat foreigners with the same courtesy shown to an American, and to be real neighbors to them, patiently helping them to learn our language and to arrive at all that is best in our American life.

We appeal to members of the American churches that they manifest a real Christian attitude toward these people, many of whom have revolted against churches which they considered tools of tyranny in other lands, and in so doing have swung far into hostility against religion itself. This state of mind cannot last. Let us, by act and word, so interpret to these people the mind of God that, when their fundamental religious nature shall again assert itself, we shall be in position to help them find Him and find peace and joy for their souls.[51]

It is not possible to give a complete account of the making of the Inter-Church World Movement report on the Steel Strike, but there

[51] Anson Phelps Stokes, *op. cit.*, II, 347.

are useful perspectives for Methodists which show the quality of some of the denomination's response.

Bishop McConnell has noted them in his autobiography, *By the Way*. It was Fred B. Fisher, chairman of the Industrial Department, who first raised the question as to an investigation at a meeting of a hundred ministers assembled in the Pennsylvania Hotel in New York. McConnell was presiding. The question was raised who would chair the special committee to carry on the investigation. "A number of prominent churchmen were asked to undertake the task, but none would accept. . . . Finally, though this is only my own guess, I was asked as a last resort." [52] There was agreement that the actual investigation of technical matters would be in the hands of expert social workers; and this was done.

The attitudes of leaders of steel are significant. McConnell says:

> The difficulties before the special committee were largely in the attitudes of the directors of the industry. . . . As far as I could see, the feeling of the steel leaders was at first somewhat of amusement, changing to surprise that the committee should think itself qualified to ask any questions, and at last of pain at being questioned. They could not see that the committee was trying to find out human situations, and that it was not concerned with technical processes except as they affected the men involved in them.[53]

One day the president of a steel company came to see the bishop. "In a polite way he said he had come to tell me what a dreadful mistake I had made in getting mixed up in a steel investigation. He conceded that I was a good enough fellow as long as I stuck to my own field, but that in dealing with wage scales and similar matters I could not possibly know what I was talking about." [54] The relevance of the gospel had not penetrated his business attitudes or understanding.

"The most surprising phase of our effort," McConnell goes on to say, "was the significance the steel group placed on their spy reports. There were about six hundred of such reports in one plant—reports on the laborers' attendance upon street meetings where all descriptions of radical speeches were made. . . . The steel people never could understand why we didn't take the spy stuff more seriously." [55]

A somewhat related problem was a conversation with an em-

[52] F. J. McConnell, *By the Way* (Nashville: Abingdon Press, 1952), p. 214.
[53] *Ibid.*, p. 215.
[54] *Ibid.*, p. 216.
[55] *Ibid.*, p. 217.

ployer of labor who could not find words strong enough to express his rage at trade unions, at their agreements to stand by one another and their profiting by the strength that came just out of union itself. "Later he told me of agreements among employers in a business in which he was an important factor, how he and his fellow controlling officials in about all the factories in that business stood together in loyalty one to another, and how much of a privilege it was to be associated with such men. This man was a worthy Methodist, in good standing among us." [56]

It took a good deal of forthright courage for the bishop to stand up to the conflict and opposition which the developing and reporting of the investigation aroused, especially for Methodist leaders in and around Pittsburgh.

I shall always deeply appreciate the attitude of the Pittsburgh Annual Conference toward the report. The natural supposition would be that this conference would be tied hand-and-foot to the steel industry, but it was not. The conference, situated as it was in the center of a group of industrial leaders, the last word in what might be called industrial self-will, was made up of a most forward-looking group of Methodists. I am quite well aware that many of them could not see what good it would do to publish the steel report, but once the publication had been determined upon, they stood by it. I am most deeply indebted to Daniel L. Marsh, then secretary of the Pittsburgh Church Union, for his courage in standing up against the criticisms of the report. [57]

There were others also who were called upon to "stand for" their bishop. McConnell notes: "There is no use denying ... that anyone who gets into an attack on a widespread industry may have to pay a price which now and again may be heavy." [58]

The report greatly influenced public opinion and this in turn affected the policies of the United States Steel Corporation. On March 7, 1920, it announced that two of the evils, the seven-day week and the so-called "long turn at the shifts" had been entirely eliminated. They also stated that an announcement about the twelve-hour day could be expected in a month or so. On April 18 the chairman of the Steel Corporation stated to the stockholders: "The officers of the Corporation, the presidents of subsidiary companies, and a majority of others in positions of responsibility are in favor of abolishing the twelve-hour day, and for this reason and *because of the public sentiment referred to,* it is our endeavor and

[56] *Ibid.,* p. 217.
[57] *Ibid.,* pp. 219-20.
[58] *Ibid.,* p. 221.

expectation to decrease the working hours—we hope in the comparatively near future." [59]

The Honorable William G. McAdoo (1863-1940), former Secretary of the Treasury, made an observation at the time which reflected a significant portion of enlightened public attitude: "The findings of such a Commission, as indicated by the recent illuminating report of the Interchurch World Movement, would inevitably have turned public sympathy in favor of the just demands of the men! And let me say here, that the report of the Interchurch World Movement on the conditions in the steel industry must shock the conscience of America." [60]

The conservative *New York Tribune* stated on July 20, 1920: "The report of the Interchurch Commission, composed of men whose good faith will not be questioned, concerning conditions in the steel trust industry, is such as to require the Steel Corporation either to refute the charges or to change its policies." [61] In writing a report to the United States Coal Commission, Zechariah Chafee, Jr., of the Harvard Law School expressed the following trenchant judgment: "If the Interchurch reports lead to the abolition of espionage, shackled assemblage, illegal arrests, police clubbing, a partial press, an uninformed pulpit, no one will have sounder cause to rejoice than the supporters of our present industrial system." [62]

The United States Steel Corporation fought back. Judge Elbert H. Gary printed and distributed a million and a half copies of an address by the Reverend E. Victor Bigelow entitled, *Mistakes of the Interchurch Steel Report.* Later Marshall Olds wrote a five-hundred page response, *Analysis of the Interchurch World Movement Report on the Steel Strike.* Churchmen like Alva W. Taylor and F. Ernest Johnson found this book marked by factual errors, garbled statistics, and mutilated quotations. F. Ernest Johnson of the Federal Council of Churches, together with Roman Catholic and Jewish leaders, attacked the defense prepared by Steel and called for the abolition of the twelve-hour day.[63] On July 6, 1923, Steel announced the end of the twelve-hour day.

It is interesting to note the generally favorable response of the Methodist press to the Report on the Steel Strike of 1919.[64] *Zion's Herald* emphasized (a) the integrity of the commission which un-

---

[59] Cited in Anson Phelps Stokes, *op. cit.*, p. 348. Italics added.
[60] *Ibid.*, p. 348.
[61] *Ibid.*, p. 348.
[62] *The Inquiring Mind*, p. 173. Quoted in Stokes, *Ibid.*, p. 348.
[63] *Federal Council Bulletin* (June-July, 1923), p. 5.
[64] See Miller, *op. cit.*, p. 213.

dertook the investigation, (b) the duty of the church to investigate, (c) the unmistakable evidence that conditions in the steel industry were bad, and (d) the need for widespread reading of the report. The *New York Christian Advocate* asked the steel officials to cease blathering about "Reds" and either disprove the statements of the commission or remedy speedily the conditions exposed in the report. The *Northwest Christian Advocate* suggested that any who say the churches are not friendly to the working-man should read this report which was made by some of America's most representative church leaders. The *Social Service Bulletin* commended the report highly. James C. Baker, in an article in the *Methodist Review*, was impressed with the report's sincerity, closeness to the facts, and sanity of judgment.[65] It must be noted, however, that the *Arkansas Methodist* and some other journals of the denomination never mentioned it.

In evaluating the response of the churches to the Report on the Steel Strike, Miller states:

It was instrumental in reorienting the attitude of the churches toward industrial questions, particularly regarding the strike as a weapon of labor. During the year 1919 clerical opinion seemed to view the strike as an un-American form of intimidation. After the publication of the Inter-Church study, churchmen tended to reserve judgments on the merits of a particular strike, and to increasingly view strikes as a legitimate weapon of labor.[66]

Stanley High in *The Church in Politics* [67] stressed the significance and the effectiveness of Protestantism in abolishing the twelve-hour day in the steel industry. At the time of the strike about half of the twelve-hour industrial workers in the United States were in the steel industry. Their employers were the last large group to yield. They yielded largely as a result of the pressure brought by the religious forces of America.

The case of steel was the most impressive from the standpoint of the social gospel movement; but there were other industrial areas where the church hardly transcended the power structure of private industry. One of these is the textile industry in North Carolina. The intensive study made by Liston Pope relates an important chapter in the interaction of Methodism and the mill villages of the South.

[65] James C. Baker, "Steel and Men," *Methodist Review*, 104 (1921), 389-97.
[66] Miller, *op. cit.*, pp. 212-13.
[67] Stanley High, *The Church in Politics*, pp. 233-34.

We shall turn to this aspect of the Methodist role in industrial relations in the following section of this chapter.

4. A CASE STUDY IN TEXTILES

Nearly every mill builder in Gaston County, North Carolina, was a churchman before he built mills. In 1900 fifteen of these were Methodists. Among the worker residents, by 1880 Baptists and Methodists about equaled Lutherans and Presbyterians who descended from original German and Scottish settlers in the county.[68] Church leaders helped to create and express public approval of textile entrepreneurs. Ministers and religious publications praised the new industrialists as redeemers of a people and a region.[69] For example, when George A. Gray, the enterprising and successful developer of Gaston County mills, died in 1912, he was editorially praised by the *North Carolina Christian Advocate*. E. W. Hardin cites other examples of commendation of mill builders in "The Attitude of the Methodist Episcopal Church, South, in North Carolina toward the Textile Industry in North Carolina." [70] In 1880 Braxton Craven, president of the largest Methodist college in North Carolina, dedicated a new cotton mill to "Almighty God," and a Methodist minister present observed as follows:

I never saw such a thing in this country before—but I do hope the example set by this company will be followed by all who succeed them in this bright Southern land. When we, as corporations and as business men, bring business and religion into daily contact and recognize formally our dependence upon divine blessing for success, we are not likely to fail to realize all.[71]

A Methodist preacher who was pastor of the uptown church in Gastonia followed the example of Lutheran pastors in encouraging the building of mills. He made it a practice to organize an industry wherever he went, "for the good of the community." Through his efforts several Gaston County mills were organized, and he subscribed for stock in a number of them, being regarded as a tower of economic strength in the community. But other factors were also applauded, notably the "moral revolution" whereby mills and prohibition displaced the whiskey business. Between 1891 and 1900

---

[68] L. Pope, *Millhands and Preachers*, p. 17.
[69] *Ibid.*, p. 21.
[70] B.D. thesis at Duke University, 1938, on which the study by Liston Pope partly draws.
[71] *Raleigh Christian Advocate* (Feb. 25, 1880). Cited in Pope, *Ibid.*, p. 24.

seventeen new mills were built and the number of licensed distilleries declined from forty to sixteen.

"The greatest contribution of the churches to the industrial revolution in the South," says Pope, "undoubtedly lay in the labor discipline they provided through moral supervision of the workers." [72] They set out to "mold transplanted farmers into stable, contented, sober citizens and industrial workers." To this end the preachers inculcated the personal virtues of stability, honesty, sobriety, and industry. Their churches provided centers of community integration other than the mill itself, and emotional escape from the difficulties of life in a mill village.

For their part the mills also contributed directly to the support of the churches. Sometimes mill owners specified where churches were to be built. In South Gastonia, for the location of fourteen mills, the owners specified a Baptist church at the southern end of the settlement and a Methodist church at the northern end. The mills contributed directly to the salaries of pastors, who either received a check through the mail or called personally at the office of the mill. Pope states: "In the case of the Methodist churches, the amount forthcoming from the mills is specified for a year in advance, and is about the same from year to year. The district superintendent of the Methodist churches calls on the mills at least once a year to secure renewal of their contributions. In addition to this regular visit, he goes to various mill owners for extra sums whenever needed, and generally gets them." [73] In 1938 out of twenty pastoral charges, eleven of them mill charges, six received direct help from mills on the pastor's salary and four received subsidies of other types, such as provision of a parsonage. However, gifts from mills comprised only 6 per cent of the total amount received by Methodist pastors in the county and accounted for 20 per cent of subsidies to preachers. [74]

Mill support for Methodist work had a broader interest in the South than in North Carolina's Gaston County. In 1910 the South Carolina Annual Conference pointed out in a resolution that "the properly manned church is a commercial as well as moral asset of the mills." It urged mill administrations to appropriate proportionate amounts to the salaries of ministers in their villages and appointed a commission to confer with the Manufacturers' Association of South Carolina on the matter. This matter has been studied by R. W. Spears in "The Attitude of the Southern Methodists of South

[72] *Ibid.,* p. 29.
[73] *Ibid.,* p. 39.
[74] *Ibid.,* p. 40.

Carolina in Regard to the Textile Industry in South Carolina." [75] His main sources were the minutes of the annual conferences and the files of the *Southern Christian Advocate*. The Western North Carolina Annual Conference, in whose boundaries Gaston County falls, adopted a resolution in 1929 requesting textile manufacturers to pay at least one half of the expense of maintaining religious worship in their mill villages.[76] In 1938 Methodist churches received direct help from the mills in about the same number and amounts as they had a decade earlier.

Because of the development of mill villages it was inevitable that the Methodist churches would tend to become class churches. In 1910 the Board of Missions was reported as appropriating forty-two hundred dollars to the thirty mission churches in the Western North Carolina Conference serving the mill people. By 1929 it was asserted that 29 per cent of the churches of the conference were composed of textile workers and others related to the industry. Of these seventy-five per cent received aid from the Board of Missions.[77] The uptown Methodist Church of Gastonia helped organize at least six new churches in the nearby mill villages, often providing pastoral service until the fledgling church could manage on its own. Support for building programs was especially common. A clear class line separated the uptown churches from the mill village churches. Some of the social forces operative to isolate the mill church included wage levels, educational achievement, housing facilities, recreational needs, and the psychological orientation of mill villagers. The class cleavage may be symbolized by the fact that when in 1923 an uptown church was erected, it cost nearly the value equal to that of all forty mill churches in the county. It is not surprising that religion in the mill villages tended to serve as an escape from economic conditions, while religion in the uptown churches was to a considerable degree a sanction of prevailing economic arrangements.[78]

Ministerial leadership is of course a matter of considerable importance in dealing with Methodist churches. "The influence and extension of a denomination over the masses of the people in Gaston County have tended to vary inversely with the degree of professional education required of its ministers. . . . The more highly educated preachers have not attracted the mill workers, who have

[75] B.D. thesis, Duke University, 1936. Cited in Pope, *Ibid.*, p. 41, 341.
[76] Pope, *Ibid.*, 41n.
[77] *Ibid.*, pp. 75-76.
[78] *Ibid.*, pp. 91-92.

come to comprise two thirds of the total population.[79] Since the denominations lost influence in the mill villages in rough proportion as its ministerial representatives became professional religious experts, it is understandable that Methodists were more successful than the Presbyterians who preceded them in strength of numbers. By comparison with Presbyterians and Lutherans, Methodist Episcopal, South standards of ministerial education were low. The denomination did not establish a college degree as a prerequisite to ordination until 1934, and until 1940 it could easily be circumvented. In 1938-39 less than half of its preachers in Gaston County had seminary training, though most were college graduates.

Methodist preachers, like Baptist ministers, having had less training in religious traditions, drew more heavily on first-hand experience in the immediate conditions of the culture of the communities in which they served. They were sensitive to immediate needs and adaptive in their programs. However, as the educational level of the leadership tended to rise, there were indications of a lowering response on the part of the workers. The educational gap creates problems for both the preacher and the pew. As the social identification of Baptist and Methodist ministers with their people in earlier decades outstripped the Lutheran and Presbyterian leaders, so they in turn "are being slowly vanquished at present by 'ignorant and disreputable' preachers of the newer sects, who are of the people and manifest an unfeigned enthusiasm for service to the people." [80] In this change the standard sociological dialectic in the evolution from sect to church to sect was re-enacted.

The mill owners in Gaston County have been concerned to control the village churches which they help to survive. Some clergy have cynically expected the mills to support an arrangement advantageous for the owners. In times of strike the workers can hardly win with the preachers against them. The preachers, in turn, are inhibited from complete freedom of expression where a mill owner provides parsonages for four ministers who lived in the village. In one case, as part of a total salary of $1,900, the Methodist preacher received a direct subsidy of $62.50 each month, and an additional $50 gift at Christmas. The mill retained title in fee simple to all church buildings and parsonages in the village.[81] In this instance the district superintendent conferred with the mill owner's

[79] *Ibid.*, pp. 107-8.
[80] *Ibid.*, pp. 114-15.
[81] *Ibid.*, pp. 152-53. Normally the annual conference retains title to church property.

son about the effectiveness of a previous minister and the requirements of a new one.

In addition to the handicaps of direct and indirect control of churches by mills, the social quiescense of the clergy may be attributed to their lack of knowledge of economic and social affairs, to their own retreat into piety from the problems of the secular order, to their lack of method in making social analyses, and to the attitudes of parishioners and employers toward their role. They were often completely submerged by the paternalism of the social situation in which they lived. Thus they lacked the freedom and the preparation to be Christian social prophets in the twentieth century. In a time of industrial crisis they contributed unqualified and effective sanction to the economic culture patterns dominant in Gaston County.[82]

5. A CASE STUDY IN COAL MINING

Not far removed from the scene of *Millhands and Preachers* are the Southern soft coal fields which we shall now consider as another case study of the response of Methodism to a distinctive industrial challenge. These coal fields comprise those which lie south of the Mason and Dixon line. The case study was made in the late forties by Arthur E. Shelton and its data, therefore, carry the reader beyond the period of the twenties. Nevertheless, it is most coherently included at this point because of the type of problem involved. Methodism has had a long history of relationships with coal mining and coal miners since the days of John and Charles Wesley, but the American pattern of relations is quite distinctive as the case study shows.

Arthur E. Shelton surveying the area in the late forties gave special attention to the situation in Eastern Kentucky, Southern West Virginia, Eastern Tennessee, and Southeastern Virginia, where the greatest amount of Southern soft coal is found. Overlapping this mining area are portions of the Holston, Kentucky, and West Virginia Conferences of The Methodist Church.[83]

[82] *Ibid.*, p. 330.
[83] F. B. Shelton wrote a B.D. thesis at Emory University in 1920, "An Investigation of the Social Life of a West Virginia Coal Mining Field" (unpublished). P. M. Conley edited *Life in a West Virginia Coal Field* (Charleston: The American Constitutional Association, 1923). N. H. Collisson prepared the report of the Coal Mines Administration published as *A Medical Survey of the Bituminous Coal Industry* (Washington: United States Government Printing Office, 1947). This study contains some excellent statistical studies of housing, hospitals, medical conditions, and church and community life. H. L. Morris', *The Plight of the Bituminous Coal Miner* (University of Pennsylvania Press,

A modern mining town is characterized by a tipple, a store, a clubhouse, and several rows of houses very much alike, usually built on the side of a mountain in the less accessible parts of the country. Ordinarily prices in the stores range higher than in other communities. Physicians available are usually those hired by the coal companies with salaries paid through the check-off system from the miners' pay. Housing generally may be divided into five classes: (a) company-owned houses. (b) rentals owned by absentee landlords, (c) rental property outside the coal company area, (d) miner-owned housing in the camps, and (e) miner-owned housing outside the camp. The most dominant type of housing, according to Collisson's study, was company-owned. In 1947, 87 per cent of the company-owned houses were from twenty to fifty years old, and only about 35 per cent were termed adequate. Ten per cent had baths as compared with 31 per cent in the private housing and 40 per cent of all houses in the United States. Health conditions were not good. In 1932 the mortality rate for children under five years of age was 88.6 per thousand compared with 22.1 per thousand for the United States as a whole.

Mining in the Southern Appalachian region began in the 1880's. The Methodist Church had already been there. The co-operation of the companies and Methodism established a fateful pattern early in mining history, that of company-owned church buildings supplied by Methodist ministers whose salaries were largely subsidized by the coal companies.[84] In 1910, Arthur E. Shelton reported, there were only nineteen appointments in the coal fields—nine of these were supplied by local preachers and ten by Conference members, the average salary being $642 per year. Of the Conference men, six were college graduates and one was a seminary graduate. By 1920 the appointments had grown to thirty-nine and the Conference men numbered twenty, the average salary being $1,359. Fifteen ministers were college graduates and one a seminary graduate. There was considerable growth in the 1920's. The number of appointments, many with large circuits, had increased to ninety-six. All the preachers were Conference men, the average salary being $1,997. Of the ninety-six, college graduates numbered forty-eight, and

1934), contains valuable material on religion. See Arthur E. Shelton, "The Methodist Church and Industrial Workers in the Southern Soft Coal Fields" (unpublished doctoral dissertation, Boston University, 1950).

[84] Isaac Patton Martin, *History of Methodism in the Holston Conference* (Knoxville: Methodist Historical Society, 1944). Dr. Martin was Presiding Elder of the area when the coal fields opened in 1883. His work is the source of the historical material on the churches. Statistics are from the Journals of the Holston, West Virginia, and Kentucky Conferences.

thirteen were seminary men. The membership stood at more than fifteen thousand persons. Then came the crash of 1929. By the end of the thirties the number of appointments had dropped to forty-nine. Of these fifteen were by accepted supplies, the largest number since the opening of the fields, and the average salary was $1,541. The number of college graduates fell to nine and seminary-trained leadership to four. While the total membership was listed at fifteen thousand, nearly 30 per cent were listed as inactive or nonresident.

When Shelton made his study in the late forties, he found that the typical Methodist church in the coal fields had a membership of 222. Company officials made up 23.6 per cent of the membership, while miners composed only 14.9 per cent. Company participation was considerable, three fifths of the church buildings being owned outright by the companies. The coal companies paid directly one third of the budget of the churches in the area. Nowhere do the trade unions own or financially support the Methodist churches in the way the companies do. Most of the remainder of the financial support for the Methodist churches was by use of the check-off among the workers in the mines.[85] This contribution, supposedly voluntary, is not always so in fact. Contributions of a dollar a month for the church have been known to be a condition of employment. In many cases the miners who gave through the check-off were personally quite indifferent to the church.

Ninety per cent of the ministers reported in Shelton's survey that the union was not friendly to the church, while 43 per cent reported that the company was friendly and co-operative. The typical miner was somewhat bitter toward the Methodist church and its work in his community. Four criticisms of the church were prominent: (1) it is company dominated; (2) it puts too much emphasis on money; (3) it is not interested in the welfare of the miner; and (4) it is against the union.

This contrasts with the company attitude. Shelton observes:

The church supplies the community with a higher type of minister than do most other denominations, and the program of Methodism appeals to the cultural level of company officials more than to any other group in the mining community. The people who make up the non-mining membership play a great part in the church as leaders and teachers. These persons are very friendly to the church but also see its need to give ministry to all classes of people in the community.[86]

[85] A. E. Shelton, op. cit., pp. 72-86.
[86] Ibid., p. 191.

The ministry to the coal fields has developed difficulties in the quality of leadership. The Methodist minister in the coal fields is, on the whole, either just starting his career or just finishing it. Moreover, most ministers in these areas have no training or preparation for the special type of community in which they serve. Lack of economic security and accessibility to his work often discourages the average Methodist minister from accepting an appointment in the mining circuit. Finally, he feels beholden to the company which dominates the financial side of the church's life.

A major problem in ministering in the coal fields is the competition of the sects. Once Methodism was almost exclusively the church that served the mining communities. The situation has changed significantly as the sects have grown.

The Church of God is the most prevalent sect group in the mining communities, and it is virtually an established denomination. There are several appeals which the sects have for miner support: (1) they oppose the social and economic pattern of the prevailing community life, thus feeding on the miners' discontents; (2) they express religion in a more emotional manner than the older denominations; (3) they exercise a kind of authority through a rigid, narrow, and absolute interpretation of the gospel.

Another set of issues involves the Negro in the Southern soft coal fields. Since World War I Negroes have been employed in greater numbers than before. Many of them were recruited by the companies from the deep South. There have been many problems of segregation and discrimination. So far as jobs are concerned there is equality without segregation. The problem is acute, however, in housing, education, church life, and all matters of close personal relationships.

Methodism is locally quite segregated, though Negro Methodist churches in the coal fields are sometimes strong institutions.

This analysis of the Methodist response to industrialism in the soft coal fields indicates the need to break with the paternalism and company domination of church and community. There is need to develop a program, strategy, and leadership properly trained for the tasks. There is need of entering into a sounder relationship with the working class in the mines. There is need for the Methodist church to assert Methodist polity in the control and operation of local Methodist churches. There is need for the church to become an inclusive church. There is need for the church to develop a program of Christian social relations concerning all the major aspects of community life, including the freedom and responsibilities of miners in their unions and church relationships. There is need to understand the nature, role, and appeal of the sects in the area. Shelton's study illustrates the general problem of Methodism's tendency to accommodate to the middle and upper-middle class groups in American society and to neglect and lose the working classes, the very groups that were so great a part of early Methodism's concern.

6. OTHER INDUSTRIAL CONFLICTS

The Methodist response to industrial conflict must be sketched so as to include the coal strike in Colorado in 1927-28. In this case the Social Service Commission of the Colorado Conference issued a pronouncement defending the miner's right to a living wage and to unionization. The abridgement of civil liberties was protested as well. In Denver the Grace Community Church opened its doors to a strike meeting. Students of the Iliff School of Theology interviewed the strikers, and the Fellowship of Reconciliation rented the municipal auditorium as a means of giving wide publicity to the findings of the students.[87]

A textile strike in New Bedford, Massachusetts, in 1928 also drew the attention of churchmen. This strike was precipitated apparently by a sudden and arbitrary wage cut which was the final blow to wage-earners already restless with grievances. The strike was long and bitter. It involved thousands of persons and paralyzed not only New Bedford but the surrounding area as well. There were the usual charges of outside agitators and Communist leaders. The Council of Churches facing the strike squarely supported the action of the pastors in having the "Social Creed of the Churches" read from the pulpits. *Zion's Herald* was alert to the situation and stated in its August 8, 1928 issue that it was not impressed with the charge that "outsiders in the pay of Moscow" were behind the movement or the unrest. "If half the tales," read the editorial, "that reiterate 'in the pay of Moscow' were true, the world today would be bankrupt. For not all the assets of all the nations of earth could possibly finance fifty per cent of the revolutionary enterprises attributed to Russia."[88] Two issues of the *Bulletin* of the Methodist Federation for Social Service defended the strikers.

While these developments were in process, the Methodist Protestants remained primarily interested in the temperance issue and

---

[87] Miller, *op. cit.*, p. 271. Rev. Charles Webber organized Denver Labor College in 1919. He was succeeded by Rev. George Lackland and he by Rev. Edgar Wahlberg. The college continued for about twenty years.

[88] Quoted in Miller, *op. cit.*, p. 267.

related problems. However, that church took an interest in national legislation in behalf of aliens. The Methodist Protestant General Conference of 1920 adopted a resolution to support congressional action for the better protection of aliens and for the endorsement of their treaty rights. Both ministers and laymen were urged to communicate with their representatives for the passage of suitable legislation.[89] At this time the *Methodist Protestant* magazine showed some direct interest in social action. An editorial seeking to secure larger support for Church papers urged that this was necessary because the secular press was increasingly unfriendly to the great moral reforms which are necessary to make the path of the Church smooth to the hearts and consciences of the people.[90] No great social issues were discussed by the journal itself in preparation of the coming General Conference that year. This attitude continued apparently, according to an editorial in 1916 which commented on the session of the Maryland Conference of the denomination as follows: "There were no rankling discussions and no radical action was taken in any direction." [91]

C. The Merger of German Methodism

In 1920 the population of the United States numbered 105,710,-610, of which 34.4 per cent were foreign-born whites. More than a third of the people lived under direct foreign cultural influences. Of the 344 out of every 1000 the following would have been the language distribution: ninety-seven would have spoken English, eighty-two German, thirty-four Italian, twenty-four Polish, twenty Yiddish, fifteen Swedish, thirteen French, twelve Czechoslovakian, and ten Norwegian. Large language groups made non-English-speaking churches possible and the decline in immigration meant that sociological forces would require major readjustments in institutional life. Taking German Methodism as an example, we may briefly analyze the relations of the denomination as a whole to the assimilation of foreign groups in the United States.

The growth of German Methodism followed closely the curve of German immigration. In 1820 the German immigrants numbered 968. By 1850 the census figures showed 310,000. The wave of emigrants following the revolution of 1848 sent the number up to almost 430,000 in 1854. Then the wave subsided until the high of 1873. Church membership in the quarter-century from 1847-72

[89] *Journal* of the Methodist Protestant General Conference, 1920, p. 37.
[90] *Methodist Protestant* (May 12, 1920), pp. 4-5.
[91] *Ibid.* (April 19, 1916).

grew 521 per cent. The next quarter-century saw the rate drop to 102.5 per cent. In the years between 1897 and 1922 there was an increase of only 1.8 per cent; in the decade from 1912-22 a loss of 2 per cent. By 1922 this branch of Methodism had become an old people's church served by preachers who numbered more men between ages seventy and eighty than between twenty and thirty and more between sixty and seventy than between twenty and forty.[92]

The sociological forces at work making for liquidation and merger are easily recognizable and familiar. In addition to the dramatic and traumatic events of World War I, there were more basic factors of cultural attrition. The immigrants adapted to American life with eagerness, and this was evident in the use of language. Moreover, many Germans were required to know English in their trades and business relations. They became bilinguists and their children and grandchildren knew English better than the mother tongue of the parents. American customs were quickly adopted in mixed neighborhoods. Many took pride in the speed with which the old-world ways were laid aside in favor of new world practices. As a result by 1924 the use of English predominated in German churches.

When immigration fell off, the use of English became even more of a practical necessity. Less frequently was German spoken at home and fewer learned it at school. Intermarriages increased the exclusive use of English. Many who knew English and used it in secular life preferred German in worship; but even those who clung to German in the home and church often did all their occupational communication in English.

The pattern of bridging the cultures and language groups in church tended to be as follows: First, English was partially used in the Sunday schools and Epworth League and other young people's gatherings. Then followed an occasional Sunday evening service in English. A next stage would see a German language service in the morning with all other services in English, except that German was also used in prayer meetings and adult Bible classes. Finally, everything was English except a German Sunday-school class and the funeral services for the older members. There were, of course, variations and combinations of this pattern of development, depending on place and rate and times of immigration.

Young people tended to drift away to English-speaking churches. The pastors followed in the trend. In 1890 there were 108 men in

[92] Douglass, *op. cit.*, pp. 210-11.

the Conference Course of Studies, but in 1922 there were only 22. Preachers sought to transfer to English-speaking conferences, 64 doing so between 1910 and 1922. The young candidates for the ministry studied in English-speaking theological seminaries in America, and some of the older ones took special studies there. Linguistic patriotism, as Douglass calls it, faded away. There were hard economic realities associated with these facts.

Though German Methodist benevolence giving was proportionally large, preachers' salaries were low and conference claimant payments were small. Advancement in the denomination as a whole was confined mostly to those who were thoroughly acculturated. Then, too, as assimilation grew, most of the parishes overlapped English-speaking ones. By 1922 the German church was stronger than the English one in only 16 per cent of the cases where the parishes overlapped.

Merger was inevitable, but some have doubted whether the rate of liquidation of German Conferences was socially and religiously sound. In 1924 the General Conference passed enabling legislation for the process of merger. The North German Conference merged that year. It also empowered the St. Louis German Conference to merge with the contiguous annual conferences during the next quadrennium. The merger took place in 1925. In 1926 the West and South German Conferences dissolved. In 1927 and 1928 the California and the Pacific German Conferences followed the fashion. By 1932 only the East, Central, and Chicago-Northwest remained. When the Chicago-Northwest Conference merged in 1933 it transferred churches from Chicago to Omaha and from St. Paul to St. Louis. When the Central German Conference adjourned that same year, its preachers took appointments from Michigan to Kentucky and from West Virginia to Indiana. Only the East German Conference still presided over Methodism's mission to the Germans in America.

There was resistance, some of it significant, to the rapid transition from ten annual conferences to none. Four considerations seem worthy of mention. They are taken from a list of eleven circulated in a protest by some of the respected leaders of the Central German Conference. They reflect chapters from the epic of sorrow that is written by any minority group as it loses its religious and social identity.

The first consideration had to do with the benevolent institutions which ranked among the best in the Church.[93]

[93] *Ibid.*, p. 217.

114

The leaders of these institutions have all, with one exception, expressed their fear that a merger with other Conferences by the dissolution of the Central German Conference at this time would create hardships for these institutions, causing insurmountable difficulties. These institutions have been founded with much prayer and have been maintained with much sacrificial service. . . . Most, if not all, direct access to the patrons and supporters of these important agencies would be cut off and their very existence would become jeopardized. In fact, a Conference merger for several of these agencies would amount to a tragedy.

A second objection had to do with sensitivity to the needs and feelings of older people, a sensitivity which the bureaucracy of a majority group seldom experiences for a minority group.

We still have among our members thousands of old people who joined the churches of this Conference in its earlier years. For most of them the disrupting of this Conference would be a great sorrow, and they will find it exceedingly difficult to adjust themselves to the new order of things. The merger should be deferred until most of them have joined the Church Triumphant, which will not be so many years hence.

Thirdly, the transfer of ministers would be of little benefit to them. Many had, as it were, preached themselves "out of a job" in their effectiveness as bilingual missioners.

While a small number may be offered a better opportunity for the future, it must be clear to every thoughtful person that most of our present men will not fare so well in English-speaking churches as they do at the present time. The fact is, that in our English Conferences there is a perfect scramble among a large percentage of the pastors for suitable places. It stands to reason that under such conditions transfers by merger could and should not expect any special consideration.

This protest was prophetic. Many leading churches of the former German Conferences went to episcopal favorites, and preachers with a strong German accent either stayed on where they were or went to the end of the appointment line.

A final protest had to do with a disregard of the viewpoint of the laity. Since then the voice of the laity has become more influential. "Living in a democratic age, country, and church, it appears to us that so momentous a step as dissolving a Conference should not be undertaken unless the majority of our laymen so wish. They have had an equal share with the ministry in building up the Conference; their official voice should be heard in dissolving the same. This has not been done."

No one who is not intimately acquainted with the life of a German Methodist parsonage or has not moved sensitively among its parishes and pastors can know the tears, the sorrow, the frustrations, the disappointments, and even the secret bitterness that attended the liquidation of this mission to the Germans in America.

German Methodism as religion created a strong personal faith and a keen sense of loyalty to America and hence inculcated strong social responsibility, but it did not encourage activity in politics. Its pietism was linked to activism, but only in a few preachers did it express a "social gospel." The German Methodists were as a rule indifferent to office-holding. Between the Civil War and 1939 twelve German Methodists served in Congress. Three or four served in the consular service. One became a governor, one a lieutenant-governor, and one a judge. A number served in lesser capacities. Much more significant was their contribution, as graduates from their colleges and seminaries, to education, the ministry, medicine, journalism, music, industry, and law. These men are witnesses of the role of Methodism in taming the energy of the frontier and making it a stable society. "It took the seething enthusiasm of the frontier and gave it the balance of a soul." [94]

In the land of liberty the preachers proclaimed the sovereignty of God, the forgiveness of sins, and the compassion of Christ in practical service. The small church became a center for the immigrant home. The small Christian college contributed to both the men and the culture of the nation. Church and college provided much of the substance of American life. They built American culture at the intersectional points of the national frontiers and the spiritual hungers of immigrants. Because of their bilingual competence, many of America's finest youth went out from German Methodist colleges and Methodist universities to study in Germany and to return, having broken open and maintained the channels of intellectual intercourse, scientific investigation, and theological and philosophical understanding between two continents.

D. Temperance and Prohibition

Temperance and general social reform had grown side by side in Methodism. In the form of Prohibition the church became deeply involved in the political problems of enforcement. Moral and legal problems were paradoxically intertwined.

In some ways the efforts to enforce Prohibition in the twenties

[94] *Ibid.*, p. 270.

were but one illustration of the American paradox in the field of law and justice. Thurman Arnold has pointed up this paradox of Americans' calling for law enforcement at the same time that they multiply the laws beyond the point of enforceability and violate them from day to day.[95] Max Lerner comments illuminatingly about this paradox:

The Americans have sought to solve the problem by alternations of neglect and enforcement, as shown by their traffic regulations, their disastrous Prohibition experiment, their gambling and betting laws, their vice and narcotic laws. They have moved between the twin beats of complacency and conscience, cynicism and Puritanism, silence and crackdown. There will be long periods of "Patterned evasion" of the legal norms through corruption and the "Big Fix." Then there will be a "crime wave" or some other index of alarm, followed by the inevitable crackdown on racketeers, "vice-kings," fee-splitters, "ambulance-chasers," narcotics peddlers and addicts, gamblers, bookies, prostitutes, gang warriors, traffic violators, or just vagrants and bums. In this crackdown the police, prosecutors, judges, press, clergy, and politicians tumble over one another in an hysteria of legal enforcement, feeling at once virtuous and inwardly silly. Then a vast apathy will blanket the community, and the silence will be as before.[96]

Beneath the paradox and breakdown in Prohibition law enforcement was a general revolution in post-World War I morals. The ongoing moral crisis which every society faces was especially acute in the "revolt of the younger generation." New freedoms were asserted in an era that saw the crest of the feminist wave and changing mores of smoking, drinking, petting, and premarital sex relations. The "revolt of youth" would have come in any case, and indeed had set in at least a decade earlier, but in the context of Prohibition youth took a clue from the oldsters armed with bootleg liquor and flouting the codes of the "blue noses." To be sure, the "revolt of youth" was partly a search for religious meaning. But it was also a flapper-and-flask "lost generation." Some of those trails were to disappear in the thirties and forties and to reappear in the fifties with widespread loss of controls involving sex, alcohol, and gambling.

The tendency of some temperance bodies to put the stress on a single cause and on legal enforcement, once the Volstead Act was passed, had serious consequences for social Christianity as a move-

[95] From *America as a Civilization*. Copyright © 1957 by Max Lerner. By permission of Simon and Schuster, Inc., p. 438.
[96] *Ibid.*, pp. 438-39.

ment. (1) The key slogan of the years of the "Noble Experiment" was "Obey the Law." (2) "The humanitarian concern for the drunkard as victim tended to be replaced by indignation at the drinker as criminal." (3) The champions of the Act claimed credit during the Volstead period for about all the social advances then going on, but for many of these they had not worked. (4) Just as the proponents overstressed the benefits of Prohibition, they understressed other social issues and tended "to make Prohibition a surrogate for the social Gospel." [97] (5) Prohibition tended to be the criterion of social responsibility, as reflected in resolutions in the Methodist Episcopal General Conferences in 1924, 1932, and 1936. The politics of the single cause tended to throw social questions out of perspective. The resolutions in 1936 said, for example, that "the moral and social decline of the last quadrennium has startled the socially minded people of the world. The long hard ascent up the heights of Christian idealism has been countered with a demoralizing avalanche." (6) The ethical failings of some of the professional "dry" politicians damaged the Church's moral prestige. "Only rarely did the dry leaders understand how much they were advancing the secularist bias of the rising generation by causing it to associate the Church simultaneously with a joyless legalistic morality and with dubious ethical practices in its achievement—in short, with hypocrisy." [98] Carter probably goes too far in this criticism, but he has a point based on a concern expressed by Bishop Edwin Holt Hughes. A leader in the Methodist Episcopal Church, South, complained that his church "used to have a Board of Temperance and Social Service. It paid mightly little attention to social service." [99] Despite the errors of their single-tracked devotion, the leaders of temperance, we must add, were devoted Christians and many had broad social concerns.

Supporters of Prohibition were bound to be concerned over the political leadership of the nation because the opposition aggressively organized all possible resources against the Volstead Act. By 1928 everyone recognized that the "noble experiment" was moving toward a showdown. Methodists threw their energies into the election of that year and influenced the outcome. The election of 1928 was not, however, a simple affair and has stimulated a number of studies, partly because one of the presidential candidates, in addi-

[97] Carter, op. cit., pp. 42-43.
[98] Ibid., p. 44.
[99] Bishop Mouzon before the Virginia Annual Conference, quoted in Carter, Ibid., p. 43.

tion to being against Prohibition, was a Roman Catholic. Some have raised the questions of Puritan moralism and religious bigotry. In any case, to vote against a Catholic for President is hardly a definition of a bigot.

Hoover's triumphant victory has been analyzed as resulting from a fourfold situation: (1) the widespread propaganda and belief that the continuance of Republican rule meant continued prosperity; (2) the negative attitude of much rural America to the Tammany background of a corrupt machine based on immigrant votes from which Smith had arisen, even though Smith had served eight years admirably as governor of New York state; (3) the deepseated opposition of many American Protestants to the elevation of a Catholic to the Presidency; and (4) the determination of the evangelical churches to retain prohibition, which Smith denounced, but Hoover called a "noble experiment." "Hoover Democrats" shattered the solid South. Republicans carried Virginia, North Carolina, Tennessee, Florida, and Texas. This was about the same pattern as that in the Eisenhower victory of 1952 when neither Prohibition nor Catholicism was involved. In 1928 Smith lost his own state, New York, and every western and border state.

Miller's summary analysis of election factors in 1928 as they affect the religious response is particularly significant.[100] Some analysts like Virginius Dabney, Gunnar Myrdal, Wilbur J. Cash, Harold J. Laski, and Gustavus Myers stress the thesis that clergymen dominated the South in the twenties and their leadership was decisive in the election of 1928. The religious issue was, however, not the decisive one, as the laity agreed with the clergy on Smith. The clergy were representing the convictions of the laity. Miller says: "When Protestants said they opposed Smith because of his wetness, they meant precisely what they said. Prohibition was not a straw man; it was the factor that more than any other determined the vote of many Americans in the election of 1928."[101] The laity did not agree with the clergy on issues involving racial and industrial justice and hence were not blind followers of alleged zealots for reform. Even outside the South prohibition was three times more influential than the Protestant-Catholic issue, as the studies by William Ogburn and Neil Talbot show. But more important in determining the election outcome than either prohibition

[100] M. Miller, op. cit., pp. 50-52. See His "A Footnote to the Role of the Protestant Churches in the Election of 1928," Church History, 25 (1956), 145-59.

[101] Ibid., p. 51.

or religion was the economic prosperity of the country which favored the continuance of a Republican as President.[102]

In 1928 the Curriculum Committee of the Methodist Episcopal Church introduced a course of six lessons "for the study of educational, scientific and personal aspects of temperance law enforcement." The International Lessons Commission recognized that the churches were facing a serious situation in the United States and Canada. They noted:

There is, especially in the cities, widespread and open defiance of laws, particularly temperance legislation, and a growing tendency to regard temperance as a matter of purely private concern. Forces opposed to prohibition are waging a ceaseless and unscrupulous war of propaganda. Moreover, during the decade since the adoption of the 18th Amendment, the program of education vigorously prosecuted prior to that event has been relaxed, both in the public schools and in Sunday Schools. A generation of youth has come to maturity which has had no vivid experience of the open saloon and its attendant evils and little systematic instruction regarding the personal and social effects of the use of alcohol.[103]

The Methodist Episcopal Church, South, being morally committed to prohibition, was bound to be deeply involved in politics in behalf of the cause. But there was a cleavage on the church's participation in politics. Bishops Edwin D. Mouzon, John M. Moore, Horace M. DuBose, and James Cannon, Jr. believed it was right for them to participate actively in party politics, and they did. Bishops Collins, Denny,[104] and Warren A. Candler strongly opposed this participation on the ground that it was wrong for the church as a church to enter the political field to advance Prohibition by supporting the Republican party, and by denouncing the Democratic party which was opposed to Prohibition and in favor of the repeal of the Constitutional amendment providing for it. Seven remaining bishops took no public stand at the time.

This controversy is instructive. Bishop Cannon (1864-1944) and like-minded advocates called a conference at Asheville, North Caro-

---

[102] *Ibid.*, p. 52.

[103] *Report of the Curriculum Committee of the Methodist Episcopal Church,* 1928.

[104] It is interesting to note that Bishop Denny was never able to support any plan of union with the other branches of Methodism. See John M. Moore, *The Long Road to Methodist Union,* pp. 131, 176, 201. Bishop Candler was also opposed to union. Both were well known for their opposition to all forms of racial integration.

lina, to organize the Anti-Smith Democrats. With the support of a good many Southern papers and the leading organs of the Methodist Episcopal Church, South, they carried on a vigorous campaign both in opposition to Governor Smith and ofttimes against the Roman Catholic Church, of which he was a member. In the heat of the campaign the following resolution was unanimously adopted by the Methodist Preachers' Meeting in Atlanta on July 24, 1928:

As patriots who hold principle above party we are undisturbed by the denunciation of party enthusiasts and partisan editors. Men of character and courage are only amused at being dubbed "dry fanatics," "intolerant bigots," "prejudiced cranks," "party disruptionists" and other complimentary epithets inadmissable here. Oh, consistency! Read us out of the party because we cannot conscientiously vote for your soaking Tammanyite, but go your limit to secure the Republican farmer-labor vote, the foreign-born, criminal wets of New York, Chicago, and similar hyphenated American cities and sections, and accept as the chairman of your campaign committee one who confesses himself "an independent" and is even now a member of the Republican club.[105]

The controversy was bitter. There were dangers in political tendencies which identified Prohibition too inherently with Protestantism.

The cause of Prohibition had in the slogan "obey the law!" an interesting connection with the field of race relations.

The Episcopal Address to the Methodist Episcopal Church, South, in 1926 included admonitions on Christian citizenship that were relevant not only to the turbulent twenties with their liquor lawlessness and lynchings, but to the period following the great Supreme Court decision on education in 1954. The bishops said:

Because we are Christians we are not therefore the less loyal citizens, but rather we should be better citizens. Our country long ago proclaimed that all governments derive their just powers from the consent of the governed. The majesty of her laws is grounded on the majesty of the people who through authorized tribunals enacted the laws for their direction and obedience; yet lawlessness now abounds: It cannot for a moment be tolerated that any man, particularly a Christian, be permitted to choose the laws he is to obey. All laws are to be obeyed. All our people must be prevailed on as a matter of conscience, as a matter of right, to be themselves obedient to all law, and to use every proper influence with others to induce them to become law-abiding. Contempt for the law of the land,

---

[105] R. G. Smith, *Politics in a Protestant Church*, p. 105.

a substitution of personal desire or judgment for law, leads straight to anarchy. We cannot be good Christians and bad citizens.[106]

When the Commission on Temperance and Social Service brought in its report it noted that the commission had co-operated as far as possible with the Commission on Race Relations and commended it.[107] The report noted that its support was moral and not financial. Moral support of this kind was fairly characteristic of the General Conferences of that era. In 1930 the Episcopal Address pointed out that the Methodist Episcopal Church, South, was not giving proper leadership in racial co-operation.

We Methodists of the South are in position to lead forward the bringing in of a better day for the colored people. Unfortunately most of us know little about the efforts this race is making to rise and the difficulties they encounter as they climb upward. Not only are many people doing nothing to assist these people, but by their attitude and conduct they are making difficult the work being done by their leaders and ours.

E. Race: Equal but Separate

When the General Conference of the Methodist Episcopal Church, South, met in 1918, there was concern over the condition not only of the 300,000 members of the Colored Methodist Church, but for the 9,000,000 Negroes living in the South. "What the Negro becomes in the process of his social, industrial, and religious development," said one report apprehensively, "is a matter of gravest concern to every white man in the South who is also an American citizen with a national vision." The apprehension continued in the following vein: "It is therefore little short of appalling to look ahead to the possibility of considerable proportion of these millions of colored people, one day living among us as alien enemies, distrustful in mood and hostile in attitude toward us. . . . It is time, then, for us to set in motion other and more constructive influences, if we would avoid the consequence here suggested." [108] Although the General Conference of 1914 had adopted the Social Creed, that creed had made no reference to race. In practical terms, if we are to judge by the reception given to an address by the Reverend

[106] *Journal of the General Conference of the Methodist Episcopal Church, South, 1926,* p. 320.
[107] The Commission on the Church and Race Relations of the Federal Council of Churches was organized in 1921. In the South the Commission on Interracial Co-operation represented the leading Christian forces. About 25 per cent of its members were ministers.
[108] *Journal,* General Conference of the Methodist Episcopal Church, South, 1918, p. 61-62.

W. J. Walls of the African Methodist Episcopal Zion Church to the Conference in 1918, both he and his white audience accepted the doctrine of "separate but equal" in matters of social relations.

There was at this time a great deal of unrest among the Negroes. As Gunnar Myrdal points out, "the upheaval in Southern agriculture prior to the First World War, the mass migration to cities and to the North, and the War itself, all acted as stimulants to the rising unrest of the American Negro people." [109] The Negroes wanted to fight in the war along with other Americans. About 400,-000 were drafted, but they were often segregated in labor camps or used as servants. "They met discrimination everywhere, and derogatory rumors about their behavior as soldiers were spread." Perhaps 200,000 Negroes went to fight in France and here had experience and a vision of a larger world than their previous life had afforded. Their experiences were eagerly reported in the Negro press and widely discussed.

Upon coming home after the war the Negro soldiers met fearful and suspicious whites. Their new industrial footholds in the North were contested by white workers and tension arose in the subsequent depression. In the South a wave of lynchings spread terror, and even more bloody race riots swept Northern cities. Myrdal says: "Without doubt the accumulated experiences during and immediately after the First World War were a most severe shock to the American Negroes and had lasting effects." [110] In the midst of this shock there was a variety of radical movements among Negroes representing labor, political, and intellectual interests. A number of leaders emerged who were important figures in the following decades despite riots, lynchings, and unemployment.

Lynching is mob action which deprives a person of his life without due process of law. In the fifty-five year period from 1882 to 1937 there were 5,112 lynchings in the United States. Of this number, 3,657 were Negroes, 1,455 were whites. A strong sentiment against lynching developed from time to time in the South, where most of them occurred. Lynchings decreased from about 200 annually in the 1890's to 10 per year in the 1930's and 4 per year in the 1940's. Many of the lynchers belonged to the group of young, propertyless, unemployed, irresponsible native whites, many even with court records.[111]

In their Address of 1922 the Methodist bishops of the South were sensitive to these tragic events:

[109] Gunnar Myrdal, *op. cit.*, II, 745.
[110] *Ibid.*, p. 745.
[111] Simpson and Yinger, *op. cit., pp.* 463-64.

We therefore urge our people everywhere to do all they can for the uplifting of the Negroes into preparation for a safe and helpful citizenship. This implies that they shall have complete justice where their lawful rights are concerned. We especially urge that everything possible be done to prevent lynchings, which are no less a disgrace to those who engage in them than they are an outrage upon the helpless victims.

The South's racial problems were as much a problem of the church as of the social environment.

A special session of the Southern General Conference was called in 1924 for the purpose of considering the first plan of unification with other Methodist churches. On this occasion there was a vigorous minority report against the plan of unification on the basis that it would not safeguard the traditional separation of the races within the church. Nevertheless, the plan was approved by the Conference and ordered submitted to the various annual conferences in 1925. When this was done, the plan failed because it did not receive the constitutionally required number of votes to be adopted. There seems to be little doubt that one of the reasons for its failure was the fear on the part of Southern churchmen that the *status quo* in race relations might not be maintained.[112] We have already noted the anxiety which was aroused in 1928 when the Northern church resolved to have the General Conference meet only in towns where equal (in this case meaning the same and integrated) accommodations were available. In handling such racial issues as these, it is apparent that in the twenties the Southern bishops were in advance of their General Conference. They consistently called for a higher conception of citizenship than prevailed in the South, and related citizenship to Christian obedience.

The period of the twenties, then, had little to show by way of church advance in race relations. A Negro leader wrote in 1925: "Of all the groups devoted to social uplift I have least hope in the white Christian ministers." [113] The policies and practices of Protestantism generally did not materially help to integrate the Negro in American life; indeed, they contributed to his segregated status.[114] However, a number of Negro leaders were in the process of training in Methodist and other Protestant colleges and theological schools. Negro and white Methodist women were active in the Association of Southern Women for the Prevention of Lynch-

[112] See John M. Moore, *The Long Road to Methodist Union*, 1943, pp. 176, 179.

[113] Quoted in Miller, *op. cit.*, p. 298.

[114] See Frank S. Loescher, *The Protestant Church and the Negro*, p. 15.

ing. Clergymen accounted for a fourth of the members of the Commission on Interracial Co-operation. Methodists within the Federal Council of Churches participated in its pronouncements for the removal of discrimination and in founding the Commission on the Church and Race Relations, later the Department of Race Relations. Through its efforts, Race Relations Sunday was first observed in 1923 and Brotherhood Month was established.

CHAPTER FIVE

The Social Creed in the Great Depression

Chronological Outline of
Major Events in American Social, Economic, and
Political History: 1930 to 1939

1930—Population: 122,775,046.

The Supreme Court rules that purchasers of intoxicating liquors are not guilty of violating the Prohibition law.

Congress passes the Smoot-Hawley Tariff Bill, with world-wide trade repercussions.

Construction of Boulder Canyon Dam begun.

The Supreme Court holds constitutional a Louisiana law permitting the state to give certain free textbooks to pupils in parochial and private schools.

1931—Supreme Court by a five-to-four decision denies citizenship to Miss M. A. Bland and to Dr. D. C. Macintosh who refused to promise in advance to bear arms in defense of the United States.

President Hoover urges reliance (June 15) on individual efforts and voluntary relief.

President Hoover proposes a moratorium for all international indebtedness. Later ratified by Congress.

U.S. Steel Corporation announces 10 per cent wage reduction, followed by Bethlehem Steel, General Motors, and other corporations.

Scottsboro (Alabama) case. Negro youths involved were defended as victims of injustice. Becomes a *cause célèbre*.

Stimson pledges U.S. to join in one-year naval holiday, provided other nations do the same.

1932—China and Japan warned that U.S. will not recognize any treaty in which its treaty rights or its citizens are impaired.

Senate passes bill granting independence to Philippines under certain conditions at the end of twelve years. House adopts it.

Roosevelt elected president (472 electoral votes) over Hoover (59).

Railroads and unions agree to 10 per cent cut in wages. U.S. Steel corporation cuts wages 15 per cent.

Democratic Party platform declares for repeal of the 18th Amendment; the Republican platform is vaguely contradictory.

"Bonus Expeditionary Army" expelled from Washington with aid of regular army.

Federal Council of Churches adopts an "advanced" Social Creed.

1933—President Roosevelt announces "bank holiday" (March 6). Congress passes Emergency Bank Bill.

TVA proposed. Passed April 26, 1933.

Industrial codes of many kinds adopted.

NRA goes into effect. By this law all child labor is forbidden.

Twenty-first Amendment adopted, repealing the Eighteenth. (Dec. 5)

U. S. goes off gold standard.

U.S. recognizes the government of the U.S.S.R.

On December 31 it was announced that $324,-428,488 had been expended for relief in seven months, and that four million workers have been employed. About twelve million men out of work.

Hitler made Chancellor by Hindenburg. German Reichstag building burned. Communists accused. Hitler given blanket power for four years.

Concordat signed between the Third Reich and the Roman Catholic Church.

1934—Roosevelt signs Tydings-McDuffie Act giving Philippines independence to become effective July 4, 1946.

Securities and Exchange Act signed.

Reciprocal Trade Agreements Act signed.

Hitler purge; Hindenburg dies. Hitler becomes absolute dictator in Germany.

Supreme Court, in a conscientious objector case, recognizes freedom of religion as directly protected in the Fourteenth Amendment.

1935—Roosevelt asks 3.5 million jobs in public works (PWA) to end dole. 22,375,000 on relief rolls.

National Labor Relations Act (Wagner Act). (Upheld by Supreme Court, April 12, 1937.)

Social Security Act. (Upheld by Supreme Court, May 24, 1937.)

Committee for Industrial Organization headed by John L. Lewis, organized within AFL; expelled in 1937; becomes Congress of Industrial Organizations (CIO) in November, 1938.

Nuremberg laws deprive Jews of citizenship and bar intermarriage.

League of Nations condemns Italy for invading Ethiopia.

Third International (Communist) decides Russia will side with democracies against Fascist states.

1936—Japan withdraws from naval conference at London; U.S., France, Britain sign pact March 25.

Spanish Popular Front (republicans and leftists) wins parliamentary elections. Spanish civil war begins. Troops led by General Francisco Franco.

Hitler sends German troops into Rhineland, defying Versailles Treaty: denounces Locarno Pact.

Zinoviev and Kamenev executed in Russia as alleged collaborators with Trotzky and Nazi secret police.

Rome-Berlin Axis formed.

Japan signs anti-Comintern treaty with Germany.

Franklin D. Roosevelt re-elected.

1937—Roosevelt's second inaugural sees "one-third of the nation ill-housed, ill-clad, ill-nourished." Sit-down strikers at Flint, Michigan, defy court order telling them to evacuate.

Roosevelt defeated in effort to "pack" Supreme Court; subsequently Justices Hughes and Roberts switched to give New Deal a majority in the court and later appointments strengthened the majority.

Japan begins undeclared war on China; fighting continues throughout World War II until fall of Japan. Neutrality Act limits sales to belligerents. F.D.R. calls for "quarantine" of aggressors.

Pope Pius XI issues encyclical, "Mit Brennender Sorge," March 14; it is read in German Pulpits on Palm Sunday.

Oxford: Universal Christian Conference on Church, State, and Community. Edinburgh: Second World Conference on Faith and Order. Vote taken to create World Council of Churches by merging Life and Work and Faith and Order movements.

1938—New Agricultural Adjustment Act signed: establishes parity payments, ever-normal granaries, crop insurance.

Fair Labor Standards Act provides forty-cent minimum wage and forty-hour week, to be achieved within eight and three years, respectively.

Nazis seize Austrian government; Schuschnigg ousted. Jews herded into concentration camps.

Munich agreement.

1939—Sit-down strikes outlawed by U.S. Supreme Court.

Madrid surrenders to Franco. U.S. recognized Franco government.

Germany and Russia sign ten-year nonaggression Pact. Germany invades Poland and annexes Danzig; Britain and France declare war.

U.S.A. proclaims neutrality. F.D.R. signs bill removing arms embargo; substitutes "cash and carry" trade with belligerents.

Roosevelt appoints Myron Taylor as his personal
representative to the Pope with the rank of
ambassador.
Einstein writes letter to Roosevelt which leads,
eventually, to the atomic bomb.

A. Judgments on the Economic Order

THE GREAT DEPRESSION PROVIDED THE PRINCIPAL BACK-
ground for the domestic social policies and legislation proposed by
the churches in the thirties. Interpretations of the causes of the
plunge from prosperity to adversity varied greatly, but accounts
of the disturbing influences included the following: (1) Overexpansion in agriculture, with American farmers producing more
wheat, cotton, corn, livestock, and other commodities than could
be sold at satisfactory prices. The results were agricultural surpluses and devastatingly low prices, decline in buying, and increased
tenancy as payments on heavy mortgages radically curtailed the
farmer's liquid assets. (2) Industrial overexpansion. Boom years
created an industrial capacity geared to produce far more than
purchasing power could consume. (3) Technological effectiveness.
Though "technological unemployment" might not be permanent,
the immediate effects were that the power of labor to buy was
reduced. Decisions to introduce labor-saving devices were not sufficiently paralleled by policies to increase wages, shorten the labor
day and the labor week, and diminish the use of women and children
in industry. (4) Capital surpluses were too high as capital kept
too much and labor did not have enough to buy its share of the
things produced. The monopolistic tendency of much American business greatly facilitated its control of prices. Much was said about
the free market when governmental control was proposed in the
twenties, but few recognized that business had learned to manage
the market and restrict competition when such policies were more
profitable than the free market. (5) Overexpansion of credit in
production and consumption alike. Following the speculative spirit
of the Coolidge era, purchasers mortgaged their futures for goods
that they often consumed before they could be paid for. (6) Im-
balance in international trade. In the tradition of protective tariffs
most Americans were slow to realize that international trade is
a "two-way street." As Americans withdrew credit in Europe,
their economies were depressed and American goods had fewer
buyers. (7) World-wide political unrest. Especially in Europe

130

Asia, and South America many countries were overburdened with governmental debts, and few national budgets were in balance.[1]

The optimism which characterized American life in the first quarter of the twentieth century was rudely shaken by the great depression which was initiated by the Wall Street "crash" of 1929. Widespread misery, ever deepening in its social and personal effects, caused many churchmen and church conferences to consider seriously for the first time the soundness of the existing economic system. The protest voices and warnings of the twenties became a flood of social criticism and demands for a better social order.

At the same time prophetic social witness found in the gospels a surer foundation. There was a coalescence of Christian idealism and realism, of urgency and relevance. Methodist-trained Charles R. Brown, dean of Yale Divinity School, asked if he was his brother's keeper, replied, "No, I am my brother's brother." [2] Brotherhood was to require a serious examination of the whole social system. The bishops of the Methodist Episcopal Church stated in 1930 that there was something fundamentally wrong "with a social system that, in the midst of plenteous abundance, dooms untold numbers of our people to unbearable poverty and distress through no apparent fault of their own." [3]

Wage workers and farmers had not shared relatively in the so-called prosperity of the 1920's. In the depression they were to endure even greater hardship. Gross inequality became a source of widespread discontent. Persons receiving incomes of $10,000 and up in 1920 had a total class income of $6,761 millions and in 1929 received $14,466 millions. Using an index of 100.00 for 1920, the figure in 1929 stood at 214.00. Wage workers as a class increased their index to only 109.1 while farmers actually declined to 72.7. Lewis Corey observed that by and large "the farther an occupation is from directly productive work, the larger the income it yields." [4] Taking the nation as a whole, 68.5 per cent of the gainfully occupied people received 41 per cent of the income, while 15.9 per cent received 51.9 per cent of the income. In the year 1928,

[1] Brookings Institution, *The Recovery Problem in the United States* (1936); W. B. Donham, *Business Adrift* (1931); F. A. Shannon, *America's Economic Growth* (1940); L. M. Hacker and B. B. Kendrick, *The United States Since 1865* (1932); Lewis Corey, *The Decline of American Capitalism* (1934).

[2] Charles R. Brown, *The Gospel for Main Street* (New York: The Century Company, 1930), p. 24.

[3] *New York Christian Advocate* (Dec. 11, 1930), p. 1527. Cited in Miller, *op. cit.*, p. 65.

[4] Lewis Corey, *The Decline of American Capitalism* (New York: Covici-Friede, 1934), p. 309.

382,241 persons in the upper-middle class, or .8 per cent of the population received 18.4 per cent of the money income or 21.8 per cent of the total income, including business savings.[5] This concentration of income meant poverty for the many and swollen incomes for the few, resulting in underconsumption among the masses and conspicuous overconsumption among the upper classes. There was widespread discontent which became critical in the years of the Hoover Administration.

In 1932 and 1936 the bishops of the Methodist Episcopal Church spoke on industrial relations. They were concerned about both the exploitation of the wage earner and the tendency of the upper classes to label honest critics of the current economy as "radicals." Two statements reflect the bishops' attention to the problem of the economic system as such and the rights of those who criticized it from the perspective of Christian principles:

It cannot be denied that the industrial practices of past decades have given us the deplorable conditions of today. Industry has as a rule given labor a grudging, insufficient wage, keeping it down by child exploitation, by suppression of legitimate organizations, and by other expedients, while at the same time huge fortunes have been amassed for the favored owners of the resources of production. Today the burden is without conscience shifted to the worker who after giving his labor for miserable financial results, is turned off to starve or beg. Thus, the machine, which might have been used to lift the load of poverty from the backs of all the people, has been used selfishly for the benefit of the few.

In 1936 they said:

The indisputable statement that Christian principles should be applied to industry is nervously met by the charge that the speaker has become a radical. Directly good men are so obsessed by an imaginary menace that they cannot see the obvious faults of the social and financial system. The critic is regarded as an enemy, whereas he may really be the long-run friend. So it occasionally happens that some of the best men are represented as the country's foes, while commercial representatives who take millions in unearned salaries or in subsidies for watered subsidiaries receive no stern condemnation. Without now debating the merit or the

[5] *Ibid.*, p. 312. Brookings Institution summarized the situation as follows: "Nearly 6 million families, or more than 21 per cent of the total, had incomes less than $1,000. About 12 million families, or more than 42 per cent, had incomes less than $1,500. Nearly 20 million families, or 71 per cent, had incomes less than $2,500. Only a little more than 2 million families, or 8 per cent, had incomes in excess of $5,000. About 600,000 families, or 2.3 per cent, had incomes in excess of $10,000." Cited in *Information Service*, 21 (June 20, 1942, No. 25) by Dr. F. Ernest Johnson.

demerit of the so-called capitalistic system, it may still be said with assurance that the best way to preserve it for its claimed service is to make an honest endeavor to purge it of its wrongs and excesses.

In 1930 the fall annual conferences, such as Wyoming, Colorado, Rock River, Wisconsin, Michigan, Northeast Ohio, and Pittsburgh, took critical account of the current unchristian social order and took particular notice of various specific problems. Colorado noted that Methodism was committed to a new economic order. Pittsburgh referred to the failures of our "present social organization." Rock River's social service commission stated that solution of present ills lies in "an economic readjustment." Wyoming spoke of "the breakdown of the present economic order." Michigan described the situation as "the economic chaos of today," and Wisconsin said that there "is something fundamentally unchristian in our economic system." Northeast Ohio made the judgment: "Just as long as the desire for private profit is the regulating principle in our modern industrial and commerical life, so long the high interests of human life will be jeopardized." [6]

The vigorous criticism of the profit motive and the economic system, which was so common among churchmen and religious bodies during the depression, seems strange amid the prosperity and complacency of the present time. Profit was a symbolic term for much more than the strict economic meaning of the word. Obviously the farmer, the cotton grower, and every businessman sought a profit. It was a "fighting word." Often those who attacked the profit system had no clear alternative to offer to American capitalism. There were those who demanded relief from the excesses of capitalistic inequalities; there were those who attacked the monopolistic tendencies of powerful corporations; there were those who supported the reforms of the New Deal; there were those who advocated consumers' co-operatives; and there were those who holding one or more of these positions espoused one or another form of socialism. Since Christians were impelled to work at the roots of social evil in the motives of men, they often attacked the capitalistic order in terms of the "profit motive." On the other hand, it was only natural that laymen who were leaders both in church life and business world felt unfairly judged by those who made sweeping moral judgments against the "profit system" but who had no immediate obligations to payrolls or stockholders.

[6] These comments were summarized in the *Social Service Bulletin* for Nov. 15, 1930. The Rock River Conference is in Northeastern Illinois. The Wyoming Conference overlies portions of New York and Pennsylvania.

In all the social criticisms of the economic order to be noted below there was a marked socialistic tendency. However, among Methodist leaders there were many "prophetic" utterances in behalf of social justice that sounded like socialism, but they actually never voted farther to the left than the New Deal program. It should also be noted that the bill of particulars in the platforms of the Democratic and the Socialist parties overlapped at many points, but the "systems" which gave them their contexts were quite far apart. Many Methodist liberals used a mixture of Christian and Marxist vocabulary in their analysis of the economic crisis. But from this fact alone it is quite impossible to determine their ultimate political commitments.[7] When it came to voting it was reform rather than revolution which received the dominant support of the Methodist laity.

Some Methodists read Harry F. Ward and the literature of the Methodist Federation for Social Service. His writings included *Our Economic Morality, Which Way Religion?, The Profit Motive, The New Social Order,* and *In Place of Profit.* Many read the writings of Kirby Page, pacifist socialist, and Harry F. Laidler, the socialist director of the League for Industrial Democracy. Some also admired the political leadership of Norman Thomas but did not vote for him. Reinhold Niebuhr's *Moral Man and Immoral Society* became epoch-making. Critical reform was encouraged in many of the books by Bishop F. J. McConnell. The crisis gave birth to a multitude of economic proposals.

Generalizations about the economic order as a whole were the most significant aspects of the church's response to the crisis, but they were coupled with specific judgments on unemployment, agriculture, race relations, civil liberties, military training and war. We can note only a few of the representative annual conference judgments. Michigan demanded for the millions of the jobless a proportionate share of the financial aid of the federal government. Wisconsin declared that "the church should not countenance the unreasonable taking of profit out of food products after they have left the farmer and before they have reached the consumer," but "should cry out against the injustice wrought by our economic order in creating a situation wherein there are the possessors of millions in wealth while millions of persons cannot purchase the necessary

[7] The treatments of the profit motive in the early 1930's are strikingly different from those twenty years later. See J. Bennett, H. R. Brown, W. A. Brown, Jr., and G. B. Oxnam in *Christian Values and Economic Life* (New York: Harper and Brothers, 1954). See also W. G. Muelder, *Religion and Economic Responsibility* (New York: Charles Scribner's, 1953.)

food for physical well being, while other millions would gladly produce to feed the undernourished and starving, but cannot afford to do so."

Northeast Ohio urged the general boards, commissions, and the General Conference to arrange for their meetings only in places where colored members and delegates would not be discriminated against. In this connection it is well to remember that Wisconsin pointed out that "discrimination against Negroes and Asiatics in hotel and restaurant accommodations makes it impossible for Milwaukee to extend an invitation to the General Conference of 1932 to hold its sessions there." Pittsburgh promised the hearty support of its churches in the effort to abolish the coal and iron police system which systematically violated civil liberties. And the Colorado Conference viewed "with shame the fact that so large a part of our national budget is expended for military purposes." In addition to statements on all the above issues several of these annual conferences put themselves on the side of education for marriage, the principle of voluntary parenthood, and legislation which would make possible the publicity needed for birth-control methods to be widely and responsibly effective.

The Methodist Federation for Social Service in 1930 carried some of its educational activities to Epworth League Institutes in Illinois and Wisconsin. Its leaders met with the Social Service Commission of the Wisconsin conference. The temper of the times is reflected in the words of a Wisconsin Methodist preacher: "Put yourself on the side of a social order based on Christian principles, and 90 per cent of the businessmen in your congregation will be against your position and classify you as a bolshevik." In Denver some Methodist church members put up cards in their windows urging milk drivers to join their union and quoting from a Methodist church pronouncement demanding recognition of labor's right to organize: "This home believes in the principles for which organized labor and the church jointly stand. . . . We will greatly appreciate seeing your union card when next you call to collect your bill." [8] In other places Methodist young people were raising the question whether warm churches should be locked up while myriads walked the streets in the cold with no place to sleep.[9]

By the fall of 1930 perhaps seven million men were out of work. In Cleveland, police broke up a Communist-led unemployment demonstration. That very day the Methodist Council of Cities meeting declared: "The piling up of large reserves for investors already

[8] *The Social Service Bulletin* (Oct. 15, 1930), p. 4.
[9] *Loc. cit.*

receiving dividends, while workers are turned out to suffer and to die, should become abhorrent to every citizen. . . . The methods too commonly employed by police forces in dealing with hungry men are in themselves a menace to the very institutions which they are designed to protect." [10] In that same city a Methodist church set up a soup kitchen at that time.

There were many voices of judgment, and they spoke out on many themes. The Methodist Youth Association (Milwaukee, 1932) : "The social order today based on profitism, we believe, is inherently unchristian since its standard of value is materialistic and selfish." Northern New York Methodist Episcopal Conference (1931) : "We are the victims, the beneficiaries, and the perpetuators of an economic system which is founded upon profit and motivated by selfish gain." Wyoming Methodist Episcopal Conference (1932) : "The present economic and industrial order stands condemned before the bar of Christian justice for the following reasons : Its central motive is production for profit instead of need . . . it increasingly places the wealth of the world in the hands of the few while the masses cry out in vain." New York East Methodist Episcopal Conference (1932) : "The profit motive must go. The acquisitive desire must be replaced by the desire to serve."

What did the various conferences regard the function of the church to be? Was it to define the task? To set an example? To make judgments? To take sides? To educate? Perhaps all of these. Rock River (1932) : "It is not our task to propose economic programs. It is ours to point out the evils . . . and to suggest some goals and ways for which religion must stand." Delaware : The church "can offer to the world an example of business procedure. . . . The church is an employer, an investor, and an administrator of funds. . . . The church and its ministers should refuse all such special favors as seem to put them under obligation to be silent on questions of social righteousness." Chicago Social Action Conference : "The dividing line in the present social conflict is between the specially privileged and the underprivileged. . . . We as ministers and church workers are members of the privileged class. . . . The initiative for the breakdown of that barrier (of class privilege) rests upon us." [11]

Ministers and laymen responded to the industrial and agricultural crisis in part through participating in a number of associations of reform. In 1932 the Religion and Labor Foundation was organized with Methodists prominently represented on its board and

[10] *Ibid.* (Nov. 1, 1930), p. 4.
[11] These statements are all cited in *The Social Service Bulletin* (Jan. 1, 1933).

staff.[12] The Christian Social Action Movement was largely Methodist.[13] Methodists participated actively in the Fellowship of Southern Churchmen and Friends of the Soil, the United Christian Council for Democracy, the Fellowship of Reconciliation, the Ministers' Union of America, the Committee for the Defense of Southern Share Croppers, the League for Industrial Democracy, the Workers' Defense League, the Social Security Association, the American Association for Labor Legislation, and others.

There was much ferment and eagerness to participate in social action on the part of clergy, theological students, and the staffs of reform societies. Miss Winifred Chappell of the Methodist Federation for Social Action spent six weeks of 1934 in the mining camps of West Virginia in support of workers' rights and interests.[14] *Zion's Herald* was greatly concerned over the labor situation in "bloody" Harlan County. Students from Boston University School of Theology marched in a textile-strike picket line in 1931. *Zion's Herald* [15] sided with the workers, and the New England Methodist Conference passed a resolution condemning the abridgment of civil liberties during the strike. In Denver the Reverend A. A. Heist gave encouragement to organized labor while serving Grace Community Church, and the students at Iliff Theological Seminary became increasingly involved. There were scores of such expressions during the turbulent days of the thirties.

Methodism moved, for a period, to the left—part of a national tendency to approach problems more from labor's perspective or from an outright New Deal or even a socialist position. In 1934 a poll of some twenty thousand ministers showed that 63 per cent favored and 13 per cent opposed (the rest doubtful) a system of compulsory unemployment insurance under government supervision. Likewise, 54 per cent favored and 12 per cent opposed national unions as opposed to local company unions. Company unions were a residue of the open-shop campaigns waged by management associations in the twenties.[16]

About the same time Kirby Page sent out a questionnaire to ministers which registered 28 per cent in favor of socialism. Of the socialist responses the denominational spread was percentage-wise as follows: Methodist (34), Evangelical (33), Congregational

[12] Francis J. McConnell, Willard Uphaus.
[13] Gilbert Cox, Paul Hutchinson, Owen Geer, W. B. Waltmire, J. Stitt Wilson, Clarence Tucker Craig, and James M. Yard were among its leaders.
[14] Miller, *op. cit.*, p. 277.
[15] *Zion's Herald* (Nov. 18, 1931), p. 1444.
[16] Miller, *op. cit.*, p. 253.

(33), Reformed (32), Disciples (30), Episcopal (24), Baptist (22), Presbyterian (19), Lutheran (12).[17] In response to a National Religion and Labor Foundation poll in 1935 about 67 per cent of the 4,700 respondents pledged themselves publicly to support old age pensions, unemployment insurance, and a child labor amendment. Equally significant were the replies of these churchmen to certain action efforts as follows: (a) 40 per cent agreed to make acquaintance of local labor leaders; (b) 32 per cent agreed to entertain union officials in their homes; (c) 21 per cent agreed to invite labor union leaders to speak in their churches; (d) 26 per cent agreed to aid labor to organize; and (e) 36 per cent agreed to resist attempts to substitute company unions for "genuine" workers' unions.

From these evidences of critical church concern it would appear that the depression confirmed the worst fears of liberals at the turn of the century that America seemed in danger of becoming a land in which the millionaires had more and more, and the rest had less and less, and where a few financiers had a strangle hold not only on the country's economic apparatus, but on its political apparatus too. But, as it turned out, some changes were called into being. Progressive conservatives today, looking back on the thirties, may be inclined to agree with the interpretation made by Frederick Lewis Allen in *The Big Change*.[18] When the country's democratic spirit and national sense of fair play was outraged, the nation went to work to change things, not by a revolution but by a series of experimental revisions in the system. In the great depression the repair work and reconstruction were quite drastic. Though some reforms were foolish, the basic principle of unrevolutionary and experimental change prevailed.

Through a combination of patchwork revisions of the free enterprise system in the form of tax laws, minimum wage laws, subsidies and guaranties and regulations of many kinds, plus labor union pressures and new management attitudes following the Wagner Act, a significant change was effected. It was, among other things, a redistribution of income from the well-to-do to the less-well-to-do. With the improvement of income and status to the lower-income groups, thus enabling them to buy more goods and expand the

---

[17] *Ibid.*, pp. 101-2. The term socialism was defined as that "represented by the Socialist Party of America, or by a new and more inclusive alignment, in which the present Socialist Party would be included." Norman Thomas was the leading personality in this party.

[18] (New York: Harper and Brothers, 1952) ch. 18, pp. 289-93.

market for everybody, America discovered a new frontier, the purchasing power of the poor.

The United States did not scrap the profit system, but demonstrated (so the progressive-conservative argues) that it could be so adapted as to combine most of the advantages of governmental responsibility and of private initiative and to avoid the disadvantages of each. In this combination governmental intervention is limited and private industry and associations have a great degree of freedom.

During the thirties when these experimental repairs and changes were taking place in the economy, the New Deal generated a great deal of heat, even passion. Marquis W. Childs observed in 1936 that a consuming hatred of President Roosevelt was beginning to permeate the whole upper stratum of society. "Regardless of party and regardless of region, today, with few exceptions," said *Time* in April 1936, "members of the so-called Upper Class frankly hate Franklin Roosevelt." [19] The economic classes who felt they were being liquidated had great difficulty in adjusting to the new relationships and power patterns in industrial relations and politics. From the perspective of 1960 it is quite evident that despite the difficulties and readjustments, the basic features of the "profit system" survived and capitalism as a whole was conserved within an adaptable "mixed economy."

Methodists who sought to come critically and realistically to grips with the economic and social crisis had continually to be alert to rightist groups of all kinds. Some of these were secular, others were related to religious organizations. In the early thirties there were also groups intent on building the military mind and on repressing critical thinking. The American Coalition, the National Civic Federation, and the American Legion operated on the level of national organizations. Locally there were associations like the Better America Federation in Los Angeles, the American Vigilante Intelligence Association in Chicago, and the Industrial Defense Association in Boston. At this time the War Department attempted vigorous propaganda in the schools. It bracketed and attacked both pacifism and internationalism. In several states the National Guard was consulted about handling unemployment demonstrations. In Illinois it circulated secretly "Emergency Plans for Domestic Disturbances." A Wisconsin city witnessed collusion by American

[19] See Arthur M. Schlesinger, Jr., *Esquire* (January 1959), for a survey of these attitudes.

Legionnaires and the local police in breaking up a political meeting of workers at which capitalism was criticized.

The Daughters of the American Revolution occasionally aroused semihumorous responses from liberal Methodists. Owen Geer, in a letter to *The Social Service Bulletin* of the Methodist Federation for Social Service, reported an incident in Kansas: "The school boys who guard the traffic for the children crossing the streets in Wichita have always carried little red flags to stop oncoming motorists. The D.A.R. found the red flags altogether too disturbing. They petitioned the school board and succeeded in getting them changed to green flags. . . . I think it is an outrage to have so much red in those Kansas sunsets." [20]

The General Conference of the Methodist Episcopal Church was convened in the spring prior to the election which brought the Democratic Party and Franklin D. Roosevelt to power. There was a reaffirmation of the Social Creed and an expansion of it through important additional pronouncements. During that same year also the Federal Council of Churches reformulated and expanded its "Social Ideals." These two documents had great similarity. The first of these is cited immediately below along with notations on similar positions taken by the Methodist Episcopal Church, South. As Dr. F. Ernest Johnson has pointed out in making a well-known inventory of social trends, much of the social legislation of the New Deal was parallel to the Social Creed demands.[21] The historic character of the 1932 version of the Social Creed and the attendant General Conference pronouncements indicates its inclusion at this point. As we shall see, it stimulated a number of annual conferences to take strong positions on many issues.

B. The Social Creed: 1932 to 1939

The Social Creed which the General Conference of the Methodist Episcopal Church adopted in 1932 has several interesting features. Its first section comprised a number of paragraphs which were substantially those of the historic Social Creed as modified in 1912. Then followed a section which called for the development of the creed. This development was expressed in "translating" the fundamental principles of Christian social ethics into several areas of application.

Section One of the creed was to be read in the pulpit on Labor Day Sunday.

[20] *The Social Service Bulletin* (April 15, 1933), p. 3. In 1933 the name was changed to *The Social Questions Bulletin*.
[21] See *Information Service*, 21 (June 20, 1942), No. 25.

To show the development of social thought in the Methodist Episcopal Church, South, the resolutions of that church are introduced in the various sections which seek to "translate" the basic principles into concrete lines of action.

1. SECTIONS OF THE SOCIAL CREED TO BE READ TO THE CONGREGATION ON THE SUNDAY PRECEDING LABOR DAY

The Methodist Episcopal Church stands for equal rights and complete justice for all men in all stations of life; for the protection of the family by the single standard of purity, uniform divorce laws, proper regulation of marriage, and proper housing; for such regulation of the conditions of toil for women as shall safeguard the physical and moral habits of the community; and for the fullest possible development of every child, especially by the provision of proper education and recreation, and by the abolition of child labor.

It stands for the abatement and prevention of poverty, by the protection of the individual and of society from the social, economic, and moral waste of the liquor traffic, by the conservation of health, and by the protection of the worker from dangerous machinery, occupational diseases and injuries.

It stands for the right of all men to the opportunity for self-maintenance, safeguarding this right against encroachments of every kind; and for the protection of workers from the hardships of enforced unemployment.

It stands for suitable provision for the workers in old age and for those incapacitated by injury; for the principle of conciliation and arbitration in industrial disputes, and for a release from employment one day in seven.

It stands for the gradual and reasonable reduction of the hours of labor to the lowest practicable point, and for that degree of leisure for all which is a condition of the highest human life; for a living wage as a minimum in every industry and for the highest wage that each industry can afford, and for the most equitable division of the product of industry that can ultimately be devised.

It stands for the right of employees and employers alike to organize.

It stands for a new emphasis upon the application of Christian principles to the acquisition and use of property.

2. DEVELOPMENT OF THE CREED

"We believe in making the social and spiritual ideals of Jesus our test for community as well as for individual life; in strengthening and deepening the inner personal relationship of the individual with God, and recognizing his obligation and duty to society. This is crystallized in the two commandments of Jesus: 'Love thy God' and 'Love thy neighbor.' " After this general statement on the de-

141

velopment of the Social Creed the ideals of Jesus were translated into a number of specific areas by the General Conference of 1932.

3. EDUCATION

Translating this ideal into education means: (a) The building of a social order in which every child has the best opportunity for development and in which is afforded adequate and equal educational opportunity for all. (b) A thorough and scientific program of religious and secular education designed to Christianize everyday life and conduct. (c) Conservation of health, including careful instruction in sex hygiene and home building, abundant and wholesome recreation facilities, and education for leisure, including a nation-wide system of adult education. (d) Insistence on constitutional rights and duties, including freedom of speech, of the press, and of peaceable assemblage. (e) Constructive education and Christian care of dependents, defectives, and delinquents, in order to restore them to normal life whenever possible, with kindly segregation for those who are hopelessly feeble-minded.

It is interesting that the section on education includes concern for civil liberties. Not only the Social Creed of 1932, but also the *Doctrines and Discipline* of the Methodist Episcopal Church, South, in 1934 and 1938 and the Social Creed of 1939 adopted at the Uniting Conference reaffirmed recognition and maintenance of rights and responsibilities of free speech, assembly, and press. They encouraged positively free communication of mind with mind as essential to the discovery of truth.

Concern for freedom, the rights of the person, and the redemption of all men was expressed in the same official conferences on prisons, courts, and the machinery of justice. Methodism underscored the values of justice, opportunity, and equal rights for all. It asked for the application of Christian principles of redemption to the treatment of offenders, with the purpose of restoring them as useful members of society. Correspondingly, it called for reform of penal and correctional methods and institutions and also for a reform of criminal court procedure.

4. INDUSTRY AND ECONOMIC RELATIONS

The General Conference of 1932 resolved that translating this ideal

into industry and economic relationships means: (a) A reciprocity of service—that group interests, whether of labor or capital, must always be integrated with the welfare of society as a whole, and that society in its turn must insure justice to each group. (b) A frank recognition that all ownership is a social trust involving Christian administration for the

142

good of all. (c) Freedom from employment one day in seven, and the eight-hour day as the present maximum for all industrial workers. (d) An effective national system of public employment bureaus to make possible the proper distribution of labor forces. (e) Economy in the home—such an arrangement of the home budget during the years of productive earning that there may be an increasing reserve for later years. (f) Adequate provision for impartial investigation and publicity, conciliation and arbitration in industrial disputes. (g) The right of labor to organize with representatives of their own choosing, and where able, to share in the management. (h) The supremacy of the service, rather than the profit motive in the acquisition and use of property on the part of both labor and capital, and the most equitable division of the product of industry that can be devised.[22]

The idea that all ownership is a social trust under God was stressed in the *Doctrines and Discipline* of the Methodist Episcopal Church, South, in 1934. The need for wider and fairer distribution of wealth by means of forms of social control was expressed in the *Discipline* for 1934 and 1938, as well as the demand to apply the Christian principle of social well-being to the acquisition and use of wealth. This included the subordination of speculation and the profit motive to the creative and co-operative spirit.

Other ideas in the Social Creed of 1932 which were echoed in the Methodist Episcopal Church, South, involved collective bargaining, hours of work, and employment. In 1934 that Church asked for mutual good will and co-operation among economic groups. Group interests, it stated, whether of labor or capital, must always be integrated with the welfare of society as a whole, and society in turn must insure justice to each group. In this context the Southern church emphasized the right of employers and employees alike to organize for collective bargaining and social action. Both should be protected in the exercise of this right.[23]

In both 1934 and 1938 the Methodist Episcopal Church, South, asked for at least one day's rest in seven and a reduction in the hours of labor as the general productivity of industry rises. The Uniting Conference of 1939 sought for the protection of workers from enforced unemployment. Both branches of Methodism had affirmed previously the right of all who were not physically or mentally incapacitated to have an opportunity for self-maintenance.

[22] Most Methodists continued to support the profit-motivated form of economy despite this pronouncement of the General Conference of the Methodist Episcopal Church. On the whole, the pronouncements of Methodism were closer to the New Deal than to a form of socialism such as is suggested in the subordination of profit to service in the above criticism of economic order.

[23] See also the Uniting Conference of 1939.

All these conferences re-echoed the historic position of Methodism on the employment of women and children. They called for the regulation of conditions of work of women such as shall safeguard their welfare and that of the family and the community. They demanded the abolition of child labor and adequate provision for the protection, education, spiritual nurture, and wholesome recreation of every child. These social-welfare goals were supplemented by broad endorsement of social insurance against illness, accident, want in old age, and unemployment, with the hope that adequate measures would be taken by the appropriate federal and state agencies to assure their achievement.

In view of the fact that the Board of Education and the church press were occasionally criticized severely for the views expressed above, it is significant to note that the southern branch of Methodism recommended a strong emphasis in its literature on pertinent social questions, such as industrial justice.[24]

5. AGRICULTURE

The General Conference of 1932 said that translating this ideal into agriculture means:

(a) That the tiller of the soil shall be encouraged in his efforts to own the land he farms, and society be protected by efficient production and conservation of fertility. (b) That the cost of market distribution from farmer to consumer shall be cut to the lowest possible terms, both farmers and consumers sharing in these economies. (c) That there shall be every encouragement to the organization of farmers for economic ends, particularly for co-operative sales and purchases. (d) That an efficient system of both vocational and general education of youths and adults living on farms shall be available. (e) That special efforts shall be made to insure to the farmer adequate social institutions, including the Church, the school, the library, means of recreation, good local government, and particularly the best possible farm home. (f) That there shall be a widespread development of organized rural communities, thoroughly democratic, completely co-operative, and possessed with the spirit of the common welfare. (g) That there shall be the fullest measure of friendly reciprocal co-operation between the rural and city workers.

6. RACE RELATIONS

The General Conference also declared that translating this ideal into race relations means:

(a) The practice of the Christian principle of the same protection and rights for all races who share our common life. (b) The elimination of

[24] Methodist Episcopal Church, South, *Yearbook, 1935,* p. 32.

racial discrimination, and substitution of full brotherly treatment for all races. (c) The fullest co-operation between the Churches of various races, even though of different denominations. (d) Educational and social equipment for the special needs of immigrants.

The great depression struck the Negroes even more severely than the white people. They lost jobs in the cities in greater numbers; they were driven down to starvation wages—especially in agriculture. When they did keep their jobs they were harassed by movements like the "Black Shirts" who organized to take jobs away from them. Those who were unemployed had less savings than the whites and became destitute sooner. The movement of creative opportunity in the arts and entertainment field collapsed. Myrdal summarizes: "Between 1930 and 1933 there was utter distress and pessimism among Negroes; practically the only ones with hope were the few who turned to communism." [25] And communism proved to be a false messianism.

It is constructive to recall the initial attitude of Negroes toward Franklin D. Roosevelt. They were frankly skeptical about him, because he was a Democrat,[26] and for other reasons rumored. In Chicago for example only 23 per cent of the Negro vote went for Roosevelt; but the support for him quickly rallied after he was in power. The New Deal meant unemployment relief, housing projects, farm security work, and other federal assistance. They were thrilled by the obvious friendliness of the President and his wife. During these years race riots died down, lynching declined, Southern liberalism was growing. All of this added up in the late thirties to less despair and pessimism among Negroes than in the early years of the decade; but there was little long-range hope as yet. Relief was not employment. There was no significant improvement on any other front. In the South the Negro's agricultural status moved from bad to worse; he became ever more dependent on the decisions of white landowners.

In the decade of the Great Depression the Southern church continued to grow in its sense of responsibility for justice to the Negro. The statements by the bishops are especially significant because in 1934 the General Conference asked and answered the question: "Who shall make public pronouncements for the Methodist Episcopal Church, South, on great social questions of national and international importance?" The answer was: "Pronouncements of the Church on great social questions of national and international

[25] Gunnar Myrdal, op. cit., p. 754.
[26] We have already noted the Negro opposition to Wilson.

importance shall come from the College of Bishops rather than from any one particular General Board of the Church." [27]

In 1934 the Committee on Temperance and Social Service made a special reference to the Social Creed of the Churches adopted by the Federal Council of Churches in 1932. This was probably the first time that the conception of *race* was positively related to the Social Creed. No concrete application of the declaration on race, however, was made.

In one of the later Reports of the Committee on Temperance and Social Service we may find a fairly strong pronouncement on racial relations. It is more a charter for goals of action than a program of commitments.

Resolved, that we, as a Church, recognize this obligation in respecting the personality of the different races constituting the body of the citizenship of our common country; that we shall appreciate the individual worth of every man, and do nothing that will hinder or retard his fullest development through education, in his religious life, and in his economic relations; . . . that we see to it that there are no legal barriers erected against [the rights of] any man, individually . . . that there be guaranteed by law the equal protection to life, liberty, and property . . . that there be no discrimination in the enforcement of the penal laws of the States, and that in the due administration of justice every man stand on his individual merit.[28]

At the last General Conference before unification of the three branches of Methodism the Episcopal Address referred to the great mission field that opened at the door of the Church, namely the ten million Negroes, three-fourths of whom were in the territory of the Methodist Episcopal Church, South. Then it added:

Whatever may be the sins of others and whatever may be pleaded in extenuation of our own shortcomings, a large bulk of omission needs to be rectified in the course of our future relations with our brother in black. The Negro wants good wages, good schools, better housing, wholesome recreation, police protection, justice in and out of the courts, a larger share of civic improvements, and a chance to make the most of himself and have the same for his children. This is nothing more than, as a human being and an American citizen, he has the right to expect. For the most part, however, he has lived since the manifest of his freedom under an

[27] *Journal,* General Conference of the Methodist Episcopal Church, South, 1934, p. 252. Reports could, of course, be made by commissions to the general conference.

[28] Report Number 9, *Journal,* General Conference of Methodist Episcopal Church, South, 1934.

economic and political system that has not always fostered his best development.[29]

After unification, as before, white churches in South and North did little to cultivate the great mission field of Negro population.

A case of special importance was that of the Scottsboro boys which began in March 1931. Nine Negro boys, caught at random from a freight train, were indicted for raping two white girls who were also on the freight, who had spent a night at a hobo jungle near Chattanooga and were traveling with a white boy to Huntsville, Alabama. Many persons and groups became interested in the case through nineteen years, but the person who gave justice its leadership was Allan Knight Chalmers, minister of Broadway Tabernacle, subsequently professor of preaching and applied Christianity at Boston University School of Theology.[30] He became head of the Scottsboro Defense Committee and saw the men involved through to their long overdue freedom.

In the context of this volume we can note only some of Methodism's concern in the case. In 1934 the National Council of Methodist Youth urged Alabama to free the boys, regarding them as victims of racial injustice. The Methodist Federation for Social Service was also active in its expressions of concern.

The *New York Christian Advocate* criticized the court decisions when they seemed to follow certain Southern mores more than the canons of criminal justice, and the *Northwestern Christian Advocate* expressed regret that the state of Alabama could not be put on trial. It editorialized as follows:

It is one of the ironies of our so-called civilization that an American state can be so complacent over its social neglect which produces such prostitutes, and over its industrial and educational policy which produces such useless men; and yet can feel perfectly virtuous over protecting the "honor" of its womanhood as represented in the vagrant girls, and feel wholly righteous in hanging the black boys it never thought of until they were accused.[31]

Such a vigorous editorial was paralleled by one in the *Nashville Christian Advocate* whose comments on the case were made in the face of indignant protests from the subscribers.[32]

[29] *Journal*, General Conference, Methodist Episcopal Church, South, 1938, p. 245.
[30] See A. K. Chalmers, *They Shall Be Free* (New York: Doubleday & Co., 1951).
[31] *Northwestern Christian Advocate* (February 8, 1934), p. 123.
[32] R. M. Miller, *op. cit.*, p. 180.

7. INTERNATIONAL RELATIONS

Once again, the General Conference stated that translating this ideal into international relations means:

(a) The removal of every unjust barrier of trade, color, creed, and race, and the practice of equal justice for all nations. (b) The administration of the property and privileges within each country so that they will be of the greatest benefit, not only to that nation, but to all the world. (c) Discouragement of all propaganda tending to mislead peoples in their international relations or to create prejudice. (d) The replacement of selfish imperialism by such disinterested treatment of backward nations as to contribute the maximum to the welfare of each nation and of all the world. (e) The abolition of military armaments by all nations except for an international police force. (f) That the Church of Christ as an institution shall be used for the prevention and abolition of war. (g) A permanent association of the nations for world peace and good will, the outlawry of war, and the settlement of all differences between nations by conference, arbitration, or by an international court.

On questions of international relations and more specifically on peace policy, the leadership of Methodism was probably much more pacifist in sentiment than the general membership. Many laymen were willing for the church and for their pastors to affirm positions which they themselves did not regard as realistic. In the polls taken of ministers, theological students, and youth, the pacifist position was strongly represented. However, many leaders of that period recall that the general sentiment in the pews differed sharply from that expressed in the pulpit on questions of war, military preparedness, and conscientious objection.

Thanks to a poll of 53,000 ministers, 19,372 of whom replied, we have a significant index of their opinion on issues of war and peace in 1931.[33] This provides a useful comparison of Methodist Episcopal opinion with that of Protestantism as a whole. The following summary states the over-all percentages and then cites the Methodist responses on individual questions. In the same way the responses of theological seminarians are indicated.[34]

[33] The questionnaire was sent out by S. Parkes Cadman, Harry Emerson Fosdick, Daniel A. Poling, W. Russell Bowie, John Nevin Sayre, Ralph W. Sockman, Reinhold Niebuhr, Kirby Page, Sherwood Eddy, and William P. Merrill. The Methodist Episcopal Church, South, was not included in the poll. In the case of the theological seminaries only Boston and Garrett are reported because of the size of the number of replies.

[34] Kirby Page, "Nineteen Thousand Clergymen on War and Peace," *The World Tomorrow* (May, 1931), pp. 138-41, 151. It is doubtful whether the laity

Of those who responded, 62 per cent expressed the opinion that the churches of America should now (1931) go on record as refusing to sanction or support any future war; 54 per cent stated that it was their present purpose not to sanction any future war or participate as armed combatants. The number who regarded the distinction between "defensive" and "aggressive" war as sufficiently valid to justify their sanctioning or participating in a future war of "defense" was 43 per cent. Forty-five per cent said they could conscientiously serve as official army chaplains on active duty in war time.

Substantial reduction in armaments, even if the United States is compelled to take the initiative and make a proportionately greater reduction than other nations are yet willing to do, was favored by 80 per cent of those replying. Only 13 per cent favored military training in public schools and civilian colleges or universities. Sixty-two per cent held that the policy of armed intervention in other lands by the government to protect the lives and property of American citizens should be abandoned and protective measures confined to pacific means. Finally, the immediate entrance of the United States into the League of Nations was favored by 66 per cent.

Turning to the theological students, it was evident that they opposed the war system even more vigorously than clergymen generally. Of the 1,101 who replied, 79 per cent believed that the churches should refuse to sanction it or support any future war; 72 per cent stated it as their present purpose not to sanction any future war or to participate as an armed combatant; and only 27 per cent said that they could conscientiously serve as official army chaplains on active duty in wartime.

There was a remarkable shift in attitudes a decade later.[35]

Included in the report on World Peace which the General Conference adopted in 1932 was an endorsement of the stand which the Federal Council of Churches had taken on the rights of conscience. The Federal Council statement was prompted in part by a five-to-four decision of the United States Supreme Court denying naturalization to Professor D. C. Macintosh of Yale University who refused to promise in advance to bear arms in defense of the United States. The position which the Methodist Episcopal General Conference made as its own stated:

---

in any such percentages as are indicated would have refused to sanction "any future war."

[35] *Ibid.*, 151.

In view of certain judicial decisions which raise fundamental questions as to the justice of our present naturalization laws, we desire to put on record the following convictions:

We hold that our country is benefited by having as citizens those who unswervingly follow the dictates of their consciences, and that a policy of denial of naturalization to aliens of such character is contrary to the ideals of a nation into whose very structure the principle of political and religious liberty has been built.

If the present naturalization law does, under fair interpretation, require the exclusion from citizenship of applicants who put allegiance to God above every other consideration, we believe that the law should be amended.

Futhermore, we believe it to be the duty of the churches to give moral support to those individuals who hold conscientious scruples against participation in military training or military service.

Going beyond this endorsement the General Conference then took an historic position on conscientious objection and military training which was to play an important role both in the 1930's and in World War II. The Methodist Episcopal Church petitioned as follows:

We petition the government of the United States to grant to members of the Methodist Episcopal Church who may be conscientious objectors to war the same exemption from military service as has long been granted to members of the Society of Friends and other similar religious organizations. Similarly, we petition all educational institutions which require military training to excuse from such training any student belonging to the Methodist Episcopal Church who has conscientious scruples against it.

We earnestly petition the government of the United States to cease supporting all military training in civilian educational institutions. We urge Methodists in all parts of the world to make a like request of their respective governments, and further to plead for the abolition of compulsory military service in countries where it is now required.[36]

In 1934 the General Conference of the Methodist Episcopal Church, South, adopted a statement which called upon all of its ministers to preach each year on the subject of world peace and which also pledged the support of the Church to its conscientious objectors:

The Methodist Episcopal Church, South, true to the principles of the New Testament, teaches respect for properly constituted civil authority. It holds that government rests upon the support of its conscientious citizen-

[36] Reaffirmed in 1936. The same basic position was taken by the Methodist Episcopal Church, South, in 1934 and the Uniting Conference in 1939.

ship, and that conscientious objectors to war in any or all of its manifestations are a natural outgrowth of the principle of good will and the
Christian desire for universal peace; and holds that such objectors should
not be oppressed by compulsory military service anywhere or at any time.
We ask and claim exemption for all forms of military preparation or service for all conscientious objectors who may be members of the Methodist
Episcopal Church, South. In this they have the authority and support of
their Church.

When these ideas were incorporated into the Social Creed of the
united Methodist Church a further sentence was added: "However,
we recognize the right of the individual to answer the call of his
government in any emergency according to the dictates of his
Christian conscience." [37]

The Methodist Protestant Church, like the other branches of
Methodism, showed a growing concern over war and international
relations. In the period from 1922 to 1936 as much space was devoted to these problems as to alcohol reform. Its General Conference
of 1936 spoke out vigorously against the national trend toward
militarism and suspected anyone who carried a gun as a potential
criminal. The pacifist trend in the denomination was strong and
hence the need for social reform on issues of war and peace was
urgently expressed.

World war and fascism are so dreadful and suicidal in their implications that the thinking forces of the world should shrink in horror from
the fatalistic doctrine that either is necessary or desirable. Let the Church
speak with no uncertain voice against involvement in "dollar diplomacy,"
in entanglements with foreign countries that no longer regard treaties as
sacred. This General Conference opposes the promotion of a jingoistic
spirit by the building of great competitive armaments as well as that form
of military training required in schools and colleges. There is the same
psychology here on a national scale as in the general placing of toy pistols
in the hands of children. We are happily past the day when every man is
expected to carry a gun. Those who do are potential criminals. [38]

The General Conferences, North and South, were keenly interested in all phases of the peace movement during the thirties.
They urged peace action. The Southern church in 1934 stated that
pastors should preach at least once a year on world peace and the
evils of war. In the North the General Conference of 1932 urged
entrance of the U.S.A. into the World Court. It criticized all
propaganda tending to mislead peoples in their international re-

[37] *Discipline* (1940), ¶ 1712, sec. 16.
[38] *Journal of the Methodist Protestant Church*, 1936, p. 64.

lations. It supported the policy of refusal to recognize territorial gains made by any nation in violation of its signature to the Pact of Paris outlawing war. It asked for the general reduction of armaments. Its stand that military armaments, except for internal police force, should be abolished by all nations was reaffirmed in the Social Creed of the Uniting Conference in 1939. In 1932 and 1936 the Northern General Conference urged establishing a department of peace in the federal government. After repeating "that the Methodist Episcopal Church, as an institution does not endorse, support or purpose to participate in war," it asked the Federal Council of Churches to try to find a way by which "the spiritual ministry of the churches to the armed forces of the United States may be performed by ministers appointed and supported by and amenable to the churches."

Apropos of the 1936 General Conference action, the leading editorial in the *Army and Navy Register* for June 20 of that year proposed (1) "that the War and Navy departments terminate under proper procedure the commissions of all Methodist chaplains in regular land or naval forces who upheld 'the peace pact of Methodists' "; (2) "that the War and Navy departments terminate, for the convenience of the government, all reserve commissions held by Methodist clergymen and laymen"; (3) "that the War and Navy departments refuse to accept for a citizen's training camp, or for instruction in collegiate officer's training corps units, any members of that Church." This vigorous response brought forth an interesting comment in the *Christian Century:* "The *Army and Navy Register's* proposals and the pronouncements of the General Conference fit together like the two parts of a tunnel that have been driven toward each other from opposite sides of a mountain until they meet to make one continuous highway." [39]

8. DUTY OF THE LOCAL CHURCH

The General Conference placed a direct responsibility upon the local church:

We believe it is the duty of every Church to investigate local moral and economic conditions as well as to know world needs. We believe that it is only as our Churches themselves follow the example and spirit of Jesus in the fullest sense—translating these social ideals into the daily life of the Church and the community—that we can ever hope to build the Kingdom of God on Earth.

[39] *The Social Questions Bulletin* (Sept. 1936), pp. 2-3. See *Christian Century* (July 15, 1936), "Let the Army and Navy reject Methodists."

With this assignment the General Conference of 1932 concluded its program of what it meant to translate the ideals of the Social Creed into action.

Against this background of a reformulated and developed Social Creed we shall examine further the peace testimony of the church during the late thirties and then turn to the crisis precipitated by the standpoints of the Methodist Federation for Social Service and the right-wing groups within and outside the church who sought a showdown in the General Conference of 1936. An additional note about race relations and Prohibition pronouncements will bring this chapter to a close.

The international situation worsened steadily during the world-wide depression. Autarchy and imperialism, fascism and communism, neutralism and intervention, and civil war spelled deterioration in international relations, moral confusion, rearmament, and war. Japanese expansion was proceeding apace in the Far East; Italy attacked Ethiopia; Hitler developed his hysterically racist "Third Reich"; Spain was aflame in a supported civil war which was a dress rehearsal of horrors to come; the League of Nations utterly lacked effect; and Germany and Russia made rapid opportunistic reversals of policy in the crisis over fascism and communism. While in America investigations of the World War I munitions industry were under way, the nation was combatting unemployment in part by reviving industry through rearmament. Neutrality or collective action was an issue that troubled the conscience of the churches.

The attitudes of various annual conferences reflect the tensions in church groups. In June 1938 the Pacific Northwest Conference, speaking of munitions, said: "We oppose all so-called war-profits legislation which rather guarantees than destroys the profits in war, and favor instead nationalization of the munitions industry and taking the profits out of war." [40] The Erie Conference held a similar view: "We recommend that the Federal Government assume exclusive responsibility for the manufacturing of munitions of war and that the sale of such materials to individuals, groups, or nations be prohibited." "We favor the nationalization of the munitions industry," said the Central Pennsylvania Conference in April 1938.

At the annual conference level there was division of opinion on the question of neutrality or collective actions. The Genesee Con-

[40] Quoted in *Social Questions Bulletin* (April, 1939), p. 2.

ference (Oct. 1938) petitioned the President and government of the United States

to take such measures as will be found practical to prevent the material and financial resources of this country, including scrap iron, oil, and gasoline, and other materials, from being used to further the invasion of China and the civil war in Spain, by altering the present Neutrality Act; and that our government ease the suffering of the Chinese people by extending a substantial loan from our great surplus of wheat and cotton to the government of China.

The Central New York Conference opposed the exportation of munitions and raw materials to aggressor nations. "We recommend non-co-operation in business with aggressor nations. We believe such a program as this will give support to those who suffer the ravages of war as in China, Spain, and Czechoslovakia, without involving the United States in the business of war."

A clear plea for collective security was made in 1938 by the New York Conference: "Having for all practical purposes abandoned the negative policy of neutrality, a positive policy in world affairs is all the more incumbent upon us as a nation and as individuals." The positive program was "the adoption of a policy of collective security upon the part of the world's democracies." This included the belated joining of the League of Nations by the United States. The following year (April 1939) the same conference resolved: "We approve the attempt of the President of the United States to put the moral and economic strength of America upon the side of the world's democracies in their apparently belated decision to take a stand against the continued aggressions of the totalitarian states." [41] The Colorado Conference condemned resort to war, but believed that some means of collective security for the democracies might be devised under the auspices of the League of Nations."

Clarence K. Streit's popular book, *Union Now,* received the approbation of the New York East Conference, but this body also said: "We will in no wise support a decision to send our army and navy to participate in armed conflict outside the national boundaries of the U.S.A." [42]

This latter testimony could have been an echo of the voice of youth in the Methodist Church. The National Council of Methodist Youth, organized in 1935, was a strong advocate of a peace testimony. Among the many liberal pronouncements, it stood firm in a

[41] Quoted, *ibid.* (Sept., 1939), p. 3.
[42] *Loc. cit.* The conference action was in May 1939.

position denouncing war as unchristian and sinful, and reaffirmed the declaration made by the General Conference of 1928 that war be made a public crime under the law of nations. The National Council of Methodist Youth strongly supported the Oxford Pledge of pacifism and took an active part in the student anti-war movement. Identification with and encouragement of the nation-wide demonstrations against war were major objectives.[43]

In 1939 at its third biennial session the theme was "The Christian Fellowship in a World of Conflict." Its report fully supported the Christian pacifist position. The Commission on Christian Action in Time of War advocated the following:

Oppose the Industrial Mobilization Act—the May Bill or its successor. Refuse to register in the event of a draft for military or industrial service. Work with other groups such as the following: Fellowship of Reconciliation, Woman's International League for Peace and Freedom, War Registers' League, Methodist Peace Fellowship, National Council for Prevention of War, labor organizations, Socialist Party, Youth Committee to Keep America Out of War.

It was also reported by this group that the World Peace Commission had the names of over five thousand Methodists who had declared they would not support war in any circumstances.

At the Fourth Conference (1940) the theme was "We Build for Thee," and the youth group remained firmly opposed to war. The leadership of the National Council of Methodist Youth continued to endorse antiwar groups and supported such causes as the "National Day of Mourning" on October 16, 1940, which was proclaimed to be the registration day for conscription for military service. The executive committee of the Council supported the "Keep American Youth on American Soil Program" and continued affiliation with the "Youth Committee Against War."

After the Uniting Conference which created The Methodist Church (1939) the National Council of Methodist Youth became a more representative organization, merged several youth groups, and was closer to an official agency. At the close of the war in 1945 its publication, *Concern*, still carried a peace testimony in its editorial policy: "There shall be unalterable opposition to war as a means of settling disputes. Christianity cannot be nationalistic; it must be universal in its outlook and appeal. War makes its appeal

[43] Al Hamilton, *Students Against War*, published by the National Council of the Methodist Youth and the World Peace Commission, 1937.

to force and hate; Christianity to reason and love." [44] This testimony was mainly a quotation from the Episcopal Address of 1944. In line with this spirit the leadership has continued to oppose military conscription and University Military Training proposals, armament and nuclear weapons. It supports the United Nations and sponsors many study seminars in co-operation with other agencies of the church.

During the crisis of 1939 the Methodist Federation of Social Service made a test poll of its membership and on the basis of the poll approved the following foreign policies: [45]

1. The boycott of Japanese, German, and Italian goods.

2. An embargo upon the shipment of arms, munitions, implements of war, secondary war materials, and upon the supplying of credit facilities to aggressor nations.

3. Selling to the victims of aggressive warfare the means of defense under conditions designed in each case to remove the risk of our being drawn into war, e.g. adaptations of the cash-and-carry principle.

4. Concerted action between the popular democratic forces in the democratic nations to promote in common the policies expressed in 1, 2, and 3 to bring about for this purpose a conference of official representatives of the nations governed under democratic constitutions.[46]

On the same day in the same city the Uniting Conference of Methodism adopted "A Social Creed" which said in part: "We insist that the agencies of the church shall not be used in the preparation for war, but in the promulgation of peace. We believe that war is utterly destructive and is our greatest collective social sin and a denial of the ideals of Christ. We stand upon this ground, that the Methodist Church as an Institution cannot endorse war nor support or participate in it." It reaffirmed the position on conscientiousness which we have noted earlier: "We ask and claim exemption from all forms of military preparation or service for all conscientious objectors who may be members of the Methodist Church. In this they have the authority and support of their Church. However, we recognize the right of the individual to answer the call of his government in an emergency according to the dictates of his Christian conscience."

The following year at the first General Conference of the United Church the resolution opposing war passed, but by no means all the delegates agreed to the church's position. In the Episcopal Ad-

[44] National Conference of Methodist Youth (August 24-30, 1945).
[45] Biennial Conference, Kansas City, Missouri, May 9, 1939.
[46] *Social Questions Bulletin* (Sept., 1939), p. 1.

dress Bishop Francis J. McConnell made the plea not to yield to the fallacy that the United States must get into war if it is to serve in establishing a new peace basis.

We can best serve by staying out . . . we deplore tendencies of churches in war times to subordinate even their preaching to war aims . . . we hold that the United States should remain out of the present conflicts in Europe and the Far East. We urge the government of the United States, in collaboration with the governments of other neutral nations, to persevere in the attempt to secure in Europe and in Asia a negotiated peace consistent with a just and fundamental solution of world problems.

Not all of the bishops were in agreement. Bishop James Cannon wrote an open letter to Secretary of State Cordell Hull urging him to use "his great influence with President and Congress to declare war against Hitler and his fellow monsters." In response to this statement Charles F. Boss, Jr., Executive Secretary of the Commission on World Peace, issued a news release protesting Bishop Cannon's open letter and stating that it was only a personal view and not that of the Methodist Church, for only the General Conference could speak officially for the whole church.[47]
The official stand of the General Conference, which owed much to the leadership of Ernest Fremont Tittle as chairman of the Committee on the State of the Church, sustained the view expressed by Bishop McConnell: "We believe that the United States should remain in a position to preserve democracy within its own borders, to provide relief for war-stricken populations, and to assist in the physical and economic rehabilitation of a war-shattered world. We hold, therefore, that the United States should remain out of the present conflicts in Europe and in the Far East." [48] It also reasserted its earlier position on conscientious objectors.
After the war broke out in Europe, but before Pearl Harbor, the Commission on World Peace convened a conference on a just and lasting peace, thus anticipating the one held in 1942 by the Federal Council of Churches. Such a Conference served to show that Methodist peace sentiment was not isolationist even when it was anti-interventionist. How effective the mobilizing of peace attitudes could be for world order is evident in the Crusade for a New World Order which was held during World War II.
Not only at the national level but also in Annual Conferences there was a significant peace witness and support of conscientious

[47] May 22, 1940.
[48] *Discipline*, 1940, p. 775-76.

objectors. California Methodism will serve as an illustration.[49] Statements like the following are typical: "Christianity must finally rule international relations or else it will ultimately become futile as a personal experience." [50] "The war system and the Prince of Peace do not belong in the same world and civilizations cannot contain both." [51] "The Church should declare that it will not, as a Church, sanction war." [52] "The agencies of our Church shall not be used in preparation for war." [53]

When the war was finally on, the church accepted the fact that the "Christian is bound to serve his own nation in all ways compatible with the Christian faith and the Christian way of life." [54]

Nevertheless, California Methodism refused to retreat from its advanced position, even after the nation had been enmeshed in the war for several years. In 1944 the Southern California Annual Conference said:

> As an Annual Conference we reaffirm the position we have taken since our country first entered the war. In 1942 our Conference said that "whatever may be the opinions, convictions, or actions of individual members of the church, the church itself is not at war. It is supra-national, supra-racial and supra-class in its nature and organization. It confesses supreme allegiance to the Lord Jesus Christ alone." In 1943 our Conference said: "The church by its very nature cannot rightfully become part of the war effort. In its origin, nature, purpose, and relation to human destiny, it is more than a national institution." And now, in 1944, without making any attempt to bind the consciences of individual members, we declare that so far as our Conference has anything to do with it, the Church will not give its moral and spiritual sanction to war.[55]

Based on the action of the General Conference asking for exemption from military service for its conscientious objectors, the Southern California Conference in 1933 requested the authorities of the state universities in California to exempt Methodist students from R.O.T.C. [Reserve Officers Training Corps] on those grounds. Two students petitioned accordingly and were denied their petition. The boys were suspended, and the church went to work in their

[49] The paragraphs dealing with California Methodism are based on S. Raynor Smith, Jr.'s, dissertation earlier cited. The source references are those in the dissertation.
[50] *Journal, Southern California Conference*, 1931, p. 104, in Smith, *ibid.* p. 389.
[51] *Ibid.*, 1930, p. 113.
[52] *Loc. cit.*
[53] *Ibid.*, 1936, p. 103.
[54] *Ibid.*, 1943, p. 164.
[55] *Ibid.*, 1944, p. 154, in Smith, *ibid.*, pp. 392-93.

defense, taking the case through the courts. Finally, the United States Supreme Court in 1934 rendered a decision against the boys involved. The church went as far as it could.

When the Selective Service Act came into effect the church established a Committee for Aiding Conscientious Objectors "to give proper help to your young people who register as conscientious objectors." [56] A Fellowship Fund was created to help support those who were assigned to Civilian Public Service Camps. In one (in 1941) case a local draft board refused a Methodist the right to register as a conscientious objector. He was sentenced to the federal prison on Terminal Island. The Methodist Church committee pledged the resources to protest the case, much to the displeasure of the United States attorney in the case. He launched an inquiry into the church's activities, and indicated the possibility of lodging criminal complaints against The Methodist Church for obstructing justice. The matter was called to the attention of the federal attorney general who called a halt to the investigation of The Methodist Church and ordered a review of the case. Subsequently the Methodist in question was released and permitted to enter the Civilian Public Service Camp at San Dimas, California. This incident shows how far both the church and the nation had moved between two World Wars.

C. The Attack on the Methodist Federation for Social Service

Having noted the fundamental questions about the nature and morality of the social-economic order which bishops, pastors, youth groups, annual conference, and the General Conference raised in the early thirties, it remains to indicate the leadership undertaken by the Methodist Federation for Social Service. Its masthead carried this aggressive assertion: "An organization which seeks to abolish the profit system in order to develop a classless society based upon the obligation of mutual service." This formulation gave a revolutionary focus to the prophetic witness of the organization and of course precipitated vigorous controversy in annual conferences and the General Conference, especially that of 1936. Abolition of the profit-seeking economy was a large order and open to misinterpretation. In the subsequent review of the work of the Federation in the mid-thirties it is instructive to note not only its militant program on domestic issues related to the Social Creed, but also its vigorous attack on the gathering forces of international

---

[56] *Journal, California Conference,* 1941, p. 212, Smith, *ibid.,* p. 400.

conflict. This meant coming to grips with Nazism, Fascism, Communism, and colonialism.

The outline of a Christian program for society which the leadership of the Federation advocated in 1936 went considerably beyond the platform of the New Deal. The program called for the transformation of our class-divided society into one that was fraternal and co-operative.[57] This meant that the profit-seeking economy around which capitalism was organized was wanting in three respects—method, motive, and end. "The method is the competitive struggle, the motive is selfishness in the form of greed, the end is the acquisition and control of property rights for the sake of the power thereby gained." These three, it was argued, have again and again been rejected in the "individual and collective statements of the Christian conscience." Therefore: "We demand and support the extension of the democratic process because it leads to the sharing of life and the creative control of our organized living, but in order to enforce its unemployment and its falling standard of living the capitalistic state is everywhere limiting or destroying democracy." This required, furthermore, the removal of the "profit-seeking economy" and its replacement "by an economic order which will provide the base for, and will lead continuously toward, the more abundant life for all the people which our gospel proclaims." [58]

The above judgment was interpreted by the Federation as an extension of positions already taken by the General Conferences since 1916. In 1916 the General Conference of the Methodist Episcopal Church asserted that the Christian conscience must protest against the manifest inequality in the distribution of wealth. In 1924 it declared that "wealth accruing to the holders through monopoly values or special privileges, or through large opportunities for costly savings, is not earned." In 1928 it asserted in behalf of "the supremacy of the service rather than the profit motive." In 1930 the bishops held that "we cannot escape the conclusion that a more equitable distribution of wealth is basic." In 1932 the General Conference said that "the present industrial order is unchristian, unethical, and anti-social because it is largely based on the profit motive, which is a direct appeal to selfishness. Selfishness is never morally right, never Christian, and eventually never benefits anybody." When laymen within and without the Methodist Church attacked the Federation for seeking "to abolish the profit

[57] *The Social Questions Bulletin* (March 1936), p. 1. The denunciation of American capitalism seemed unreasonable to those who regard capital as an economic need for growth and the profit motive as a spur to enterprise.

[58] *Ibid.*, p. 2.

160

system," the leaders of the organization replied that the attack should really be leveled against the General Conference for "all that we have done is to demand the removal of that part of the present industrial order which makes it 'unchristian, unethical, and anti-social.'" As a substitute for the profit-seeking economy the Federation urged a "planned and planning social economy which continuously adjusts our economy efforts to measured needs, cultural as well as material."

Such a program and goal inevitably precipitated much controversy. The Federation leadership represented a small minority of the membership of the Methodist Church. Speaking to the issue raised by the Federation and similar groups in other denominations, F. Ernest Johnson wrote in 1935: "These minority movements and advanced creeds *belong within* the church, but they cannot be identified with it without falsification." [59] They are movements within church bodies which function as educational and pressure-action forces, but "to commit the entire membership to what they themselves may be agreed upon at any particular time is another matter." [60] Johnson viewed organizations like the Methodist Federation as sect-type groups within the church itself. This relationship inevitably involves tension between the minority organization and the whole body. He says,

Only thus, can the church be kept alive and made to feel the most exacting demands of the Christian ideal upon the conscience in terms of social effort, and of that individual discipline which citizenship in the Kingdom requires. The small group of adventurous and prophetic souls, bent on a radical attack upon society as it is, may thus maintain for themselves a fellowship of thought, feeling, and action, and in so doing may gradually lift the entire membership to a higher spiritual temperature.[61]

There is no assurance, of course, that the minority group has in all respects a solidly defensible position.

During the quadrennium from 1932 to 1936 the Federation leadership issued eighteen "Crisis Leaflets" written to raise discussion concerning the steps necessary in the crisis to implement the positions taken by the General Conference in 1932. Six issues dealt with the breakdown of capitalism, and six dealt with the question of how to get from the old to the new economy. The author of these leaflets was a controversial personality, not only among

[59] F. Ernest Johnson, *The Church and Society* (New York: The Abingdon Press, 1935), p. 86.
[60] *Ibid.*
[61] *Ibid.*, pp. 216-17.

conservative businessmen in the church, but also among some of the quite liberal and progressive leaders of social action in Methodism and in other denominations.

In 1933-34 and again two years later Harry F. Ward made a coast-to-coast trip holding seminars among members in an effort to clarify the judgment of the members on the main issues involved and to get unity among the socially minded forces of Methodism as the basis for action in the crisis.[62] The opponents of the Federation attacked not only the basic position being developed by Ward on the economic order but also the appropriateness of the use of the name Methodist. They also demanded a disclaimer of speaking officially for Methodism. Then, too, some of the opponents proposed instead an official Commission on Social Action.

The Methodist Federation for Social Service made clear that its name was not official, but insisted that it wanted the world to know that its members comprised a company of Methodists. Since 1936 was a General Conference year, it was important to bring into the open the most basic issues. On the question of the name and official control the Federation proposed as follows:

The remedy for those who dislike to be associated in the public mind with those who have our views is neither suppression nor official control. Both are impossible. There will always be an organized group of Methodists holding advanced views on the meaning of religion in social thinking and action who will be objectionable to the conservatives. No disclaimer of official connection will remove the association that will be made in the public mind. The only remedy for the reactionaries is that which they are now taking, namely to organize themselves, develop publicity, and let the world know that there are two kinds of Methodists. Thus the issue can be thrashed out, as it should be, by the process of discussion.[63]

The reference to two kinds of Methodists was an error based on an emotional judgment. Despite the feelings which divided men into antagonistic groups, Methodists were hardly either reactionaries or protagonists for the Federation. There were, of course, ultraconservatives in the church, but there were also followers of the policies of the national government which worked toward reform within the profit system rather than toward radical reconstruction. Methodists covered the whole range of the political and economic spectrum. The Federation was within its rights in appealing to resolutions and legislation which had passed annual conferences and the General Conference. Many laymen and clergy

[62] *The Social Questions Bulletin* (April 1936), p. 2.
[63] *Ibid.*, p. 3.

contended that the radical statements of official Methodist bodies regarding the profit motive and, by implication, the profit system were both ambiguous and unrepresentative. What it means for any statement on social questions to be "representative" of Methodism has never been clearly determined. In any event many who disagreed with the social philosophy and the program of the Federation ardently defended its prophetic function and freedom in the church. Others could not tolerate the thought of the word Methodist being associated with either its philosophy or its program.

We shall note below some of the groups that led in the attack at the time of the General Conference of 1936. Before noting these it is interesting to indicate the reasons given by the Federation against displacing the unofficial Federation by an official commission. (1) The Federation felt that the chief proponents for an official agency were in fact reactionaries who opposed social action and were interested only in control and censorship. (2) Experience in other denominations showed that an unofficial voluntary society was important because "an official organization cannot speak out clearly and positively on certain vital points." (3) The proposal would weaken the denominational position since it would centralize in one bureau the social education and action that had become diffuse in the several boards and agencies. (4) Co-ordination of the work of these boards would strengthen their work without adding machinery or expense. (5) Since temperance is not presently a political issue, some part of its funds might wisely be used in an educational campaign against the war which seems so imminent. Rather than quarrel about a name or an official agency the Federation besought the General Conference to face the basic issue: "Whether this Conference is going to utter any word of leadership for mankind in the most widespread crisis the human race has ever confronted. In all parts of the earth millions are threatened by destruction in wars they do not want, which can gain them nothing." [64]

The attack on the Federation was part of a heavy barrage against "the Methodist Reds." This attack grew with mounting fury not only against churchmen but was directed against actual Communists and various kinds of socialists indiscriminately. In addition it denounced the Democratic Party and especially the administration in Washington.

This era of the New Deal may be called, despite the protest of upper-middle class Methodists and others like them, the era of

[64] *Ibid.,* p. 3.

the Methodist social ethic. Much for which the Social Creed had stood in its social legislation, with the exception of Prohibition, was in the process of political and economic formulation and enactment. Of all the churches the Methodists' formulations of the social gospel in the General Conferences and various Annual Conferences from New York to California were closer to the New Deal programs than were those of any other denomination, though on some issues the Congregationalists came quite close. In the New Deal the much denounced "profit system" was retained and many Methodist aims were achieved. Harry F. Ward, the executive secretary of the Methodist Federation for Social Service, embraced and advocated, of course, a much more radical Christian socialist ideology and program than did the President; but the actual platform of the Federation and the programs of leaders like Bishop McConnell, Bishop Baker, and President Oxnam (and later of Bishop Hartman, then editor of *Zion's Herald*) were remarkably akin to the spirit of the legislation which makes of the 1930's a great political watershed in American history.[65] The Federation was always a loosely knit organization.

Some of the attacks on the Federation and its leaders came from outside the church. William Randolph Hearst syndicated a series of articles to the effect that the "Reds" were using the clergy in a drive to destroy the institutions of the United States. Hearst had another series entitled "Rid the M.E. Church of 'Red' Incubus." Its author attacked the social movement in the church, and such specified matters as collective bargaining, minimum wage laws, old-age pensions, and social security legislation. He expressed the hope that the Methodist Episcopal General Conference "will deal with the McConnell-Ward-Chappell radical aggregation without gloves."

A columnist in the *Philadelphia Inquirer* accused the Federation program of involving the breakup of the family and taking away all private property. He concluded by asserting that it is impossible to be a Methodist and a Communist and asked why then does the Methodist Church allow itself to be exploited? In Los Angeles the police chief suggested to the president of the District Newspaper Association the widespread use of an editorial on "Communism in Churches" which especially attacked the Methodist Church because of what the Southern California Conference said about the "profit system." During the controversy which ensued Bishop

[65] Bishop Herbert Welch, one of the founders, disagreed vigorously with Ward's position. Oxnam was president of DePauw University.

James C. Baker sent a statement to be read in the churches: "that The Methodist Church in keeping with the traditions of the Church universal did not propose to take its message from the President of the United States, the Governor of the State, the Mayor of the City, or the chief of police, but from God." [66]

In some cases the attack on the Methodist Church was linked to general attacks on the Federal Council of Churches and its efforts in church co-operation on social questions.

From within the church there were attacks like those of the Reverend Rembert Gilman Smith, of The Methodist Episcopal Church, South. His pamphlet, *Methodist Reds*, proposed: "Ought not the name to be changed from Methodist Federation for Social Service to Marxist Federation for Social Strife?" Miller points out that Smith's volume, *Moscow over Methodism*, which appeared in 1936, enjoyed wide popularity. He organized the Methodist League against Communism, Fascism, and Unpatriotic Pacifism, which claimed membership in ten states.[67]

In addition to individuals there were groups of laymen who wished to head off "radicalism" in the church. In 1935 under the chairmanship of Henry S. Hennschen, president of the Chicago Bank of Commerce, a few laymen organized the Chicago Conference of Methodist Laymen. The secretary was Wilbur Helm, president of the Illinois Society of the Sons of the American Revolution. The avowed purpose was "for renewed emphasis on the spiritual phase of the life and work of the church." They discussed "the growing radical propaganda and hostile attitude toward business and the established order which are being disseminated," and proclaimed that "the economic system had done an amazingly creditable job of maintaining employment," and that there is "not the slightest proof that the economic system has failed in its essential service to society." Looking toward the General Conference, they said in the press: "We are going to demand settlement of the status of the Communist-influenced Methodist Federation for Social Service, and of clergymen and church officials who use their positions to preach Socialism and Communism." The *Chicago Tribune* and the Hearst press gave such statements wide publicity.

The principal target of the Conference of Methodist Laymen was the Methodist Federation for Social Service. It should be noted also that liberals directed a great deal of extreme criticism on this group of conservative laymen. Charges of "Communism" were met by

[66] *The Social Questions Bulletin* (May 1936), p. 1.
[67] R. M. Miller, *op. cit.*, p. 124-25.

counter charges of "incipient fascism." The Conference of Methodist Laymen represented a conservative group who sincerely held to the capitalist system and believed that it was hardly the function of the church to pass judgments on secular affairs.[68] Such an attitude was widespread in the church. In the heat of controversy and the turmoil of economic upheaval some conservatives charged that socialists could not be Christians and some liberals denied the same of capitalists. Eventually the church was to assert that Christianity cannot be identified with any *ism*.

Another group, the Methodist Laymen's Committee, with one hundred names on its letterhead, besought the General Conference to "take definite action to correct the existing situation by adopting such measures as will eradicate those sinister influences that have insinuated themselves into the church." They made special reference to the Methodist agencies that have to do with the training of youth.

Patriotic organizations of various kinds used the Hearst articles and the pamphlets of the Methodist laymen's organizations widely. Some of the phrasing of these lay statements corresponded to that employed by the *National Republic,* the official organ of a coalition of 117 "patriotic" groups. Material printed by the American Liberty League was distributed at meetings. The latter group was the creature of great utility, munitions, steel, copper, and other interests. An investigation by the Senate Lobby Committee showed that the interlocking group of "patriotic" organizations were in general all supported by the same group of financiers. These groups distributed tons of printed propaganda, devised intricate "charts," "blacklists," list of "doubtful speakers," "red networks," and carried on a continuous attack against the Federal Council of Churches, liberal and left-wing church groups, pacifist and radical organizations. They lumped together in an indiscriminate manner Communists, Socialists, pacifists, Christian pacifists, liberals, and the New Deal administration. In addition they personally attacked leaders like President G. Bromley Oxnam, then at DePauw University, and E. F. Tittle, because of their stand on war.[69]

The controversy was not a single line-up of clergy versus laymen. It cut across both parts of the church. Many laymen came to question the social order and some organized on the issues involved. A laymen's Religious Movement, which was Methodist Episcopal, unofficial and not affiliated with any other group, was started in

[68] *Ibid.,* p. 125.
[69] *Social Questions Bulletin,* pp. 3-4.

Chicago and had officers from Wisconsin. It was endorsed by two hundred laymen from thirty states. They said: "The present leadership of The Methodist Church is standing true to the spirit of the Gospel." Preachers also disagreed on the over-all problems. Bishop Adna Leonard instructed the Pittsburgh social service commission in 1935 not to sponsor the Methodist Federation for Social Service conference held in that city, and publicly attacked the secretaries of the Federation. Bishop Herbert Welch, one of the organizers of the Methodist Federation for Social Service, came to look upon it "with some concern."

As the Federation saw the basic issue on the eve of the Methodist Episcopal General Conference of 1936 it was

between those, both preachers and laymen, who want a purely personal "regeneration of the heart" gospel, leaving economic and social matters alone, and those who seek the Christian way of life in organized society as well as in personal behavior. This is also the division between those who find that the Christian way of life and the needs of humanity now require the transforming of the present economic order and those whose interests are best served by its continuance in its present form and who therefore want religion to keep its hands off.[70]

Many extreme conservatives would have agreed to this, but the General Conference adhered to a union of liberal and conservative support as reflected in the Social Creed, but not so strongly put as in 1932.

What did the General Conference do? It was at this conference that official action was taken on the unification of Methodism. To this topic attention must be given subsequently. But the desire for a united Methodism in the economic order and the method of unity was to be "united study." The General Conference rejected a proposal asking for an official commission "to represent the church in the public announcements and findings of the General Conference on social, economic, and political questions and . . . to interpret the attitude of the church toward such questions" between General Conference sessions. With respect to the question on the use of the word Methodist it adopted a report which declared that unofficial groups of Methodists cannot be denied the use of the word Methodist, which "includes all who belong to any branch of the Wesleyan family." The report noted that such groups have a "moral obligation to make their unofficial relationship clear at all times." This was standard practice in the Methodist Federation for Social Service.

[70] *Ibid.*, p. 4.

Generally speaking, the social resolutions of 1936 were more conservative than those in 1932. The attack on the Methodist Federation for Social Service was symptomatic of other efforts to reduce the effectiveness of liberal leadership in the church. A dramatic instance of this was the dismissal of Owen Geer and Blaine Kirkpatrick of the Young People's Department of the Board of Education. At the Columbus General Conference of 1936 Bishop Edgar Blake was replaced as chairman and Bishop Adna Leonard became the head. We have already noted the militant sentiments of Bishop Leonard during World War I and his role in forcing Dr. Ryland out of the Methodist ministry in California because of his Christian pacifism. We have also noted his open hostility to the Methodist Federation for Social Service. When Geer and Kirpatrick were not reappointed on July 1, 1936, the specific reason given was "to relieve tension and promote greater harmony and efficiency." In commenting on this development in the Board of Education, Bishop Blake said:

> When I was told three months ago that plans were on foot to rid the Board of Education of its liberal leadership, I refused to believe it. When I was told by one in authority that certain of my episcopal colleagues were in the plot, I denied it. I said, "It can't happen here." But it has happened. Two of our most brilliant and effective leaders have been sacrificed to please a small group of Methodist reactionaries and the Hearst press.[71]

How effective had the Geer-Kirkpatrick leadership, program, method, and techniques been? During the five-year period from 1930 to 1935 while Methodist church membership decreased by 300,000 and Sunday school enrollment by 400,000, Epworth League membership increased by over 42,000. There was substantial board agreement as to the respect and confidence in which these leaders were held by the young people of the church. To them, as the Secretary of the Board observed, the removal came as a "terrible shock." The liberals in the whole church were shocked too, for it showed the power of the conservative opposition.

When the National Conference of Methodist Youth met at Berea College they took action on the Geer-Kirkpatrick dismissal:

> For several years a steady line of attack has been aimed at the social effectiveness of their Christian convictions. Their removal from office rests directly upon their social effectiveness. Yet it is this implemented Christianity which has challenged us. . . . Therefore, we express our profound disapproval of the actions of the Board of Bishops, the executive secretary

[71] *The Social Questions Bulletin* (Sept., 1936), p. 1.

168

of the Board of Education, and the Board of Education itself, which resulted in the removal of these men.[72]

There were other evidences of aroused conservative attitudes as reported by the Reverend Charles Webber, a new secretary of the Methodist Federation. In the fall of 1936 he visited and spoke at fourteen annual conferences and noted in general "a tendency on the part of Conference Social Service Commissions to recommend continued study of, rather than action on, social issues; to procure peace at any price, to avoid creating antagonisms, in brief to make tacit surrender to the power of conservative inaction." [73]

Despite this conservative tendency noted by Webber, the election returns of 1936 gave Roosevelt 523 out of 531 electoral votes. Nevertheless, the great popularity of the President did not ensure continued major reforms through social legislation. With the back of the depression broken, the New Deal and much of the nation ran out of reformist zeal. Though not much new was undertaken, many of the reforms remained in operation.

D. Progressive Concern: Illustration in California

An illustrative instance of progressive concern and conservative response to the critical social conditions of the thirties can be found in California Methodism.[74] With almost twenty-five million people out of work, *The Christian Advocate* took this opportuntiy to call attention to the fallacy of undisciplined free enterprise: "Adam Smith . . . taught that unrestricted self-interest would work for universal good. . . . The conception given was that, if we should set a lot of strong, aggressive men to work, each pursuing his own selfish way, some way out of the combined selfishness of all of them would work good for everybody. To our great hurt we have found that that is not true." [75] While exposing the fallacy, the church did not conceive itself qualified to propose plans for industrial reconstruction. Its role was to set the goal and describe the spirit.

[72] *Ibid.* (Nov., 1936), p. 3.
[73] *Ibid.* (Nov., 1936), p. 4. Charles Webber had been on the staff of Union Theological Seminary. He was a graduate of Boston University School of Theology.
[74] This material is dependent on the unpublished dissertations of S. Raynor Smith, Jr. "The Attitudes and Practices of the Methodist Church in California with Reference to Certain Significant Social Crises, 1847 through 1949" (1955), and Ernest W. Thacker, "The Methodist Church in Southern California in Relation to the 'Social Gospel,' 1928 through 1941" (1952), both at the University of Southern California.
[75] "Out of Work," *The Christian Advocate*, 80 (Dec. 17, 1931), 7 and "Grapes of Thorns," *ibid.* (Nov. 19, 1931), p. 6.

Within this context the church felt called on to speak out against the individualism of the day.

In May, 1932, the Southern California Conference held a special Conference on Social Action to consider the church's responsibility to the increasing social chaos. The following month the California Conference drew up a strong indictment based in part on the General Conference pronouncement of the same spring.[76]

When the Southern California Conference met, its action went considerably beyond the thought of setting goals and defining a spirit. It requested the President of the United States to appoint a Commission to suggest solutions to the economic disorder, and made the following proposals for consideration:

1. The replacement of our present policy of unplanned competitive individualism by a planned industrialism definitely aiming at the assurance of economic security.
2. Modification of our antitrust laws.
3. The granting of the right of industry to organize in a definite way and regulate itself under federal supervision.
4. The creating and empowering of a Commission or Commissions to regulate the industries organized under this permissive way.
5. The offsetting of technological and general unemployment by shortening the hours of labor.
6. The introduction of compulsory unemployment insurance, accident and disability insurance, old-age pensions, planned and administered on the sound basis of actuarial experience.
7. The abolition of child labor.
8. The investigation of the needs of the Nation for public works to be carried on by federal, state, and municipal agencies in periods of business depression and unemployment.
9. The suppression of gambling (e.g. stock speculation).[77]

Many of these proposals were to find concrete expression in the New Deal in the subsequent quadrennium, without abolishing the profit system.

The call for pioneer social action met with some stiff resistance. Church leaders in California had persistently to explain the relevance of the gospel for social action. In 1934 Bishop James C. Baker spoke to the fact that many people were "confused and dismayed by

[76] *Journal, California Annual Conference,* 1932, p. 57.
[77] *Journal, Southern California Conference,* 1932, p. 100.

the idea that religion should make a difference in our social, political, and economic life." [78] A number of laymen felt that religion was going beyond the limits of its valid concern in relating itself to social issues. They issued a release which made the following protest:

We recognize that a proper field of action for our Church would be that of creating a Christian conscience in each individual citizen—a conscience that will continue to be operative, and will keep men continually Christians as they impinge upon one another in their social and economic relations. But this does not justify making our Methodist Churches places for the delivery of politico-economic sermons by those not specially trained in economic thinking and therefore not qualified as economic leaders."[79]

The objections of these laymen were both general and specific. They disapproved the social emphasis of the churches' ministry and they specifically objected to the criticism of the economy as "un-Christian, unethical, and antisocial." [80] When the Committee on Social Problems made its report in 1935 they raised serious objections, especially to the critique of the profit motive.[81] They held that the conference action was "a subversive and radical pronouncement." [82] The position of the church seemed to them both morally wrong and economically absurd. They organized themselves as the Methodist Laymen's Committee and presented a memorial to the General Conference of 1936 requesting a modification of the position of the church on social issues. The memorial failed and the laymen's organized movement faded away. The modification which it requested, however, continued as a significant factor in Methodist life.

Dr. Roy L. Smith, in evaluating the consequences of this lay opposition, points out that thereafter the church became less aggressive and more conciliatory. Methodism felt it was "essential that we be not divided as a Church on questions of economic and political policy." [83] When the Southern California Conference received the report of its Social Problems Committee in 1937, observers said it was "packed with dynamite but well padded." [84] It may be noted that the Conference was only illustrating the

---

[78] "The Social Task of Religion in These Chaotic Times," *The Christian Advocate*, 83 (April 12, 1934), 2.

[79] "The Church and the Social Question," *ibid.*, 85 (Feb. 6, 1936), p. 12.

[80] Ernest W. Thacker, *op. cit.*, p. 98.

[81] "The Profit Motive," *The Christian Advocate*, 84 (Aug. 29, 1935), p. 2.

[82] *Ibid.*, 85 (Feb. 6, 1936), p. 12.

[83] *Journal, Southern California Conference*, 1936, p. 46.

[84] "Southern California Conference," *The Christian Advocate*, 86 (July 1, 1937), p. 33.

dilemma of the church which as a voluntary society can lead only if it carries its followers along. The church lives in the tension between its spiritual autonomy under Christ on the one hand and its social involvement on the other. It belongs to the social nature of the church to be both committed and accommodated. After 1936-37, it may be added, most church pronouncements in the economic field were less radical than in the previous quadrennium or two. The similarity of trends in church pronouncements on social questions and the modification of reform zeal and effectiveness in the New Deal provides evidence for the thesis, cited in Chapter One, that the social gospel may be interpreted, in part at least, as an accommodative movement in the church. When did the New Deal come to an end? Richard Hofstadter has suggested the state-of-the-union message of January 3, 1939, in which no new legislative proposals were made by the President to Congress.[85] Both the social resolutions of the churches and the reforms of the New Deal were responses to profound historical forces at work in American society. The major reforms of the New Deal have not been repealed.

In summarizing this long discussion we may note: (1) that the Methodist Federation leadership represented but a minority voice in the Methodist Episcopal Church; (2) that the attack on the "profit motive" and the "profit system" in the official legislation of the church did not provide a specific alternative to the dominant American economy; (3) that many of the specific aims of the legislation of the General Conference were realized in the New Deal without a destruction of the "free-enterprise" system; (4) that the controversies of the thirties confused in many cases motives, goals, programs, and ideologies; (5) that the tensions which developed over the role of the church in social questions had a generally constructive effect in establishing the responsibility and freedom of the church in this part of its ministry.

E. The Aftermath of Prohibition Repeal

During the period of contest over repeal, the church-school and youth literature was full of materials on the problem of alcohol. The *Epworth Highroad* in 1932 had some discussion in every issue —either a lesson, an article, or a cartoon. A study of this same periodical in 1936 reveals the same emphasis and persistence of instruction. During 1936 there were numerous articles in the *Adult Student* and beginning in October of that year a five weeks' course entitled, "Alcohol and Human Life."

[85] *The American Political Tradition*, p. 342.

The official weekly of the Anti-Saloon League was named *The American Issue* and for many Methodists and evangelical Protestants Prohibition had become *the* issue before America. Consequently, with its repeal went a deep sense of tragic failure. As has already been noted, temperance and the "social gospel" went along together in the first two decades of the twentieth century. Then the most ardent champions of the social message of Christianity were vigorous temperance leaders. Yet the Prohibition movement had tended to become a socially autonomous cause. When Methodists said temperance they usually meant total abstinence. Sermons on temperance became one of the religious folkways of America.

During Prohibition there was a tendency, as we have already noted, for many Methodists to substitute Prohibition for the whole social gospel. To the extent that this is true, it was based not only on the tendency to make temperance a single all-consuming cause, but also on the fact that many millions more of church people had been systematically educated against the evils of alcohol than on the central issues of the economic order and their responsibilities for society as a whole. Within the reports of the boards and agencies to the General Conference there was lack of coherence between the analyses made by the champions of Prohibition and those by the advocates of social reform in the committee on the state of the church.

If the advocates of Prohibition tended to claim all social good in the twenties as due to the Eighteenth Amendment and the Volstead Act, they tended to evaluate the quadrennium following its repeal by the fact alone rather than by the great social revolution that had taken place in the first four years of the New Deal, Wagner Act and all. In the twenties Prohibition was claimed as a cause of the lower death rate, the higher standard of living, the improvement in general public health. It had "relieved distress of poverty, . . . opened new lines of commercial opportunity, . . . given to labor greater efficiency." [86]

In 1924—amidst the Teapot Dome scandals—the Methodist Episcopal Church adopted a resolution rejoicing in "the good that is found in the public life today," and declaring that "in quantity it far exceeds the evil." [87]

In 1936 the generalization was that "the moral and social decline of the past quadrennium has startled the socially minded people of

[86] Paul A. Carter, *op. cit.*, p. 42.
[87] *Daily Christian Advocate*, 20 (1924), 593.

the world. The long, hard ascent up the heights of Christian idealism has been countered with a demoralizing avalanche." [88]

After repeal came, some anti-Prohibition groups and individuals outside Methodism remained active in the so-called "Liberty League" and opposed the New Deal in the congressional elections of 1934, thus illustrating a tie between these ultra-conservatives and the repeal movement, on the one hand, and a continuing link between the Prohibition movement and the liberal humane forces of an earlier generation, as noted in Chapter One.

Many Methodists North and South concurred in the sentiment expressed in the Episcopal address of the Northern Church in 1936:

> Since the closing of the last General Conference the Eighteenth Amendment has been repealed. Our voters, being desperately tried economically, were terribly tempted morally, . . . We now proclaim to our country and to the World the intent of the Church to continue a relentless fight against the beverage liquor trade. The liquor traffic is inherently immoral. Legalizing it did not change its character.

One of the great weaknesses in the situation was that the cause of temperance had not been well integrated into the Social Creed. The methods of social change approved by Methodism had never been fully or consistently integrated in theory or in practice. Prohibition employed a principle and degree of state intervention into private industry and habits which went far beyond anything advocated in the other social legislation of the church or by the Methodist Federation for Social Service. The three branches of Methodism endorsed a philosophy of state action in the economic sphere which made national or federal coercion decisive, which it justified on pragmatic grounds, and which Prohibition's proponents have often repudiated on issues like race relations, where the appeal has been to regionalism and jurisdictional patterns of life. No path is thornier than the road to sound temperance policy.

The greatest need of the temperance movement in Methodism in the next twenty-five years after repeal has been to find a coherent philosophy and theology of education and action that makes it, as it should be, part and parcel of the personal and social witness of the whole gospel. Temperance ethics is still often wedded to economic individualism and pietistic moralism and not sufficiently to the inclusive solidarity of social responsibility. There is growing interest in the current efforts to achieve this goal in the church.

[88] *Ibid.*, 23 (1936), 369. Quoted in Carter, *op. cit.*, p. 43.

CHAPTER SIX

World War II and a New World Order

Chronological Outline of the
Major Events in American Social, Economic, and
Political History: 1940 to 1945

1940—Population: 131,669,275

Dunkirk evacuation. German "Luftwaffe" launches all-out attack on England. Churchill tells England he has "nothing to offer but blood, toil, tears, and sweat."

U.S.A. trades fifty over-age destroyers to Britain in return for right to lease sites for eight naval bases in British possessions. F.D.R. declares U.S.A. to be the "Arsenal of Democracy."

Selective Service Act signed: Over sixteen million register on October 16.

Serious religious and social conflict in Holyoke, Massachusetts, over birth-control issue.

The Supreme Court makes religious liberty applicable to state cases (Jehovah's Witnesses cases).

F.D.R. re-elected.

1941—F.D.R. signs Lend-Lease Bill.

Hitler attacks Russia. U.S.A. pledges all possible aid to U.S.S.R.

Atlantic Charter (Aug. 14): F.D.R. and Churchill agree on war aims.

Pearl Harbor (Dec. 7). U.S.A. and Britain declare war on Japan (Dec. 8).

Germany and Italy declare war on U.S.A., Congress declares war on these countries (Dec. 11).

U.S. government decides to build more than six hundred chapels in military camps available to the three faiths, extends chaplain services, co-operates with national religious organizations in the U.S.O. and so forth.

1942—Consumer rationing begins—tires and gasoline. F.D.R. signs price-control legislation.

U.S.A. forces on Bataan surrender. Corregidor surrendered.

May 30—one thousand RAF planes smash Cologne in one of the war's mightiest raids.

Nazis begin occupation of all France.

Federal Council of Churches holds Study Conference on Just and Durable Peace, Delaware, Ohio.

Japanese-Americans evacuated from west coast. Methodists and others minister to them in relocation centers.

1943—Casablanca Conference. Churchill and F.D.R. agree on unconditional surrender goal.

German 6th army surrenders at Stalingrad; turning point of war in Russia.

Third International (Comintern) dissolved in Moscow.

F.D.R. signs withholding tax. Uses war powers to break mine strike under Lewis.

Mussolini deposed. Italy surrenders.

Race riot in Detroit points up international implications of Negro problem in U.S.A.

October 19-November 1—Moscow Conference: Hull, Eden, Molotov pledge unity to win war and establish world organization; promise democratic Italy and free Austria.

November 22-26—Cairo Conference: F.D.R., Churchill, Chiang Kai-shek pledge defeat of Japan, freeing of Korea.

Supreme Court decision in the Gobitis flag-salute case, an important event for religious freedom.

Chinese Exclusion Law, long opposed by most American churches, repealed.

China placed on the same quota basis as other nations.

The U.S.S.R., relaxing its active anti-religious propaganda, permits the installation of the Patriarch of All Russia of the Orthodox Church and the training of priests.

1944—D-Day (June 6) : Allies land in France.

Rome falls to Allies.

Paris liberated.

F.D.R. re-elected.

1945—Yalta agreement.

F.D.R. dies (April 12) ; Truman is President.

April 25—UN parley opens at San Francisco— charter signed June 26; goes into effect October 24.

Americans and Russians meet on Elbe.

33,000 inmates of Dachau concentration camp freed by U.S. forces.

Berlin falls; Germany surrenders unconditionally.

July 16—A-bomb test at Almagordo, New Mexico (announced August 6). Some scientists oppose on ethical grounds, advise bomb not be dropped on Japan. (Franck Report) Potsdam Conference.

July 26—Attlee becomes British Prime Minister Churchill is out.

August 6—A-bomb blasts Hiroshima, Nagasaki (August 9).

September 2—Japanese sign surrender terms aboard battleship "Missouri" (V-J Day).

Truman, Attlee, and Mackenzie King (Canada) decide in Washington Conference that A-bomb secrets will not be shared until UN adopts control plan.

American Communist Party told by Jacques Duclos to cease wartime co-operation with government and return to militancy; Earl Browder excommunicated, replaced by Foster.

A. The United States in World War II

AS IN WORLD WAR I, SO IN WORLD WAR II THERE WAS A COAlescence of national unity and national ethics. We can understand the place and purpose of The Methodist Church best if we note, however briefly, the inclusive context of the total patriotic and moral effort. The prosecution of the war effort in response to the external threat to the national community solidified the people to a marked degree in a temporary unity.[1]

There were many appeals to such a unity: laying aside partisan politics; feeling the common "I am an American" principle amid the numerous minority elements of the nation; forgetting the class struggle on the production line and submitting to a "no-strike pledge"; accepting the egalitarian procedures of rationing and priorities; working side by side with persons of other races in new places and new jobs; building a united morale in the armed forces; and establishing interfaith community among Jews, Protestants, and Roman Catholics. The rallying cry was the common social purpose to defeat totalitarianism and racist Nazism in the name of the dominant American ideals. "To win the war" meant everything from the munitions plant and the war-bond counter to civilian defense, ration books, and the beachheads of Iwo Jima and Normandy.

Patriotic zeal was organized into a positive psychological and ethical attack on the enemies of American ideals. Hitler and Hirohito were the symbols and the alleged embodiment of racism, antidemocracy, hatred for personal rights, subjugation of religious and cultural liberties, suppression of free labor, militarism—in short, of all totalitarian threats to individual dignity and common humanity. War against the Axis served to place behind the ethics of the "American Dream" the propulsive power of nationalism. The uttermost in human self-sacrifice was linked to consciousness of the highest social values.

The unity movements and slogans of the "duration" were not only stimulated by catastrophic threats from abroad; they were stimulated by crises and divisions at home. "Total" war heightens and exaggerates all social problems and tensions, makes for stereotyped thinking and scapegoating, and tempts men to exalt the procedures of violence in efforts to win during conflict. More than a hundred thousand Japanese-Americans were removed from their homes and relocated; there were serious race riots in parts of the United States; and there were numerous clashes among white and non-Caucasian workers. There were countless scrapes in schools and on playgrounds. There was a rising tide of anti-Semitism; bigotry was

---

[1] See Walter G. Muelder, "National Unity and National Ethics," *The Annals*, "Controlling Group Prejudice" (March 1946), pp. 10-18. The next few pages reproduce sections of this article.

accentuated; and anti-Catholicism was promoted. Discrimination was still practiced in the armed forces. Labor felt that it was hamstrung by the no-strike pledge, and waited for the termination of the war to renew its demands with strength. Black-market practices stirred derisive resentments. And soldiers were propagandized against organized labor with its high wages. Many GIs had, of course, honest resentments against labor.

Thus the war abroad had its counterpart in the social struggle at home. The tensions of the pluralistic society were everywhere evident. To meet the crisis, civic and national unity movements were promoted on every side. To be sure, the World War II soldier was far less starry-eyed than his counterpart in World War I.

The unity programs were heavily weighted with ethical judgments. However, the country fought with a moral passion which made her patriotism almost indistinguishable from religion. The war was fought ostensibly to make the "Four Freedoms" secure everywhere in the world. Statesmen affirmed the following: to give "to decent people everywhere a better chance to live and prosper in security and in freedom and in faith"; "to uphold the doctrine that all men are equal in the sight of God"; "to destroy the world-wide force of ruthless conquest and brutal enslavement"; to preserve "this new-world love of education and dignity of the common man"; to abolish "discrimination between people because of their race, creed, or color"; to repudiate the "monstrous philosophy of superior race and conquest by force"; to embrace "loyally the basic principles of peaceful processes"; to defend "free schools"; and to realize "faith in life, liberty, independence, and religious freedom." Such ideals were generally summarized in the Four Freedoms as President Roosevelt formulated them: "Not only freedom of speech, freedom to worship God each in his own way, but freedom from want and freedom from fear as well."

These wartime ideals were represented not only as lofty civic traditions, but as realizable now and as having the immemorial sanction of Jewish and Christian faiths. Statesmen often closed major addresses with prayerful clauses. If the churches did not agree that the war was "holy," and in general they did not—they often emphasized that it was "just." After detailing the Four Freedoms the President added: "That is no vision of a distant millennium. It is a definite basis for a kind of world attainable in our own time and generation." "There must be no compromise between justice and injustice; no yielding to expediency; no swerving from the great human rights and liberties established by the Atlantic Charter itself." All these freedoms are "a part of the whole freedom

for which we strive." Other leaders said that we are "one in the
prayer for the victory of the principles of Christian civilization."
Before us lies "the great constructive task of building human freedom and Christian morality on firmer and broader foundations than
ever before." In this task the voice of the United States is to express
the aspirations of mankind as it goes forward to its destiny. "The
soul of that destiny is a maximum freedom of the human spirit."

Some observers have pointed out that there was significantly less
hate in World War II than in World War I. "The Hun" referred to
all Germans. One could hardly say this of Nazi. But when it came
to epithets about the Japanese—hate hardly knew any bounds.

B. Pacifism and Participation

Between December 4, 1940, and February 5, 1941, *The Christian
Century* ran a series of articles by ten Christian leaders on the general subject "If America enters the war—what shall *I* do?" Three
of the ten were Methodists: Albert E. Day, Francis J. McConnell,
and Ernest Fremont Tittle. This proportion reflects both the concern and the leadership which Methodists were giving to the critical
issues.[2]

Day's position was that he could not reconcile active, purposeful
participation in the imminent war with the Christian way of life.
The madness of racialism and nationalism evident in the European
conflict was equally beyond the reach of even a military victory
and seemed likely to be only intensified by a victory. "Some of us
believe that there is a more effective resistance to evil—a disciplined, determined non-violence that is unafraid of prison or concentration camps or death, that offers the enemy an opposition he
cannot reach with his bombs, but an opposition which at the same
time appeals to his better nature and clears the way for God into
the very center of the conflict." Day eschewed any assumption of
moral superiority or presumption of sainthood, but affirmed a refusal to accept an ultimate dualism between ethics and politics, or
to believe that the only choice is between hypocrisy and vengeance,
or to retreat to a morally impotent mysticism. He felt obliged to
confront "a pagan order with certain creative truths which, if not
doubted, may sometime become the experienced truth of the race."

Bishop McConnell said: "If the United States enters the war, I
shall support it as long as it remains on a defensive basis." He made

---

[2] Other writers: John C. Bennett, John Haynes Holmes, Reinhold Niebuhr,
Charles P. Taft, Albert W. Palmer, Harry Emerson Fosdick, and Henry P.
Van Dusen. Day and Tittle were recognized pacifist leaders; McConnell was
not.

clear that he did not mean the doctrine that the offensive is the best defense. The more serious consequence to a democracy, he felt, would be the debauchery of the public mind during the war. He noted, as we have earlier in this volume, that some of the most scandalous wrongs in the history of the United States against civil liberties were perpetrated after World War I. Then, too, he insisted that should war come he would on every possible occasion discuss openly the terms on which war is to cease. Such would include the question of surrendering some national sovereignty for the sake of international adjustment. Another question would be the deadly inadequacies of the capitalistic system. "The economic factor is not the only one to be considered as making for war, but there is excellent reason for calling it the chief factor."

McConnell anticipated the anticommunist hysteria that was to come later. "If the fascists should conquer Britain and start toward the United States, all they would have to do to capture outright large sections of our materialistic tories would be to promise to save the United States from communism, whether there was any danger from communism or not." This minority of tories, he went on to say, clamor for a new emphasis on the old-time individual religion. Finally, McConnell noted he would keep right on holding that the conscientious objector "even of the absolute type, is absolutely indispensable in wartime as holding on high the Christian ideal of protest against war."

Ernest Fremont Tittle spoke as one who in 1917 left a wife and three children and went to France. He later became convinced, as the Oxford Conference in 1937 put it, that war is "a defiance of the righteousness of God as revealed in Jesus Chirst and him crucified." And so he affirmed that if the United States became a belligerent in Europe or in Asia, he would undertake to contribute in some way to the good of his country, but he would not "support" the war. "Christian pacifists," he said, "do not proclaim that tyranny is better than war; they proclaim that tyranny cannot be overcome by war." He insisted that war as we now know it cannot pave the way for the doing of good. "When the fighting ends, the people who make the peace are the same people whose ambitions and practices created the situation which bred the war." He also insisted that war as we now know it cannot even hold evil in check.

Tittle's position was that of Christian pacifism based on the Christian faith that the cross of Christ is the supreme revelation of God's method of dealing with evil. The relevance of this to the American scene meant that as a national policy pacifism would require the United States to set its own house in order. He said:

It would seem a real solution (which peacetime conscription is not) for the problem of unemployment and equality of opportunity for all Americans, including Negroes. It would require the repeal of the Oriental Exclusion Act and the placing of Orientals on the quota basis which now governs immigration from other countries. It would call upon the United States to abrogate its present unequal treaties with China and to establish its relations with China on a basis of complete equality and reciprocity. It would require the United States, in the formation of its domestic policies, to have a lively and continuing regard for the welfare of the rest of mankind. This would forbid such selfish—and shortsighted—conduct as the Smoot-Hawley Tariff Act and the Silver Purchase Act of 1934. It would lead the United States to become indeed a good neighbor, concerned that all nations should have equal access to raw materials and needed markets for their industrial goods.

When the General Conference met in 1940 the nation was not officially at war. When it next met in 1944 the war was far advanced. No official utterance of the denomination as a whole therefore could guide the annual conferences and the local churches. However, the Council of Bishops spoke and gave some direction. In addition the Commission on World Peace was zealously at work. After the outbreak of war the bishops said:

Our country has stood, always and unequivocally, for the democratic way, and therefore the clash was inevitable. . . . There can be no peace in the world until the totalitarian threat against the liberties of all freedom-loving people is thoroughly eradicated.

We roundly condemn the processes of war even while accepting the awful alternative, not of our making, forced upon us by the selfishness and the perversity of men. From a measure of the guilt of this, none of us is free.[3]

The last sentence of this quotation indicates a long journey in the church's thinking since World War I. At the Oxford Conference of 1937 representatives of the Protestant churches had come to recognize that "war can occur only as a fruit and manifestation of sin." They recognized, further, that it was impossible to reconcile the pacifist and the nonpacifist positions, but that both views were sincerely held by Christians. That war is sin they held to be a "truth [which] is unaffected by any question of what may be the duty of the nation which has to choose between entry upon war and a course which it believes to be a betrayal of right, or what may be the duty of a Christian citizen whose country is involved in war."[4] The great

---

[3] "The War Time Message of the Council of Bishops, *Zion's Herald*, CXIX (December 24, 1941), 1166, 1180-81.
[4] "Message" of the Oxford Conference of 1937.

Oxford Conference, along with the vigorous dialogues between liberals and neo-orthodox, between pacifists who were socialists and pacifists who were individualists, between interventionists who were militarists and interventionists who had no illusions about the fruits of war—had prepared the churches to embrace the following attitude: "If war breaks out, then pre-eminently the Church must manifestly be the Church, still united in the one body of Christ, though the nations, wherein it is planted fight one another. . . . (The) fellowship of prayer must at all costs remain unbroken. The Church must also hold together in one spiritual fellowship those of its members who take differing views concerning their duties as citizens in time of war."

Against this doctrine of the church the attitudes of Methodist Annual Conferences, General Conferences, and the crusade for world order take on a new perspective and special significance. How did the organized Methodist people respond? The aggressions of Hitler and Mussolini and the attack on Pearl Harbor presented the church with a new situation.

James W. Gladden's study of The Methodist Church in relation to war and peace examined a number of annual conference pronouncements during World War II and portrays some interesting variations among the several jurisdictions.[5] It reflects the fact that after the war began many of the conferences dropped the stand taken by the denomination in 1940.[6] Gladden's digest follows: In 1940-41 all sixteen of the conferences examined in the Northeastern, Northcentral, and Western Jurisdictions had set up committees, were opposed to the church participating in war, forbade war use of the local church or the national agencies, urged exemption of individual conscientious objectors, and wanted the United States as a nation to stay out of war.

In the Southeastern Jurisdiction only five had committees. Four spoke out against the churches being a part of war; four wanted individual conscientious objectors' exemption, and none asked the nation to stay out of the European conflict.

Whereas all sixteen conferences of the Northeastern, the Northcentral, and the Western Jurisdictions covered by the study were opposed to church participation, only ten mentioned this position in 1942. Six failed to restate the earlier conviction and said nothing about the use of church agencies in and for war. Thirteen spoke

---

[5] James W. Gladden, "The Methodist Church and the Problem of War and Peace: An Analysis in Social Understanding." A preprint of an abstract of a doctoral dissertation, *University of Pittsburgh Bulletin*, 42.

[6] See above p. 194 in manuscript.

specifically in support of conscientious objectors. Only three of the sixteen spoke of international organization, although ten supported study conferences which expressed such a need. In the Southeastern Jurisdiction in 1942 only Virginia and North Carolina showed a measure of insistence upon the stand taken by the denomination in 1940. The Alabama Conference went all out in support of the war.

By 1943 only eight conferences refused church support of war. Only six out of thirty-two said, "We cannot bless war." Nineteen conferences before the war insisted on the right of the conscientious objectors; this number had fallen to ten by 1943. "Only four actually endorsed the war effort, but the language of the speakers and the reports of the other committees suggest that there was a majority feeling in other conferences that the Church was 'in the war.'"

The third General Conference of United Methodism convened two and a half years after the nation was officially at war. Could the church maintain its prewar stand? The response to this question reflected and caused at the time as deep a rift as any that has occurred on a social issue since unification. Behind the phrases finally adopted were basic issues which were often confused and which some defined differently. Many saw the conflict in the General Conference as a contest simply between those who were for and against pacifism. In reality, as Georgia Harkness [7] has pointed out, it was a matter of the church as *Church* (not in its individual members) participating in the war, so far as the majority report (which eventually lost) was concerned. The minority report (which finally carried) referred to both the role of individuals and the position of the church.

The majority report was recommended out of committee by a vote of seventy-seven to forty-four.[8] It was an effort to reaffirm the official position of the church expressed in 1940. In presenting the majority report, "The Church in Time of War," Ernest Fremont Tittle, Chairman, stated that by common agreement of both the majority and minority members of the Committee on the State of the Church, two amendments were to be inserted into the majority report. These paragraphs are of historic interest as showing views on which there was virtual unanimity in 1944.

The church cannot be indifferent to the issues at stake in the present conflict. It is deeply concerned in the human values in jeopardy and in the ultimate effect of the conflict upon the cause of justice, freedom, and

---

[7] Memorandum to author, March 26, 1960.
[8] Dr. Tittle was chairman of the Committee on the State of the Church. In 1952, Mr. Parlin was made chairman.

brotherhood. As a corporate body seeking to declare the will of God, it must express its moral judgment and use its moral force against tyranny, aggression, persecution, and all forms of political dictatorship and totalitarianism which run counter to our Christian belief in the worth and dignity of every individual.

We call upon the Church to pray for the welfare of those in the armed forces, for the maintenance of their Christian faith and ideals and their safe return to our homes and churches, if this be possible. Believing that God has a stake in the victory of peace with justice in the present conflict, we commend our cause to Him, praying "Thy Kingdom come, Thy will be done." [9]

A minority report by 17 members, of whom 14 were laymen, was presented by Charles Parlin. When the vote on the floor was taken, 203 laymen voted for the minority report and 131 voted against it; 170 ministers voted in favor and 169 against, thus giving the minority report the sanction of both groups.

Crucial paragraphs in the minority report as finally adopted stated:

In this country we are sending over a million young men from Methodist homes to participate in the conflict. God himself has a stake in the struggle, and he will uphold them as they fight forces destructive of the moral life of men. In Christ's name we ask for the blessing of God upon the men in the armed forces, and we pray for victory. We repudiate the theory that a state, even though imperfect in itself, must not fight against intolerable wrongs.

While we respect the individual conscience of those who believe that they cannot condone the use of force, and staunchly will defend them on this issue, we cannot accept their position as the defining position of the Christian Church. We are well within the Christian position when we assert the necessity of the use of military forces to resist an aggression which would overthrow every right which is held sacred by civilized men. [10]

The close vote among the ministers and the clear division among the laity are indications of the long way that Methodism had come in the years since World War I. Such a vote would have been unthinkable at that time. The troubled conscience of Methodism was shared by many church bodies in America and Europe.

As has already been noted, whether pacifist or nonpacifist, whether defined in terms of the church as such or in terms of individual members, Methodist people developed a sustaining conviction about international responsibility and the need for a responsible

[9] *Journal* of the 1944 General Conference of The Methodist Church, p. 366.
[10] *Discipline* (1944), ¶ 2016.

world political organization. The story of a major aspect of that development in education and action must now be told. It preceded the General Conference of 1944.

C. The Crusade for a New World Order

The Crusade for a New World Order was a model educational and action campaign for a connectional denomination like The Methodist Church. It was an effectively organized effort (1943-44), initiated by Bishop G. Bromley Oxnam, to register the opinion of the members and constituents of The Methodist Church on the question of the participation of the United States of America in such international co-operation as would be necessary to establish world law and order. In December 1942 the Council of Bishops voted to spend a week in Washington in conference with the leaders of government, to make inquiry concerning plans for the postwar world. The council was in Washington from February 22 to 26, 1943 and conferred with more than twenty such leaders, including also representatives of foreign governments, business, and labor. Immediately prior to the Washington meeting Bishop G. Bromley Oxnam, then resident in the Boston area, made a proposal that the council appoint a commission of twelve bishops to consider a crusade to draft plans for its execution, to organize and direct the movement.[11] Two bishops were elected from each jurisdiction. The proposal was adopted, the commission was created,[12] initial meetings were held in April and July, and the plan was reported to the regular council meetings in July and December 1943.

The mobilization of the church was a phenomenal achievement. It rested on a threefold conviction and on a solidly constructed Christian platform.

The threefold conviction was:

First, the religious forces of the nation must become influential at the place decision is made, *before it is made,* so that their convictions may be regarded as creative and cooperative contributions. Religious forces must not wait until decision is made and then protest.

Second, Methodists, after more than a century of missionary service throughout the world and more than a quarter century of education in

[11] G. Bromley Oxnam, *The Crusade for a New World Order: A Report by the Chairman* (April 5, 1944). The material in this section is largely taken from this report.

[12] Bishops Baker, Baxter, Holt, Jones, Kern, King, Lowe, McConnell, Moore, Oxnam, Selecman, and Wade. Bishop G. Bromley Oxnam was chairman, Bishop Paul B. Kern, vice chairman, and Bishop Raymond J. Wade, secretary.

the field of international relations, are world-minded and desire world order.

Third, the members of The Methodist Church, as citizens, desire such action by the United States Government as will insure full participation in, and continuing cooperation with, such international organization in the political, economic, and other fields as may be necessary to end war, to establish world law and order, economic and racial justice, and to guarantee the freedom of the individual.

The crusade platform stated:

The peoples of the world must choose between *international collaboration,* in which lies the possibility of enduring peace; and *isolationism,* in which lies the certainty of continuing war.

As Christians, we choose international collaboration and such international organization as, in the judgment of experts, may be necessary to establish world law and order based upon justice and brotherhood.

As Christians, we reject isolationism which subordinates the well-being of the world to national self-interest, and denies the Christian doctrine that all men are children of one Father and are members of one family.

Jesus Christ is the Saviour of the World.

The World is our Parish.

Co-operation with the Federal Council of the Churches of Christ in America was an organic part of the bishops' crusade. Indeed, the Crusade for a New World Order was organized to complement the work of the Federal Council as represented in its Commission to Study the Bases of a Just and Durable Peace. John Foster Dulles was the chairman. Fourteen members of the commission were Methodists, including the executive secretary.[13] The presence of both leading pacifists and nonpacifists illustrates the fact that the peace movement in Methodism was solidly linked with international solidarity and world responsibility both before and during the war.

The crusade deliberately chose to emphasize those concepts which had been developed at the co-operative council table of national organizations. Thus the movement recognized that the "Six Pillars of Peace," as formulated by the Federal Council, represented proposals which were at once moral and practical. Methodism gave widest publicity to them and incorporated them in the curricular material of the study classes in church school and summer institutes. In the same spirit it used the pronouncements of the International

---

[13] Eugene E. Barnett, Harold Bosley, James Cannon, Jr., Ralph S. Cushman, Mark A. Dawber, Albert E. Day, Georgia Harkness, Stanley High, Harry N. Holmes, Sallie Lou MacKinnon, John R. Mott, G. Bromley Oxnam, Ernest Fremont Tittle, and Walter W. Van Kirk.

Round Table at Princeton, which were sponsored by the Federal Council and by the Canadian United Church Commission on Church, Nation, and World Order. Such co-operation shows responsibility both in the original formulation of policy and in efforts to express the policy in action.

The Six Pillars of Peace which formed the skeleton structure of much of the educational activity affirmed the following propositions:

1. The peace must provide the political framework for a continuing collaboration of the United Nations and, in due course, of neutral and enemy nations.
2. The peace must make provision for bringing within the scope of international agreement those economic and financial acts of national governments which have widespread international repercussions.
3. The peace must make provision for an organization to adapt the treaty structure of the world to changing underlying conditions.
4. The peace must proclaim the goal of autonomy for subject peoples, and it must establish international organization to assure and to supervise the realization of that end.
5. The peace must establish procedures for controlling military establishments everywhere.
6. The peace must establish in principle, and seek to achieve in practice, the right of individuals everywhere to religious and intellectual liberty.

As the initial announcement of the crusade went out, it proposed a flow of letters from the people to their representatives in Congress and in the executive branch of government. The letters were to be written by individuals, expressive of their own hope for an ordered world. This expression of opinion, it was hoped, might reach the dimension of a million letters at times when measures embodying moral principles were under consideration. The crusade clearly recognized the line of separation between church and state, but it also recognized that churchmen are citizens, and as citizens they are responsible for the expression of their opinion in a democratic society.

At the time of the crusade (1943) Methodist denominational membership stood at 7,955,085, worshiping in 41,059 churches and led by 25,377 preachers. There were 114 Annual Conferences and 578 district superintendents. With such an organization from the Council of Bishops to local churches and a number of great boards and commissions, the church could move from national and world policy to local parishes with dispatch.

The crusade involved a number of action elements: (1) mass meetings, (2) local parish services, (3) house-to-house visitation, (4) preparation and distribution of literature, (5) writing of letters, (6) special acts of consecration and dedication, (7) widespread use of the media of mass communication, and (8) co-ordination of education, worship, and action. Leadership by the bishops and pastors symbolized the action of the whole church. Co-operative leadership by the boards and commissions showed how specialized resources could be co-ordinated in a powerful witness for freedom, justice, and peace.

It is instructive to note specifically how the boards and commissions co-operated. The Board of Missions and Church Extension (through its Divisions: the Foreign Division, the Home Division, the Woman's Division of Christian Service, and the Division of Education and Cultivation) organized and directed the mass meetings, produced and distributed the literature of the crusade mass meetings, and shared in the house-to-house visitation. Its executives served as members of the speaking teams, and as representatives of the board in the afternoon meetings. It underwrote the expenses of these meetings, the production of literature, and the leaflet, "Your Part," which was distributed in the homes during the house-to-house visitation.

At this point a further word about mass meetings and house-to-house visitation is in order. The functions of the mass meetings were to give initial impetus to the writing of letters to the representatives of the people, to impress the membership with the fact that since the church is a large and powerful body it has co-ordinate responsibilities, and to inspire the leaders to carry the message of the crusade to the parishes and homes. Mass meetings were held in seventy-six great centers of population in January of 1944. The total attendance was 193,957. These meetings followed a similar pattern. In the morning the resident bishop spoke on "The Meaning and Objective of the Crusade." Two addresses followed: one on "A Christian America," and one on "A Christian World." The afternoon had two features, the presentation of the specific activities of the co-operating boards and commissions and the "Act of Dedication." As a "token and pledge" made by all to register their opinion on the question of international collaboration, the fathers and mothers, relatives, and loved ones of the sons and daughters in the armed forces were called upon to write a postcard to those in the armed services of the nation. In the evening there was a service of song followed by two major addresses on "The Coming Peace" and on "The Prince of Peace." Twenty-five teams of speakers toured the nation, composed of thirty bishops, twelve ministers, four laymen, and five lay women. In the afternoon presentations 408 different individuals participated.

For the house-to-house visitation the Woman's Division of Christian Service and the Board of Lay Activities were especially responsible. Visitors went out two by two, calling in the homes, presenting the issue and leaving the pamphlet entitled *Your Part*. Two million of these leaflets were distributed during the house-to-house phase of the crusade. To prepare the representatives in government for the receipt of the letters, Bishop Oxnam wrote personal letters to the President, each member of the cabinet, and each senator and representative. This action in itself had a notable response from Washington.

A word must be added about the use of art and music in the crusade. A poster was painted by Howard Chandler Christy. It was unveiled at the meeting in Worcester, Massachusetts, and copies were sent to all Methodist Churches. The painting also was reproduced on countless postcards for use in the crusade. Three hundred thousand were mailed to servicemen. Dean Earl B. Marlatt and Professor William L. Stidger of Boston University School of Theology wrote the crusade hymns, one to the tune of the Russian Hymn, the other using Finlandia.

We return now to the role of other agencies of the church. The Board of Education (the Division of the Local Church, the Division of Educational Institutions, and the Editorial Division) produced the literature necessary to undergird the movement with education. It gave generous and important space to the crusade in all its periodicals and story papers; organized the church school for full participation in the crusade; and revised the curriculum of its youth divisions and adult classes, producing altogether nearly one hundred articles, pamphlets, booklets, and study courses.

The educational effort was impressive. The basic document was *Primer of Action. The Crusade for a New World Order. The Methodist Church*. This booklet gave direction to the area bishop, the district committees, and the pastors. It recorded the specific cooperation offered by each board and commission and gave practical instructions on writing representatives in the federal government. It included some materials like "The Six Pillars of Peace," which had already been made available by the Federal Council of Churches.

The Board of Education's own program was worked out in co-operation with Annual Conference boards of education and included the following:

(1) Conference-wide meetings in more than two hundred summer camps, institutes, and assemblies for youth and young adults;

(2) More than five hundred district and subdistrict youth meetings featuring the bishops' crusade;

(3) A covenant of reading and prayer for a new world order, employing special bibliographies on Christian World Order;

(4) Emphasis on this theme in the regular youth, young adult, and adult classes, together with the corresponding leadership training programs;

(5) Emphasis on motivation in the materials for opening services in church schools;

(6) World Order Youth Forums on the Six Pillars of Peace and related subjects;

(7) Distribution of materials prepared by the bishops and making organizations and facilities available for promoting the crusade;

(8) Co-operation with other churches. The board urged Methodist churches to co-operate with other churches and agencies in the community in holding conferences for a study of postwar problems and in other constructive community enterprises.[14]

Motive magazine gave the crusade prominent attention. *Power,* a book of daily devotions for young people, emphasized the theme of international co-operation.

The Methodist Publishing House published most of the crusade literature under rush order and at a time when labor and material were in short supply. It set up the book exhibits at all mass meetings. The *Upper Room,* with a circulation of 2,000,000 (200,000 sent to the armed forces) devoted its January 1944 daily studies of scripture and prayer to the crusade theme. *The Christian Advocate* ran numerous inspirational and feature articles. Similarly the independent journals, like *Zion's Herald* and the *Conference Advocates* and the *Pastors Journal* gave wide publicity to the movement. *The Methodist Woman* devoted two issues to crusade material, thereby reaching the 1,300,000 organized women of the church. Methodism's missionary journal, *World Outlook* (200,000 circulation) devoted the January issue to the crusade. It carried letters by President Roosevelt, Vice-President Wallace, Secretary Hull, Wendell Wilkie, and Alfred M. Landon, commending the crusade.

[14] John Q. Schisler, "Educating for a Christian World Order," The Division of the Local Church, June 1943.

The Board of Lay Activities, as indicated above, shared the house-to-house visitation with the Woman's Division of Christian Service. The crusade was made a major item in the recommendations of the board for the year 1943. Laymen filled the pulpits in circuit churches on the climactic Sunday of January 30, 1944.

The Commission on World Peace organized the district committees, served as a clearing house for follow-up plans, prepared and distributed at its own expense "The Christian Citizen's Opinion on World Order" and the "Order of Service for the Day of Consecration," to which further reference will be made below. It is a significant fact, regarding Methodism's role in preparing the nation for the United Nations charter reception, that the Commission distributed approximately one third of all the Federal Council materials that reached the Protestant churches.

The Day of Consecration, referred to above, was promoted by the Commission on Evangelism, the order of service having been prepared by the Commission on World Peace. The former commission prepared a tract, *Christ the World Saviour,* and carried a Consecration Day sermon in *Revival Pulpit* and an article in *Tidings.*

The Commission of Public Information played inevitably a unique role and was in charge of all publicity and the radio programs. Nation-wide broadcasts were arranged over NBC, CBS, and the Mutual. In addition the Crusade Radio Committee, in co-operation with the Institute of Oral and Visual Education and the Boston University Radio Institute, produced thirteen fifteen-minute transcriptions. These were used by 243 stations, in most cases once each week for thirteen weeks, in some cases once each day for thirteen days. The stations used these transcriptions as features without cost to the church. The Office of War Information gave three worldwide broadcasts on the crusade and its objectives, stressing to enemy countries the war aims of the democracies as seen in the crusade, as well as pointing out the freedom of the churches in democratic lands.

The response of the press was particularly important as measured not only in news coverage but in fully two hundred editorials. Said the *Atlanta Constitution:* "No more important movement for the establishment of an international brotherhood of nations, for the end of selfish, blind isolationism, has been undertaken than this by the Methodists of the United States." Generally speaking, the editorials showed full understanding and real appreciation of the movement. *Time* used two stories, including a reproduction of the Christy poster. *News of the Day, a* Metro-Goldwyn-Mayer release, made a special sound recording of the New York meeting for its audience of twenty-two million. Walter W. van Kirk gave prominent time to the crusade in several of his broadcasts of "Religion in the News" over NBC. Several commentators discussed the crusade, particularly the influence of the letters as they came by the ten thousands into Washington. The impression was profound; Senator Capper, an old-line Kansas conservative, had the Methodist proposal placed in the *Congressional Record* along with his enthusiastic endorsement of it.

How should such a crusade be evaluated? Its chairman, Bishop Oxnam, has made a number of basic observations. The church was eager for its education for peace to be complemented by action. The crusade showed how impressive action could be when fully mobilized throughout the church. Then, too, the crusade made its points clear by using basic propositions like the Six Pillars of the Federal Council; but "had the Crusade sought to win support for a particular blueprint plan of postwar organization, it would have divided the Church in fruitless discussion before the Church had been united on the general and fundamental proposition." In addition, the churches would need to call for an early and definite statement on foreign policy, believing that the nation has the right to know for what it fights both at home and abroad.

In the next place, the crusade showed that since church action can be effective, the church has a continuing obligation to be vocal and politically potent. This it can do without crossing the line that separates church and state. Moreover, the leadership of the church must study ways to make the mind of the church known and ready for continuous action in support of world order. Also, the world mission of the church must be reinterpreted to the people. In all this, the place of faith in determining the conduct of nations is seen to be primary. The church has a duty to express a common faith and give it life in a common purpose. Finally, the crusade revealed that creative forces of great significance lie dormant in parishes across the nation. The movement must flow into maturer and more effective Christian education and action.

When American Protestantism in 1945 rallied behind the United Nations Conference in San Francisco, the moral and political voice of the United States had, in part at least, been shaped by the tremendous and brilliant Crusade for a New World Order.

What happened to the Methodist pacifists during the war? What kind of people were they? We have already noted that the General Conference asked that conscientious objectors be given the same legal recognition as members of historic peace churches. It has been noted that one of the most surprising facts during the war was the number of conscientious objectors who came out of the non-peace churches. The Methodist Church had almost as many conscientious objectors as the Quakers. Methodists participated in the National Service Board for Religious Objectors and kept a registry from 1936 on.

Herman Will, Jr., who was thoroughly familiar with Civilian Public Service Camps (C.P.S.), in 1948 made some significant observations about the 199 Methodists he studied in C.P.S. There were 941 Methodists in all who served in C.P.S. He writes,

Of the 199, thirty-five are either ministers or ministerial students, nine are missionaries, thirteen are engaged in relief work, seven serve as Y.M.C.A. secretaries, and four are full-time workers for peace. College instructors number twenty-nine, high-school teachers seven. Some sixteen are employed in hospitals, as doctors, or in behalf of better care for mental patients. The consumers' cooperative movement has hired fifteen of these former C.P.S. men. Students make up the bulk of those remaining with a scattering in other vocations.[15]

Many Methodists accepted alternative service for conscientious objectors. The continued idealism of these men is indicated when one makes an analogy with the percentage of the one million Methodists who served in the armed forces. If the same percentage had entered the full-time ministry or mission service, there would be fifty thousand recruits to swell the depleted ranks of the ministry and to carry the Christian message into every part of America and the world. Similarly, there would be more than thirty thousand teachers, twenty thousand doctors and medical workers, fifteen thousand employees for co-operatives, and fifteen thousand to undertake relief projects overseas.

Methodism incurred a debt of honor to the historic peace churches because of Civilian Public Service Camps. In 1947 it was called to the attention of Methodists that a debt of $225,000 was still to be paid to the small peace churches which had carried most of the burden.[16] Eventually of a total obligation of $485,000 the church

[15] Herman Will, Jr., *et al*, "What Happened to the Pacifists?" A Symposium. *Motive*, 8 (April 1948), no. 7, 12.
[16] *Unfinished Business for Methodists*, 1947.

paid $425,000 when it was advised by the peace churches to stop and to use the rest on peace programs.

D. Witness on Race in Wartime

Nazism and Hitler's international aggressions made racism and the problems of race relations acute wartime issues.

The Methodist Church had just been organized as the union of three separated branches on a jurisdictional plan which had its Central Jurisdiction based on race. Another branch, the Colored Methodist Episcopal Church,[17] with strong ties to the Methodist Episcopal Church, South, did not come into the union, but continued in the same relationship as before. This arrangement was confirmed with the recommendation "that financial support of the Colored Methodist Episcopal Church be continued by those jurisdictional divisions with which said church is historically related, and to such an extent as those jurisdictions may deem wise." [18] This provision has appeared with each subsequent edition of the *Discipline*.

The Central Jurisdiction presented a more difficult problem at the time of unification than the C.M.E. Church because the nineteen Negro conferences which made up its constituency existed within the Northern church. In the Plan of Union these nineteen conferences plus the Negro Mission Conference and other Negro missions in the United States were segregated. The Methodist Church did not, however, accord inferior status to the Central Jurisdiction as an organization. Constitutional provisions in the denomination's policy guaranteed for the Negro membership equal participation in the denomination-wide General Conference, General Boards, Council of Bishops, and the like, and reserved to the Negro membership the right to elect its own leadership and establish many of its own policies and procedures. Below the top associational level, however, the Negroes were segregated. Negroes, therefore, were not segregated at the general administrative and legislative level of The Methodist Church, but they were at all other levels, with two significant exceptions. Some Negro churches in the Western and Northeastern Jurisdictions were included in the Annual Conferences of those regions. Moreover, The Methodist Church did not

[17] The correct title of this denomination is now the "Christian Methodist Episcopal Church." In 1939 it had some 374,440 members and 4,248 local churches.
[18] *Discipline*, 1956, ¶ 46. See J. Philip Wogaman, *Methodism's Challenge in Race Relations* (Boston: Boston University Press, 1960), ch. I.

specify that any person may be denied membership in any local church fellowship because of his race. "Constitutionally, the Central Jurisdiction is defined by its Negro churches and conferences, not by any provision requiring all Negro Methodists to belong to it." [19]

During the war Methodism was a pretty thoroughly segregated type of church life at the local level. Dwight W. Culver, basing his figures on the response of 71.5 per cent of the district superintendents of the denomination to an inquiry mailed them in 1946, reported that only about one hundred of the more than twenty thousand "white" Methodist pastoral charges were integrated with even one Negro member.[20] Culver found also that Southern institutions of higher learning related to The Methodist Church were segregated. In some Northern theological seminaries there were important exceptions to this pattern. However, in most non-Southern institutions there was small, token, or no integration, and in some integrated institutions there was discrimination in such matters as housing.[21]

These facts do not tell the whole story. A considerable number of Methodists, as we have already noted in previous chapters, continued to seek to eliminate racial barriers in the church. The issue loomed large in the thinking of many who opposed unification. Their thinking was further stimulated by the tragic fate of the Japanese on the West Coast and the general plight of Negroes in American life.

In 1942 Americans witnessed the spectacle of their fellow citizens in concentration camps because they were Japanese by racial origin. This situation is related to unfortunate episodes in the history of American-Japanese relations, including the joint political maneuvering of Southern anti-Negro interests and anti-Oriental interests in California. This conspiracy of injustice resulted by an Act of Congress in 1924 in the exclusion of Japanese from the quota immigration plan. The churches protested this unneighborly act which, at most, kept 150 would-be immigrants from American shores each year. In California, the church response was especially significant because of its stand during World War II.

Building on the firm statement of the General Conference of 1932

[19] Wogaman, ibid., p. 2.
[20] Dwight Culver, Negro Segregation in The Methodist Church (New Haven: Yale University Press, 1953), pp. 143-51.
[21] Ibid., pp. 129-33.

the Southern-California Annual Conference had in 1934 developed a series of pronouncements and urged a program:

Against the background of this (General Conference) statement, we deplore the presence of lynching.

We protest against the practice of the importation of immigrant groups to flood the labor market in profitable times and the companion evil of failure to recognize the responsibility to this same group when their labor is not so profitable.

We insist that racial differences shall not lessen the concern of Christian people for justice in all labor disputes.

We urge a policy of fellowship and acquaintance between churches of various racial groups.

We recommend that the Board of Education assist in the organization of round-table discussions and conversations upon inter-racial problems.

We insist upon the equal treatment and recognition of all delegates at conference and conventions connected with the Methodist Episcopal Church, regardless of race or color.

The statement recognized that all the principles of the Social Creed applied to all races alike.[22]

This philosophy received its focal test in the case of the Japanese, both citizens and aliens, during the war. The response of the church to this crisis among the Japanese from 1942 to 1945 is a high point in the history of race relations in California Methodism's witness.[23]

At the beginning of the war there were about 100,000 persons of Japanese ancestry living in California. Their cause had already been a concern of the church, for in 1930 the Conference had asked for a reform in immigration policy. In 1941 the Japanese were the scapegoat of general anti-Oriental hostility and organized groups. When all Japanese were ordered in 1942 to be relocated, The Methodist Church opposed the action as un-American and unchristian. The uprooted Americans were transplanted to Relocation Centers, but they were followed by the church. Indeed, many local churches identified themselves with the evacuees by having services and meals with them on the day they were rounded up for the concentration camps. Once the Japanese were in the camps, Methodists cooperated with the federated churches that were set up in the Relocation Camps, there being thirty-one Japanese Methodist ministers in these camps.

[22] *Journal, Southern California-Arizona Conference*, 1934, pp. 117-18.
[23] See S. Raynor Smith, *op. cit.*, pp. 314, 322. The term Japanese will be used for all persons of Japanese ancestry involved in this crisis regardless of status.

During the summer of 1942 the Methodist churches in various communities adjacent to loading and sending centers helped the Japanese prepare for their forced migration. This meant helping dispose of and lease their homes and businesses; storing property or selling cars, equipment, and furniture; providing for livestock and preparing for an indefinite absence. Methodist churches at Sacramento, Berkeley, Oakland, San José, Fresno, Alameda, San Francisco, Bakersfield, Palo Alto, and Brawley made space available for the storage of household goods. Within the camps Christmas presents, Japanese books, recreation equipment, church supplies, office furnishings, educational materials, and many other things were supplied. Methodist pastors and others visited frequently and tried to make relations as normal as possible under very trying circumstances.

The Southern California-Arizona Conference stated in 1942:

The all-inclusive fellowship of the Church embraces with profound sympathy the Japanese who have been uprooted by the evacuation orders. We are not unmindful that powerful interests, popular war hysteria, provincialism, and vigilantism, as well as military precaution enter into the situation. We do not join in a wholesale suspicion of disloyalty on the part of the Japanese of any generation. We deeply regret that the citizenship rights of many of them have been violated. We urge our church people to join in a positive movement to protect these people from threats of permanent loss of civil and economic rights. We seek with them for a new birth of freedom.[24]

The threats to the future loss of civil and economic freedom were real, for powerful vested interests were seeking to use the passions of war to prevent the return of any Japanese to California. They sponsored an amendment to the state constitution to prevent any Japanese alien from owning or leasing any kind of property in California. This amendment would also have closed the fishing industries to the Japanese. The church launched a vigorous opposition to the proposed measure, and when the sponsoring petition failed to secure the necessary number of signers, Methodists felt that they had had a significant share, along with other church and civic groups, in defeating the assault on this minority group. The church was further gratified when the Alien Land Law, which it had op-

[24] *Journal, Southern California-Arizona Conference*, 1942, pp. 161-62. Methodists were by no means unanimous in their support of the Japanese evacuated from California. Many laymen and some ministers felt that the government's action was right and justified.

posed in the past, was declared unconstitutional by the Supreme Court in 1948. Looking back over the war years, the California Conference said in 1946: "We are humbly grateful that the Methodist Church expressed a spirit of aggressive good will in seeking to uphold their (Japanese) fundamental rights." [25] This gratitude was also expressed in many acts at the end of World War II which helped mold public opinion to a place where the Japanese were received back without undue incident.[26]

The field of race relations was marred not only by the relocation of Japanese but by lynchings and race riots involving Negroes. In 1918 there were sixty-seven lynchings; in 1941 there were four reported. There was widespread discrimination in industry, in labor union practices, in housing, and in almost every phase of national defense. The President issued Executive Order 8802 on June 25, 1941, and appointed the Committee on Fair Employment Practice. In September he sent an intra-government letter in which he asked all heads of departments and independent establishments to examine "their personnel policies and practices to the end that they may be able to assure me that in the Federal Service the doors of employment are open to all loyal and qualified workers regardless of creed, race, or national origin." In March 1942, President Roosevelt authorized FEPC to obtain employment data from all government agencies and departments. These actions brought results.

In addition to economic disadvantages, Negroes continued to suffer from political ones. The poll tax in the South had by 1940 been effective in disfranchising not only Negroes but millions of whites as well.

There is ample evidence that it was partly designed for this purpose. Gunnar Myrdal pointed out that "in 1940, Oklahoma . . . had 60 per cent of its adult citizenry voting compared to 18 per cent in Arkansas; North Carolina had 43 per cent compared to 22 per cent in Virginia; and Louisiana, which has been without the poll tax only since 1934, had 27 per cent compared to 14 per cent in Mississippi." [27] It has been estimated that in the presidential elections of 1944, 10 per cent of the potential voters voted in the seven poll-tax states, as against 49 per cent in the free-vote states. The President's Committee on Civil Rights estimated that in the

[25] *Journal, California Conference*, 1946, p. 423.

[26] See Carey McWilliams, *Prejudice Japanese-Americans: Symbols of Racial Intolerance* (Boston: Little, Brown and Co., 1944), for an analysis of the social forces at work in this whole crisis.

[27] Gunnar Myrdal, *op. cit.*, I, 483.

Congressional election of 1946, the first such election after the war against Hitler, Nazism, fascism, and racism, the figures were 5 per cent for the poll-tax states and 33 per cent for the free-voting states.[28]

The war ended with a long agenda of challenges to the nation and to the churches in the field of race relations.

[28] *To Secure These Rights* (New York: Simon and Schuster, Inc., 1947), p. 39.

CHAPTER SEVEN

The Postwar Social Witness

Chronological Outline of
Major Events in American Social, Economic, and
Political History: 1946 to 1956

1946—First meeting of the United Nations General
Assembly in London. Security Council Con-
venes. Trygve Lie installed as UN General
Secretary.

Nuremberg war criminal trials. Ethical and
legal protest against them by Robert A. Taft.

Truman ends all price and wage controls, except
on rent, sugar, and rice.

Judge Goldsborough fines John L. Lewis $10,000
and the United Mine Workers Union $3,500,-
000 for contempt in disobeying Federal Court
order.

UN Atomic Energy Commission recommends
(10 to 0) the U.S.A. Control Plan; Russia and
Poland abstain.

UN Security Council and public opinion force
withdrawal of Russian troops from Iran.
British-French withdraw after complaint of
Syria-Lebanon from that territory.

1947—Russia rejects U.S. plan for UN Atomic Energy
Control.

Truman Doctrine announced; policy of contain-
ment of Communism.

General Motors settles wage dispute with United
Electrical Workers (CIO); sets "cost of living" pattern.

Marshall Plan adopted to assist European recovery.

Taft-Hartley Labor-Management Relations Act passed over Truman's veto.

India, freed by Britain, becomes independent state.

UN investigating committee recommends that Britain give up control of Palestine and that Arab and Jewish states be established.

General Assembly votes commission to set up free government for all of Korea.

The Supreme Court in the Everson Case decides that the New Jersey law permitting free transportation of parochial school pupils is not unconstitutional.

1948—Jan. 30 Gandhi assassinated.

Communists seize power in Czechoslovakia.

Nation of Israel proclaimed (May 14); British end mandate at midnight; Arab armies attack.

General Motors grants eleven-cent hourly wage increase; first escalator clause.

Berlin airlift begins June 21; ends May 12, 1949.

Henry Wallace runs for President on peace issue; Truman re-elected.

U.S. Supreme Court by an eight-to-one decision in the McCollum case (Champaign, Ill.) states that religious instruction by representatives of the churches in public-school buildings is unconstitutional.

UN General Assembly approves Universal Declaration of Human Rights.

First assembly of the World Council of Churches, Amsterdam, Holland.

Pan-Orthodox congress of the Eastern churches held in Moscow.

1949—Cease-fire in Palestine, armistice between Jordan and Israel.

Truman proposes Point Four Program to help world's backward areas.

Beginning of North Atlantic Treaty Organization (NATO).

German Federal Republic (West Germany) established.

Russia sets off atomic explosion.

Eleven top Communist leaders in U.C. found guilty of advocating overthrow of government.

Minimum wage raised to seventy-five cents.

Nationalist Chinese government moves to Formosa.

The Netherlands transfers sovereignty over Indonesia to Indonesian Republic.

1950—Population: 151,132,000.

Truman orders development of hydrogen bomb.

Senator Joseph R. McCarthy (R. Wis.) states that Communists are working in State Department.

Communist China is refused admittance to United Nations.

North Koreans cross 38th parallel to invade South Korea. Truman orders U.S.A. air and sea aid to South Korea. Security Council calls on UN members to help repel North Korean aggression. Chinese open massive offensive; turn UN forces back.

Eisenhower named commander of NATO forces in Europe.

1951—General Assembly condemns (44 to 7) Communist China as aggressor in Korea.

Truman removes General MacArthur from all Far East commands.

Truce talks begin in Korea.

U.S.A. orders construction of world's first atomic submarine.

Atomic test explosions begun in Nevada; become a world issue.

Japanese peace treaty signed in San Francisco by forty-nine nations.

1952—Truman seizes steel industry to prevent nationwide strike.

Supreme Court (6-3) rules Truman's seizures of steel mills unconstitutional; mills returned to owners; United Steel Workers Union goes on strike.

Eisenhower elected, ending twenty years of continuous Democratic administration.

The Supreme Court bars railway "Jim Crow" cars.

1953—Stalin dies.

Dag Hammarskjold begins term as UN Secretary General.

Eisenhower signs Off-Shore Oil Law giving states rights to all minerals in submerged lands within their claimed off-shore boundaries.

Korean armistice signed.

Moscow announces explosion of hydrogen bomb.

Eisenhower launches "atoms for peace" campaign at UN General Assembly.

1954—First atomic-powered submarine, "Nautilus" launched at Groton, Connecticut.

April 22—June 17—Army vs. McCarthy inquiry; subcommittee report, August 31, blames both sides.

May 17—U.S. Supreme Court unanimously bars segregation in public schools.

Eisenhower (September 6) launches world atomic pool without Russia.

December 2—Senate "condemns" Senator McCarthy on two counts by 67-22 vote.

Second Assembly of the World Council of Churches, Evanston, Illinois.

1955—Scientists approve Salk vaccine.

Supreme Court leaves school desegregation to regional Federal Courts.

"Summit Conference."

International Scientific Community effectively re-created.

Eisenhower cancels Dixon-Yates contract on power production.

AF of L and CIO merge partly into AF of L-CIO.

UN admits sixteen new members.

1956—U.S. releases 40,000 kg. Uranium 235 (worth $1,000,000) for peaceful atomic power at home and abroad.

Archbishop Makarios of Cyprus is sent into exile by Britain.

First aerial H-bomb tested over Namu I, Bikini Atoll (ten million tons TNT equivalent). Scientists report radiation is peril to future of race.

U.S. withdraws its offer to help Egypt build Aswan Dam on Nile.

Egypt announces seizure of Suez Canal control.

Poland restores Gomulka to power.

Hungarian revolt violently repressed by Soviets. UN General Assembly condemns Russia for aggression (55 yes, 8 no, 13 abstaining).

Eighty-two nations agree at UN on new International Atomic Energy Agency for peaceful use of atom. U.S. offers the agency 11,000 lb. of uranium 235.

Israel, French, and British attacks on Egypt condemned by U.S., and UN manages cease-fire. Anglo-French forces withdraw.

Eisenhower re-elected with Opposition Congress.

A. Civil Liberties: "I Protest"

MOUNTING REACTION IN THE POSTWAR WORLD GAVE GREAT concern to constructive civil liberties groups and to the church.[1] The era was to carry the name of an irresponsible Senator, Joseph McCarthy of Wisconsin. He whipped up and rode the tide of anti-communist hysteria. At the peak of the hysteria the churches spoke out—and one churchman, a Methodist bishop, was to play a heroic role. What was the state of the public mind? The American Civil Liberties Union issued its annual report for 1948-49 under the significant title, *In the Shadow of Fear, American Liberties 1948-49.* It stated that the present "hysterical atmosphere . . . exceeds in its severity, intolerance, and fears any such period in the Union's 29 years of activity; and the dangers of enduring damage are therefore the greater, as well as the obligations to combat them." This atmosphere had serious effects in many parts of social life. Con-

[1] See Alan Barth, *The Loyalty of Free Men;* Robert E. Cushman, *Civil Liberties in the United States;* G. Bromley Oxnam, *I Protest.* As an example of the reaction see John T. Flynn, *The Road Ahead: America's Creeping Revolution* (1949), distributed by the so-called Committee for Constitutional Government.

gress continued to be unable to enact any civil rights legislation; no significant relief was given from shackles in existing legislation against labor's rights; an unprecedented array of barriers to free association rose; forced declarations of loyalty, black lists, purges, taboos on progressive programs and principles were in effect. The consequences of the anticommunist hysteria were in this way not primarily those inflicted on the civil liberties of Communists. Possible treason or actual espionage could hardly be ignored in the "cold war." The chief misfortune was the damage done to the independent thinker, even if he were anticommunist. Able and loyal men were prevented from giving their best service to the government and to society.

Laws to ban or outlaw the Communist Party had serious consequences beyond the violation of the civil liberties of Communists.

The Communist Party is threatened with outlawry either by federal legislation . . . or by the government's current prosecution of its leaders under the Sedition Act of 1940, charging a criminal conspiracy solely for advocating historic Marxism as interpreted by the Communists. Bans on Communists and those associated with agencies held to be under Communist control, past or present, have been rapidly extended during the year to cover not only all federal employees, but thousands of employees in private firms working on government defense orders, all those receiving atomic energy fellowships, and all registrants for the draft.

There were grave effects in education as leading institutions and associations banned Communists from the teaching profession in moves "unprecedented in academic life in singling out membership in one political party as a disqualification in itself, without regard either to other equally valid disqualifications or to the consequences of discouraging independence among teachers or of encouraging heresy-hunters and informers." Excommunists and noncommunists who refused to take loyalty oaths suffered extensively. Inevitably the F.B.I.'s functions greatly expanded under laws penalizing opinions and associations; and this expansion was a democratic risk since, for the first time in American history, it created a virtual secret political police system with an array of informers and undercover agents.[2]

In 1948 the General Conference meeting at Boston heard a

[2] American Civil Liberties Union, *In the Shadow of Fear. American Liberties*, 1948-1949. See also Carey McWilliams, "Battle for the Clergy," *Social Questions Bulletin*, 38 (Nov. 1948), No. 7. This article was reprinted from *The Nation* (Feb. 7, 1948), pp. 150-52.

stirring Episcopal address presented by Bishop Oxnam. One of its key themes was freedom. The General Conference made a portion of the Episcopal address official:

A prophetic ministry can come only from a free pulpit. Recognizing the severe tensions today that often create an intolerant spirit and restrictive procedures, be it resolved that we affirm our belief in the necessity of maintaining freedom for the Methodist pulpit. We deprecate the tendency to label our ministers as "hopeless conservatives" on the one hand, or "dangerous radicals" on the other hand, when they honestly proclaim their interpretation of the truth in a given situation. Our ministers must be kept free to call to judgment those who are guilty of either personal or social sin. We would, with emphasis, reaffirm this statement from the Episcopal Address: "We are determined that free preachers, occupying a free pulpit, preaching to free laymen in a free land, shall proclaim the freeing truth of the religion of Jesus. Methodism is determined not to allow the intimidation of its clergy. We call upon our laymen, whose freedom is equally involved, to join our preachers in maintaining this freedom in the presence of social systems that deny it, so that our people may progress steadily and surely, and above all peacefully, toward a society worthy of the term, 'The Kingdom of God.' "

The Committee on Un-American Activities of the United States House of Representatives issued a report entitled "100 Things You Ought to Know about Communism and Religion." Its declared intent was to inform churchmen what would happen to them and their church if Communism ever takes over the United States of America. In passing it attacked the Epworth League, which went out of existence in 1939, as if still active, or ever infiltrated by Communism, and it attacked the Methodist Federation for Social Action as a "tool of the Communist Party."

The report drew a strong statement by the Council of Bishops which said in part: [3] "As the Bishops of the Church, we desire to affirm our full confidence in the patriotism and religious devotion of the hundreds of thousands of Methodist youth and to express our deep resentment of any attempt to question their loyalty." Referring to the methods of the Un-American Activities Committee they said: "We do not here comment upon the procedures of this Committee and the way its hearings at times have been conducted. We do declare that the publishing of falsehood concerning individuals who

[3] Enacted and signed by the Council of Bishops meeting in Cincinnati, Ohio, December 2, 1948, and released by Bishop James C. Baker of Los Angeles, president of the Council, through the office of the Council's secretary, Bishop G. Bromley Oxnam, 150 Fifth Avenue, New York City.

have never been interviewed, who have had no opportunity to refute allegations, in a word, for a body to act as a court, jury, and executioner, without the individual or organization concerned being heard, is contrary to American tradition and in effect is to jeopardize our freedom."

The bishops also objected to the way the committee entered the area of religious organizations, and said: "Nor, do we, at the moment, do more than call attention to the strange fact that only Protestant organizations are attacked in this report. We have far more confidence in the painstaking and patriotic procedures of the Federal Bureau of Investigation than in the hearsay and un-American procedures of this Committee that now enters the field of religion, regardless of its disavowal of that fact."

It is significant also that in developing their rebuke to the Committee on Un-American Activities the bishops appealed to their own Episcopal Address of 1948, to the position of the Federal Council of Churches taken in 1946, and to the declaration of the World Council of Churches made at Amsterdam in 1948.

For five years after 1948 the civil liberties situation in the United States worsened. During the first session of the 83rd Congress in 1953, three major committees conducted investigations of Communism. They were the Permanent Investigations Subcommittee of the Senate Governmental Operations Committee, whose chairman was Senator Joseph H. McCarthy; the Internal Security Subcommittee of the Senate Judiciary Committee, whose chairman was Senator William E. Jenner; and the House Un-American Activities Committee, whose chairman was Representative Harold H. Velde.

These congressional committees were not constituted as courts and did not have the safeguards of court procedures. When investigating individuals they often did not state what was charged against a witness but merely implied, by their questions, that the individuals were guilty of subversion. In many cases the accuser was not identified and did not appear before the committee. When the accuser did appear, little attempt was made to examine or discover the truth or error of his testimony. Thus inconclusive or unsupported evidence was often accepted by the committees as proof. Moreover, unverified and unevaluated material was at times released to the press. The accused, when allowed to appear, were permitted to have legal counsel, but such counsel could not make statements or ask questions of the committees or of other witnesses. Consequently to many observers, within and without the churches, the committees' procedures did not seem to be aimed at determining whether the accused was guilty of subversion or had been associated with "subversive" ideas, but rather that the purpose was to discover whether the accused met the committees' conceptions of loyalty.[4]

Critics of the committees' hearings felt that the disservices were fivefold: (1) they exaggerated the existence and threat of Communism; (2) they gave political significance to anyone who posed as an anticommunist leader regardless of his views on other crucial issues before the people; (3) they made people think that security against the threat of Communism would make them secure in every respect; (4) they gave a few persons the power to define Americanism and to press their definitions through fear and intimidation; and (5) they led the public to confuse Communism with "liberalism" and in this way employed a method typical of Communist techniques.

The Protestant churchman whose name became identified in heroic proportions with resistance to the worst methods of the investigating committees was Bishop G. Bromley Oxnam.[5] In June 1953, he demanded a hearing before the Committee on Un-American Activities of the House of Representatives.[6] Says Bishop Oxnam,

For seven years, that Committee had released so-called "files" containing false material concerning me. These releases appeared upon official letterheads of the Committee, and were signed by an official clerk. Later, in response to my insistent inquiries, the chairman of the Committee declared that the Committee did not vouch for the accuracy of the material released, and that such releases did not represent a conclusion or an opinion of the Committee. The releases carried no such disclaimer, in my case.[7]

When Bishop Oxnam requested a hearing, efforts were made to put the request in a bad light. One Congressman had said that the Bishop served "God on Sunday and the Communist front for the balance of the week." The Baltimore Conference of The Methodist Church unanimously demanded an apology "for (the Congress-

[4] See Rhoda E. McCulloch, *Loyalty and Freedom*, a pamphlet prepared at the request of the General Department of United Church Women, National Council of Churches of Christ in the U.S.A. See also "The Battle over McCarthyism: An Evaluation," *Social Questions Bulletin*, 44 (March, 1954), No. 3.

[5] G. Bromley Oxnam, *I Protest* (New York: Harper and Brothers, 1954).

[6] The Rev. Jack R. McMichael and Dr. Harry F. Ward also appeared before the Committee but on later dates. McMichael's evaluation, "The House Committee Hearing," appeared in *Social Questions Bulletin*, 43 (June 1953), No. 6. Oxnam disassociated himself from McMichael under questioning.

[7] *I Protest*, pp. 11-12.

man's) disrespectful remarks to our distinguished bishop and the affront given The Methodist Church."

Bishop Oxnam made a brilliant presentation and appearance before the Committee on July 21, 1953. The next day the committee, on motion of Congressman Clyde Doyle, voted "that this Committee has no record of any Communist Party affiliation or membership by Bishop Oxnam," and Congressman Morgan M. Moulder of Missouri said,

After hearing and careful consideration of all evidence, it is my opinion that Bishop Oxnam is not and never has been a Communist or a Communist sympathizer. On the contrary, he convinced me that he has vigorously opposed Communism, and has fought hard against the philosophy and conditions which breed Communism. However, I do believe Bishop Oxnam to be a liberal, but not more so than Thomas Jefferson or Theodore Roosevelt. It is my opinion that he is a loyal American citizen and is intensely possessed with the spirit of God and the work of the church he serves.[8]

In his book, *I Protest,* Bishop Oxnam has formulated a number of theses which have become part and parcel of the Methodist and ecumenical witness on the issues involved:

1. I protest against the use of the House floor to defame. It is at once ungentlemanly and un-American to abuse the privilege of immunity by broadcasting a falsehood from the House of Representatives. There is no Congressional immunity from the Biblical injunction, "Thou shalt not bear false witness."

2. I protest against procedures that are in effect the rule of men and not the rule of law; procedures subject to the prejudices, passions and political ambitions of Committeemen; procedures designed less to elicit information than to entrap; procedures that cease to be investigation and become inquisition and intimidation.

3. I protest against the inexcusable incompetency that has characterized too many members of the research staff of the House Committee on Un-American Activities, an incompetency that has both duped and embarrassed members of the Committee.

4. I protest against the release of unverified and unevaluated material from the so-called files of this Committee on official letterhead and signed by an official clerk, a practice particularly reprehensible since the Committee refuses to vouch for the accuracy of the material and insists it does not represent an opinion or a conclusion of the Committee. The alleged inclusion of a disclaimer, disavowing responsibility or accuracy, is

---

[8] *Ibid.,* pp. 19-20. See R. Niebuhr, "Communism and the Clergy," in D. B. Robertson (ed.), *Niebuhr: Essays in Applied Christianity* (Meridian Books, 1959), pp. 117-23.

no justification for the release of falsehood because to release it is in effect to validate it.

5. I protest against the un-American assumption that underlies many utterances of these Committeemen, namely, that accusation constitutes conviction. The uncorroborated identification of a citizen as a Communist by an unknown informer is not proof, and the publication of the names of persons thus identified is a vicious and un-American practice.

6. I protest against the "Big Bully" spirit and the bad manners of some Committeemen who lecture and berate a witness, and who through insinuation misrepresent the views and activities of the witness as well as secure headlines for themselves in the press. A witness is forced to listen to the homilies of the ignoramus, the misrepresentation of the unscrupulous, and the brow-beating of the bully. I protest against such degrading and un-American procedures.

7. I protest against the apparent determination of the Committee to save face rather than to face facts. I protest against its unwillingness to clean up its files and to revise its procedures so as to eliminate its abuses. Neither ignorance nor inertia can longer be tolerated. Congressmen who have introduced bills designed to bring investigating committee procedures into harmony with American tradition deserve the support of the public whose patience is well-nigh exhausted.

8. I protest against the failure of the House Committee on Un-American Activities, after spending hundreds of thousands of dollars of tax funds, to propose sound legislation to end the Communist menace or to suggest constructive proposals to remove the causes that produce Communism or creative measures to make us impregnable to Communist infiltration.

9. I protest against the constant use of the phrase "It is cited" without informing the public that most citations are not conclusions reached after careful research and confirmed by responsible bodies, but in the case of this Committee and of many State Committees are often the result of incompetent study, the collection of unverified rumor and staff listing. The use of the phrase "It is cited" is a device designed to discredit. It is sheer duplicity and is subject to the severest condemnation.

Bishop Oxnam's protest did not stand alone. Major Protestant denominations issued clear rebukes to the irresponsibility of certain Congressional committees and the National Council of Churches made a definitive study and pronouncement.[9] In addition significant

[9] American Baptist Convention, May 25, 1953; the General Council of the General Assembly of the Presbyterian Church in the U.S.A., October 21, 1953; Advisory Committee of the Executive Committee of the General Council of the Congregational Christian Churches, March 12, 1953; House of Bishops of the Protestant Episcopal Church, Nov. 12, 1953; General Board, National Council of the Churches of Christ in the United States of America, March 11 and Sept. 16, 1953 and again March 17, 1954. There were many other denominational pronouncements.

voices outside the church were deeply concerned, some having been outspoken for many years.[10] "The Message to the Church" prepared by the Methodist Council of Bishops and released on December 11, 1953, takes its significant place following the protest noted above and in the context of these other actions. The bishops said:

It has been the conviction of The Methodist Church for years, never held more strongly than now, that the right to be free implies not only freedom of the body, but also the freedom of the mind, and the freedom of the spirit.

In this time of fear and irresponsible accusation, areas of freedom of speech and thought are being narrowed all over the world. In communist lands thought control uses the techniques of absolute censorship, spying of secret police, torture, imprisonment, and death.

In our land, when we protest against such types of control, self-appointed guardians of the liberty we want for ourselves and all men may, by the calling of names, unfounded accusations, and the assertions of guilt by association, destroy the priceless heritage they claim to defend.

In the United States today there are people, some of them in our church, who are being made to believe false statements about their leaders until the human mind is filled with suspicion and the human spirit is shackled. In such an atmosphere suspicion becomes a fear, fear becomes hatred, and hatred sets a man against his neighbor, friend, and brother.

We resent unproved assertions that the Protestant ministry is honeycombed with disloyalty. We are unalterably opposed to communism, but we know that the alternative to communism is not an American brand of fascism.

Our time-honored and self-authenticated procedures for determining guilt and disloyalty can so easily be discarded in fanatical investigations, that we must oppose those who in the name of Americanism employ the methods of repression, who speak with the voice of democracy but whose hands are the hands of tyranny.

Victory over communism belongs to the triumph of spiritual idealism which has made our nation and given it any leadership it merits among the nations of the world. The President of the United States in a compelling speech last spring emphasized that victory over communism is possible only through a great spiritual movement.

In the continuing conflict between freedom and totalitarianism, religion has been and is the unfailing bulwark of free men. Faith in the sovereign goodness of God and in the inherent dignity of man has sustained the people of every nation who have dared to stand for moral right and have

[10] Zachariah Chafee, *Free Speech in the United States* (Harvard University Press, 1941) ; Elmer Davis, *But We Were Born Free* (New York: Bobbs Merrill Co.) ; George B. Galloway, "Congressional Investigations—Proposed Reforms," *Law Review* of the University of Chicago, Vol. 18 (Spring, 1951), No. 3.

refused to surrender their dreams of universal peace. This simple and stalwart faith lingers in the souls of unnumbered millions, though sometimes half-buried beneath our fears and selfish interests. The most pertinent need of this hour is a spiritual reawakening, and a turning to Almighty God.

We therefore call upon the Church to proclaim the evangel of Jesus Christ with renewed confidence and insistence in the face of every opponent, and to interpret its relevance to the fears and problems that confront us.

We call upon our people that they remember the rock out of which they are hewn, that they hold fast their Christian heritage; that they stand steadfast against every attempt to shackle the human spirit; and that with humble mind and dedicated life they pray and labor with all who confess the Lordship of Christ to the end that all men may be redeemed by his grace and his kingdom may be established on earth.

B. The Methodist Federation for Social Action and the General Conference

An equally dramatic sequence of events developed with regard to the Federation. In 1944 the Methodist Federation for Social Service (unofficial)[11] was commended by the General Conference. In 1950 the Board of Publication asked the Federation to move its offices from 150 Fifth Avenue. The Council of Bishops commended a recommendation within the Federation membership that the word "Methodist" be dropped from its title. In 1952 the General Conference requested "the Methodist Federation for Social Action (unofficial) to remove the word 'Methodist' from its name" and approved the above-mentioned action of the Board of Publication. Behind this change in official attitude by the General Conference lay a complex series of events related more to personalities and to leadership than to basic changes in the historic position of the Federation or in the outlook of its members. At significant points the controversy over the Federation shared in the confusion of the anticommunist hysteria from 1947 to 1953, which we have just discussed, and in part the controversy related to serious tension within the organization itself.

Accusations of communism and communist-front activities on the part of churchmen and church organizations in the period under review were widespread and often irresponsible. They created a great stir in Methodism as in most Protestant denominations. Their sources were both without and within the churches. From Los

[11] In 1947 the name was changed to the Methodist Federation for Social Action.

213

Angeles, "Spiritual Mobilization," for example, organized a relentless attack on everything associated with the "social gospel." In 1952 it editorialized that "the social gospel will be this year's most serious church issue." [12] The editor had his eye on both Congregational and Methodist assemblies. "The main inspiration of the new movement," said Irving E. Howard in a feature article, "was non-Christian." [13] Three years earlier John T. Flynn in *The Road Ahead* attacked the Federal Council of Churches and specifically Methodists like Bishop G. Bromley Oxnam and E. Stanley Jones. In addition he lashed out recklessly against such leaders as John C. Bennett and J. Henry Carpenter. He charged that an organization had grown up which was a "a clique of Christian ministers and laymen to poison the minds of the Christian churches in America with the principles of radical socialism." [14]

Flynn's book was widely distributed by the Committee for Constitutional Government,[15] more than 400,000 copies being distributed in a special edition in 1949. The tendency of the special edition was to identify communism with socialism, to set any form of socialism in sharp contrast with any form of Christianity, and to link with socialism the "Fair Deal" of the Truman Administration. A similar type of reasoning was employed by an influential columnist of the Scripps-Howard press chain in his coverage of the 1947 annual meeting of the Federation at Kansas City, Missouri, December 27-29.[16] We shall deal more fully with this incident below because it had a direct relationship to the General Conference of 1948 and caused serious misunderstanding in the church about the fundamental position of the Federation and many of its officers and members.

Fuel was added to the fire of misunderstanding and bitterness by a wholesale attack written by Stanley High in *Reader's Digest* in an article entitled "Methodism's Pink Fringe." [17] This repeated

---

[12] *Faith and Freedom*, 3 (May, 1952), 2. Spiritual Mobilization at first operated from the study of James W. Fifield, Jr., pastor of the First Congregational Church of Los Angeles. Later it was organized separately as a nondenominational organization.

[13] *Ibid.*, p. 3.

[14] *The Road Ahead* (New York: The Devin-Adair Co., 1949), p. 107.

[15] This secular organization had headquarters at 205 East 42nd St., New York City 17.

[16] A full analysis of the meeting and the errors of alleged communist contentions were discussed in early 1948 by the Alabama, Michigan, Mississippi, North Carolina, and Virginia *Advocates*, by the Christian and Central *Advocates*, and by *Zion's Herald*.

[17] February, 1950.

many of the earlier unproved charges and added other charges based on published materials taken out of context. Efforts were made by leading Methodists, including G. Bromley Oxnam, to have the *Reader's Digest* publish a reply which would clarify the facts and refute the allegations and insinuations, but the journal refused. Earlier the magazine had printed a digest of Flynn's *The Road Ahead*.[18]

High's article upset many ministers and laymen. Other attacks came from such unofficial, self-appointed groups as the "Committee for the Preservation of Methodism," which published lists of "Methodist Termites," and Circuit Riders, Inc., who issued a number of pamphlets. One of the latter's more aggressive pamphlets was entitled *Information Concerning the Methodist Federation for Social Action* and appeared in February 1952 with an eye to the General Conference of that year.

A book that received wide attention was *Moscow over Methodism* by Rembert Gilman Smith. It had first appeared in 1936 and grew out of an article entitled "Methodist Reds" in the Tulsa, Oklahoma, *Tribune*. Stimulated by the national sensation which accompanied *The Road Ahead* and Stanley High's article, Smith brought out a new edition of his book in July 1950. Most of the material which these persons and groups published was as unreliable as the files of the Congressional committee which we have noted in connection with Bishop Oxnam's book, *I Protest,* in the previous section.

It is significant that the crescendo of the attack on the Federation and certain of its officers and members should have reached its peak in the quadrennium from 1948 to 1952. Attacks and criticism were not new. We have already noted the severe attacks on the Federation in 1936 after it had taken a more radical position during the depression than previously. On more than one occasion the Methodist Episcopal Church had taken a critical look at its unofficial social education and action agency. These evaluations are instructive.

In 1924 the General Conference of the Methodist Episcopal Church appointed a commission to study the whole question of social service in the denomination. This commission was chaired by Bishop Adna W. Leonard, a recognized leader with conservative convictions who was not likely to be prejudiced in favor of the Federation. He presented the report of the study commission in

---

[18] See the response by Walter G. Muelder, "Mr. Stanley High's Fringe of Conscience," *Zion's Herald* (Feb. 15, 1950). Bishop G. Bromley Oxnam's "The Reply the *Reader's Digest* Refused to Publish," with an appended statement by Ralph E. Diffendorfer, was published as a pamphlet.

1932. It concluded with words of commendation for the Federation: "Our study of the work of the Methodist Federation for Social Service leads us to the conclusion that the peculiar and exceedingly important work which has been undertaken by this body of Methodists can best be prosecuted through an agency organized and operating in the manner which has characterized this Federation during the last quarter of a century." The report also stressed the fact that the "Federation does not speak, nor does it attempt to speak, officially for the Church," and concluded: "The recommendations of this social agency which, from time to time, have been given by the General Conference, have been fully justified." [19]

At that time and during the ensuing years there developed a growing interest in some kind of official agency in this field. After the unification of the three branches of Methodism in 1939, it was natural that the General Conference would take this whole question seriously into consideration, inasmuch as there were official agencies in the related fields of temperance and world peace. In considering this broad question the work of the Federation was again reviewed in 1944. Then, as part of the resolution on "The Church and Economics" the General Conference said: "For three generations the Methodist Federation for Social Service (unofficial) has pioneered in the field now under consideration. It has a history of achievement in stimulating thought and action of which the Church is proud. The work must be carried forward by some effective method." [20] In 1948 a commission was set up to study the matter of an official board or agency and in 1952 the Board of Social and Economic Relations was created. Thus the church was making up its mind about an official agency at the very time that a storm of controversy was raging concerning the Federation.

The turning point in the relation of the Federation to The Methodist Church generally must, in retrospect, be placed in 1944. In that year its two most prominent leaders retired: Bishop McConnell, who had been its president since 1912, and the editor of the *Bulletin*, Harry F. Ward, who was also its executive secretary.[21] There was some consideration at that time as to whether the Federation should continue, but the membership expressed a desire to continue and the Rev. Jack McMichael was named executive secretary. He was also editor. McMichael's leadership was increasingly controversial within the Federation from the beginning. By 1948 there was more discussion about him and more energy and time

[19] Quoted in above pamphlet by G. Bromley Oxnam.
[20] *Discipline*, 1944, ¶ 2022.
[21] Charles Webber, an associate secretary, also resigned in 1944.

devoted by officers and executive committee members regarding his methods, stands, relationships, and leadership than to the goals for which the organization existed. When the organization was reproved by the General Conference in 1952, it was already torn by dissension and had lost a number of its most respected members, largely because of the leadership issue. In addition a number of its strong chapters on the West coast, in the Midwest, and in New England had become disaffected—again, not because of the historic posture of the society, but because of lack of confidence in Mc-Michael's policies.

Important resignations antedated the controversies of 1947 and 1948. Others were to come in 1951, a full year before the General Conference in 1952. Some long-time leaders like Bishop Oxnam and Diffendorfer resigned because of conflicts over McMichael's point of view on foreign affairs and questions of basic policy. On June 9, 1947, Oxnam resigned as vice-president and as a member of the executive committee. He says: "I resigned from the Methodist Federation for Social Action because I objected to the continuous attacks of the Editor of the *Bulletin* upon John Foster Dulles, Martin Niemoeller, and Kagawa." [22] Bishop Oxnam had, moreover, not been happy with certain socialistic tendencies in the leadership of the organization by Harry F. Ward since the early thirties. In his testimony before the Congressional committee headed by Mr. Velde, Oxnam stated that he objected to the socialist objective in the masthead of the *Bulletin* as formulated in 1932. "I disagreed with that fundamentally.... Now there was one answer there, either get out or try to change it. I did the best I could. I did not change it, and I am sorry." [23]

Diffendorfer of the Board of Missions stated that he resigned from the Federation on July 20, 1948 because of a difference of opinion regarding his own views and the interpretation of an address given by John Foster Dulles before the General Conference that year. Diffendorfer said:

At that time I advocated the policy that all missionaries going into countries where communism was an issue should be trained in Russian ideology and practices of communism so as to be able to meet this issue intelligently in their fields of labor. My letter of resignation called the comment of the Federation on this speech "untrue and misleading" and "treated flippantly my stand on this matter in a manner entirely uncalled for." In this letter of resignation, I also objected to the criticism of the

[22] G. Bromley Oxnam, *op. cit.*, p. 8. See Roy, *op. cit.*, pp. 316-22.
[23] *I Protest*, p. 143.

address of Mr. John Foster Dulles before the same General Conference. The Federation *Bulletin* reported Mr. Dulles "as advancing the country along the road to war." The fact is, the speech of Mr. Dulles before the General Conference was an appeal to the world not to be stampeded into war—just the opposite of the *Bulletin's* inference.[24]

In the next four years many other leaders developed opposition to and lack of confidence in the editorial policy and practice of the *Bulletin*.

Between the resignations of Oxnam and Diffendorfer came the attack by Frederick Woltman, columnist for the *New York World-Telegram*, who covered the annual meeting at Kansas City in December 1947.[25] Having seen an advanced copy of the program, he wrote his first article prior to the first session with the lead-in sentence: "The prestige of the Methodist Church will be used in Kansas City, Missouri, this week to furnish a national sounding board for communists and fellow travelers to expound the gospel of the communist line." He held that the Methodist Federation for Social Action was a politically powerful adjunct of The Methodist Church and had closely followed the Communist party line on many issues.

This accusation was deeply resented by the officers and many members of the Federation. Bishop McConnell despised Communism with all his soul, as did all the other bishops who were members of the organization. Other officers had militantly fought communism and communist-front affiliations on the part of churchmen for many years. Woltman's accusations were repeated in a number of daily papers. When the real facts were given to the *New York Times*, that paper retracted statements it had printed. The material of the Woltman articles was reissued and used to impress the delegates at the General Conference in Boston that the Federation was an affront to the church.

When it became clear that enemies would try to make an issue of the Federation at the General Conference of 1948, the society made preparation to defend itself.[26] The delegates were given material repudiating what the organization regarded as a smear. There was

[24] Dr. Diffendorfer's statement was appended to Bishop Oxnam's, "The Reply the *Reader's Digest* Refused to Publish."
[25] Mr. Woltman was a *World-Telegram* staff writer and Pulitzer Prize winner. His articles were reproduced with other material in a pamphlet called "The Facts" and distributed at the General Conference in Boston in 1948.
[26] See Walter G. Muelder, "What About the Federation?" *Zions Herald* (April 7, 1948), pp. 315-17. See also Ralph Lord Roy, *Apostles of Discord* (Boston: The Beacon Press, 1953), pp. 308-36, "The Struggle within Methodism."

serious consideration of a libel suit. Memorials seeking to deny the Federation the use of the name Methodist or otherwise seeking to repudiate it were considered by the appropriate committee but none of these memorials was recommended for approval. A number of bishops, pastors, and laymen prepared and circulated a "statement concerning the Methodist Federation for Social Action" and distributed it at the Conference. The statement endorsed the Federation and asked that the commendation given it in 1944 be repeated. No official action was taken. And so, it survived the crisis of 1948, but worse crises were to come.

Although general charges of being "red" and "communistic" were absurd with respect to the organization as a whole and its membership in particular, all was not well within the society under McMichael's leadership as executive secretary and editor of the *Bulletin*. While no one within the organization regarded him as a Communist, many wanted him to express a more forthright and objective Christian position in handling international relations and domestic issues in which Communist fronts also had an interest. The hope was that such a position would make clear how Christian ethics brings both capitalism and communism under Christ's judgment and how this applies to the foreign policies of both the U.S.A. and the U.S.S.R. By 1950 there was very general distrust of McMichael's leadership among many who were aware of the confusion and unrest within the organization.

Several key leaders requested McMichael as editor to write a critical article on the Soviet Union, its methods, and policies, to make clear the Federation's Christian criticism of communism. Although the editor in October 1950 prepared a statement on "The Federation and Communism Charges," it fell far short of what was expected.[27] When by spring such an acceptable article was not forthcoming several key members of the executive committee resigned.[28]

Meanwhile the church was upset by the article of Stanley High which had appeared in *Reader's Digest* and which repeated unfounded remarks of Woltman. In response several of the bishops, as in Los Angeles, Syracuse, and Boston wrote open or pastoral letters on the irresponsible journalism of the *Reader's Digest*. Bishop Ledden[29] pointed out that he had personally attended the Federation

---

[27] J. R. McMichael, "A Friendly Reply to Our Critics—Methodist and Otherwise," *Social Questions Bulletin*, 40 (Oct., 1950), No. 7, 30.

[28] L. Harold DeWolf was one of these. He had been influential in converting a Communist organizer to Christianity. See Lewis R. Shultz, "I Turned from Communism to Christianity," *Zions Herald* (March 1, 1950), pp. 201-2.

[29] To the Ministers of the Syracuse Area, Feb. 17, 1950.

meeting in Kansas City in December 1947 and knew that the press had received an unjustified and maliciously distorted story of that session. He vigorously criticized the article by Stanley High. Bishop Lord wrote an Open Letter to the Editors of *Reader's Digest*. He said: "In these days of hysterical judgments when the pathological has become the normal and we see the freedoms that were America turn to fears, it is surprising, disappointing, and disheartening to find the editors of *Reader's Digest*, through irresponsible journalism, adding to the problem rather than to its solution." [30] As a protest of conscience he cancelled his subscription.

This attack and that of the previous year by Flynn could not be overlooked by the Council of Bishops. The Bishops also could not overlook the anxiety that many felt because of the use of the name Methodist in the title of the Federation. In anticipation of this situation some Federation leaders proposed that the organization change its name so as to clarify its unofficial character in the minds of the church members and urged that this be done prior to the announced meeting of the bishops in April 1950. When the Council of Bishops met, they were under the impression that the Executive Committee of the Federation favored this action.

Some of the external opposition to the Federation had little to do with alleged Communism or socialism as such, but arose from regional interests and stands taken on racial issues. After the attack by Stanley High, the *Alabama Advocate*, for example, took up the crusade. The editor acknowledged that the Federation leaders were not advocates of Communism, but wanted the organization to come out of hiding and reveal its stand on segregation. This was a surprising demand, for the Federation had vigorously opposed racial discrimination and had consistently stood for brotherhood and equality in race relations. Bishop Edgar A. Love has pointed out that Negro Methodists owe to the Federation under Bishop Hartman's leadership[31] gratitude for their role in opening the doors of the cafeteria in the Methodist Building in Washington, and that at the University of Oklahoma the Federation chapter had a part in opening the University doors to all.[32]

When the bishops met in April 1950 they expressed pride in the achievements of The Methodist Church in the field of social action. They referred to the Social Creed as a kind of Christian Magna Charta for the churches of Protestantism. They quoted from the

[30] March 6, 1950 at Boston, Massachusetts.
[31] Bishops Hartman and Love were at various times presidents of the MFSA.
[32] *Social Questions Bulletin*, 42 (June, 1952), p. 28.

Episcopal Address of 1948 endorsing the free pulpit and rejecting communism. They noted the independent nature of the Federation, commended the reported intention to drop the word "Methodist," and said further that they deplored and sharply disagreed with "certain positions taken and statements published of late in the Federation's official Bulletin." [33] They also noted that members of the Federation had recently made clear similar judgments of criticism. The bishops were indignant over Flynn's attack on Methodist leaders, on Protestantism, and on the Federal Council of Churches. They explicitly questioned the competence of Flynn, renewed their expressions of confidence in the Federal Council, and rose to the defense of G. Bromley Oxnam and E. Stanley Jones. "These men have our abundant confidence and we take a justifiable measure of pride in the outstanding contribution which they are making to world Christianity."

The question of the word "Methodist" was not settled to the satisfaction of the bishops or that of a number of leaders in the Federation, and continued to be part of the tangle of issues which confronted the membership. Most of the officers believed that a change of executive secretary was desirable and this conviction was brought to his attention in 1950. In early 1951, when McMichael chose not to resign, several members of the executive committee announced that the nominations committee would have to choose between their continued membership on the committee as officers and the nomination of McMichael. The renomination of McMichael resulted in the resignation of Bishop L. O. Hartman, Walter G. Muelder, and L. Harold DeWolf. The latter withdrew from membership as well.

During the same spring some basic conflicts arose over Mc-Michael's handling of the Korean War, especially the reports of the investigating committee on the UN.[34] *Zions Herald* published articles on the subject and Emory S. Bucke wrote an editorial, "What Hope for the Federation?" which was directed to the nominating committee. The editorial stated a view held by many who were close to the situation:

It is obvious that Mr. McMichael has no intention of resigning despite repeated requests and even demands from Federation members that he do so. It is also obvious that many members of the Federation who do not

[33] The specific positions and statements were not indicated in the formal statement by the bishops.

[34] See Walter G. Muelder, "Truth and the Social Zealot. McMichael and the U.N. Commission on Korea." *Zions Herald* (March 14, 1951) pp. 243-45. See also L. Harold DeWolf's article in the same issue dealing with McMichael and Willard Uphaus.

support Mr. McMichael, but who want him to resign, are reluctant to vote for his dismissal because they don't want to oust him "under fire." The continued work of this controversial figure has meant that in many areas the Federation has deteriorated and become merely an organization "on paper." [35]

The Boston University School of Theology chapter of the Federation invited McMichael to talk over the whole situation. After an unsatisfactory interview the chapter formally withdrew from the Federation and became an independent organization known as Action for Truth and Christ.[36] During that year there were chapter defections in several parts of the nation and at least one voted to join with the new Boston University organization.

As The Methodist Church prepared for the 1952 General Conference, where the question of the Federation was bound to come up because of the expected report of a commission on an official social action agency, the delegates were prodded by attacks from *The Methodist Challenge* and Circuit Riders, Inc. These two attacks, one an individual project and the other organized, must now be briefly noted.

The Methodist Challenge (formerly Bob Shuler's Magazine) is the private project of the long-time pastor of Trinity Methodist Church in Los Angeles. It advocates a 100 per cent conservative and orthodox Methodism. On social issues the editor waged a relentless attack on any form of liberalism. A single issue included such sentiments as these: "If I must either die or become a brother of the atheistic butchers of the Kremlin, I choose death," an attack on both the National Council and the World Council of Churches; a personal attack on the social views of Bishops Baker and Oxnam; a defense of "right to work" laws; an attack on the Jews, on Walter Reuther, and on UNESCO. The influence of *The Methodist Challenge* was not as great as that of the more highly organized Circuit Riders, Inc.

The Circuit Riders, Inc., was organized explicitly "to support those bishops and other leaders of The Methodist Church who oppose the spread of Socialistic and Communistic theories in our Church"; "to oppose all efforts to propagate Socialism and Communism and all other anti-American teaching in the Methodist Church"; "to assist in obtaining any action which may be necessary to require the Methodist Federation for Social Action to drop the

[35] March 21, 1951.
[36] The reasons for withdrawing were published in *Zions Herald*, May 16, 1951, "To Our Brethren of the Federation."

word 'Methodist' from its name and remove its influence from our Church." Circuit Riders, Inc., accused the Federation of seeking "to use the Church and its agencies to promote Socialistic and Communistic theories and anti-American activities. This is particularly evident in some phases of the youth program, in certain aspects of women's work, in some theological seminaries, and in the preparation of some of our Church and Church School literature." [37]

Circuit Riders, Inc., was particularly active prior to the General Conference of 1952, seeking to identify the Methodist Federation for Social Action with the communist line and with communist front organizations. The executive secretary was M. G. Lowman. One of the members of the executive committee was John C. Satterfield of Mississippi. Charles Parlin, who in 1952 became chairman of the General Conference's committee on the state of the church and who in the following year was to be attorney for Bishop Oxnam before the Velde Committee, was a distinguished member. Both Mr. Satterfield and Mr. Parlin resigned from Circuit Riders, Inc., after the General Conference of 1952 and have not been active in the organization since. Circuit Riders, Inc., accomplished one of its basic purposes "to assist in obtaining any action which may be necessary to require the Methodist Federation for Social Action to drop the word 'Methodist' from its name, vacate its office in the Methodist Headquarters Building, and remove its influence from our Church." [38] This attack on the Federation contained a fear of possible socialist influence in any official agency which might be established to displace or succeed the unofficial Federation. Circuit Riders, Inc. said:

It has been suggested that in 1952 there again be set up an agency to speak for the church in the realm of social action, to be known as the "Board of Social and Economic Relations." It would be instituted with the same good intentions and honest hope that inspired so many of the church leaders who set up the Methodist Federation for Social Service in 1912. But there is little reason to believe that control of its policies

[37] The officers of the M.F.S.A. were Bishop Francis J. McConnell, President; Vice-presidents: Bishop J. W. E. Bowen, Dr. Dillon W. Throckmorton, Rev. Edgar Wahlberg; Recording Secretary, Rev. Sumpter M. Riley, Jr.; Treasurer, Rev. Lee H. Ball; Ass't. Treas., Mr. William W. Reid. Rev. Jack R. McMichael was Executive Sec'y. and Editor. Associate Secretaries were W. T. Brown and Rev. Mark Chamberlin.

[38] "Information concerning The Methodist Federation for Social Action" was compiled and presented by Circuit Riders, Inc. in February, 1952. In the Circuit Riders organization, in addition to above officers, the following were on the executive committee: Clarence Lohman, Texas; Paul Sturtevant, N.Y.; Mrs. Gifford S. Adams, Michigan; M. G. Lohman, Ohio; Charlton DuRant, South Carolina; J. W. Ford, Maryland; C. Paul White, M.D., Illinois; G. Spencer Wice, California.

and actions would not drift into the hands of the same Bishops, educators, ministers, and other Methodist leaders who have dominated the Methodist Federation for Social Action during the past twenty years.[39]

Most of the charges and the information which Circuit Riders, Inc. made were the kind we have already noted in the attacks by Woltman, Flynn, and High. They also used the unevaluated materials of the House Committee on Un-American Activities against which Oxnam made his historic protest later. In 1948, the committee published a pamphlet entitled *Communism and Religion.* Question 92 asked, "What is the Methodist Federation for Social Action?" Answer, "A tool of the Communist Party, denounced by numerous loyal American Methodists." The chairman of the House Committee, John S. Wood, wrote a letter on May 10, 1951 in which he stated, "This committee has made no investigation of The Methodist Federation for Social Action, and therefore is unable to furnish you information in regard to that organization." [40] Thus in 1948 the House Committee announced a conclusion and in 1951 its chairman stated that no investigation had been made. Circuit Riders, Inc. invited its readers to review their files of the *Social Questions Bulletin* but failed to note the disclaimer by John S. Wood while repeating the charges.

What Circuit Riders, Inc. so basically overlooked was that the ethical judgment on economic life expressed by the leaders it attacked represented in effect an emergent consensus of both responsible clerical and lay opinion. Circuit Riders, Inc. was not representative of any great body of business, government, and labor judgments on American economic life. A significant consensus of enlightened leadership in these fields emerged in a series of conferences convened under the auspices of the National Study Conference on the Church and Economic Life. The basic social perspectives embodied in the reports and findings of these study conferences, though not so socialistic as those of Harry F. Ward, are broadly similar to those expressed by McConnell, Webber, Oxnam, Hartman, and others in the Federation over a quarter of a century. When one places this emergent interdenominational consensus among conservative and liberal leaders in industry, government, and church alongside the pamphlets of Circuit Riders, Inc. one can

---

[39] Circuit Riders, Inc. relation to General Conference in 1952 is described in Roy, *Apostles of Discord*, p. 326.

[40] Quoted in G. Bromley Oxnam, *I Protest*, p. 116. The letter was written to Reverend Edgar Wahlberg, M.F.S.A. Vice President. See *Social Questions Bulletin*, 41 (Nov., 1951), 30.

understand why Roy classified the latter among the "apostles of discord." [41]

Leaders like Parlin and Satterfield have emphasized the changed character of Circuit Riders, Inc. since 1952. In this latter period the organization continued to reprint earlier charges and to distribute unevaluated material even after Oxnam's vindication before the Velde Committee, after the publication of *I Protest,* and after the Methodist Council of Bishops sent its message to the church on December 11, 1953 on the whole matter of irresponsible investigations.

After the 1952 General Conference, Circuit Riders, Inc., gave wide circulation to Joseph Zoch Kornfeder's "A Compilation of Public Records, 2109 Methodist Ministers." The compilation was by its structure and profile an uncritical but vigorous effort to discredit a large number of devoted and responsible Christians. In 1957 in recognition of the fiftieth anniversary of the Federation, Circuit Riders, Inc. published "Fifty Years of Un-Methodist Propaganda." In *Recognize Red China?* it linked once more quite uncritically the Methodist leadership in the National Council of Churches to other leaders in a fresh "exposé" of participation in the World Order Study Conference held in 1958. In 1960 the pamphlet, *30 of the 95 Men Who Gave Us the Revised Standard Version of the Bible,* was cited as a source for the charges in the *Air Reserve Center Training Manual* (Student Text: NR. 45-0050, INCR V, Vol. 7) prepared by the Lackland Military Training Center in Texas. The charges were that thirty of the persons who served on the translation project have been affiliated with procommunist fronts, projects, and publications. Thus Circuit Riders, Inc. has shifted from attempts to purge Methodism to a much wider circuit of denunciations.[42]

In the midst of national turmoil, agitation within and without the churches, confusion and controversy in the Federation, and interest in an official agency for the field of social and economic relations, the General Conference of 1952 convened. After covering much of

[41] Roy, *Apostles of Discord,* pp. 326 ff. The reader may wish to compare the consensus referred to above with the pronouncements and program of the Federation and with such a book as H. R. Bowen, *Social Responsibilities of the Businessman,* chs. 5 and 6.

[42] The General Conference of 1960 adopted a report entitled "Attacks upon Churches and Churchmen" which included a specific judgment on Circuit Riders: "We regret that any Methodist contribute either money or leadership to such organizations as Circuit Riders, Inc. which utilize 'guilt by association' and 'fellow-traveler' approaches as they stir up unjustified suspicion and develop unfounded fears." (*Daily Christian Advocate,* May 9, 1960, pp. 429, 596-98.)

the same ground which the bishops had considered earlier, the Conference resolved as follows:

I. That we affirm the historic position of The Methodist Church that the General Conference of The Methodist Church is the only body authorized to speak for The Methodist Church.

II. That The Methodist Church does not approve many of the statements and policies of the Methodist Federation for Social Action (unofficial).

III. That the General Conference announces and emphasizes that the Methodist Federation for Social Action (unofficial) has no right to take any action which in any way might be construed as speaking for or reflecting the sentiment or position of The Methodist Church.

IV. That we do hereby request the Methodist Federation for Social Action (unofficial) to remove the word "Methodist" from its name; and we approve the action of the Board of Publication in requesting said federation to terminate its occupancy of quarters in the Methodist Building at 150 Fifth Avenue, New York City.

V. That we do reaffirm the historic position of The Methodist Church of the right of its people to interpret the Christian faith in the field of social and economic relations and to work to bring our social order more nearly into conformity with the teachings of Christ in accordance with the dictates of their own consciences.

VI. That these resolutions be printed in the 1952 edition of the *Discipline*.[43]

This resolution was a serious blow to what by 1952 survived of the Federation. Nevertheless, when the membership were circulated about a change of name, they decided to retain the name Methodist. The power and effectiveness of the organization has materially declined since 1952, partly due to the controversy over McMichael,[44] and partly to the role in the church assigned to the Board of Social and Economic Relations which was created at that time.

Did Methodism need an official agency? Among Presbyterians and Congregationalists official social action agencies had been organized for many years. Moreover, specific groups of problems had already called forth official Methodist agencies in the areas of temperance and world peace. What of social and economic questions, the most seriously controversial of American problems? For its part the

---

[43] *Discipline*, 1952, ¶ 2031.

[44] Albert Barnett, Chairman of the nominations committee in 1951, resigned because of conflicts with McMichael's procedures and policies. Bishop Edgar Love resigned because he had accepted the presidency on condition that McMichael would resign as Secretary and McMichael's resignation did not then materialize.

unofficial Federation had for more than twenty years intermittently supported the idea of an official board or commission in this field. Many of its outstanding leaders consistently supported the idea, but noted also the desirability of continuing a prophetic unofficial society which would pioneer in new areas and goad an official body to take action beyond that represented by the conventional opinions of complacent church membership.

In 1928 at the General Conference, Oxnam and others proposed an official agency. In 1944 the idea was presented to the General Conference again and a special committee was appointed. This commission made a recommendation to the General Conference of 1948, but members of the Committee on the State of the Church thought the matter too controversial, and the commission was continued another four years.[45] The *Christian Advocate* supported the idea when it was discussed prior to the General Conference of 1952 but editorialized that "the membership of such a board would need to be elected with great care." It added: "We hope that the membership will be chosen with extreme caution." What this meant was that "any effort to capture the board for one point of view, or to bar any point of view from membership, should be firmly resisted. All ideas ought to have a chance, no matter how far to the left or right, as the board discusses the Christian implications of all plans and methods and comes up with a viewpoint that can represent a democratic Church like ours."

One of the crucial issues in the prophetic tradition is involved in the phrase "represent a democratic church." What is the meaning of representation? What is the normative role of a democratic majority on a controversial moral issue in a Christian church? What is the relationship of the judgment of God to a "representative" opinion poll among the church membership? This problem has a more difficult answer, perhaps, in an unofficial organization on social questions than in an official agency which must "represent" equally all jurisdictions of the church and both laymen and clergy. The moral dilemmas of leadership are most acute at this point.

The four principal functions of the proposed Board of Social and Economic Relations were (1) to make available resource materials and provide local church groups with information and guidance; (2) to lead in and encourage the implementation of the Social Creed of the church; (3) to co-operate with other general agencies in

---

[45] Editorial, "Officially, Social Action," *The Christian Advocate* (April 3, 1952), p. 10. This issue carried several brief articles on the subject. See also Walter G. Muelder, "Social Action in the Methodist Church," *Zions Herald* (Feb. 6, 1952), pp. 128-29.

service projects, including pioneering ventures; and (4) to stimulate social thinking and acting within the church. These functions will be elaborated in Part II on the Structure of the Methodist Response.

C. Labor Issues and "The Right to Work"

The struggle for civil liberty and for sanity amidst anti-communist hysteria and McCarthyism is only one of the major crises in current American life. A second is industrial relations and can be symbolized by the "right-to-work" laws and the campaign to make them general in the several states. This type of campaign has its historical roots in open-shop philosophy of the "American Plan" which made headway especially during the twenties.[46]

The "right-to-work" movement, like the forces behind the enactment of the "Taft-Hartley Act," was a counter attack against organized labor's great gains under the New Deal and during World War II. Membership in all unions moved from a low of less than 3,000,000 in 1933 to over seven million in 1937, 10,500,000 in 1941, and 15,500,000 by 1947. Industries like steel and autos, which had once been the citadels of antiunionism, furnished membership power in labor growth. Trade unions had become powerful and were afflicted with the problems of power. They found themselves in favorable relationships to the Federation Administration and active in the councils of cities where formerly they had been only tolerated. Cities like Detroit and Pittsburgh were politically transformed, along with industrial and cultural change. It was inevitable that countermovements would develop.

Unpopular strikes, jurisdictional disputes, racketeering, featherbedding, Communist infiltration, and lack of democratic internal controls afflicted the labor movement in conspicuous places, though they did not characterize the labor scene generally. There developed a widespread feeling that labor was getting too strong for its own good and that it needed to be put in check. Because of their power some unions, it was believed, had misused their strength instead of bargaining "in good faith." The bulk of the charges actually brought to the attention of the National Labor Relations Board seem to have related to collateral issues affecting bargaining rather than to outright refusal to negotiate. Collective bargaining is one of the main reasons for the existence of labor organization.[47]

[46] S. Perlman and P. Taft, *History of Labor in the United States, 1896-1932* (New York: The Macmillan Co., 1935).

[47] John A. Fitch, *Social Responsibilities of Organized Labor* (New York: Harper and Brothers, 1957), pp. 38-39.

In 1947 the Congress passed the National Labor Relations Act, commonly called the "Taft-Hartley Act." Section 14, 6, provides: "Nothing in this Act shall be construed as authorizing the execution or application of agreements requiring membership in a labor organization as a condition of employment in any State or territory in which such execution or application is prohibited by State or territorial law." This section of the "Taft-Hartley Act" opened the way for the so-called "right-to-work" campaign in the various states, and the drive was encouraged by the National Association of Manufacturers, the United States Chamber of Commerce, and the American Retail Association. When F. R. Hartley retired as Congressman, he accepted leadership of the National Right-to-Work Committee. The campaign has been successful in about nineteen states, most of them nonindustrial and many located in Southeastern United States. The fundamental issue has to do with the legality and right of union security clauses in collective bargaining contracts.

By the close of the war, protected by union security provisions of one kind or another, organized labor increased its membership nearly 50 per cent. Of a total membership of 14,000,000 in 1945 the A.F. of L. could claim some 6,300,000 and the C.I.O. approximately 6,000,000. Along with this tremendous growth and attendant power came a stiffening of various public attitudes toward labor. At the beginning of the war the Federal Council of Churches passed a resolution affirming that labor not only has a right to organize but also "that it is socially desirable that it does because of the need for collective action in the maintenance of standards of living." [48] This position was coherent with the general view developed in many church bodies that organized labor makes a positive contribution to democratic life and opportunities for personality development. The growth of the church's appreciation for organized labor was often in contrast to the highly organized antilabor activities of the National Association of Manufacturers. When labor crossed the great watershed of the New Deal period, it did so in the face of fierce organized opposition. But the disclosures of the LaFollette Committee concerning the methods used by corporations to fight unions, including spies and well-stocked arsenals, as well as the more complex technique of strike breaking called the Mohawk Valley Formula, had an important effect upon public opinion and on corporations who found it expedient to adopt policies that could stand the light of day.

The popular attitude toward unions has been very pragmatic and

[48] Federal Council, *Pronouncements on Religion and Economic Life* (New York: Federal Council of Churches, 1947), p. 10.

hence capable of significant shifts from period to period. In 1937 the American Institute of Public Opinion conducted a poll in which it asked: "Do you think the attitude of the Roosevelt Administration toward labor is too friendly or not friendly enough?" The answers are significant.[49]

Group	Too Friendly	Not Friendly Enough	About Right
National cross-section total	46%	13%	41%
Republicans	80%	12%	8%
Democrats	29%	15%	56%

Once in the war the public would have little to do with strikes. An opinion poll in December 1942 found that 89 per cent favored the forbidding of all strikes during wartime.[50] During the war the American people went along with increasing labor organization and union security, but were watchful for any interference with the war effort or undue show or use of power.

At the end of the war and in subsequent years there has been confusion in the public mind and lack of generally accepted criteria.[51] The Federal Council had a positive and constructive appreciation of labor's role, but a firm insistence on democratic methods in solving disputes. In the Labor Sunday Message of 1946 the treatment of issues showed a bipolar treatment of the industrial order, stressing both union responsibility and management responsibility. It commended both for the stability which had been given industry. The following year it said: "Clearly the Church must reject both the idea that most employers are greedy conspirators who combine in gigantic soulless corporate entities and the idea that organizations of employees are usually rabble led by demagogues. . . ."[52] At the same time it saw the need for drawing both power groups together for better understanding and co-operation.

When the Taft-Hartley Act was passed, *Information Service* observed that "it is a big victory for the employing class and a corresponding setback for organized labor, no matter how it is viewed ethically."[53] Yet the article was cautious in its specific criticisms. An editorial in the nondenominational *Christian Century* observed

[49] Hadley Cantril (ed.), *Public Opinion, 1935-1946* (New Jersey: Princeton University Press, 1951), p. 881.
[50] *Ibid.*, p. 819.
[51] *Ibid.*, p. 201.
[52] Federal Council of Churches, *Annual Report, 1947*, pp. 131-32.
[53] *Information Service*, June 28, 1947, p. 1.

that "The Taft-Hartley law may turn out to be a good thing . . . if it prods the unions back into self-reliance and thus lessens government activity in labor relations." [54]

The "right-to-work" laws, of course, increase the role of government in industrial relations by intervening against union security clauses despite the rank-and-file attitudes of workers. Until the provision was eliminated in 1951, the Taft-Hartley law required that a union had to secure majority approval through a secret ballot, conducted by the National Labor Relations Board, in the bargaining unit before the union could request any form of the union security provision. From August 1947 to October 1951, the NLRB conducted 46,119 union shop authorization polls among employees. The union shop was favored in 44,795 of these polls or 97.1 per cent. This meant that more than 5,500,000 votes were cast for the union shop, or 91 per cent.[55]

After the "right-to-work" campaign was under way, the American Institute of Public Opinion under Dr. Gallup made a coast-to-coast survey of union members on the question: "Some states have passed 'right-to-work' or open shop laws that say each worker has the right to hold his job in a company, no matter whether he joins the union or not. If you were asked to vote on such a law, would you vote for it or against it?" A representative cross-section of America's sixteen million union members responded as follows: vote for law—33 per cent; vote against law—61 per cent; no opinion—6 per cent.[56]

In 1954 the Bureau of Labor Statistics analyzed 1,716 agreements covering 7,404,600 workers and found that 79 per cent of these agreements covering 81 per cent of the workers had union security provisions.[57] It is quite evident, therefore, that the "right-to-work" campaign comes as an effort to weaken union security on the part of groups in the community not themselves part of the labor movement.

When the issue was considered in the Division of Christian Life and Work of the National Council of Churches, the judgment was rendered "that union membership as a basis of continued employment should be neither required nor forbidden by law; the decision

[54] "Second Thoughts on the Taft-Hartley Law," *Christian Century*, 64 (1947), 918. During the same year, of twelve editorials involving labor eight were sympathetic and four displayed neutrality or disapproval.

[55] United Steel Workers of America, *Work for Rights* (Pittsburgh, Pa.: 1958), p. 18.

[56] *Ibid.*, p. 19.

[57] *Ibid.*, p. 20. See U.S. Dep't of Labor, *Monthly Labor Review*, June 1955.

should be left to agreement by management and labor through the process of collective bargaining." [58]

Methodist leaders participated on both sides in the discussion over union security and their statements have been used in various state campaigns. Bishops Hazen G. Werner and Richard C. Raines favored "right-to-work" laws in Ohio and Indiana respectively. The statements by Bishop G. Bromley Oxnam and Dean Walter G. Muelder were widely used against the laws in numerous states. In the fall of 1958 efforts to pass such laws failed in five of six states. As we have noted, however, all the states in the Southeastern Jurisdiction have passed such laws.[59]

The Board of Social and Economic Relations took the view that these laws constitute a real menace in restricting freedom. The Board's resolution states:

Under present federal legislation, it would appear that the right to work is a general right, not to be denied to men in the aggregate, but the right to work in a specific industrial plant or business can be subject to special conditions. This is simply to assert what has long been true in the United States, namely that man has the right and the duty to work for his livelihood. However, the conditions and terms under which he will work are subject to general social laws of health and welfare as well as rules adopted by any particular industry as a condition of employment.

It now appears that certain states by means of "right-to-work laws" would inject further restrictions by law. Such states would forbid union maintenance agreements even when mutually satisfactory to management and labor.

Such laws are miscalled "right-to-work laws" since they do not oblige anyone to give an individual a job. Their real menace lies, however, in denying by law the possibility of increasing the quality of individual freedom.

We believe that the role of the state is that of regulation so that individuals may have the maximum freedom of choice consistent with the welfare of the group, while groups may have the maximum freedom for the group action consistent with the welfare of the nation. Therefore, we hold "that union membership as a basis of continued employment should be left to agreement by management and labor through the process of collective bargaining."

However, it must be recognized that the limitation of any individual's

---

[58] Voted by the Executive Board of the Division on Christian Life and Work, June 5, 1956, as modified by the General Board on June 6, 1956 and in February 1960.

[59] In Martinsville, Virginia, the state "right-to-work" law was used to destroy the Amalgamated Clothing Workers Union in 1949. The story has been told by Charles Webber in "The Death of a Trade Union."

right to freely seek employment when such power of limitation is vested in a group places upon that group and its leaders a high degree of moral responsibility. They are only temporary trustees of rights that rest ultimately in the individual. Unless democracy and justice are the guiding principles and practice of such groups, government regulation may become necessary to return to the individual surrendered freedom. On both labor and management rests the burden of proving that this limitation of the individual's freedom is warranted in the total justice it preaches for all who labor.[60]

The stiffening of public attitudes toward organized labor is reflected in the recent Senate investigations of labor-management corruption and the current efforts to enact labor-reform legislation. The Board of Social and Economic Relations of The Methodist Church noted in its resolution on this problem that the Senate committee investigating labor-management corruption "in no way intended to reflect on the overwhelming majority of the labor unions and business men of the nation, of whose integrity the committee is firmly convinced." The resolution noted seven abuses that need correction: "(1) Lack of democratic procedure in some unions. (2) Unwarranted control by an international over a local union. (3) The misuse of union funds, particularly expense accounts, pension funds, and health and welfare funds. (4) Collusion between employers and union leaders. (5) Illegal and improper actions by certain managements, unions, and industrial relations consultants. (6) Infiltration of gangsters into some unions. (7) Lax policies of law enforcement."

In giving its judgment to the church and community for discussion and action, the board made nine suggestions in the area of legislation. Existing statutes regulating labor-management relations needed revision in the light of twelve years of experience since the Taft-Hartley Act, and some new legislation was indicated. The proposals were more comprehensive and specific with respect to legislation than any made by a General Conference since unification in 1939. Reforms would include:

(1) A requirement for all unions to hold elections at regular intervals (not less than every four years) conducted by secret ballot, without restraint and upon due notice and to conduct the business meetings of the union according to customary democratic procedures.

(2) A requirement for all unions to file with the Department of

[60] See *Contact* (May 15, 1959), pp. 3-5.

233

Labor, and/or proper state authorities, adequate financial reports, these reports to be furnished to all union members.

(3) A requirement for financial reports of all pension, health, and welfare funds, including those administered by management, to be filed with the Secretary of Labor and/or proper state authorities. For example, the report should include the amount of rebates and commissions and to whom and when paid.

(4) In order that there be no conflict of interest, a requirement for unions, union officers, and employers to file with the Secretary of Labor and/or local state authorities reports of any financial transactions between them other than bargaining agreements.

(5) A requirement for a clear delineation of the rights and authority of the international and member local unions one to another.

(6) A requirement for a secret ballot on all strike votes with due notice to the entire membership.

(7) A requirement that striking union members may participate in decertification elections.

(8) A requirement that unions may strike "farmed-out work."

(9) A requirement that there be proper supervision of union trusteeships.

The Board of Social and Economic Relations emphasized matters not only of legislation but also of personal integrity in both labor and management groups and encouragement on the part of unions to undertake internal reform measures. No governmental legislation nor changes within the corporate structure of the union can substitute for the basic need of personal integrity. "The Church must encourage men of integrity who are presently in leadership in labor unions and encourage others of similar qualities to be willing to accept leadership." [61]

D. Toward the Elimination of Discrimination

Stimulated by its crusade for world order and the various study conferences which looked to a just and durable peace, the General Conference of 1944 prepared its own resolution on "Conditions of Peace." [62] It drew on Episcopal addresses, the Social Creed, the Delaware Conference of 1942, the Princeton Conference, and the like. Part of the comprehensive statement of "Conditions of Peace" dealt with race relations and was itself a syllabus covering many phases of this problem. The General Conference made the portion of the Episcopal Address of 1944 dealing with race an integral phase

[61] *Ibid.*, p. 4.
[62] *Discipline*, 1944, ¶ 2015.

of its official preamble to proposals for action. It stated: "No one race is superior or self-sufficient. God created us not for independence but interdependence. The divine law is that we help ourselves by helping others. It is not possible to obscure the rights and claims of other races without suffering ourselves. To impair humanity at one point is to impair it as a whole."

The General Conference asked for a Study Commission "to consider afresh the relations of all races included in the membership of The Methodist Church and to report to the General Conference of 1948." The whole endeavor rested on a specific comprehensive goal: "We look to the ultimate elimination of racial discrimination within The Methodist Church." The equality of races was urged as a basis in writing the peace treaty. The church urged "the repeal of existing discriminatory legislation against the immigration and naturalization of Orientals of friendly nations, and as soon as possible of all nations." It asked that "American citizens of Indian ancestry should be regarded as citizens and no longer as wards of the government" and contended for their corresponding opportunities and responsibilities. It deplored the rising tide of Anti-Semitism and called for the promotion of better understanding with Jews. The paragraphs on the Negro have special interest in view of the subsequent discussions in Methodism and among the members involved:

We stand for the recognition of the rights of the Negro. To this end we urge:

(1) The foundation within our schools and colleges of special courses and activities promoting racial understanding.

(2) Equal opportunity in employment, upgrading, and conditions of work, in exercise of full rights of citizenship, in access to professional and business careers, in housing, in transportation, and in educational facilities. We endorse the principles underlying the Fair Employment Practice Committee and urge all agencies involved in the administration of the act to improve that administration.

(3) Equal protection through the agencies of law and order.

On the question of the Japanese-Americans the General Conference commended the work of the War Relocation Authority for its policy of finding homes and employment for the Japanese-Americans then living in relocation centers. It called upon Methodist churches to help, "especially in the preparation of communities to welcome and assimilate these persons into American life." It looked to the restoration of their full rights as citizens and the right to return to their former residences and occupations at the end of hostilities.

The conference also insisted that all Latin Americans employed in the United States be accorded just, fair, and friendly treatment.

Finally the resolution outlined certain broad procedures of courageous indictment and patient mediation. Corporate influence was to be exercised by having "interracial commissions appointed in nation, state, and every community where racial groups are to be found." Educational projects were urged at all levels and groups, including specifically the Woman's Society of Christian Service. On the minister and lay leader in every local church was placed a direct responsibility to lead out in the community by promoting racial understanding and good will.

The failure of the local churches to act boldly in implementing interracial programs was to bear strange and bitter fruit a decade later. What the church neglected to do within her own fellowship intensified her impotence in the community outside her doors of worship. The community had not learned to expect from the local church special leadership on social questions. The popular image of the church had little in it of social education and action, especially in racial matters.

The Woman's Division of Christian Service worked out a number of specific legislative proposals in the field of civil rights. One of the jurisdictional officers of the society, Mrs. Dorothy Tilly of Atlanta, Georgia, served on the President's Committee on Civil Rights. Immediately the report of that committee, published under the title, *To Secure These Rights*, taken from the Declaration of Independence, was made basic material in the society's study course, "The Bible and Human Rights." Among the legislative proposals in 1948 were: (1) A federal anti-lynching bill, (2) legislation prescribing procedures of investigating committees of Congress so that accused persons may have rights of defense, (3) anti-poll tax legislation, (4) a permanent fair employment practices commission, and (5) legislation to protect women against discrimination in economic, civil, political, and social life. The social education and action program of the Woman's Division of Christian Service has been the most forward-looking and locally effective of any of the work of the church as measured by actual instances of interracial fellowship and specificity of programming. In communities and areas where the ministers and laymen held to the segregated jurisdictional lines of the church's polity, the women often crossed these lines successfully in their meetings.

The General Conference of 1948, stimulated by the report of the President's Committee on Civil Rights and the pointed thrusts of the Episcopal Address, made a vigorous pronouncement: "The principle of racial discrimination is in clear violation of the Christian belief in the Fatherhood of God, the brotherhood of man, and the kingdom of God—the proclamation of which in word and life is our gospel. We therefore have no choice but to denote it as un-Christian and to renounce it as evil. This we do without equivocation." [63] The follow-through was declared but not specified in the statement: "We, as Christians, must address ourselves with patience and perseverance to the infinitely complicated task of removing racial discrimination, root and branch, from our common life, both in the church and in the nation in which we live."

President Truman pleased some Methodists by his appointment of an able committee on Civil Rights and he asked the Congress to follow out its excellent recommendations. The opposition of a powerful minority of Democrats prevented such legislation from being enacted. The national Democratic convention in 1948 became the scene of a sharp debate on civil rights. When strong civil rights planks were inserted in the platform, it became clear that the Democratic party was committing itself to the extension of civil rights in this country regardless of the strong disapproval of some members of the party. This minority group registered its protest by nominating Governor Thurmond of South Carolina as candidate for President.[64]

In two years prior to the elections of 1948 the Republicans were in control of both houses of Congress and had an opportunity to make good their 1944 platform pledges on civil rights. The energy of the party leadership went into tax cuts and military preparations rather than real assistance to minority peoples, to such an extent that the executive secretary of the N.A.A.C.P. complained of "the abysmal failure of the Republican-controlled 80th Congress to help carry out any of the pledges of the 1944 Republican platform to enact federal legislation against lynching, the poll tax, and employment discrimination. The scuttling of public housing and slum clearance at the behest of the powerful real estate lobby—all of these were obviously believed to be unimportant because the people apparently were 'ready for a change.'" [65] The optimism of the Republicans was shattered by the re-election of President Truman.

When the General Conference of 1952 convened in San Francisco, it once again took a position on civil rights and asserted that "there is no place in The Methodist Church for racial discrimination or

[63] *Discipline*, 1948. The same idea was repeated in 1952 and 1956.
[64] "Methodist Pronouncements Compared with Political Platforms," a booklet published by the Methodist Federation for Social Action, New York, 1948.
[65] Quoted in *Ibid.*, p. 14.

racial segregation." [66] It related this judgment to the world situation and noted the promulgation by the United Nations of the Universal Declaration of Human Rights (1948). Realizing that it was up to the church "to free itself utterly from racial discrimination and segregation, the General Conference recommended five specific and feasible immediate steps: (1) full participation in all activities of the Methodist fellowship without discrimination or segregation; (2) equality of accommodations at national and international conferences of the church; (3) "that the institutions of the church, local churches, colleges, universities, theological schools, hospitals, and homes carefully restudy their policies and practices as they relate to race, making certain that these policies and practices are Christian"; (4) that the agencies and institutions of The Methodist Church employ their staffs without racial discrimination; (5) that the churches of the Central Jurisdiction be especially apprised of the enabling legislation whereby they could become members of another jurisdiction and thus move out of their segregated status. In 1956 the General Conference ordered a study of the whole jurisdictional structure of the church and reiterated many of the points just outlined. It facilitated the process of transferring Negro churches.

Because of its monumental consequences for education and the whole field of race relations, the Supreme Court decision of 1954 has been pivotal on the American scene since that date. On May 17 in an historic and unanimous decision the U.S. Supreme Court outlawed all public school segregation. Chief Justice Earl Warren said, in part: "We come then to the question presented: Does segregation of children in public schools solely on the basis of race, even though the physical facilities and other 'tangible' factors may be equal, deprive the children of the minority group of equal educational opportunities? We believe it does. . . . We conclude that in the field of public education the doctrine of 'separate but equal' has no place."

The first official group of The Methodist Church to speak following the Supreme Court's decision was the Woman's Division of Christian Service. In May 1954, they said:

We affirm anew our determination to work with greater urgency to eliminate segregation from every part of our community and national life and from the organization and practice of our own church and its agencies and program. We rejoice that the highest tribunal of Justice in this land, the Supreme Court of the United States, proclaimed, on May 17, 1954, that segregation in public education anywhere and everywhere

[66] Many of these points had been urged from time to time over a twenty-year period. *Discipline*, 1952, ¶ 2027.

in this nation is an infringement of the Constitution and a violation of the Fourteenth Amendment.[67]

When the Council of Bishops met in November, 1954, they issued the following official statement:

The historic decision of the Supreme Court abolishing segregation in the public school system is in keeping with the attitudes of The Methodist Church. In our official pronouncements, including the Social Creed and Episcopal Address adopted by the 1952 General Conference, our position has been clearly stated. The Supreme Court recognized that such a ruling brought with it difficulties of enforcement, and therefore made provision for sufficient time to implement its decision. . . . The ultimate success of the ruling will be determined in the hearts of people of the nation. Thus the church is furnished with an unequaled opportunity to provide leadership during this period in support of the principles involved in the action of the court.

The next major agency of the church to express itself was the Board of Social and Economic Relations which issued a "Message on Race Relationships" in January, 1955. It rooted its message in the General Conference utterances of 1948 and 1952. After acknowledging the difficulties involved in implementing the Supreme Court's decision it recommended:

(1) That the decision of the Supreme Court be accepted graciously and gracefully. (2) That our people . . . practice the conviction that no one should be discriminated against on the basis of race or color. (3) That we practice and preach our belief that we are all children of the same Heavenly Father. . . . Therefore, we encourage our churches everywhere to move resolutely forward toward the goal of full participation of the people of all races in the life of the church and the community.

The racial crisis within the church is one of the most serious problems that has confronted it in the present century. The dilemmas of leadership reflect the sectional tensions and conflicts involved. The bishops of the Southeastern Jurisdiction have not always stood with their brethren in the Council of Bishops on the matter of public-school desegregation, and they have been subject to considerable criticism for abdication of leadership in implementing the pronouncements of the church. On the other hand, they experienced considerable pressure from the constituency which elects them through the Jurisdictional Conference.

[67] *The Methodist Woman*, 14 (July-August, 1954), 483.

Racial problems abound in all sections of the United States. Each has its own minorities to understand, integrate, accommodate, or assimilate. In no state are attitudes on race unanimous, but divided. Since the Negro population is still more largely concentrated in its traditional American location, Southern views and practices are peculiarly decisive both in the churches and in national politics. By 1959 nine of the Southern states having laws requiring segregation had begun compliance with the Supreme Court's decision on segregation in the schools. Several large cities in four of the remaining eight Southern states began actions of compliance within a few years of the court decision.

There are regional complications sometimes within states. But in four states political leaders have played on majority opinion to work to by-pass the decision legally or to defy the ruling. Many white Methodists in the South support the Supreme Court decision and the action of the General Conference. The Negroes overwhelmingly support these positions. Some Methodists are profoundly disturbed about the thought of integration in church or community and have organized vigorously to combat it. Some of these are active members of White Citizens Councils and combine their efforts with continued participation in Circuit Riders, Inc., to whom we have referred above. We shall have more to say about race and the jurisdictional system when we consider the structure of the Methodist response below.[68]

Indicative of various local responses are statements and actions in places like Houston, Texas; Atlanta, Georgia; Little Rock, Arkansas; Montgomery, Alabama. One hundred seventy-three Houston Area ministers, in October, 1957, urged "every God-fearing citizen to encourage respect for our courts and obedience to all decisions." "The Supreme Court," they said, "has ruled on an issue which affects our public schools and the sacred American concept of the basic dignity and worth of every individual. . . . We believe that for an individual or group to defy decisions with which he or they are not in agreement is to encourage other dangerous elements in our society to follow the same destructive procedure for their own ends." [69]

Methodists were leaders among the eighty ministers of Atlanta,

[68] In Alabama some Methodists have organized the Methodist Laymen's Union with the purpose of saving The Methodist Church from integration and disunion. In 1959 they succeeded in getting state legislation favorable to their holding churches or their property should secession take place. Analogous legislation was passed in Mississippi in 1960.

[69] Houston *Post* (Oct. 18, 1957). Quoted in *The Road to Brotherhood* (Chicago: The Board of Social and Economic Relations, 1959), p. 19.

Georgia, who in November 1957 issued a manifesto containing six principles of basic importance for "our thought and conduct." [70] These meant:

(1) Freedom of speech must at all costs be preserved. (2) As Americans and as Christians we have an obligation to obey the law. (3) The public-school system must not be destroyed. (4) Hatred and scorn for those of another race, or for those who hold a position different from our own, can never be justified. (5) Communication between responsible leaders of the races must be maintained. (6) Our difficulties cannot be solved in our own strength or in human wisdom . . . but only through prayer.

One of the most tragic aspects of the new crisis in the South is what it revealed of the lack of real communication across racial lines in many communities, including ministers and even bishops. Hearings held in centers like Baltimore, Maryland; Orangeburg, South Carolina; New Orleans, Louisiana; and St. Louis, Missouri, under the Commission to Study the Jurisdictional System, showed that many white Methodist ministers had no real awareness of their Negro colleagues and churches serving in the same towns and cities. This lack of communication is itself a product of the philosophy that separate can be equal.[71] So persistent is this point of view in parts of the South and elsewhere that the Board of Social and Economic Relations in a study book, *The Road to Brotherhood*, felt obliged to include a chapter which defends this doctrine along with that genuinely expressed in the official pronouncements of the church.

Thus W. B. Selah of Jackson, Mississippi, says: "The policy of separate but equal opportunity fits the conditions under which the races live in the South and commends itself to the reason and conscience of good men of both races." [72] There is no suggestion in the argument presented by Selah that the present attitudes of persons in local churches on such an issue ought to be changed or that the ministry ought in Christ's name to seek to do so.

Capitulation to local mores and customs or accommodation to regional traditions in race relations compounds the dilemmas of

---

[70] *Loc. cit.* This group has since grown to more than 300. See Atlanta *Constitution* (Nov. 2, 1957).

[71] Harry F. Richardson stated in *Dark Glory*, published ten years earlier (New York: Friendship Press, 1947) that the co-operation of the white ministers with the colored pastor and his church is not nearly as great as that of the white laymen (p. 159).

[72] *Ibid.*, p. 42.

leadership when fundamental moral issues present themselves. The racial crises in Montgomery, Alabama, and in Little Rock, Arkansas, are examples. Throughout the world men have acclaimed the "Stride Toward Freedom" represented by the successful bus boycott in Montgomery led by Martin Luther King, Jr. Roger Baldwin has said that "no event in the long struggle for racial equality in the United States was so novel and triumphant as that of the Negro community of Montgomery, Alabama, against segregation on public buses . . . no story like it has come out of the conflict of races!" [73]

Part of the opposition to the bus boycott was from persons like the Reverend E. Stanley Frazier, then minister of St. James Methodist Church,[74] and one of the most outspoken segregationists in Methodism. Here we see the church in conflict with itself, for Martin Luther King, though Baptist, was trained at Methodism's Boston University School of Theology and was applying the theology and Christian social ethics he studied there to the problems his people encountered in the deep South.[75] On the other hand, the Reverend Mr. Frazier was quite an aggressive organizer of the Alabama delegates to the General Conference in 1956 in resisting the development of the church's position on race. His "Information Bulletin" [76] stated: "Many of us at the General Conference favored the idea of a study commission as a barrier to any radical action that the Conference might have taken following heated debate; but we protested including in the resolution creating the commission any statement that declared segregation to be unchristian or which would be regarded as an instruction to the Commission to rid The Methodist Church of all segregating factors."

In his campaign Frazier attacked such leaders as Waldo Beach of the Duke Divinity School and Albert E. Barnett of Candler School of Theology for their integrationist ideas and attacked the Methodist publications for printing such sentiments as those of Beach. What drew the special fire of Frazier with respect to Barnett was the latter's statement in *The Christian Century* [77] supporting the N.A.A.C.P. A powerful group of laymen in Alabama have organized to resist any and all desegregation and integration in The Methodist Church.

In Little Rock the Methodist ministry in the fall of 1957 found

[73] Martin Luther King, Jr., *Stride Toward Freedom* (New York: Harper and Brothers, 1958).
[74] *Ibid.*, pp. 115-18.
[75] *Ibid.*, pp. 100-107.
[76] See *Information Bulletin* (August-September, 1957) issued by Association of Methodist Ministers and Laymen, Montgomery, Alabama.
[77] May 30, 1956.

itself along with the leaders of all the churches caught in a massive political and violent resistance to educational integration.[78] Little Rock's school board had long been on record with an intent to comply with the Supreme Court decision of May 17, 1954; but on September 2, 1957, the Arkansas National Guard surrounded Central High School under orders from Governor Faubus and on September 4 the Guard refused nine Negro students to enter. On Friday, September 20, Federal Judge Davies directed Governor Faubus to stop interfering with integration at Central High. Conflict grew intense and in due course the United States Army intervened under orders from President Eisenhower.

Pettigrew and Campbell, who made a careful study of the role of the ministry in these critical circumstances, are convinced that "the Protestant ministry is potentially the most effective agent of social change in the South in the decade ahead." But a review of clerical activity in Little Rock revealed that the ministry has not provided the united and forceful leadership needed and expected.[79] The "Protestant dilemma" is between "the organizational concerns of money and members and the effective expression of principle." There was need for unified ministerial action, for early, precrisis indications of sentiment, and the full use of moral sanctions. It is important to place the stress on the concept of dilemma, for Methodism at least played a role that was ambivalent, and hence rather ineffective. Moreover, it was internally divided in its episcopal counsels, despite the official position of the denomination as a whole.

After the federal troops had taken over the protection of Negro high-school students and tension ran high in the city of Little Rock, Paul E. Martin, Methodist Bishop of Arkansas, wrote in the *Arkansas Methodist* for Oct. 10, 1957 as follows:

Never have the Christian forces been given a greater opportunity to exert an influence for good than in this present crisis. . . . The real Christian must stand for obedience to law and orderly process for settling differences within the framework of our government. . . . We recognize the differences of opinion shared by sincere men and women concerning the matter of integration in the schools. . . . Now is the time for the Christian Church in the spirit of prayer to call upon all good people to encourage the forces that will unify rather than divide our people. . . . In this crisis, let the church be the church.

[78] Ernest Q. Campbell and Thomas F. Pettigrew, *Christians in Racial Crisis: A Study of Little Rock's Ministry* (Washington, D.C.: Public Affairs Press, 1959). The foreword is by Walter G. Muelder.
[79] *Ibid.*, p. viii.

Support of law and order had earlier been pledged by fifteen ministers in a protest against Governor Faubus' action, with Methodist clergy the largest single group represented; but none of the major church administrative officials in Little Rock signed the protest.

A year later the situation was worse in several respects. When the schools were closed, the city's leading Methodist Church was used for tutorial sessions. The Highland Methodist Church was used by the Faubus-spawned Little Rock Private School Corporation. A council of Methodist laymen, which spoke threateningly of the need for formation of a new Methodist Church, South, was formed in Little Rock in the fall of 1958.[80] Stout segregation sentiments were expressed at the organization meeting, attended by some three hundred persons. Some prominent lay leaders voiced the idea that their "ministers' minds were befuddled." On the other hand, the Woman's Society for Christian Service rallied its forces to combat the deteriorated and chaotic situation.[81] By and large the response of the church was confused by decades of default in implementing its resolutions.

E. In Support of the United Nations

International concerns in The Methodist Church in the postwar period are clearly oriented to the idea of World Organization. On this major issue it has confirmed the positions developed by the great ecumenical organizations like the National Council of Churches and the World Council of Churches. Indeed, Methodism has taken every occasion to state its own position in relation to these great bodies as part of the emergent ecumenical concensus on Christian social ethics. In 1944 the General Conference said: "The time is at hand when the Church must rise in its might and demand an international organization which will make another war impossible." Bishop James C. Baker and Walter Van Kirk were Methodists prominently present as consultants at the San Francisco conference which wrote the United Nations Charter and brought the United Nations into existence. Charles F. Boss also served as an accredited nongovernmental representative there.

The Commission for World Peace said: "We rejoice in the existence of the United Nations organization which offers the opportunity of international cooperation for world security and survival. This organization must now be made to work for the ends of justice,

---

[80] *Ibid.*, p. 114.
[81] In 1959 the constructive forces for integration handed Governor Faubus his first significant defeat on the school issue.

security, and peace." The Commission also recognized the limitations of the UN organization and operation, but asked that Christians give it the support of prayers and political action. They saw it as a base on which a better political order can be developed. "We look toward the development of a true form of world government out of machinery already established and functioning in the United Nations." [82]

Support of the United Nations has been expressed in every General Conference statement on world order from 1948 on and is in the Social Creed of 1960. Concerns on specific issues in international life have been expressed as well as general commitments.

When in 1948 the "Marshall Plan" was being vigorously discussed, the Woman's Division of Christian Service stated that "it was regrettable that the 'Marshall proposal' was not made through the United Nations Economic Commission for Europe." Support for the European Recovery Program was expressed by the Commission on World Peace, but it qualified this endorsement by expressing "the hope that the program will not be an extension of American imperialism in Europe, that the nations helped will be free to choose their own basic economic patterns, and that the door will be left open for participation in its work and scope by other nations." [83]

Between 1944 and 1948 one or more major Methodist boards or agencies urged the following actions: entrance of the U.S.A. into the UN; prayerful support of the UN; co-operation with a UN resolution against "false reporting and inciting to new war"; entrance of the U.S.A. into various subsidiary organs of the UN; appropriations for UNESCO's program of "defense of peace" comparable to appropriations for military defenses; continuation of UNRRA or its equivalent; placing the territories in the Pacific occupied in the recent war under the Trusteeship Council; extension of reciprocal trade agreements; assistance to Greece and Turkey through the UN; and relief and rehabilitation for Europe through the Economic Commission for Europe.

In 1944 the General Conference had requested the Congress to postpone action on postwar conscription until after the war. A few months after the conclusion of hostilities, the Council of Bishops (December 5, 1945) adopted a position opposing universal military conscription or compulsory training in peacetime. They reaffirmed this position in 1947. The pamphlet supporting this pronouncement stated that universal military training was too costly, that it did not

[82] Quoted in *Methodist Pronouncements Compared with Political Platforms,* (1948).
[83] *Loc. cit.* (1948).

contribute to research, and that hastily trained men would actually weaken national defense, not help it.[84] The Commission on World Peace was much more vigorous in its attack on military training, asked for further legal recognition of the conscientious objector, and opposed the R.O.T.C. on Methodist College campuses. In this connection it stressed the point that civil liberties were based on the gift of God and not a gift of government.[85]

Methodists believed in waging peace-making. The church which in 1944 had been deeply divided now pulled together and moved forward. Thus the 1948 General Conference placed its authority behind vigorous action for peace. Numerous seminars were held thereafter in Washington and New York as a co-operative venture of the Commission on World Peace, the Board of Missions, and the Methodist Student Movement. The agenda comprised the crucial international issues then under national consideration, such as the Marshall Plan, Point-Four Program, a German peace treaty, the expansion of world communism, problems of displaced persons, and the like. The Board of Education also carried on programs of positive international understanding through work camps. Methodist agencies sought to provide understanding amid the rising tide of anti-communist hysteria and asked for real study of communism, of the U.S.S.R., of the major issues before the United Nations, and of the termination of "cold wars" by positive means. Consistently the Commission on World Peace sought reduction and control of armaments and pointed out the dangers of the militarization of the U.S.A. The Commission withheld support of the North Atlantic Pact and urged further study of its various aspects.

Prior to the Korean War, the Commission on World Peace suggested *de facto* recognition of Communist China's government while withholding approval of its Communist character. After the outbreak of the Korean War in 1950 the Commission at its annual meeting, though not denouncing the United Nations' action or passing judgment on existing facts, analyzed the situation critically and the evil events that led up to the war. By way of contrast, the Central Committee of the World Council of Churches supported the intervention of the UN.

In 1952 the General Conference adopted an extensive resolution on "The Church and War and Peace." This statement, based on

[84] *National Defense? Yes. U.M.T.? No.*

[85] Annual Meeting of the Commission in 1951. After a considerable struggle in the Subcommittee, of which Georgia Harkness was chairman, a significant agreement was achieved and the basis laid for a forward program in world peace to be adopted by the General Conference.

the historic achievement of 1948, provides a comprehensive statement of the position of the church and will therefore be considered more fully in the next section of the present volume, where systematic interpretations of the church's position will be presented. Several characteristics of the Methodist response to the challenge of war and peace as expressed in the *Discipline* in 1952 may be noted, however.

In the first place, the church reaffirmed its general position of 1944, incorporated since then in The Methodist Social Creed: "Christianity cannot be nationalistic; it must be universal in its outlook and appeal. . . . The methods of Jesus and the methods of war belong to different worlds." The church must, accordingly, use its spiritual power to destroy war. Secondly, its rejection of the idea of preventive war was expressed as concurrence in the Report of the Federal Council of Churches' Commission on the Christian Conscience and Weapons of Mass Destruction. Similar concurrence was expressed in the third phase with the Universal Declaration of Human Rights. Fourthly, it reinforced the Episcopal Address as it dealt with disarmament and the earlier action of the Council of Bishops in their opposition to any system of universal military training. In this way the positions developed by various boards, councils, and agencies were brought into a comprehensive official position by the church as a whole.

Other positions of special significance included an emphasis on the moral and spiritual conditions of peace; a program of relief of suffering through Church World Service and the Methodist Committee for Overseas Relief; a defense of the UN as "our best political hope of peace"; a call for the revision of the UN charter in such manner "as to enable that body to enact, interpret, and enforce world law against aggression and war"; rejection of R.O.T.C. installations in church colleges as a violation of the separation of church and state; rejection of the ideology and practice of Communism, along with improved negotiations with the U.S.S.R. through the United Nations; proclamation of the undying interest in the freedom and political self-determination of all peoples; urging increased resources for Point Four and technical assistance programs through the UN as much as possible. The resolution ends with a resounding defense of civil liberties, and criticizes not only the "thought control (which) uses the techniques of absolute censorship, surveillance by secret police, torture, imprisonment, and death" as practiced in some countries, but also the techniques of "social rejection, calling of names, demands for 'loyalty oaths,'

247

denial of employment, irresponsible accusations, and assertion of 'guilt by association' employed in others." [86]

In 1956 most of these points were repeated and emphasized, the church relating its general perspective to that of the Assembly of the World Council of Churches in 1954. The resolutions of 1952 and 1956 have, with slight modifications, made the perspectives of the Commission on World Peace the official view of the church.

[86] *Discipline*, 1952, ¶ 2026.

PART TWO

The Structure
of the Methodist Response

CHAPTER EIGHT

Itineracy and the Conferences

A. Itineracy and Episcopacy

IN THE FRONTIER PERIOD THE WORK OF THE CIRCUIT RIDER was one of the most important factors in Methodism's success. He covered ofttimes one or more states, went from place to place on his horse in all kinds of weather—baptizing, marrying, teaching, counseling, preaching, distributing religious literature from his saddlebags, organizing Sunday schools and churches, administering informal justice, and otherwise advancing personal and social righteousness. Usually he visited each station of his circuit once a month, and these visits were often community events. Both the federal government and the state of Oregon have paid tribute to the circuit rider. The federal government sanctioned the fine statue of Francis Asbury (1745-1816), the greatest of the circuit riders, on a prominent place in Washington, D. C. The state of Oregon erected "The Circuit Rider" in front of the Oregon capitol. President Theodore Roosevelt wrote of frontier Methodism and its preachers as follows:

Its essential democracy, its fiery and restless energy of spirit, and the wide play it gave to individual initiative, all tend to make it peculiarly congenial to a hardy and virile folk, democratic to the core, prizing individual independence above all earthly possessions, and engaged in the rough and stern work of conquering a continent. . . . The whole country is under a debt of gratitude to the Methodist circuit riders, the Methodist pioneer preachers, whose movement westward kept pace with the movement of the frontier, who shared all the hardships in the life of the frontiersman, while at the same time ministering to that frontiersman's spiritual needs and seeing that his pressing material cares and the hard and grinding poverty of his life did not wholly extinguish the divine fire within his soul.[1]

[1] Quoted in Anson Phelps Stokes, *Church and State in the United States,* I, 660.

251

Perhaps T. R.'s implications are a little more military than is consistent with Methodist peace doctrine. When he said "conquer" a continent, he meant literally that—at the expense of the Indians!

The itinerant system has served the personal and social witness of the gospel in the twentieth century as well as in the pioneer period of the nation's history.

Space does not permit a thoroughgoing study of the theory and practice of the system at mid-century, but a few relevant points are in order. It makes possible a periodic review of effectiveness; the best matching of problems and personnel; the security of professional tenure if not in a particular church then at least in the conference; a town, city, county, district, and conference-wide strategy for assessing problems and building programs; and introduction of new talent and ideas in difficult situations. With a prophetically strong bishop and an alert, committed cabinet of district superintendents the itinerant system linked to a well-conceived connectional program can accomplish a great deal.

There are handicaps to itineracy as well as benefits, depending on the other leadership factors in an annual conference. Prophetic spirits may be removed from situations where they are needed in order to keep the wrong kind of peace; men may be kept moving too frequently to develop effective programs of social education and action; courageous and intelligent preachers may be "sent to Siberia" if the hierarchy wishes to punish them; and men with a popular touch and a knack at money raising may be given preferment and kept in prestige pulpits or in leading churches which fail to lead their people anywhere but to institutional success. There is, finally, the almost inevitable temptation to try to curry favor with those having the power of appointment, this leading to silence or flattery. The consequences for both bishop and minister may be tragic.

All in all, itineracy becomes what the appointive powers make it —an instrument of courage, experimentation, and innovation or an instrument of complacency, conformity, and worldly compromise. On such matters the crux of the problem may be "prophet" versus "pastor" and not itineracy as such.

Volume Four will deal fully with the theory and practice of strategy. We should note, however, that the individual minister has a number of reference points which he must take account of as he seeks to bear witness to the whole gospel of Christ for persons and society. Each of these has some bearing on itineracy and on the structure of the Methodist response to social events and conditions.

First of all, the minister has his own understanding of the gospel, his own commitment to Christ and the Kingdom, and his own inner integrity. The threshold of compromise is determined to an important degree by the prophetic consciousness, talent, and dedication of the individual pastor.

The second reference point is the pastor's fellow ministers. Innovation or the lack of it depends to a great extent on how a man seeks to stand with his peers and how they rally to him and support him. Here the fellowship of the Annual Conference plays a determining role in the lives of many men. Oftentimes whole conferences tend to be "liberal" or "conservative" depending on the quality of the interaction among the men over a period of years. Leadership among one's peers is a significant social category.

A third reference point is the administrative officers of a conference, the district superintendents and the bishops. How they act in crucial times of testing may make or break a pastor in a social crisis. The great socially minded bishops of the church are great not only because of the positions they have publicly taken, but because of the positions they have solidly taken behind men who deserved and needed their help. The connectional system can keep ministers from being isolated and broken by reactionary forces.

The fourth reference point is the program of the Annual Conference integrated into that of the area, the jurisdiction, and the General Conference. Men need resources from the General Boards and Agencies and from organized men's and women's groups. But above all, they need to be effectively related to the great body of official legislation which The Methodist Church has developed. Individual ministers have a duty and a right to stand on the Social Creed—and to know that their church is solidly behind them when they take a stand.

The fifth point of reference for a clergyman is the membership of the church, the whole body of the laity. We have seen in our discussion of race relations how vulnerable a minister may be at this point. So long as Methodism is built on the voluntary parish membership plan, the dilemma of leadership will be real. In most places people do not have to be Methodists to be religiously served—and a man who has lost his members is a "problem" pastor. The dilemma is the more acute because in the midst of high mobility of population most laymen do not give vigorous leadership on controversial issues a high priority in their churchmanship.

These five points of reference must be cumulatively and mutually supporting if the structure of Methodist response in a local church is to be effective.

Itineracy as a social reality is not what it once was. It must, accordingly, not be treated as a static norm. Preachers, district superintendents, and bishops do not itinerate as they formerly did. In an age of accelerated mobility in many phases of American life, including above all the general population, Methodist clergy tend to move less often than formerly. Often the minister remains and the congregation moves. Especially urban clergy complain that they preach to a parade. Thus from an historical perspective there has been a marked decline in itineracy. Function for function there is quite a difference between a "presiding elder" and a "district superintendent," though they refer to the same office in the polity. The episcopacy was once quite itinerant and has become essentially diocesan in many instances. It is certainly more sectional, jurisdictional, and parochial than it once was—despite a bishop's many trips to board and commission meetings. At all levels of denominational structure and function the posture of Methodism's response has changed and is changing as far as itineracy is concerned, thus affecting the leadership of the church in society.

The privilege and the price of the mission of the church is leadership. If leadership is abdicated, the mission is betrayed. This betrayal may be deeper than the relatively practical question of compromise, tactics, or strategy. The local pastor faces the theological fact that the church is not an association of private individuals who decide on the spiritual and moral rules of their club, but the church has a head, Jesus Christ, who calls forth a present witness to the righteous love of God, which is the Holy Spirit. It is God who lays upon the redeemed community the obligation to lead the secular community into the paths of righteousness. In all types of social questions, economic or racial, for example, this principle of leadership holds. Often the moderates in the church, not wishing to stir up or experience tension and conflict, lapse into silence and inaction. In so doing they invite the worst forms of evil and violence. They forsake the community to the uncompromising fanatics and extremists and give no effective ministry to the confused majority. As Harry S. Ashmore has said, "When responsible men default, irresponsible men take power." [2]

This last principle holds as much for bishops, annual conferences, jurisdictions, and the General Conference as for the pastor and the local church. All of these may succeed in building a strong social institution which they name the church and still betray Christ and

[2] Harry S. Ashmore, *An Epitaph for Dixie* (New York: W. W. Norton, 1957), p. 44. See V. O. Key, *Southern Politics in State and Nation* (New York: A. A. Knopf, 1950).

his church which through their compromise they may not really have built. Many people are intimidated today because they are bewildered and confused. They are frequently intimidated in race relations, as Ashmore says, "not so much by the militant segregationists as by the smothering mores of the Southern community." This majority group remains impotent because it remains, for the most part, without public or private leadership.[3] Analogous comments can be made on most social issues in every part of the nation.

The bishops of The Methodist Church have special responsibility not only to their respective areas, but to the whole country. Their leadership affects the pervasive and integrating function of religion in all aspects of our interpenetrating culture. They must, therefore, address themselves continually to those values and norms, those meanings and processes, which give cohesive meaning and value to society, not merely to the institutional growth of the church as a specialized society. There is a marked tendency for the dominant values of society and the controlling values of religion to coalesce, for they interact in an interdependent whole. Either religion will aggressively shape and guide the energies and purposes of society in its most basic relationships and institutions or religion will be transformed by the other power centers of society—or the church may become a world apart, a ghetto of ineffective spirituality. As the chief pastors of the church, the bishops have responsibility to lead not only the gathered community, the people of God, but also to bring every institution of society captive to Christ and the kingdom of God.

The bishops have provided a number of types of leadership. Some have contributed to the basic literature of the "social gospel" movement; some have been active members and officers of unofficial bodies like the pioneering Methodist Federation for Social Service; some have headed investigating committees in industrial areas; some have been chairmen of major reform boards of the denomination; some have skillfully gathered outstanding leadership for social causes to their areas; some have been directly involved in political action; some have served on ecumenical commissions and been resource leaders for great study conferences; some have given the prestige of their personalities and office to unpopular causes; some have protested in person unjust process in civil liberties matters; some have protected younger ministers from persecution and reprisals, though some have thrown them to the wolves; and some

---

[3] *Ibid.*, p. 31. Quoted in *The Perkins School of Theology Journal* (Spring, 1958), p. 12.

have sponsored new and creative forms of ministry. The combined roles of prophet, priest, and administrator have given Methodist bishops great spiritual, moral, and social power.

National and international problems require national and international leadership. When the bishops have addressed themselves to these problems, they have generally won the plaudits and respect of their fellow ministers. A few bishops have been pre-eminent in exercising ecumenical and national responsibilities.

There is a real question whether the present jurisdictional system tends to circumscribe the image which a Methodist bishop has of his role in social leadership. It is, of course, not a question of choosing between area administration and world administration. Both dimensions of the church's work are integrally related. But it is a question of goals. Goals determine administration and canalize the energy of the church. Jurisdictional goals are not sufficient to meet global challenges. Bishops, therefore, need to be locally effective and relevant in the light of world-wide Christian values.

As a group the bishops have exercised historically significant leadership through their Episcopal Addresses. In the South, before unification, these utterances were often the chief and sometimes the only voice which the church expressed as a whole. Since there was no unofficial body for many years like the Federation and no Peace Commission, there was no continuing body apart from the bishops to prepare and stimulate the General Conferences in social legislation.[4] Their statements, therefore, have enjoyed special prestige. Since unification there have been numerous occasions when General Conference committees have incorporated paragraphs from the Episcopal Addresses and made them part of the official voice of The Methodist Church. Boards and Agencies like to quote the words of the Council of Bishops in their recommendations and ecumenical documents and have frequently used these statements in support of positions they are developing.[5]

The leadership of the bishops is especially crucial in the crises of national and international life that arise between sessions of the

[4] Bishop Nolan B. Harmon in *The Organization of The Methodist Church* says (p. 91) that "In the former Methodist Episcopal Church, South, the College of Bishops was frankly entrusted with the duty of making pronouncements upon 'great social questions of national and international importance,' and other groups and bodies were discouraged if not forbidden to give out statements in the name of the church." See *Discipline*, 1938, ¶ 137-a.

[5] The Episcopal Address is usually the work of one of the bishops. It develops through several stages one of which is a full and critical discussion by the bishops as a whole. All must finally sign it for approval. The principal author reads it at General Conference.

256

General Conference. Since we shall consider this problem below, we only call attention to the fact that both world wars broke out in such situations and it fell to the bishops to give guidance without special instructions from the whole church. During the second world war the bishops organized, as we noted earlier in this volume, one of the most important social education and action programs in the history of Methodism, the Crusade for a New World Order.

B. The Annual Conference

We have noted that the Annual Conference is an important point of reference for social action at the local level. For most ministers and churches it is the essential unit of legislation, leadership, and program emphasis. In this book we have not been able to analyze the Annual Conference critically. Only in a few instances has a critical historical study of an Annual Conference been made. There is need for a number of definitive appraisals of Annual Conferences. Some, like the New York East Conference, the Rock River Conference, and the New England Conference, have been closely related to pioneer efforts in social Christianity. Others have illustrious but not so well-known records of creative initiative and effectiveness. As an illustration of some of the high points and criticisms which may be made of the Annual Conference, we shall note the Southern California-Arizona Conference simply because its record has been analyzed and made available.[6] Before using it as an illustration we may note some of the creative possibilities and problems which confront an Annual Conference as a bearer of the church's social witness.

Annual Conferences may set the pace for a denomination, memorialize the General Conference, and make significant experiments. We have seen that a number of Northern Annual Conferences did this prior to the adoption of the Social Creed in 1908. In 1913 the Missouri Annual Conference of the Southern church wrote a memorial urging the creation of a Department of Social Service within the Home Department of the Board of Missions and with a commitment to the Social Ideals adopted by the Federal Council of Churches in 1912. In 1927 that same conference adopted group insurance. In 1937 it took a vigorous position on international affairs, implementing the General Conference resolutions of 1934. Again in 1946 it opposed compulsory peacetime military training as a denial of the Atlantic Charter, as contrary to the democratic tradi-

---

[6] S. Raynor Smith's dissertation covers one hundred years of the Southern California-Arizona Conference.

tions, as a step toward fascism, and as a threat to the moral life of youth. It supported the United Nations, Fair Employment Practice Commissions, and the much debated Methodist Federation for Social Service. Thus in initiating and supporting the positions of the general church an Annual Conference plays a crucial role.

We may take another illustration from the Texas Annual Conference of the Methodist Episcopal Church, South. In 1909 it set up a committee to investigate the state penal institutions and propose legislation whose primary purpose should be the reformation of the criminal classes, especially those of "more tender years." It urged the separation of first offenders from others so that this goal might be more readily achieved. In 1921 it was one of the first Annual Conferences to recognize and respond to the rise of "mighty race consciousness" and to urge co-operation with the Interracial Commission. In 1925 it took a vigorous stand against lynching in Texas. In 1933 it took a courageous stand on religious affiliation questions for public school and college applications. Again, in 1947, it supported, as did many conferences, the Methodist position against compulsory military training.

Experiments in Annual Conferences may be like those related to the Rev. Charles C. Webber and the Rev. Emerson Smith in industrial relations. In May 1944, Bishop McConnell, presiding at the New York East Conference, appointed Webber as a secretary of the Methodist Federation for Social Service and field secretary of the Amalgamated Clothing Workers of America (CIO). The following year Bishop Oxnam renewed the appointment with the concurrence of the necessary two-thirds majority of the members of the conference. Under Bishop McConnell, Webber was stationed in Knoxville, Tennessee, and under Bishop Oxnam he was stationed in Chambersburg, Pennsylvania. Later he was transferred by the Amalgamated to Richmond, Virginia, to organize the employees of the Crawford Manufacturing Company. While there he was elected president of the Virginia State CIO and director of the Virginia CIO-PAC (Political Action Committee). This brought a protest from a Methodist layman and precipitated a situation where it was necessary for the Rev. Mr. Webber to go before the Conference Relations Committee to face a request that he accept the supernumerary ministerial relationship. The Committee unanimously voted to approve Bishop Oxnam's continuing him in active ministerial relationship, and so the Bishop appointed him Chaplain to Organized Labor.

Protests were made by conservative white Methodists to Bishop Oxnam and to Bishop W. W. Peele of the Virginia and North Carolina Conferences and requesting the former bishop to move him back to New York East Conference and keep him there. Bishop Peele felt that the "Chaplain" was an embarrassment to him, the main issue being that he felt that the union organization was hurting the reputation of The Methodist Church. Bishop Alexander P. Shaw, Bishop of the Negro churches in the Central Jurisdiction in Virginia, on the other hand, was not embarrassed at Webber's appointment as "Chaplain to Organized Labor" because the CIO unions had both Negro and white workers in their locals and were practicing economic and political brotherhood in their day-by-day activities. The Negro Methodists agreed with Bishop Oxnam's statement, "I see more religion in ending Jim Crow than in preaching abstractions about brotherhood." [7] This case stimulated the Council of Bishops to set up a special committee to study the matter of this type of appointment. In 1947 the appointment as "Chaplain to Organized Labor" was withdrawn, but Webber continued as a member of the New York East Conference and president of the Virginia CIO to complete seven years, after which he was national CIO Representative, with headquarters in Detroit. He is now a member of the Detroit Annual Conference.

The experimental appointment of the Reverend Emerson Smith is quite different, though related closely to industrial problems.[8]

Bishop Lord appointed Smith as a full-time "Chaplain of Industrial Relations" as representative of the 781 churches in the four Annual Conferences of the Boston area. He was responsible to the bishop, the conferences, and an area committee created to supervise and advise his work. His ministry was not oriented to individuals so much as to groups such as churches, management, and labor unions. His task was to promote understanding and reconciliation between the often conflicting forces of industrial life. The Rev. Emerson Smith made himself an expert in the intricacies of union-management relationships. As an independent church-paid Christian minister he functioned as friend, often adviser with technical understanding, to the leaders on both sides of the bargaining table. To the churches he brought a better understanding of the realities of industrial life. In co-operation with Boston University School of Theology he developed a special summer Ministers-in-Industry seminar. After he joined the regular staff of the Board of Social and

---

[7] Charles C. Webber, "Chaplain to Organized Labor," *Michigan Christian Advocate* (Oct. 24, 1946).

[8] Clair Cook, "A New Industrial Chaplaincy," *Christian Century* (Sept. 1, 1954).

Economic Relations as associate secretary, his successor, the Rev. Luther Tyson, has continued the same profile of ministry.[9]

Annual Conferences have the opportunities to initiate creative projects, but there are limitations in the field under discussion as well. The conferences, meeting once a year, often get little beyond the resolutions stage. Between sessions there is seldom any agency to speak on new issues that arise. Frequently the resolutions are hastily drawn and insufficiently debated. Inadequate study of technical questions prevents the actions from being as useful in many concrete situations as is desirable. Some of these limitations will be high-lighted in connection with the case history, briefly presented, of the Southern California-Arizona Conference.

Annual Conferences have often been pioneers in responding to social questions, with the General Conference following after. Thus the Southern California Conference in 1907 was one that memorialized the General Conference of 1908 to create a Department of Labor and to establish a "Commission of Labor which shall work to bring about a better understanding between the church and organized labor, and for a sane and safe solution of the present difficulty between capital and organized labor." [10] When the Social Creed was adopted, California Methodism hailed it as a most important event. This was true also as to the Federation for Social Service. A California Conference Branch was organized with a "goodly list of ministers and laymen as charter members." [11] *The Christian Advocate* gave publicity to various projects of the Federation, as for example the observance of a special Sunday in tribute to labor. "At that time it is expected that the church will seek a closer, clearer, fellowship with those who work at manual toil." [12]

The Annual Conference seldom participates directly in political action, but in the case of the recall of Mayor Shaw in 1938 the church's moral crusade led to direct political involvement. Feeling that the social life of Los Angeles had become chaotic the Southern California Conference expressed itself vigorously:

The City of Los Angeles, the fifth largest city in America, is caught in a great system of political corruption and vice exploitation. The youth of

[9] See Clair M. Cook, "The Industrial Chaplains," *Christian Century* (August 31, 1955), for a general survey of various types of chaplaincy in industry.

[10] *Journal, Southern California Conference*, 1907, p. 92. Cited in S. Raynor Smith, Jr., *op. cit.*, p. 223.

[11] *Journal, California Conference*, 1909, p. 96.

[12] "Labor Sunday and Labor Organizations," *California Christian Advocate*, 59 (May 6, 1909), 3.

our city are being demoralized through gambling and illicit sale of liquor. Rackets are being built up, "Bookie" establishments operate unmolested, houses of prostitution have spread openly throughout the city, gambling devices are to be found in every corner drugstore, Chinatown is utterly demoralized by the mad rush for easy money in gambling and lotteries. Our Negro people are being shamelessly exploited. The Police Department, our only defense against lawlessness, is used not only to protect vice but is made the weapon with which to bomb and terrorize those who dare to raise a voice against their political machine. We are fast on the way toward the building up of a political machine that will put to shame even Tammany Hall in its palmiest day, or the Pendergast machine in Kansas City. Decency in Los Angeles is fighting with its back to the wall and the Church has a tremendous stake in that fight.[13]

Since the issues here were liquor, vice, and gambling, there was great unanimity among Methodists. The church felt that Mayor Frank L. Shaw had forfeited all rights to the respect of honest citizens. It supported the idea of a recall election.

Methodist ministers and a prominent Los Angeles layman demanded and helped initiate a citizens' Independent Vice Investigation Committee which was later sponsored by civic authorities. The efforts of the committee were criticized by the mayor, and the district attorney hindered the efforts at investigation. These actions called for further efforts, and the Methodist District Superintendent called a meeting of all Methodist ministers and the ministers of other denominations who cared to attend. At this meeting a representative committee was appointed which was to meet with various political and civic organizations and carry on a joint investigation of civic corruption. This group soon had public enthusiasm for civic reform glowing. An interdenominational meeting was held in the First Methodist Church attended by representatives from 250 church, labor, and civic groups. They organized a Federation for Civic Betterment.[14] This Federation voted unanimously to support the recall movement. When the Southern California Conference met in June 1938, it voted unanimous approval of the action taken by Los Angeles Methodism.[15] Methodist ministers spoke on the issue from their pulpits, they asked over the radio for the recall of the mayor, and they helped with petitions to assure a recall election. This all went forward as planned. The Federation chose a reform

---

[13] *Journal, Southern California Conference*, 1938, pp. 605-6. For the whole story see Smith, *op. cit.*, pp. 383-87.

[14] "L. A. Churchmen Aroused," *Christian Advocate*, 87 (Feb. 21, 1938), 19.

[15] *Journal, Southern California Conference*, 1938, p. 570.

candidate, and Methodism gave him full support. In September Mayor Shaw was recalled, and Mayor Bowron was elected.

A representative instance of the attitude of Annual Conferences during the war is the following one on behalf of sanity and service.

> We appeal to our churches to minister sacrificially to war victims and sufferers, both here and abroad; to keep in touch with our youth in national service, military and civilian; to pray for them constantly, and give evidence of our love and care; to protect them from exploitation by forces of greed, especially the forces of liquor and vice; to co-operate with chaplains and with civilian agencies ministering to men in national service; to support the Red Cross and the U.S.O.; to give financial as well as moral support to our youth in Civilian Service Camps; to prevent unnecessary suffering on the part of those who have been evacuated or dislocated because of war conditions; and to assist, in any way possible, the work of the Methodist Commission on Camp Activities which deals with the needs and work of local Churches in camp areas.[16]

This same conference made a vigorous effort to co-operate with the Bishops' Crusade for a new world order as part of its responsibility to constructive peace-making.

C. The Jurisdictional System

The jurisdictional plan of Methodist organization was a constituent aspect of the long effort to reunite the Methodist churches. It was one element in a pragmatic effort to solve some of the historic issues that led to the separations of 1828 and 1844, the former leading to the organization of the Methodist Protestant Church on the question of lay representation, and the latter involving the power of the General Conference as exercised on the institution of slavery. The jurisdictional idea was formulated and consistently championed by the South, and emphasized two objectives. The first was the goal of a flexible administration, providing opportunity for local and regional self-determination in a united church. The second, which many regard as the more basic, was that the Southern minority must be safeguarded against any sudden majority vote of a General Conference. Proponents of the idea point out that every plan of union included the jurisdictional conception within it.

It is important to keep in mind the place of the jurisdictional principle of polity in the context of the total constitution of The Methodist Church, the attitudes of the various sections to it, and its relation to questions of racial segregation. There were at least five

---

[16] *Journal, Southern California-Arizona Conference*, 1943, p. 165.

major problems which the commissions on union and constitution sought to resolve: (1) the question of lay representation; (2) the question of Central Conferences; [17] (3) the question of the judiciary or Judicial Council; (4) the question of the Negro membership; and (5) the question of the powers of the General Conference. Lay representation is firmly established in the Annual Conferences, the jurisdictional conferences, and the General Conference. This fundamental concept of lay expression has strengthened the democratic aspects of Methodist polity and made the church more responsive to local church attitudes and opinions. Central Conferences embody the jurisdictional idea and antedate the plan of union, having in this way relatively little to do with the regional aspects of the jurisdictional system in America. The Judicial Council carries over into the Methodist system the valuable principles inherent in the independence of the judiciary as observed in the separation of powers in the federal government of the United States. It has no organic connection with the jurisdictional aspects of church government.

The questions of the powers of the General Conference and of the Negro membership are focal issues intimately involved in the philosophy of regional and racial organization.

Jurisdictionalism as a plan of union provides for certain values in but is not a separate principle of general Methodist polity. Regionalism is provided for but is not the basis of Methodism as one people. Lay representation, itineracy, the conference principle, episcopacy, and judiciary are all more fundamental and pervasive principles of Methodist Church government than the idea of sectional interests or regional self-determination. Though strongly advocated by the South, the idea of autonomous regions was never popular in the North. The latter was either strongly opposed or at most lukewarm, and accepted jurisdictionalism as a pragmatic compromise at the time of Union.

To Northern Methodists the idea of a powerful General Conference was never a bugbear or source of fear. They were proud of it. The conception of regional self-determination, on the other hand, seemed to them a serious division in the idea of the church itself. For them it has never been a constitutive principle of church government. They agreed to it more as a permissive idea or a concession to their Southern brethren than as a philosophic ideal. This difference in attitude is reflected in the general indifference with which the work of the jurisdictional conferences has been carried out in

[17] Central Conferences are organized for the work of the church outside the United States of America. See Constitution, Sec. V and VI, *Discipline*, 1956, ¶ 16-20.

the Northern and Western parts of Methodism. Bishops are elected in them, but nothing else of great importance occurs. There is thus a wide difference in the motivation for and evaluation of jurisdictionalism as a philosophy of polity. Those regions which have not intensively used the jurisdictional machinery have found in lay representation, itinerancy, the growing democratic spirit in the church, the Annual Conference, and the area organization, adequate avenues for expressing decentralized interests and promotional effectiveness. On the other hand, those regions employing a strong jurisdictional organization have developed a genuine appreciation for its contributions.

Since the South has championed the jurisdictional system as a conserver of regional values, it is well to inquire what these values are and whether the jurisdictional system is needed to protect them. No explicit list of such values has ever been developed. It may be that regional values embedded in the mores, folkways, and customs have local power of a kind that is essentially unaffected by the jurisdictional institutions. The latter may be more a symbol than a positive power. In New England, the Mid-West, and the Northwest, for example, details in manners of church life vary widely despite the negligible use of the jurisdictional apparatus. Even the great mobility of population in recent decades has not destroyed broad regional patterns of culture. We must conclude that jurisdictional organizations make little difference to the spirit of a local congregation or the style of conduct of the affairs of an Annual Conference.

Nevertheless, it must be recognized that the proponents of the jurisdictional philosophy view it as the principle of unity in diversity which guarantees initiative and self-expression. Closely related to this principle is the idea that the regions making up The Methodist Church should be guaranteed equality of representation and participation. Whether one agrees with the need for a strong independent Jurisdictional Conference or not, there is general consensus on the values of unity in diversity, initiative, and self-expression, on the one hand, and geographical representation and participation on the other. Any differences of judgment have to do with means, not ends.

Champions of the jurisdictional idea usually have insisted that its basic motivations and goals have had nothing to do with race. Such a contention is highly misleading, though its proponents would probably contend that even if the race issue were not involved, they would still defend the idea of regional or sectional control. Bishop Collins Denny of the Southern church flatly stated that if the General Conference of a united Methodism "should elect a Negro Bishop to preside over the whole church, there would be no Methodism in the South for him to preside over." [18] The debates on the Plan of Union at the General Conference of that church in 1938 reflect a marked concern over race.[19] Moreover, as Carter points out, what kept up the Negro opposition to the Plan of Union, so that their delegation to General Conference voted 36-11 against it, was the feeling that segregation had been made a constitutional part of the church's structure, and that this fact was a backward step for Methodism. When the Northern Conference voted 495-47 to support it, the driving force was unity. Northern opposition, as articulated by Lewis O. Hartman, was a refusal "to endorse unification at the price of the Negro." [20]

The growing determination to reassess the processes of the jurisdictions has been intimately related to questions of race and racial segregation. There has existed a clear correlation between intense feelings about the jurisdictional system and feelings about segregation. It must be remembered that the Negro conferences and Negro members were not suddenly segregated at the time of Union. They had already been separate entities in the Methodist Episcopal Church for many years, though the tendencies in the North had been towards integration, in contrast to the South. The persistence of Negro conferences as segregated bodies has created a complex problem which affects both jurisdictional philosophy and transcends it. Segregation has always intersected jurisdictional church polity but would not be overcome by the abolition of jurisdictionalism alone. The jurisdictional system has protected regional patterns of segregation in church and community life while affording opportunities of Negro representation on a formula of equality at the top connectional level of Methodism.

The jurisdictional system has, therefore, a significant relationship to the race issue as reflected in the Central Jurisdiction and in the uses that are made of it to perpetuate segregation or to rationalize it. In the present constitution all jurisdictions are represented in the general boards and agencies of The Methodist Church. It is urged by some that The Methodist Church is integrated because its highest bodies and officers, including episcopacy and judiciary, are open to all races and regions alike. It is further argued that the jurisdictional system gives equal representation

---

[18] Quoted in Carter, *op. cit.*, 197-98.

[19] See Carter, "The Negro and Methodist Union," *Church History*, XXI (March, 1952).

[20] See Carter, *The Decline and Revival of the Social Gospel*, pp. 196-99. See *Zions Herald*, CXIV (March 4, 1936), on the social gospel issue involved.

and voice to minorities. The reality of integration, however, must be measured by the quality of interpersonal relations at the level of local church and community life. A church cannot define its actual Christian character at the associative level of boards and general agencies so well as by what happens at the table of the Lord in a local church.

During the two decades after unification vast social changes have taken place in the South as in the nation as a whole. Industrialization, the massive mobility of the population, urbanization, the raising of real wages and standards of living, the fusion of popular art and national values through mass media of communication, and the democratic drive for equal opportunity in every aspect of life— all have had significant consequences for church life and organization. These factors are modifying regional distinctiveness. Each part of the nation is steadily drawn out of its isolation and sectional introversion into dynamic interaction with the whole world. Nowhere is the rate of industrialization and the urban way of life more accelerated than in the Southland. For these reasons the roles of regional, cultural, and racial minorities are dynamically different from what they were in 1939. The prospect for the future is greater homogeneity and unity in the national character of the United States.

The United States has resolutely set its face on equal opportunity and the removal of legal barriers to the intermingling and integration of the races, though with strong resistances expressed in various parts of the nation. Likewise The Methodist Church has clearly expressed the doctrine that there is no place for racial discrimination in its fellowship. Consequently, the Central Jurisdiction has been placed in the line of ultimate extinction and the problems of all jurisdictions have been given the assignment of making manifest the barrierless fellowship of Christ's Church. By 1956 the dilemmas of the Central Jurisdiction had become painfully real and doubts had been raised about the jurisdictional system as a whole. It was generally agreed, however, that basic issues of the jurisdictional idea now transcended those of racial segregation.

The philosophy of the jurisdictional system must be firmly evaluated by its effectiveness in the total institutional life of the church and its contribution to the evangelical mission of Methodism.

The jurisdictional system as a method for maintaining the Central Jurisdiction confronts the growing conviction that the pattern of racial segregation existing in our nation is morally wrong and the leadership of the church is judged by this conviction. Since the Central Jurisdiction is a symbol of segregation, it being by definition designated as Negro, there is growing opposition to it as segregation enforced by the law of the church. Under these circumstances it cannot be surprising to note a decline in the number of persons received from preparatory classes and on profession of faith in the Central Jurisdiction and hence that its percentage of membership in the total church has declined (4.2 per cent in 1940 to 3.8 per cent in 1957) since unification. This Jurisdiction also shows the greatest loss in pastoral charges, the greatest loss in effective ministers, and the smallest average number of members per charge during this same period.

It is generally admitted that communications in many places between the Central Jurisdiction churches and the churches of other jurisdictions are very poor or nonexistent. A number of workshops and other meetings have somewhat improved this situation, but the situation is extremely bad. This makes effective work very difficult in new urban areas or in cities to which Negroes and others have migrated. Central Jurisdiction churches, as we noted above, are not keeping up with the change and increase of Negro population. This weakness in churchmanship is compounded by the fact that Methodism has not served the manual laborer well enough in the urban areas, and this is the occupation class of the bulk of the Negro population.

In a summary of Interracial Leadership Conferences held in a number of urban areas, the Board of Social and Economic Relations shows that discrimination and/or segregation in Methodist institutions is much more prevalent than was previously recognized. Population shifts have resulted in many white churches' being the only Methodist churches located in areas largely Negro. Although the response of such churches varies widely, with the exception of areas like Detroit and Chicago, the principal solution employed seems to be for congregations to move out. To a larger extent than is often recognized there is discrimination in hospitals, nursing homes, homes for aged, and children's homes. We have noted the situation in Methodist colleges and universities. A number of churches have consciously developed policies of freedom from discrimination and the removal of restrictive practices. The success of full fellowship is closely related to the overcoming of discriminatory practices throughout American culture as a whole.

One of the greatest costs of the segregated system in Methodism has been the decline in community leadership on the part of the Negro church. Whereas the church was for many years the focus of community leadership, this leadership is increasingly passing into the hands of educated Negro business and professional groups. Salaries have been such as not to attract the educated Negro into the ministry in sufficient numbers to maintain the leadership role in the community. Forty-seven per cent of the ministers have only high-school education, while less than 19 per cent are seminary trained. Nevertheless, says the Board Summary, religion has remained as the rallying point for social advancement. In the South the churches have provided the institutional focus for major issues. In the North many educated religious leaders have transferred activities to such organizations as N.A.A.C.P. However, in none of this has the Methodist Central Jurisdiction been prominent.

The problems of the jurisdictional system were officially debated in 1960 at the General Conference and are now before the whole church. They are admittedly complex and dilemmatic.[21] We have noted in the previous section of this volume the various attitudes that exist on the racial ideal and the abolition of the Central Jurisdiction. Many Negro leaders fear that the removal of structural barriers will not remove or change attitudes. Many are apprehensive that a radical change in the jurisdictional system will mean white leaders over Negroes but not the opposite. In addition, there is the institutional fear that the use of the present constitutional method of transfer between and among jurisdictions will result in draining the financial and personnel leadership from the Central Jurisdiction, leaving it increasingly ineffective to do its work. In the South the churches tend to be relatively small and ineffective. For example, in Florida 65 per cent of the Negro Methodist churches have fewer than 100 members, while 23 per cent have fewer than twenty members. In other areas a few large churches, with middle-class congregations, carry a large share of the financial burden and possess a large share of the leadership. In the advance across jurisdictional lines the laymen seem at present to be the most enthusiastic; the ministers are less enthusiastic; and the episcopal leadership seems to be the least enthusiastic. The hesitancy of the Negro bishops has been used as an argument by the opponents of basic change among the whites.

D. The General Conference

A major point of reference for setting social goals and defining standards is the General Conference. When the Social Creed became official in 1908 in the Northern church and subsequently in the

[21] The General Conference voted not to change the basic plan of geographical jurisdictions.

other branches of Methodism, it provided a firm historical foundation for social legislation. This book includes an extensive commentary on the development and modifications of the Social Creed. In united Methodism its authoritative place has not been minimized. It provides a unity of ideals which gives coherence to the social responsibilities of the church and other Protestant bodies which have been related to the Federal and National Councils of Churches.

In their present form the Social Creed and the miscellaneous resolutions on social questions provide a fairly comprehensive and systematic body of social doctrine.[22] The doctrine is spelled out primarily in terms of application to concrete issues. Volume III of this series makes evident how much the official resolutions have elaborated their theological foundations.

The pronouncements of General Conferences are dynamic; that is, they are modified from quadrennium to quadrennium and reflect the shifting pressures of social events and the power struggle within the political life of the church. Nevertheless, the Social Creed has been quite stable and on numerous issues a significant consensus has developed, as Part Three of this book demonstrates. It is interesting to note how the specific emphasis of General Conference resolutions relates to the responses of the MESTA questionnaire.[23]

The General Conference is the agency through which Methodism is principally reminded of its supranational character. Other agencies are the Board of Missions and the ecumenical bodies to which the denomination belongs. Because the composition of the General Conference is world-wide, its social legislation is always discussed in a global context—and this setting has a salutary effect on much of the debate in committees and in the plenary sessions. Thus we read: "Christianity cannot be nationalistic; it must be universal in its outlook and appeal." Many of the resolutions, even apart from world peace, are explicitly international in their points of reference.

From a national point of view, it is strategic that the Conference convenes in the spring of election years. At this time domestic and

---

[22] These doctrines and resolutions are sifted through the Committee on the State of the Church. Then those viewed with favor by the Committee are brought to the floor of the General Conference for debate and action. Since the delegates most concerned with social issues tend to choose this committee, what comes out may represent a higher (or at least different) social insight than the church as a whole has. Nevertheless, the opportunity for debate and for minority reports assures that over the years the social thought of the church accepts the leadership which the committee gives.

[23] This questionnaire is described in the Introduction to Part Three.

world issues are quite clearly drawn and vigorously discussed in the secular mass media of communication. There is always interest in what The Methodist Church has to say on major questions, for a body representing more than nine million Americans has political significance. The large number of Methodists in the Congress, even though they have widely disparate interests, lays a special obligation on the church to develop its judgments clearly and vigorously.

Christian responsibility in lawmaking is increased with the presence of churchmen in legislative halls. In the 86th Congress the Roman Catholics numbered 103, a gain of ten over the previous session. Methodists, long the largest group, often express anxiety that their number has dropped from 105 to 98. Of these, 17 are in the Senate where they lead in numbers, and 81 are in the House where they are second. There are 12 Roman Catholics in the Senate and 91 in the House. Protestants in general total 412. There are 12 Jewish members, 1 Hindu, and 5 who have not indicated an affiliation. The 68 Presbyterians comprise the second largest Protestant group, followed by 64 Baptists and 63 Episcopalians. There are 26 Congregationalists and 21 Lutherans.

No one has seriously debated the question of Methodist sanctions on congressional members who support legislation opposed to the resolutions which the total church has adopted. This is a church-state issue with a traditional answer. No one has made a full study of correlations between Methodist social pronouncements and the votes of Methodists in committees, in the House, and in the Senate. There is not much evidence that voters are well informed about or influenced by these pronouncements, as we shall see in the concluding chapter of this book. Congressional leaders are more sensitive to their voters' opinions than to denominational statements. In the case of Prohibition and the Crusade for a New World Order we have instances of great political power directly exercised by an aroused church.

Although the General Conference meets during national election years, its quadrennial character diminishes its political and social power. Crises occur for which no leadership or guidance was specifically provided. The Southern church had a General Conference in 1914 and not again until 1918; meanwhile, World War I broke out with American involvements in 1917. The Northern branch convened in 1916 and not again until 1920. The crash of 1929 fell between General Conference years, as did much of the epoch-making New Deal legislation. There was a quadrennial session in 1940, but America was in the war late in 1941—and no guidance was given officially by General Conference until the war was two and a half years old. The great bishops' crusade was carried out without benefit of the highest legislative body of the church. Again, this body convened in 1952 and the historic decision of the Supreme Court on desegregation came in 1954.

Such situations have thrown a great deal of responsibility on the leadership of the bishops and on the general boards of the church. We have already noted some aspects of episcopal leadership, but we must now note that an increasingly powerful role falls to the boards, commissions, and other agencies of the church. Bishops and boards tend to make the policies of the church, to develop the programs, to write the legislation, and hence to determine the profile of values enacted by General Conference. The power of bishops and board secretaries is enhanced by the fact that they are continuously at work in administration, control personnel selection, and have national oversight of programs and promotion. In the most recent quadrennium there is evidence that the proposals of the boards tend to become the basis of the legislation adopted at General Conference. Rivalry among boards has at times become a significant political fact in the power structure of Methodism. Whyte's "Organization Man" may be found in many places as "status seekers" clamor up the denominational ladder. Unofficial voices tend to become weaker, and good public relations tend to take over.

CHAPTER NINE

The Educational System

A WELL-KNOWN SOCIOLOGICAL DICTUM STATES THAT EDUcation is the most significant factor in vertical mobility from class to class in the United States. Lloyd Warner has shown graphically how by means of education men and women move from one economic class to another more rapidly than in any other way. Education has been the ladder to new realms of opportunity. More recently C. Wright Mills in *The Power Elite* and Vance Packard in *The Status Seekers* have contended that class lines are hardening and that the upper classes are now perpetuating themselves through a horizontal cycle composed of exclusive preparatory schools, selected colleges, and suburban self-absorption. While the vertical climb is slowing down, youth still seek opportunity through higher education which is becoming more important for many aspects of "status-seeking." Methodists have sought to make such opportunity spiritually and socially responsible.

A. Colleges and Universities

For more than two centuries the Methodist movement has strongly supported education. John Wesley anchored this passion for education in Oxford University. It is providential that on the American frontier Methodist leaders could point to their spiritual father as both a scholar and an evangelist. Space does not permit the retelling of the westward movement of Methodism across the continent, which left in its wake schools as well as churches. It is still building both, in the outposts of statehood and in the midst of the population boom. The circuit riders were pioneers in building colleges and universities. They have left a priceless heritage and an incalculably rich asset to virtue in learning and piety.

The greatest contribution of these educational institutions is their very existence as the bridge of opportunity for a mobile population. In 1956 they numbered nine universities, ten schools of theology, seventy-one colleges, seventeen junior colleges, seven secondary schools, and three others—one hundred seventeen in all. Some can be counted as among the oldest in their respective states.

In relation to the present project, the contributions of these educational institutions are too numerous to be mentioned. We have selected some illustrations that bear on the kinds of issues which have been reviewed above. Who can estimate the leadership which they have poured into church and secular life? The battle for freedom of the mind, for academic freedom, and for truth has seen some noble encounters on college campuses. Philosophers have blazed new trails of understanding personality and ultimate reality and laid solid foundations for moral analysis and social philosophy. Scientists have participated in unlocking the secrets of nature, society, and man. On many Methodist campuses the wellsprings of intergroup understanding have been tapped and guidance has been given to domestic policies and world order.

There have also been ignoble reverses in the field of academic freedom. Some administrations have been notoriously autocratic. Christian colleges have been sold out to business secularisms in some instances. Segregation has been practiced in some institutions of higher education long after alternative policies were possible. Colleges and universities have sometimes followed the times rather than led in the battle for truth and freedom.

At Boston University the administration achieved freedom in handling the R.O.T.C. and has maintained a very high tradition of academic freedom.[1] At Southern Methodist the administration in 1958 stood solidly behind a student project known as "A Case Study on the Communist Conspiracy." In the 1920's Hendrix College played a leading role in the fight to prevent the enactment of a proposed anti-evolution measure by the Arkansas legislature. Somewhat earlier, Emory at Oxford in Georgia stood by the academic freedom of a professor who had dared to write a liberal article on the Negro in the *Atlantic Monthly,* though the executive committee of the trustees felt obliged to accept his resignation.

In the field of antidiscrimination it is noteworthy that in 1956 the Trustees of the University of Denver adopted a resolution concerning the university and fraternity relationship. The university recognizes a responsibility for reviewing the policies and procedures of organizations identified with it and reaffirms the dictates of

[1] The references in the following paragraphs are drawn from responses to a MESTA request for case histories illustrating the manifold community activities of Methodist-related universities and colleges.

its charter that "no test of religious faith shall ever be applied as a condition of admission." The officers of fraternities were instructed to make periodic reports of progress.

At Scarritt College a liberal policy has been in operation for a long time and the college has desegregated as rapidly as it is permitted to do under law. Long before the Tennessee legislature revoked its law forbidding white and Negro students to study in the same school, Scarritt was known as the one place in that area, other than Negro colleges, where interracial meetings were welcomed, where Negroes were included as lodging guests and where white students worked in Negro centers, as part of their college practicum. In 1954-55 it had a Negro on its faculty. At Illinois Wesleyan College faculty members, as members of Wesley Methodist Church, formulated a resolution opposing the nonacceptance of Negroes at Brokaw Hospital.

The special talents of a teacher of government at Nebraska Wesleyan University have brought the college into close touch with social and labor legislation. *The Lincoln Star* in 1958 reported: "Nebraska owes to Dr. E. Glenn Callen, of the Nebraska Wesleyan faculty, an expression of thanks for his non partisan, competent survey of the state's unemployment compensation program."

The University of Chattanooga has established an Industrial Research Institute which gives service to local area industry and to federal research enterprises. Boston University has developed a Human Relations Center which combines instruction and research with community service. In Evansville, Indiana, urban transition from an area of substandard housing to one of industrial development left a Neighborhood House stranded. The college participated actively in a survey looking toward relocation of the Neighborhood House. At Millsaps College students from the department of religion and the department of sociology co-operated in an investigation project set up by the Mississippi Children's Code Commission. Community studies have been conducted by a great many Methodist colleges in all parts of the nation. Many of these overlap the fields of social work and social action.

The main task of the college is education, and when this is done well it has made an important contribution to the church's goals. At the present time there is a growing awareness of the dilemma of leadership in all of the Methodist colleges and universities. To win support in numbers and finances, these institutions have often sacrificed principle and compromised tradition. The latest quadrennial (1956-60) program sought "to interpret to our church-related colleges and universities their place and function in the life of the church and the obligation of these institutions to be Christian in teaching and in practice." It sought also "to interpret to our people of The Methodist Church the distinctive function of our institutions of learning in the church and in society. . . . These institutions, dedicated to Christian ideals, must as heretofore be evangelists in the field of higher education, to the end that the Christian concept of God and man may become the dominant element in American culture."

B. The Theological Schools

Methodism has established twelve theological seminaries. Their development reflects the church's desire to be provided with an educated ministry. For many years a seminary education was a permissible way of preparing for admission to a conference and as a step toward ordination. Today a theological education at an accredited seminary is the regular and not just a permissible road of preparation for admission on trial and ordination alongside the other requirements indicated in the *Discipline*. Some of Methodism's schools of theology have been among the best in the whole field of theological education and have given unusual leadership in ecumenical affairs and the development of social Christianity in America and the world.

Of special interest to this present volume is the development of the teaching of social ethics. Theological seminaries began instruction in this field and its cognate subject, sociology, about eighty years ago. Its place in the theological curriculum reflects the influence of the social gospel in American Protestantism. Seminaries in The Methodist Church have produced some of the greatest of social prophets, statesmen, and teachers in the twentieth century. Though not the earliest institutions to provide instruction, some of them had been active participants in the social gospel movement for a decade before the Social Creed was formulated in 1908.

Concern for social reform carried with it a demand that the seminaries modernize their curricula. Richard T. Ely urged about 1890 that half the time of the ministerial student be devoted to social studies, and he argued further that seminaries were the natural habitats for intensive work in the social sciences. Fifty or more years later Liston Pope noted, however, that there were in the accredited seminaries of the U.S.A. but thirty-two teachers of social ethics who had their primary teaching responsibility in this field. There were forty-six others whose primary listing was in other fields, but who offered work in social ethics. In 1948 social studies probably did not exceed 10 per cent of the courses in any seminary.[2] When John L. Seaton conducted a survey of theological education in The Methodist Church in 1946 and 1947, his report indicated general satisfaction with the amount of attention given to this field in most of the seminaries of the church, though there was, and still is, considerable variation among them. Some which were lamentably weak a decade ago are now developing substantial stature.

The older Northern seminaries naturally have played a more significant role in the Methodist social response in the twentieth century than have the Southern schools because of the dates of founding and for other reasons. Leadership in social ethics has a definite relationship to general standards of educational development. The founding years of the ten seminaries in full operation at the time of this writing have some historical importance for understanding their respective contributions: Boston University School of Theology, 1839; Garrett Biblical Institute, 1854; Drew Theological Seminary, 1867; Westminster Theological Seminary (now Wesley), 1882; Iliff School of Theology, 1892; Gammon Theological Seminary, 1894; Candler School of Theology, 1914; Perkins School of Theology, 1915; Duke Divinity School, 1926; School of Religion, University of Southern California (now independently Southern California School of Theology), 1940. Two additional seminaries have since been established, one in Kansas City and one near Delaware, Ohio.

Northern and Western seminaries had been involved in the social gospel movement for many years before the major Southern seminaries were founded. Moreover, they had weathered the crises of criticism regarding the historical interpretation of the Bible and the relation of science and religion before the storm over such issues broke in the South. At Boston University, Borden Parker Bowne established the philosophical movement of personalist idealism in its main outlines before 1900. Though Bowne was himself not a great social liberal, his emphasis on personality as the key to reality began an unbroken tradition which had important consequences for the development of ethics, philosophy of religion, and theology in Methodism. Herbert W. Schneider notes: "It (personalism) has been useful in breaking down the sectarian intellectual barriers of The Methodist Church, which had inherited the evangelical fear and scorn of unrevealed doctrines, but which in giving

[2] See Walter G. Muelder, "The Function of Social Ethics in a Theological Seminary," in *Education for Professional Responsibility* (Pittsburgh: Carnegie Press, Carnegie Institute of Technology, 1948), p. 181.

ear to its personalist theologians has become accustomed to philosophical forms of speech and mind." [3] Men like George A. Coe, R. T. Flewelling, A. C. Knudson, and E. S. Brightman, in relating personality not only to metaphysics but to value theory, profoundly influenced a significant portion of Methodist leaders for several decades.[4]

Many men trained in the personalist tradition found it natural to adopt social views like those of Walter Rauschenbusch and to be involved in putting personality above property values. By 1895 Edgar J. Helms was at work at Morgan Memorial and laying the foundations of a program of self-help that developed into The Goodwill Industries. When the Methodist Federation for Social Service developed its first literature on the social ministry of the church, an important contributor was Harris Franklin Rall, then president of Iliff School of Theology and later professor at Garrett Biblical Institute. Throughout his long and influential career Rall related theology effectively to social responsibility.[5] Rall was not a personalist, but his Ritschlian orientation made him concerned for social ethics. Another contributor to *Social Ministry* in 1910 was Charles J. Little, president of Garrett. Harry F. Ward, one of the founders of the Federation, was prior to his career at Union Theological Seminary a professor at Boston University School of Theology. When the Southern seminaries were founded, the leadership of social responsibility was enriched in due course by their alumni or teachers like John N. Shackford, Paul Kern, W. A. Smart, and more recently Albert Barnett. A number of Methodism's outstanding social leaders were educated at non-Methodist institutions such as Vanderbilt, Union Theological Seminary, University of Chicago, and Yale Divinity School. In the last two decades the theological emphases in a number of Methodist seminaries have reflected the influences of recent European thought, as earlier they did those of the idealists Schleiermacher and Ritschl.

From the standpoint of content and purpose the emergence of social ethics was dependent on the reformist aspects of the social gospel movement. Sociology and reform were congenial partners,

[3] Herbert W. Schneider, *A History of American Philosophy* (New York: Columbia University Press, 1946), p. 467.

[4] Leaders like F. J. McConnell, James C. Baker, Walter Van Kirk, G. Bromley Oxnam, L. O. Hartman, Edgar Love, Willis King, Georgia Harkness, Charles F. Boss, L. Harold DeWolf, Harvey Seifert, and T. Kagawa belong to this tradition.

[5] Professor Rall edited *Religion and Public Affairs*, a group of essays in honor of Bishop Francis J. McConnell. Rall wrote the essay on McConnell (New York: the Macmillan Company, 1937).

the former supplying social facts for religious education and for social evangelism. Sociology recognized religion as a social force and gave apparent scientific sanction to the contentions of the social gospel activists that religion needed to be thought through in social terms if it was to serve the present age. Ministers and theologians were active in founding the first professional societies of sociologists and economists.

Reciprocity in the two fields is reflected in the attitudes of two Methodists, one a seminary teacher, the other a popular sociologist. "If the future of mankind depends upon religion becoming scientific and therefore social, it equally depends upon science becoming social and therefore religious," said Harry F. Ward. Charles A. Ellwood noted: "The scientific study of institutions reinforces ethical religion, in that it inspires men with faith in the possibility of remaking both human nature and human social life." [6] A vast literature has developed on the relation of theology to social science and on the relation of church to society.

At the turn of the century the term "Christian sociology" was in vogue; it has not been entirely abandoned, though it has been under vigorous attack by both sociologists and theologians within and without the seminaries. The term serves to indicate the problems which confront the teacher of social ethics and the ministers whom the seminaries train. On the one hand, they face the traditional ethical and theological universals of conventional Christianity, and, on the other hand, they face the disciplines of present-day sociology which are deeply impressed by the ideals of objective description and quantitative measurement of social process. They are confronted also by the unconventional norms of philosophical ethics and the imperatives of contemporary theology. In recent decades the seminaries have been the scene of lively debates and conflicts in Christian ethics and its bearing on social education and action. Volume III of this study deals explicitly with the relation of Methodist theological perspectives to social issues and relates these to both theological method and emergent ecumenical conceptions in the field.[7]

---

[6] Quoted in *Education for Professional Responsibility*, p. 182. For a study of a number of Methodist leaders like Charles A. Ellwood of Duke, E. Stanley Jones, Francis J. McConnell, and Harry F. Ward, see J. Neal Hughley, *Trends in Protestant Social Idealism* (New York: King's Crown Press, 1948).

[7] The critique of the social gospel tradition by neo-Protestantism is reflected in the work by Hughley cited above. Later works by Robert Moats Miller, *American Protestantism and Social Issues*, and Paul A. Carter, *The Decline and Revival of the Social Gospel*, considerably modify the perspective and over-all evaluation of Hughley.

Having responsibility for the intellectual leadership of the church, the seminaries have a major duty to keep abreast of the times in Christian social ethics and the related disciplines. The present general situation in American seminaries calls forth special effort on the part of Methodist seminaries. In their study of theological education, Niebuhr, Williams, and Gustafson express disappointment at what they have found in seminaries as a whole. They say:

> Ethics is rarely completely ignored, but it receives only minimal attention in a large number of schools. It should be said further that too often the one required course in ethics gives a general approach to basic principles, quite necessary in itself but rarely probing concrete personal and social issues in the common life except for some attention to problems of pastoral ethics.[8]

Where ethics is a major subject the school has generally a large faculty.

In their criticisms these authors go further with respect to sociology:

> The sociological doctrines are even less frequently represented. Action without regard for what human beings are and how they behave in their various groupings can be futile or destructive. The growing concern for this introduction of theological students to sociological concepts stems from the desire to relate Christian ethics, and indeed all understanding of Christian faith, to those aspects of human life with which sociologists are concerned. Studies of group power and conflict, of caste and class, of ideology and social strata, authoritarian and democratic social forces, the relation of freedom and order . . . describe forces which shape the common life and spirit. The Church is itself a social group, acting in human society. The meaning of Christian community in the Body of the Church cannot be absorbed in sociology, but it cannot be understood apart from its sociological aspects. . . . The student who discovers the way in which psychology or sociology or literary criticism can function as a mediating discipline between the Gospel and contemporary man's search for faith has one of the prime requisites for a lifetime of fruitful reflection.[9]

The Methodist Church has expected much service from its theological seminaries over and above the preparation of men for

[8] See H. Richard Niebuhr, D. D. Williams, and J. M. Gustafson, *The Advancement of Theological Education* (New York: Harper and Brothers, 1957), pp. 101-2.
[9] *Ibid.*, p. 102.

ordination in the annual conferences and in the more specialized ministries. Sometimes the calls have been burdensome and costly to the educational program. A close co-operative relationship obtains between the general administrative boards and agencies and the schools of theology. Ideas developed in any place of significant leadership have been rapidly communicated elsewhere. The seminaries have been the locations for innumerable workshops covering the whole range of social problems including family life, race relations, town and country life, industrial areas, labor relations, urban planning, alcohol studies, and international relations. Students have sometimes vigorously memorialized the General Conference on such issues as race relations. Faculty members have been related to both official and unofficial action programs.

Increasingly the church as a whole has turned to the seminaries to conduct research in problem areas and to advise on fundamental policies and programs. For example, the educational curriculum of the church school has had the benefit of theological review and methodical criticism by seminary faculties; church surveys have been conducted; and ideological movements like Communism have been analyzed from the perspective of the Christian faith. Thus in many fundamental respects the strength of the schools of theology is basic for an adequate response by Methodism to the social forces of the twentieth century.

Concern for the social witness of the church has occasionally been isolated in the social ethics department of the seminary. Specialization of this type has been inimical for the welfare of theological education since all branches of theology should normally interpenetrate each other. It has also been bad for the development of social Christianity, for the latter needs thorough grounding in biblical studies, historical and systematic theology. No less required are the disciplines of practical theology. Conversely, these disciplines take on added meaning and relevance when they are organically related to the work of the church in the community, nation, and world.

Some of the Methodist seminaries have attempted significant interdisciplinary projects in Christian social thought and action and have produced statements, essays, and research materials of outstanding quality. Much work remains to be done in relating the ultimate perspectives of the Christian ethic to the provisional judgments of policy and program. Just as these ultimate dimensions of the faith need to be adequately related to practice, so the assumptions in practical programs and policies need to be specified, clarified, and where necessary, corrected. Theological education needs to become more integral and concretely relevant.

C. The Church School

This section deals with the role of the church school in Methodist social thought and action. The church school, as used here, refers to the local church program of Christian education as represented primarily in the Sunday church school and the various youth programs and activities. The significance of the church school in this study is indicated by the fact that over the years six out of ten persons becoming members of The Methodist Church have come directly through the church schools. The relation of the church school to social thought and action is discovered primarily in the curriculum and program materials used over the years in Christian education in the local church.

The Sunday school, which was the forerunner of the more comprehensive educational program that now goes under the term "church school," had its origin in the social concern of Robert Raikes, who began the first Sunday school to combat the juvenile delinquency of his day and to improve the lot of "the lower orders of mankind." John Wesley very soon adopted the plan for the Methodist societies, and the second Sunday school to be organized in America was begun by Francis Asbury.

There is much evidence that the church school over the past sixty years has not only maintained the social concerns of its origin, but has enlarged them as it has sought to make the teachings of Jesus more relevant to human life. In 1908 the Editorial and Publications Department of the Methodist Episcopal Church emphasized that

The Sunday School of today must face the problems of today, and that which was perfectly suitable twenty-five years ago would be wholly inadequate now . . . in the Methodist Episcopal Church, outside of a limited number of ultra-conservatives who are hostile to any change, this view prevails and in our Sunday School literature we are endeavoring to maintain a progressive conservatism that is open-minded to all new truths but which also has reverent regard to the traditions of faith.[10]

For almost half a century since it appeared in *The Adult Student* of the Methodist Episcopal Church, South, the following quotation has been fairly representative of the viewpoint in Methodist church-school materials:

[10] *Yearbook of the Department of the Sunday School of the Methodist Episcopal Church*, 1908, p. 110.

Christianity does not call us to turn our back on the world and live a life of selfish isolation. On the contrary, it bids us to take our places among our fellows and discharge our social obligations courageously and faithfully. Wherever there are needs to be met, wrongs to be righted, sufferings to be relieved, fallen ones to be lifted up, and great tasks to be accomplished for the good of humanity, there it is the Christian's duty to take his place and to help to the utmost of his ability.[11]

It is true "the wrongs to be righted" and the "great tasks to be accomplished" have had different emphases at different times, but running throughout the youth and adult curricula, particularly, are materials dealing with the great social issues of the day. In this regard it is significant to note that across Methodism church schools have consistently enrolled more adults than either children or youth.

The task of generalizing concerning the two larger branches of Methodism before unification is made easier by the fact that by 1916 the editor of Sunday-school publications of the Methodist Episcopal Church could say that 75 per cent of the Sunday-school literature of the Methodist Episcopal Church and the Methodist Episcopal Church, South, both graded and uniform, was identical.[12] In 1925 mention was again made of the close relationship in producing Sunday-school materials.

In general, the lesson materials for youth and adults have been "Bible centered" but they have dealt rather consistently with the implications of the biblical teaching for the problems of the day. *The Adult Student* over the years had a section of each lesson entitled "The Lesson in Daily Life" which dealt with the application to personal and social life and action. A survey of the adult materials indicates that it was rare for lesson periodicals to appear without articles on social issues accompanying the lessons. However, units of study which could be labeled "social action" units appear primarily at the older youth and young adult levels in the regular curriculum. For adults they appear, with the exception of temperance and missions lessons, as "elective" units, and for youth they are found mostly in the evening meeting materials.

The Adult Student, published by the Methodist Episcopal Church, South, will serve to illustrate some of the emphases for adults. Its initial volume (1908) sets forth in a series of lead articles, entitled "The Christian in Society," the idea that the mission of Christianity is to save society as well as the individual:

[11] *The Adult Student,* 9 (1916), 99.
[12] *Yearbook of the Board of Sunday Schools of the Methodist Episcopal Church, 1916,* p. 108.

The Christian recognizes the principles enunciated in the Sermon on the Mount as final authority in society. He believes that in these, and in these alone, can be found a cure for all our social ills, the solution for all our social problems. In the social teachings of Jesus, he finds the only foundation on which a stable and permanent society can be built.[18]

In line with this emphasis is a statement of the joint Committee on Curriculum made in 1925. In its statement of principles one of the three objectives of religious education is stated as "wholehearted participation in and constructive contribution to the progressive realization of a social order controlled by Christian principles." [14]

The implications of these basic principles are made very explicit in *The Adult Student*. The September 1912 issue dealt in a very forthright way with "Religion and Politics." It stated that the national political campaign "involves great problems of economic justice and social righteousness and no Christian can afford to be neutral or indifferent." The first elective adult study courses introduced in 1914 had as the second unit a series on poverty and wealth. Dealt with were such things as: the moral causes of poverty, disease, and undernourishment, public health, inadequate housing, unemployment, the democratic control of natural resources, the ideal of distributive justice, the wage system and its relation to Christian ethics. In 1925 the guaranteed annual wage in industry is advocated. In the early 1930's a series of lessons contrasts Communism and Christianity as a way of life. Robert E. Speer wrote that the communistic principle means the death of individual freedom; that the issue in the world of that day was not between Capitalism and Communism but between despotism and liberty.

As early as 1913 the problem of juvenile delinquency was dealt with as a concern of the church, and a series dealing with the divorce problem appeared.

The Adult Student from the very beginning dealt with race prejudice and discrimination. This emphasis was particularly strong during the 1930's and 1940's. These are typical statements made: "There is but one race—the human race. Unless we are willing to have all men as our brothers, we cannot have God as our Father"; "The spirit of Christ must govern each person in his treatment of every other of whatever rank or condition or color." Series of lessons appeared with such titles as "Living as Christians

---

[18] *The Adult Student*, 1908, p. 324.
[14] Report of Curriculum Committee of the *Methodist Episcopal Church, 1925*, p. 14.

with other Races." They dealt primarily with relationships between the Negroes and whites in the South and with the Christian solution to the problems that exist. Discrimination against the Negro is outlined and Christian ways of dealing with it are suggested.[15]

The area in which *The Adult Student* has been the most thorough is that of temperance. There were regular quarterly lessons as well as more comprehensive elective units preceding the adoption of prohibition. The emphasis in these lessons and articles changed from personal to social over the years between 1908 and 1917. After the advent of prohibition, the regular quarterly temperance lessons were discontinued and temperance was dealt with only incidentally in lessons dealing with social conditions and in articles which stressed mostly the importance of prohibition enforcement. Occasional lessons reappeared in 1929 and the emphasis was again quite pronounced by 1932 and has continued to the present.

Some indication of the attention given to social issues in the study materials for youth is given in a spot check of intermediate and senior-high materials in the periods: 1911-15; 1941-44; 1949; 1956-58. In this particular survey 425 items are noted dealing with social issues. These fit into the following categories listed in order of frequency: international relations (62); race relations (48); politics (35); marriage and family (33); pacifism (28); vocations (27); social outreach (24); church and state (22); temperance and prohibition (21); social action (21); civil liberties (18); ecumenics (14); economics (13); world order (11); public education (10); crime and penal justice (10); international organization (8); Communism (8); labor and management (7); and health and welfare (5).

There are some notable shifts in emphases in the periods surveyed. In the first period, race relations ranks first along with temperance and international relations. In the second period it ranks third; in the third period, second; and in the fourth period, fifth. International relations continues to rank first in the three succeeding periods, while temperance drops to sixth in the second period and to eighth in the third and fourth.

Marriage and family is in fourth place for the first two periods, in fifth place in the third, and ends up in second place in the fourth period. Vocations goes from fifth place, to sixth, to fifth, to third. Pacifism ranks in third place prior to World War I, drops to fifth place during World War II, is in fourth place in 1949, and drops back to fifth in the late 1950's. Economic issues are not dealt with

[15] *The Adult Student*, 25, 651 ff.; 29, 516 ff.

in the first period, are in fourth place in the second, in ninth place in the third, and twelfth place in the fourth period. Civil liberties ranks second in the first period, fifth in the second, ninth in the third and fourth. Labor and management emphases dropped from fourth rank in the first period to sixth in the second, tenth in the third, and fourteenth in the fourth. Communism goes from fifth place in the first period to eighth in the second, to ninth in the third, and to thirteenth in the fourth.

A survey of the youth publication of the Methodist Episcopal Church, South, *Epworth Highroad*, during the 1930's shows major attention being given to race relations, war and peace, and temperance. Scarcely an issue appeared without a cartoon, an article, or lesson material on the liquor problem. Typical of the emphasis in the area of race relations are these words:

> Those of us who attend young peoples' conferences and Christian gatherings talk a great deal about race prejudice and learn how tremendously evil it all is, and then go home and do little or nothing about it. But this lesson today looks us squarely in the eye and asks us why we do little or nothing about it.[16]

Thus we see that there was an attempt to deal effectively in the church school with social issues in the light of the Christian gospel. The effectiveness has no doubt been limited by the fact that so often the most direct and comprehensive approaches were through elective courses and in evening youth programs which reached only a part of the total people in the church. Too often in the Bible-centered units the extent to which the biblical teachings were applied to social issues in everyday life depended largely upon the interests and concerns of the teacher.

D. The Women's Educational Programs

Adult education in The Methodist Church takes place with unusual effectiveness in the Christian Social Relations program of The Woman's Division. It constitutes a comprehensive and often a brilliant aspect of Methodism's effort to express in every place a voice of Christian social concern and intelligent action. The tributary societies to the Department of Christian Social Relations provided important historical precedents and sources for the present program of education among the women.

During the First World War the Ladies Aid Societies became agencies through which women were mobilized for action against

[16] *Epworth Highroad*, I, 50.

alcoholic beverage consumption, for Red Cross work, and for pledge programs on Food Conservation. Methodist women helped organize some of the first Parent-Teacher Associations. In states like Massachusetts following World War I they endorsed bills for licensing all day nurseries and having them inspected by the State Board of Health. In other states the Ladies Aid Societies were deeply involved in temperance education and in the thirties had broad programs which dealt with racial prejudice, rural dilemmas, and unemployment.

Beginning in 1928 there was in the Woman's Convention of the Methodist Protestant Church a Department of Christian Citizenship. The major emphases were in the realms of world peace and temperance, but educational programs also included voting, community betterment, and justice in the economic system.

In the Methodist Episcopal Church, South, the Bureau of Social Service of the Woman's Missionary Council has roots of social concern going back to 1910. During the first fifteen years of their program some of the leading topics included: Condition and Status of Women (1913); Intemperance (1914); Institutions for the Care of the Sick, Dependents, Defectives, and Delinquents (1916); Sabbath Observance (1918); Making Democracy Safe (1919); Labor Reconstruction in America (1920); Homes and Housing (1925). One of the council's early leaders, Miss Belle Bennett, knew the value of welfare legislation, noting:

> Law is a great educator and every local auxiliary ought conscientiously and courageously to work for enactment and enforcement of righteous laws in both our local and state governments. One good law for the protection or betterment of the helpless, defective, or submerged classes will do more to change and ameliorate conditions than all the eleemosynary and philanthropic institutions we could establish in half a century.[17]

The organization played a vital part in creating the General Commission on Interracial Co-operation of which Will W. Alexander became the director. The service of the women in the bureau was noted also for the Leadership Schools for Colored Women that were developed. A summary report in 1936 states:

> One of the by-products for the individual woman has been the building of new interests. Delving into the causes and cures of war, the effects of legalized alcohol, child labor and its abuses, neglect of dependent chil-

---

[17] "Social Service (or Christian Social Relations) in the Woman's Missionary Council of the Methodist Episcopal Church, South, 1910-1940." (Undated mimeographed essay, p. 2).

dren, deliberate violations of the Bill of Rights, the effect of indecent motion pictures and magazines, the plight of the share-cropper—all these and many other matters are becoming topics of interest to women, who, save for their attendance on the missionary societies, would never realize the absorbing interest of such affairs. . . . We have been enabled to give every woman something to do that she *could* do to help in such issues.[18]

In the Woman's Home Missionary Society of the Methodist Episcopal Church the Department of Temperance took an active social stand from the time of its organization in 1905. It "attempted to attack all the evils of the land with Miss Frances Willard's book, *Do Everything*, as its guide." [19] By 1917 there were sixty-five conference secretaries assisting in the work of the temperance movement in the church. Though interested in all reform and welfare movements, especially in the crusade against child labor, increasing attention was given to temperance, prohibition, and law-enforcement. Then, in 1928, "A Call to Patriotism" was issued which summoned the women to wider fields of action. The "call" said in part:

Active participation in all matters which relate to government and public welfare, through the use of the ballot, is the patriotic duty of every woman of voting age . . . Our objective as home missionary women is the winning of America to Christ. This objective can be reached only by purifying the political, social and economic conditions of our country . . . Our missionary task is not alone the establishment of settlements, the alleviation of suffering and distress, and the care of underprivileged women and children; it is also to discover what gives rise to poverty, inefficiency, child-labor and kindred conditions, and to abolish the cause.[20]

The response to the broader program during the thirties developed to the point that in 1939 there were 77 conference, 227 district, and 3,369 auxiliary secretaries of Christian Citizenship and about 200 chairmen of citizenship departments in units of the Wesleyan Service Guild.

The Wesleyan Service Guild grew out of a need felt by individual women who wished to participate actively in the women's work of the church but could not do so because of the limitations made by the hours of their gainful employment. Two slogans describe important emphases in the Guild's program: (1) "Every member an

---

[18] *Ibid.*, p. 7.
[19] Ada Townsend, "Christian Citizenship in The Woman's Home Missionary Society of the Methodist Episcopal Church" (mimeographed essay, p. 1).
[20] *Ibid.*, p. 1.

intelligent voter" and (2) "Christian business women for a Christian business world."

In the field of World Citizenship there was a striking development between 1931 and 1940 in the Women's Foreign Missionary Society of the Methodist Episcopal Church. The Committee on World Citizenship combined education and political action on topics which included the World Court, conscientious objection to military training, the Nye Committee for Investigation of the Munitions Industry, the quota system for allowing Orientals to enter the United States, a movie code to control block booking, and a protest against increasing appropriations for naval and military purposes. On the subject of prohibition repeal a "Loyalty Pledge" was sent out to eighty thousand, and thirty-five thousand were returned, pledging personally to abstain from alcoholic beverages. The Committee co-operated on a number of projects with the Board of Education in the preparation of study materials.

With unification in 1939 the newly organized Woman's Division moved forward on the bases of these earlier approaches and developed a strong and comprehensive program, providing positive action leadership along with well co-ordinated local study groups. Miss Dorothy McConnell and Mrs. E. R. Bartlett represented the Woman's Division at San Francisco when the United Nations was organized. Mrs. C. A. Bender has for many years been an official representative of the Division at the United Nations. Miss Thelma Stevens has given continuing leadership in Christian Social Relations for twenty years. In 1946 Clare Booth Luce placed into the *Congressional Record* a copy of the report which the Department of Christian Social Relations had proposed at its meeting on December 1, 1945 at Buck Hill Falls, Pennsylvania. In introducing the program report in the *House of Representatives* Mrs. Luce said, "I recommend a close scrutiny of the social creed of these Methodist women. Here is the conscience of America at work. Neither communism, with its regimentation, and its godlessness, nor reaction with its laissez faire, and mere lip service to Christianity can take any comfort from this document. This is as comprehensive and as Christian a program as any Member of this House is likely to come upon in this session of Congress." [21] The comprehensiveness of the efforts of the Department of Christian Social Relations precludes a summary of its various aspects. They may be illus-

[21] *Congressional Record* (79th Congress), Extension of Remarks of Hon. Clare Booth Luce in the House of Representatives, January 16, 1946.

trated, however, by some of the highlights of a past quadrennium, 1956-60.

In 1956 the department urged study to create a climate for an acceptance of a changing world where people in many lands question American leadership. Thousands of groups studied the fact that many peoples question the foreign policy as well as the racial practices in the United States. These study groups recognized that constructive action for peace must recognize how other peoples fear the United States' motives and military strength. In the field of race relations it was noted that as of June 1, 1956 eighty-two conferences and all jurisdictions had ratified the department's Charter of Racial Policies.

The Woman's Division recommended in January, 1957 that a "Check List on Racial Policies" be prepared to guide Methodist women as they took stock of progress in church and community. Programs on "World Understanding" pointed up the importance of the impact of the missionary enterprise on the political and social life of the peoples in many places in the world. The theme *Understanding Other Cultures* was implemented by a study book with that title. Seminars to the United Nations became a regular part of the Christian Social Relations program.

In 1958 the work of the Woman's Division took note of the fact that the World Council of Churches was ten years old, that the Social Creed marked its fiftieth birthday, and that the Universal Declaration of Human Rights was ten years old on December 10, 1958. Along with *Understanding Other Cultures* there were in use *Youth in a Responsible Society, In Every Place a Voice,* and *Contemporary Man and the United Nations.* Other subjects in 1958 and 1959 were on housing, juvenile protection, temperance, public morals, education, and peace. Responding to the emphases in World Refugee Year the Woman's Division called for a revision of the McCarran-Walter Act and offered some principles which should govern immigration policy. A typical paragraph in its 1960 appeal to the administration and the Congress stated:

The allocation of visas to immigrants should contain no implication of discrimination on grounds of race, national origin, or religion. The principal test for admission should be based on individual qualifications which are related to good citizenship. And additional criteria should be based on (a) the reuniting of families, (b) the right of asylum, (c) special needs to relieve refugee and population pressures, (d) general immigration.[22]

The comprehensive character of the study program of the Woman's Division makes it one of the major institutions of any Christian denomination.

[22] See *World Outlook* (May, 1960), pp. 244-47.

CHAPTER TEN

Boards and Agencies

THE CONNECTIONAL SYSTEM IS EXPRESSED NOT ONLY IN
the structure of the local church and the conferences which comprise Methodist polity, but in a vast network of boards and agencies.
These boards and agencies reflect specialized functions and responsibilities. Though distinctive in purpose and duties, they reflect a
common spirit and relate in varying degrees to social education
and action. None is entirely outside the scope of the social witness
of the church as reflected in the formulation of social doctrine, social work, or social action. Altogether they represent an impressive
institutional structure attached not only to the General Conference,
but also permissively to the jurisdictional conferences and again
specifically to annual conferences. Local churches are related to the
various boards and agencies in a somewhat uneven organizational
pattern.

It is a distinctive trait of The Methodist Church not to let issues
and legislative decisions dangle in the air. When the church takes a
stand, it assigns some responsible agency to follow through in implementing it. Many of the social concerns of Methodism are dealt
with by several agencies which may in turn emphasize them in
their educational or study outlines, as features in periodicals, as
emphases in workshops and consultations, as subjects for special
promotion, and as themes for proposed legislation. Even when the
main function of a board or agency falls to one side of the dominant
concerns of General Conference social legislation, it often impinges
on it at least indirectly. Certainly no agency of the church would
regard its central task to fall outside the range of social education
and action entirely. Of major concern are the Board of Temperance,
the Board of World Peace, and the recent Board of Social and Economic Relations. But other boards are inevitably involved in Methodism's response to the sick, the poor, the migrants, the minority
groups, alcoholics, the mentally ill, the blighted areas of cities, the

291

rural revolution, the dynamics of urban life, the vocations of men and women, and the ministry to youth and children in a period of universally rapid social change.

The impressive historical contributions of the various boards deserve full treatments which are precluded by the limitations of the present volume. Apart from this spatial limitation is the additional fact that definitive historical essays of most of them are lacking as background resources. Here is a much neglected area of research. In an effort to give comparable treatment to all, we shall cite only the name and structure of each, and the official purpose as given in the *Discipline* for 1956. Taken together, these organizations comprise the auxiliary structure through which the whole church helps the conferences and the local churches, as well as individual members, to bear a social witness and to be of service. Certain problems which arise as a result of their bureaucratic structure will be noted below and in the evaluative chapter at the conclusion of this book. A number of the organizations will be cited again in connection with the topical treatment of social questions in Part III of this volume. In the following statements, the order is that used in the *Discipline*.

A. The Co-ordinating Council

Directly responsible to the General Conference, co-ordinates the work of the general administrative agencies. Its relationship to social education and action is indirect.

B. The Council on World Service and Finance

Composed of members who are elected by the General Conference. Generally speaking, its relationship to the subjects of this volume is indirect. However, it has the direct function to "require each world service agency to follow uniform policies and practices in the employment and remuneration of personnel, recognizing differences in local employment conditions." [1]

C. The Methodist Publishing House

Under the direction and control of the Board of Publication. The objects of the former are:

The advancement of the cause of Christianity by disseminating religious knowledge and useful literary and scientific information in the form of books, tracts, and periodicals; the promotion of Christian educa-

---

[1] *Discipline*, 1956, ¶ 1120, sec. 2.

tion; . . . publishing, manufacturing, and distributing books, tracts, periodicals, materials, and supplies for churches and church schools; and such other business as the General Conference may authorize and direct.

This agency has an important relation to social welfare not only in the matter of the quality of materials produced and the industrial relations which it promotes among its own management and workers; but also in the fact that "the net income . . . shall be appropriated to no other purpose than its own operating requirements and the conference claimants." [2] The Board of Publications elects quadrennially a book editor and the editors of general church periodicals. It defines their respective duties. In this latter connection, the work of the editors is organically related to the purposes of the various boards which are ordered and authorized by the church, and which have their respective goals in relation to social education and action.

D. Interboard Commission on the Local Church

To relate the local church effectively to the work of the administrative boards. It co-ordinates the policies and activities of the Board of Missions, the Board of Education, the Board of Evangelism, the Board of Lay Activities, and "any other general agency for which the General Conference may hereafter provide a commission in the local church." This commission refers certain policy problems to the Co-ordinating Council cited above. The boards here referred to are described in the following paragraphs.

E. Board of Missions

Has as its supreme aim

to make the Lord Jesus Christ known to all peoples in all lands as their divine Saviour, to persuade them to become his disciples, and to gather these disciples into Christian churches; to enlist them in the building of the Kingdom of God; to cooperate with these churches; to promote world Christian fellowship; and to bring to bear on all human life the spirit and principles of Christ.

This board is a large and complex organization organized into several divisions. The divisions which are of special relevance to the present study are the Division of National Missions and the Woman's Division of Christian Service.

In the Division of National Missions all the departments have a

[2] *Ibid.*, ¶ 1125.

direct bearing on the concerns of social education and action. These departments have to do with city work, town and country work, the Goodwill Industries, and research and survey. Provision is made for co-ordinating and joint planning wherever the work of various agencies impinges upon one another. The whole nation, with its rapid changes in city and rural life, its minorities and new communities, comes under the attention of this division. In some sense, all types of social problems are related to it.

The Woman's Division of Christian Service is one of the co-ordinate administrative divisions of the Board of Missions. It embraces both world-wide and domestic responsibilities and functions. Its purpose is

to develop and maintain Christian work among women and children at home and abroad; to cultivate Christian family life; to enlist and organize the efforts of Christian women, youth, and children in behalf of native and foreign groups, needy childhood, and community welfare; to assist in the promotion of a missionary spirit throughout the church; to select, train, and maintain Christian workers; to co-operate with the local church in its responsibilities; and to seek fellowship with Christian women of this and other lands in establishing a Christian social order around the world.[3]

The dynamic and prophetic purpose of this last clause brings the work of this society into the closest relationships with the historic concerns of the church in social action.

Within the Division the Department of Christian Social Relations is committed to an aggressive program of community service and the changing of social attitudes and structures. In this respect its purpose is more explicit than that of any board thus far enumerated: "It shall seek to make real and effective the teachings of Jesus as applied to individual, group, racial, and world relationships. It shall endeavor to enlist the participation of church women in such questions as have a moral or religious significance or an important bearing on public welfare." [4] As in the case of other agencies, it has a mandate to co-operate with other agencies of the church having similar purposes, "endeavoring to develop Christian fellowship and to deepen concern for the total responsibility of the church." [5] The continuing contribution of the Woman's Division through the Department of Christian Social Relations is

[3] *Ibid.,* ¶ 1242.
[4] *Ibid.,* ¶ 1248, sec. 1.
[5] *Ibid.,* ¶ 1248, sec. 2.

one of the most impressive in the whole of Methodism. This is due in part to the quality of its leadership, the content of its education program, and the thoroughness of its organization in the local church related to the total conference structure.

F. Methodist Committee on Overseas Relief

Provides for a continuing participation of Methodists in the relief of human suffering around the world. It contributes to the interests of social education and action by reminding the church at all times of the world character of the denomination and the necessity of defining social goals with global perspectives. In this it shares with the Board of Missions an educative role in the formulation of legislation and programs.

G. Board of Education

Like the Board of Missions, is a massive and complex organization. "The purpose of Christian Education," according to the official mandate, "is to learn, to teach, and to use [Jesus'] way by which persons of all ages are related to God as Father and to all men as brothers." [6] We have already noted the educational structure of Methodism in terms of its colleges and universities, its theological schools, and its program in the local church. Its Division of Educational Institutions represents The Methodist Church in all activities connected with secondary, higher, and ministerial education. One of its principal objectives is "to create and maintain an atmosphere in the institutions conducive to the development of a Christian philosophy of life, to the end that all members of the college and university communities may possess a knowledge and understanding of the Christian faith, and that students may emerge from their educational experiences prepared to witness to the Gospel in every area of life." [7] In this aim The Methodist Church concurs in the emphasis on the ministry of the laity in society which has become a hallmark of the ecumenical movement.

Through the Division of the Local Church a comprehensive and unified program of Christian education is developed for children, youth, young adults, and other adults in local churches. This division seeks to translate into educational experience the goals of the church as a whole, the work of the various boards and agencies, and the legislation of the General Conference. Committees of various types have been set up to effect a constructive and co-operative

[6] *Ibid.*, ¶ 1324.
[7] *Ibid.*, ¶ 1351, sec. 2.

relationship among all the organizations that depend on education in the local church to accomplish their goals and purposes.

H. Board of Evangelism

Reflects an historical concern which is sometimes interpreted as indifferent to or critical of social concerns. However, the aim of the present board includes common ground with church organizations in the field of reform and rehabilitation of society. "The aim of evangelism is to bring all men into living, active fellowship with God through Jesus Christ as divine Saviour and through the regenerating power of the Holy Spirit; to gather them into the fellowship of the Church; to lead them to express their Christian discipleship in every area of human life that the Kingdom of God may be realized." [8] The emphasis is on changing the man who creates social problems and social concerns.

I. Board of Lay Activities

Has the purpose "to deepen the spiritual life of the lay members of the church and to cultivate among them an increasing loyalty and interest that they may become an active working force in each local church." [9] As outlined in the *Discipline*, the board has a program with fourteen categories. Three of these have explicit relationships to the main theme of this volume, namely Christian stewardship, benevolences, and the Christianizing of personal and community life. Lay activities are often organized to promote the maintenance function of a local church more than its mission and prophetic function. Nevertheless this board has the future possibility of being organically related to broad social concerns due to the idea of the ministry of the laity. Should this Reformation conception come alive in Methodism, the laity would recognize that they stand in daily life at the frontier positions of the kingdom of God. The major transformation of society will come through the ministry of the laity in the world.

J. Board of Christian Social Concerns

Until 1960 Methodism's historic concern for social salvation was officially represented in the work of three boards and an Interboard Commission on Christian Social Relations. The function of this commission was "to act as the coordinator of the policies and activities of its boards, namely: the Board of Temperance, the Board

[8] *Ibid.*, ¶ 1464.
[9] *Ibid.*, ¶ 1490.

of World Peace, and the Board of Social and Economic Relations." [10] When in 1960 the General Conference united these concerns in the General Board of Christian Social Concerns, the boards became divisions within the new structure designated as follows: Division of Temperance and General Welfare, Division of Human Relations and Economic Affairs, and Division of Peace and World Order.

1. DIVISION OF TEMPERANCE AND GENERAL WELFARE

It is the responsibility of this division "to conduct a program of research, education, and action centering around the following Christian social concerns: alcohol problems; addiction to injurious habits such as use of tobacco and drugs; gambling; pornography; juvenile delinquency and crime; penal system and rehabilitation; mental health and medical care; problems associated with the aging population, and planned parenthood; traffic safety; and such other concerns as the board may specify." [11]

The 1880's saw the rise of new temperance organizations in American society and a drive for the regulation of the beverage alcohol industry. In 1880 legislation of The Methodist Episcopal Church required a committee on Temperance in each pastoral charge. This branch of Methodism established in 1904 the first permanent and official Temperance Society, but left it without a budget. Opponents argued that the Methodist Church itself was a great temperance agency and that there was no need for a separate agency. In the General Conferences of 1908 and 1912 a budget was authorized if the Society could raise the funds. Clarence True Wilson served as executive secretary from 1910-1936, with Deets Pickett as research secretary from 1913-54, founding *The Voice* and *Clipsheet* as agency organs. In 1916 the Society became The Board of Temperance, Prohibition, and Public Morals with its headquarters in Washington, D. C. The Methodist Building was begun in 1917 and completed in 1924.

The Methodist Episcopal Church, South, was less militant than the Northern branch at the beginning of the twentieth century, carrying on most of its temperance work at the Conference level. In 1918 it created the Commission on Temperance and Social Service, with a broad scope of activities including industrial, interracial, and international relationships, although the main concern was prohibition. This agency, like its counterpart in the North, had

[10] *Ibid.*, ¶ 1516.
[11] *Discipline*, 1960, ¶ 1535.

meager resources for its task; and its work was mainly carried on by Bishop James A. Cannon, Jr., from Washington, D. C. In 1926 it was made a board of the church and was given financial support from General Conference funds.[12]

In the 1920's each board was fighting for the financial support of its church and for an enforcement of prohibition in the society at large. In 1927 the Southern board issued a "Statement on Labor Conditions in Southern Industry," a quite responsible pronouncement indicating the scope of its concern; however, the board was rebuked for "meddling in politics." Both boards opposed Al Smith in the 1928 presidential campaign with reasons divided between his being a "wet" and a Roman Catholic. Both faced acute financial problems in 1933, and so neither waged a major campaign against the enactment of repeal legislation.

1933 was a crucial year for the temperance movement within and without the church, as it faced the defeat involved in repeal. The Methodist Episcopal Church, South, had its General Conference the following year at which the Board of Temperance and Social Service was dissolved on the basis of economy and efficiency and in the interests of temperance education as opposed to political action. The traditional concern for temperance was not questioned and the Board of Christian Education assumed responsibility for temperance education, while the College of Bishops was responsible for pronouncements on social questions; and industrial, interracial, and international problems were assigned to the Board of Lay Activities. Bishop Cannon had been a symbol of the work of the board and had made many enemies; the dissolution of the board took temperance work in Southern Methodism out of his hands.

In the Methodist Episcopal Church the Commission on Reorganization appointed at the 1932 General Conference recommended combining the work of the Board of Temperance, Prohibition, and Public Morals in the proposed Division of Educational Service. In 1936 the shock of repeal and the reaction against temperance leadership were farther in the past. The depression was a less critical problem, and the church was primarily concerned with the impending union of 1939. The General Conference never voted explicitly

[12] Joseph L. Allen, Jr., notes that the growth in denominational agencies parallels the growth of financial support and power of the General Conference in Northern and Southern Methodism. There was no official board of Temperance in The Methodist Protestant Church. Much of the material in this section is drawn from Allen's Ph.D. dissertation, "The Methodist Board of Temperance as an Instrument of Church Policy" submitted to the Yale University Graduate School in 1957.

on the continued existence of the Board of Temperance, Prohibition, and Public Morals; yet in 1939 the Uniting Conference produced in The Methodist Church a Board of Temperance with few changes from its predecessor in the Methodist Episcopal Church. There was little change in concerns or goals and the only structural change was the election of board members from the Jurisdictions rather than from General Conference (plus some members at large elected by the Board itself).

The late 1930's and early 1940's were a period of readjustment for the temperance movement. Bishop Edwin Holt Hughes had been the leading figure in the Methodist Episcopal Church as president of the board from 1932-40. Ernest Hunt Cherrington, who had worked with the Anti-Saloon League since 1902, was executive secretary of the board from 1936 on into the united church and until 1948. He brought an approach more avowedly educational and more restrained. From repeal on, the temperance forces were on the defensive. On the one hand, there were criticisms of the earlier tactics of the boards and of the existence of separate boards. On the other hand, the church gave increasing attention to problems of church union, race, industrial relations, and others incident to World War II. Since the war there has been a reawakening of interest in temperance and an expanded program of the board.

Several new issues for the Board of Temperance emerged in the 1940's. One was concern for the protection of men in the armed forces. A second concern was the advertising of beverage alcohol in interstate commerce. Earlier boards had co-operated with the Anti-Saloon League and the Women's Christian Temperance Union. From 1943 the board has worked more closely with the Yale Center for Alcohol Studies, Alcoholics Anonymous, and similar agencies. This signified a new concern for alcoholism and for the victims, with leadership from Bishop John Wesley Lord, who became a member of the board in 1948 and president in 1956, emphasizing the church's pastoral responsibility for alcoholics. A 1944 court decision established the right of the Board of Temperance to influence legislation and still retain its tax-exempt status. However, the board has never considered itself to be a lobbying agency in the sense that the Friends' Committee on National Legislation is a registered lobby in Washington.

Caradine R. Hooton became executive secretary of the Board of Temperance in 1949 and has stressed a "positive" approach, emphasizing that abstinence is one expression of a positive Christian life. Total abstinence for the individual and some form of restraint for the alcoholic beverage industry still remain the two main goals of Methodist temperance activity.

Political goals have not been replaced but have received relatively less attention in the last few years. Legislative effort has been centered on the restricting of advertising of alcoholic beverages and on the banning of alcoholic beverages from airlines, but there have also been programs on the state and local level. Personal dedication has been symbolized by Commitment Day, begun as a church-wide special observance by the General Conference of 1948.

The pastoral responsibility for victims of alcoholism has provided a major emphasis on rehabilitation. In 1955 the board sponsored a consultation for professors of pastoral counseling in Methodist seminaries. The educational emphasis has involved modern media of mass communication and leadership training with church and youth leaders. There has also been an increasing concern with theological problems and wider appreciation of social problems related to alcoholism and drinking.

This latter appreciation of other problems has meant closer co-operation with the Boards of World Peace and of Social and Economic Relations. This co-operation is symbolized in jurisdictional briefing conferences co-operatively sponsored and first established by the General Board of Temperance. The board was instrumental in initiating the new common publishing venture *Contact*. The General Conference of 1956 made the merger of the three boards permissible at the annual conference level. About 50 per cent of the annual conference boards merged. In some cases mergers dissolved after a trial period. The whole program is in a dynamic stage of creative effort as this volume is being written; it is concerned with positive education, commitment to abstinence, rehabilitation, and legislation. In 1960 commissions on Christian Social Concerns became mandatory at the local church level.

2. THE DIVISION OF PEACE AND WORLD ORDER

It has the responsibility to conduct a research, education, and action program in the following areas: "American foreign policy; United Nations and related international organizations; disarmament and nuclear weapon control; space control; foreign aid; tariffs, and trade; immigration and naturalization; military policy and conscription legislation; conscientious objectors and the draft; and such other concerns as the board may specify." [13]

Methodism has the distinction of being the first Protestant de-

---

[13] *Discipline*, 1960, ¶ 1538.

nomination in this country, and probably throughout the world, to establish a special agency for the advancement of peace. Already in 1924 the Methodist Episcopal Church had created a Commission on World Peace. At the time of union in 1939 it was continued and the General Conference in 1940 made it one of the regular World Service agencies. In 1952 it was renamed the Board of World Peace. Its first executive secretary, beginning in 1936, Charles F. Boss, Jr., has been a personal symbol and safeguard of the "apostolic continuity" of its work. In 1956 he became Executive Secretary of International Affairs. Daniel Taylor came to the board in 1957, was made General Secretary in 1958, and resigned in 1960.

The *Discipline*, 1956, defines the purpose of the board as follows:

It shall be the purpose of the Board of World Peace to advance the interests of the Kingdom of our Lord through international justice and the spirit of good will throughout the world; to endeavor to create the will to peace, the conditions for peace, and the organization for peace; and to organize effective action in the church for the advancement of peace.

Its extensive range of functions include:

To keep the Church informed concerning the actions of the National Council and the World Council of Churches as these relate to the field of world peace and world order.

To teach the Christian meaning of peace with freedom and justice.

To help analyze current situations and facts in an effort to better understand the problems of world peace in our day.

To help the Church create the will to peace, the conditions of peace, and to support international organization and programs for peace.

To see that The Methodist Church is organized in accordance with provisions of the General Conference in the local church, district, conference, and in areas and jurisdictions where these are found to be desirable.

To provide for the churches programs for peace and essential organizational and promotional materials.

To educate concerning the United Nations and its work, and in appropriate ways to support it as the existing international agency through which peoples may co-operate in creating the conditions of peace and in maintaining peace.

To conduct conferences or seminars on world peace for Methodist leaders in co-operation with the United Nations and in Washington in co-operation with the Department of State.

To maintain—as we have since 1945—consultative relationships with the United Nations, bringing the purposes and principles of the Church to bear upon UN policies and programs.

To maintain unofficial consultative relationships with appropriate divisions and personnel of the Department of State.

To seek to render aid in the peace programs of Methodist leaders throughout The Methodist Church.

To witness before appropriate Committees of Congress when legislation bearing upon war or peace is under consideration.

To exercise responsible action when questions of freedom of conscience among Methodist conscientious objectors are involved.

To co-operate as one of the World Service agencies among the boards and other agencies of the church in the advancement of the total program for the establishment of the kingdom of God on earth.

The Methodist peace witness displays a constant interaction and tension between two chief emphases, which we for convenience sake may call "pacifist" and "nonpacifist." The Commission and later the Board of World Peace reflect the shifting configurations of these two tendencies and have in turn been a chief voice and instigator in their development. Whereas its leadership long showed a pacifist orientation, this has particularly in the postwar period been supplemented, and in part overshadowed, by a pronounced interest in the United Nations and related organizations for international co-operation.[14]

[14] Many Methodists belong to the Fellowship of Methodist Pacifists. The specific accomplishments of Methodists on behalf of a more peaceful world include a wide range of activities. Some like Donald Temmerman, Daniel L. Marsh, and Alfred Moore were active in combating the compulsory R.O.T.C. program. Some like Annalee Stewart and John Swomley were active in preventing the passage during World War II of the Nurses' Draft and the Labor Draft. Many like E. F. Tittle and Henry Crane were ardent leaders in legal recognition rights of conscience and in developing a nonmilitaristic and near-pacifist mood in the churches. Methodists were active in many peace organizations such as the Fellowship of Truth for Peace, the National Council for the Prevention of War, the American Friends Service Committee, the National Peace Conference, the Women's International League for Peace and Freedom, the Church Peace Union, the National Council against Conscription, and the Church Peace Mission.

The peace witness in Methodism, including the strongest pacifist emphasis, has been internationalist and broadly related to the whole range of social tensions. Examples are abundant of those who have served in the Fellowship of Reconciliation: Claud Nelson and Constance Rumbough, Southern secretaries; Charles Webber, industrial secretary; James Farmer, student and race relations secretary; Orval Etter, Glenn Smiley, and Herman Will, regional sec-

The statement of the General Conference of the Methodist Episcopal Church in 1924 is an aggressive projection of the task ahead: "We are determined to outlaw the whole war system. . . . The world is now open to a crusade for peace. . . . America should lead the way. . . . We set ourselves to create the will to peace. . . . We set ourselves to create the conditions for peace. . . . We set ourselves to create the organization for peace." Revulsion against war on religious, moral, or humanitarian grounds, frequently coupled with isolationism, was part of the national sentiment at the time. While combating the isolationist mood in certain circles, the Commission on World Peace shared in the general rejection of war; but, like the historic peace churches, it persisted in doing so when it had ceased to be fashionable and opportune.

Less official than General Conferences or Councils of Bishops, it was able to speak out more concretely and forthrightly on abolition of armaments, war propaganda, R.O.T.C., and other forms of peacetime military training, exemption for conscientious objectors, and so forth. In 1934 and 1935 it urged the forthcoming General Conference to enact legislation looking toward the withdrawal of Methodist ministers from the chaplaincy. In 1944 it appointed Rev. Carl D. Soule as full-time chaplain for Methodist conscientious objectors, and the present board maintains a registration service for conscientious objectors.

The outbreak of the Second World War confronted the Christian conscience with a difficult dilemma, and many reluctantly changed their minds. But still in 1941 the Commission went on record opposing entry of the United States into the war in Europe or in the Far East. The basis for the Commission's persistent opposition to conscription was forcefully expressed in an address by its executive secretary:

We are convinced that peacetime universal compulsory military training is, in the United States, *unnecessary, inexpedient, undemocratic, and bad international policy.* The proposal, we believe, is not only inexpedient and unnecessary, but *wrong,* when weighed in the scales of the Christian Ethic, and when judged in the light of the Christian testimony.[15]

The marked pacifist note in the Commission's work in the thirties

retaries; George Houser, projects secretary; John Swomley, executive secretary; Perry Saito, interpreter of the Japanese-Americans and relocation camps; Charles Iglehart, Japan; and numerous Methodists who have served on the National Council of the F.O.R.

[15] Charles F. Boss, Jr., *Conscription and the Christian Testimony* (Chicago: Commission on World Peace, 1946), p. 14.

and early forties, and still observable in such issues as peacetime military training, is further evidenced by the fact that the Commission in these matters frequently sided with the historic peace churches.

The denunciation of war and all forms of militarism has from the beginning, and increasingly in the postwar period, been coupled with a constructive interest in the larger problems of world order. Thus in times when nationalism and isolationism were rife, the Commission gave vigorous support to the League of Nations and even expressed itself in favor of an international police force. It urged the United States government to adhere to the World Court at The Hague and to take part in disarmament conferences.

With the outbreak of the Second World War and the crumbling of the League of Nations, the Commission launched out on a trail which eventually should lead to its current broad-gauged involvement in world affairs. Under far-sighted leaders like Bishop Oxnam, Dr. Sockman, Dr. Tittle, and its own executive secretary, it rapidly assumed a vanguard position among the religious groups which realized that the foundation for a just and lasting peace must be laid during the war. Even before Pearl Harbor the Commission, expressing its "conviction that the world has now far more to gain by a *negotiated peace* than by another dictated peace," laid down a series of guiding principles for a new world order, which are worth quoting *in extenso:*

The United States should immediately declare its willingness to cooperate with other governments in the formation of a world order based on these principles: (a) each nation shall reserve to itself the right to determine its own form of government and way of life; (b) every nation shall surrender the claim to absolute national sovereignty, that is, the alleged right to seek its own interest at any cost to other nations; and (c) nations shall together seek a just solution of such problems of international concern as the administration of colonies, access to raw materials and markets, the determination of tariffs, and the stabilization of currencies. It follows that the United States should declare its willingness to cooperate with other governments in establishing whatever international organization may be needed to realize these ends.[16]

From then on, the Commission remained closely associated with the Federal Council's Commission on a Just and Durable Peace and its endeavors to evolve Christian policies and to arouse public opinion. It has provided signal leadership in the national study confer-

[16] "An Appeal for Justice, Reconciliation, and Peace," statement adopted Dec. 17, 1940.

ences on world order sponsored periodically by the Council.[17] It played a major part in the Bishops' Crusade for a new World Order in 1943.

The postwar period has seen a remarkable expansion of the sweep and drive of the Commission, as a rapid glance at its various program areas will indicate.

The board carries out an extensive program of education and promotion, designed to activate the concern for peace and to create a well-informed Christian opinion about world events and appropriate attitudes thereto. The staff keeps up a continuous program of speaking, preaching, conducting seminars at all levels throughout the country, and since 1950 All-European Methodist Seminars on World Peace. It conducts thirty to forty United Nations Seminars a year. Specialized seminars on the United Nations are held in New York. A monthly four-page bulletin, *Methodist Peace Courier*, appeared after 1954 until it was replaced by *Contact*.

The board has testified before Congressional Committees on such problems as draft renewal, universal military training, foreign economic aid, atomic energy legislation, immigration, and reciprocal trade agreements.

In its educational activities and its relations to other bodies, the board serves not only as an interpreter of the corporate mind of the church as articulated in the pronouncements and actions of General Conferences and other units. Similar to other specialized agencies, it also functions as a watchtower and an idea-laboratory for the church in matters of peace, thus providing constructive guidance in the formulation of positions and policies. The closely knit interactive structure of the denominations offers numerous opportunities for such an outreach. Many official actions of the church in this field quite naturally originate with the board. It was deeply involved in the quadrennial emphasis on World Order during the years 1952-

---

[17] In May 1941, the Commission convened an Exploratory Conference on the Bases of a Just and Enduring Peace, in Chicago, Bishop Oxnam serving as convener and chairman, and Charles F. Boss, Jr., as secretary. The report, *When Hostilities Cease*, was used extensively during the war years and reflected the co-operative thinking of Methodist agencies and the Federal Council. Reports included the Christian Faith, presented by Ernest F. Tittle; Economic Foundations, presented by S. Paul Schilling; Agricultural Proposals, presented by Earl J. Sawyer; Political Structure, presented by Earl Cranston; the Contribution of Missions, presented by Wade Crawford Barclay; and the Program of the Church, presented by Harold C. Case. The effect of this Exploratory Conference was multiplied many times by the excellent publicity which it received through both the religious and secular press, made possible by the recently organized Department of Publicity, directed by Ralph A. Stoody.

56. It co-operates closely with the Department of Christian Social Relations of the Woman's Division of Christian Service, which vies with the board in its zeal to make Methodists conscious of the fact that world-mindedness begins at home.

It proved difficult to bring about fully profitable co-operation among the boards specializing in Christian responsibilities in society. However, the Interboard Commission on Christian Social Relations was set up by the General Conference of 1952 to remedy this situation. These boards jointly issued the informative bulletin entitled *Contact*.

It lies in the nature of the case that the board performs much of its work through broad-range contacts and consultations with other peace organizations. Particularly its executive, Dr. Boss, has shown outstanding ability in developing such "connectional" relationships. He has served as an accredited observer and consultant at assemblies and committee meetings of the United Nations, beginning in 1945 with the San Francisco Conference on International Organization; has been chairman of the Council on Non-Governmental Representatives Section at the United Nations on the Peaceful Use of Atomic Energy; and participates frequently in "Background" conferences arranged by the State Department on foreign policy matters. The board has a close tie-in with the Department of International Affairs of the National Council of Churches, whose membership includes a notably high percentage of Methodists.

A statement by Dr. Boss in his quadrennial report of 1952 aptly describes the developing role of the board as an agent of Methodism's dynamic concern with world affairs: "The Commission on World Peace has developed, one might say, from a resolution on peace to an international-wide program for peace. It has moved from actions largely directed to issues in the United States to a program resting upon universal and ecumenical relations."

3. THE DIVISION OF HUMAN RELATIONS AND ECONOMIC AFFAIRS

The Division of Human Relations and Economic Affairs takes over the functions of the previous Board of Social and Economic Relations. As indicated in the narrative section of this study, this board from 1952 to 1960 was the official successor to the controversial and unofficial Methodist Federation for Social Action. Like the other divisions it has the responsibility to conduct a program of research, education, and action. Its principal concerns are: "race relations; civil liberties; public policy on education; church and state relations; civic responsibility; labor-management relations;

agriculture; conservation; government and private economic policy and practice; technological change; unemployment; housing; and such other concerns as the division may specify." [18]

The program activity has featured a number of conferences, seminars, study groups, publication, and a number of co-operative ventures with other church bodies and groups. In the field of economic life are the industrial relations and the agricultural seminars. The former bring clergy and laity into close relationships in America's increasingly industrial society, pointing up the responsibility of the church in industrial life. The latter are designed in rural areas as training programs for Annual Conference and local church chairmen and members of Commissions on Social and Economic Relations.

In the area of race relations the board's field program consists of interracial conferences. Twenty such conferences have been held in all jurisdictions and have provided not only substantial information beyond that previously known, but also practical results in increased interracial fellowship and work.

Much of the board's program requires co-operative relationships with other boards and agencies. This has been necessary in order to develop aids for the local church Commissions on Christian Social Relations. There has been close co-operation with the Department of Christian Social Relations of the Woman's Division, with the Television, Radio, and Film Commission, and with the Curriculum Committee of the Editorial Division. In 1958 the Board of Social and Economic Relations in co-operation with six other agencies sponsored the first Industrial Relations Conference; and in 1959 the first church-wide Human Relations Conference was sponsored with nine other agencies. In both of these efforts the board served as the co-ordinating agency and assumed responsibility for implementing the policy developed by the general planning group.

The work of this board, as is the case in others also, has prepared a considerable body of literature for general distribution and has sponsored study books and some major research studies. There have also been important visual aids. *The Modern Samaritan,* written by Clair M. Cook, has been popular and useful. During the McCarthy period it produced *The Sound of a Stone,* which dealt directly with the problem of character assassination, the dangers of slander and gossip, and the Christian responsibility to maintain an objective and honest appraisal of the current civil liberties situation. It also produced *Understanding and Preventing Juvenile Delinquency,* the

[18] *Discipline,* 1960, ¶ 1541.

only book of its kind, in relating this field to the churches, a co-operative venture with Haskell M. Miller. In the *Road to Brotherhood* the board attempted a presentation of the wide range of viewpoints on race relations, containing not only the case for integration, but also the case for the "separate but equal" policy. In *Security in the Modern World,* written by Elizabeth E. Hoyt, the board has sponsored a book dealing with the economic aspects of security and takes as its case study social security legislation. It also deals with the personal responsibility of individual Christians and their churches. There has also been a study on *Christianity and Communism* which deals with the theological conflict between these two rival faiths. Within this general research and study aspect of the board's work must be included the four volumes of the present series on Methodist social thought and action.

One of the new lines of activity initiated by this board is in the field of church-state relations. In many ways this is the most ambiguous issue facing the Protestant churches today. Work in this field is still in a preliminary stage with specific study and action projects for local churches and annual conferences under way.

The work of the General Board of Christian Social Concerns as an integrated agency falls outside the scope of this book, but its structure may be noted to include a general secretary, who is Dr. Caradine R. Hooton, and three associate secretaries assigned to the three divisions respectively.

K. Board of Hospitals and Homes

The social witness of the church is made through social doctrine, social action, and social welfare. Social welfare is not generally included in the category of social education and action, though it is closely related to them in various ways. This volume has had to exclude any major concern with the hospitals and homes of The Methodist Church. Nevertheless, they are an expression of the compassionate service of the Christian community. "Human welfare," as the Episcopal Address of 1956 stated,

owes its origin to the Church's concern . . . the increasing public concern for health and social services is a tribute to the Christian Church which first sponsored them and a testimony to the continued need of the Church's interest in their provision and direction . . . efforts to create more church-related hospitals and homes are gaining momentum . . . spiritual insight, professional proficiency, and personal dedication are needed to convey the Master's healing touch.

The program of the Board of Hospitals and Homes brings it into a co-operative relationship with the church nationally and with public health and welfare departments. It has a concern to develop homes for older persons; to develop health and diagnostic centers in unserved rural areas; and to develop centers for the care of the chronically ill. The over-all program also includes the extension of hospital services and facilities, child-care homes, rehabilitative services for unwed mothers, the enlargement of chaplain's work in hospitals and homes, and the recruitment and training of quality personnel for Christian centers in the fields of health and welfare.

The structure of the Methodist response through the Board of Hospitals and Homes includes the making of surveys, consultation in fund-raising plans, providing architectural data, formulating standards, sponsoring the National Association of Methodist Hospitals and Homes, and providing consultation on all forms of operation in its affiliated institutions. The Gold Cross organization combines the promotional societies of the Northern and Southern groups which assisted hospitals and homes before 1939. Gold Cross has proved to be a popular philanthropic agency of the church.

There are forty-eight Methodist child-care agencies and homes for children. They provide group care, foster homes, or adoptive services for about six thousand children annually. Methodist homes for youth provide wholesome living and understanding. Seven of the homes for youth and deaconesses serve 778 young persons annually. There are special homes for unwed mothers and their babies. Methodist homes for older persons offer security and encourage a sense of independence. These homes add "Life to years and years to life" through sympathetic service, understanding, and individual attention. The seventy-seven homes now care for seven thousand persons.

In 1958 Methodism operated seventy-four hospitals in twenty-eight states. The capacity of these hospitals totalled 18,409. They served in that year 705,522 in-patients and 689,008 out-patients. Except in the mental hospital field, The Methodist Church has developed a highly significant network of hospitals, some of them truly great.

At the present time there is a pronounced interest in interdisciplinary work among the helping professions. Nursing, social work, medicine, and the ministry are finding interpenetrating areas of service and complementary roles of work. Social doctrine, social welfare, and social action form a natural whole. This should reflect itself in the plans, policies, and programs of the great agencies of the church. As life expectancy increases, men and women naturally credit the advances of medicine for much of it. It is well to remember that the improvement in social conditions attending the implementation of the Social Creed has probably been an even more important factor in improving the nation's health. Through the church, social service and social action become partners in redemption.

This cursory survey of the structure of the Methodist response as provided by its boards and agencies invites a few summary comments and observations to which we shall also allude in the final evaluative chapter of this book.

1. Methodism has developed an impressive range of instrumentalities to deal with the total scope of personal need and social institutions.

2. An adequate account of the work of these boards and agencies cannot be had until intensive research has been undertaken on the history, development, program, and contribution of each one.[19]

3. When properly motivated, co-ordinated, and informed, these boards and agencies have a tremendous power for social education and action.

4. With few exceptions the major boards and commissions of the church reflect a pervasive concern for the quality of social life and destiny of the individual person.

5. The structure of the Methodist response in these boards and agencies is highly institutionalized and deeply implicated in the complex bureaucracy of Methodism.

6. Institutional promotion consumes a great deal of energy in this complex institutional group of operations.

7. Balance of representation and power among the jurisdictions is reflected in the control of the general administrative boards. The principle of equilibrium among sections and jurisdictions is sometimes a threat to the prophetic witness of the church. Emergent policies are often compromises affecting the essentials of Christian social ethics. On the other hand, jurisdictional representation makes the emergent resolutions more truly the voice of the church, at least in a parliamentary sense of the term.

8. Massive bureaucratic competition for the attention of the Methodist public tends to cause the boards and agencies to measure effectiveness in quantitative terms, including the tons of literature distributed.

9. Methodism has yet to solve the problem of how the local church

---

[19] It is a matter of special regret that the work of the Department of Christian Social Relations of the Woman's Division of Christian Service has never been adequately studied. Dissertations have been written on the Board of Temperance and the Board of World Peace.

can be a truly effective unit in changing social attitudes and being a voice for those who have no voice and a home where every man can be at home.

10. Official Methodist agencies cannot displace the leadership role of the individual layman and clergyman and unofficial expressions of prophetic concern, protest, and action.[20]

[20] The General Conference of 1960 created the Board of Christian Social Concerns with three special emphases: the Division of Temperance and General Welfare; the Division of Peace and World Order; and the Division of Human Relations and Economic Affairs. The General Conference requires the establishment of a Commission of Christian Social Concerns in every Methodist church. *The Methodist Story* for June 1960 summarizes the implications of the General Conference actions for local churches and presents program planning outlines in great detail, including resources and emphases in all areas of the church's life and work.

PART THREE

Major Areas
of Methodist Concern and Action

Introduction

THE HISTORICAL REVIEW IN PART I HAS PRESENTED MANY facets of the Methodist response and initiative in the political, social, and economic life of America. Beginning as a Social Creed with a limited range of social concerns, the Methodist witness has become a powerful and comprehensive expression of doctrine and activity. Almost wholly separate concerns, such as temperance and world peace, have become integral aspects of a total gospel to the whole world. Though integral they are as yet coherently related neither to all of the church's official concerns nor to the life and work of the local church. In Part II we have noted the structure of the Methodist response. We now turn to specific areas of *concern*.

The research team developed a questionnaire which has been used to find a scientific sample of Methodist beliefs and attitudes on the problems discussed in the four volumes of this study. It will be referred to as MESTA. In presenting the materials of this part of the witness of twentieth-century Methodism the original numbers of the questions are included. The reader will find the whole questionnaire and the percentage scores on each question in the appendixes of volumes three and four.

This part of the book attempts a systematic statement of Methodism's social pronouncements on major social questions. In each section the responses of the questionnaire will be included. Where useful the percentages are indicated also for each Jurisdiction. Attention is given to the relation of Methodist thought to the pronouncements and analyses of ecumenical bodies. This has proved to be a significant relationship. Finally, the actions of the 1956 General Conference are presented in such a way as to provide a clear statement of the church's official position.

CHAPTER ELEVEN

Human Rights and Liberties

METHODISTS HAVE INHERITED, CONSERVED, AND DEVELOPED a profound concern for human rights and liberties and have a significant consensus concerning the grounds on which such human rights are based. The MESTA survey showed that for the respondents:

20. HUMAN RIGHTS SHOULD BE SAFEGUARDED BECAUSE

Their recognition will lead to a
happier society ....11.3 per cent

Man is ultimately responsible to God
alone, and must be free to fulfill his
responsibility ....27.0 per cent

People should have unlimited opportunity to develop their capacities
as children of God ....42.3 per cent

Man by nature is a being of inherent
dignity and worth ....14.3 per cent

Write-in .... 1.4 per cent

No report .... 3.7 per cent

These convictions can be clearly translated into such areas as the freedom of action of school teachers and ministers. No special commentary is needed to interpret the meaning of Methodist opinion on the following two tables.

31. A SCHOOL TEACHER SHOULD

Join only those organizations approved by the institution employing him .... 8.6 per cent

Be free to join any "cause" organization (such as the League of Women Voters, National Association for the Advancement of Colored People, Citizens Council, Americans for Democratic Action, American Legion) as long as his membership does not interfere with the effectiveness of his teaching ....70.4 per cent

Be able to join any "cause" organization ....12.1 per cent

Join no "cause" organization ...... 2.1 per cent

Write-in .... 2.9 per cent

No report .... 3.9 per cent

In the Southeastern Jurisdiction the freedom which won 70.4 per cent of the total responses received 56.6 per cent of them.

32. A METHODIST MINISTER SHOULD

Be free to take a position on controversial issues if it is in accord with the Social Creed .... 9.7 per cent

Be free to take a position on controversial issues as long as this does not interfere with his parish ministry ....14.4 per cent

Be free to take, on controversial issues, any position which he regards as Christian ....68.4 per cent

Not speak on controversial issues .. 1.6 per cent

Speak only on issues on which there is agreement in his local church .. 1.8 per cent

Write-in .... 2.2 per cent

No report .... 1.9 per cent

This heritage is rooted in a profoundly cherished tradition.

The struggle for human rights and civil liberties is one of the most glorious chapters in the records of human civilization. Its landmarks in the history of the Western world are familiar: The British Magna Carta (1215), the U.S. Declaration of Independence and the Bill of Rights, the French Declaration of the Rights of Man and of the Citizen. In our times, totalitarian regimes wielding the power of virtually unlimited political, economic, and psychological control over their subjects have sought to make human rights and civil liberties a government concession and severely restricted their exercise. Also in democratic societies, including our own, the rapid extension of government influence into widening areas of public life, the pressures of fanatical groups, and the many "hidden persuaders" exploiting the mass media provided by modern techniques, are subtly eroding the domains of human freedom and responsible choice. However, this is fortunately only one side of the picture. The very enormity of the crimes against humanity, perpetrated by forces of tyranny and oppression, has called forth a rigorous counterattack. Freedoms long taken for granted, at least by their beneficiaries, have again for many become a highly prized possession worth fighting for—not as a privilege for the few, but as the birthright of all.

And whereas "the freedom trail" heretofore has been a Western trail, mankind as a whole is now joining in the forward surge. The political emancipation of hundreds of millions of people in East Asia and Africa, and their tumultous struggle to attain civil, social, and economic rights which thus far have been the white man's prerogative is an event of momentous consequence in the quest for freedom. A new dimension is unfolding in our time—an emergent gathering resolve to define man's rights and liberties more inclusively and to secure their recognition and observance more universally.

The dynamic awareness of widening ranges of the subject has not yet been focused in commonly accepted definitions. But a preliminary delineation of its scope will be in order. Rights may, in the first place, refer to certain inalienable moral claims upon society, growing out of the very nature of the human person. Their ultimate basis is variously found in the supreme worth of every individual as a rational being or in man's creaturehood as a child of God. We speak in this connection of the rights, for instance, of life, liberty, and the pursuit of happiness. Liberties or freedoms indicate the ability or opportunity to exercise rights. In accordance with a long tradition in Western history, the expression "civil liberties" frequently carries a polemical thrust; it is used to stake out protective limits of governmental control. The classical rights thus conceived include freedom of speech, press, assembly, religion, the rights of *habeas corpus*, due process of law, and so forth. Again another and broader meaning of the concept is based on a more positive view of government as called to promote the liberty and welfare of citizens. The social, economic, and cultural rights which play such a prominent role in contemporary discussions of the subject may be instanced as such liberties balanced and safeguarded by law.[1]

It is the legal embodiment and enforcement of such concrete rights of individuals and groups that is the center of controversy today. Basic to the various theories is the belief that man is endowed with certain rights and liberties which political authority cannot grant or deny, but is morally bound to protect and promote.

The efforts of the United Nations[2] in this field, though so far crowned with only limited success, are a pioneering attempt to develop the principle that the safeguarding of human rights is not a responsibility of national government alone; it is an international responsibility which must find appropriate expression both in international and domestic jurisdiction. The Preamble of the UN Charter reaffirms "faith in fundamental human rights, in the dignity and worth of the human person, in the equal rights of men and women and all nations large and small." One of the stated purposes of the organization is "to achieve international co-operation . . . in promoting and encouraging respect for human rights and fundamental freedoms for all without distinction as to race, sex, language, or religion" (Art. 1, Sec. 3).

The Universal Declaration of Human Rights adopted by the UN General Assembly in 1948 has set up common standards of achievement for the nations which deserve alert and vigorous support on the part of Christians. The declaration and its tentative implementation in two draft covenants form, in fact, a comprehensive outline of a code of ethics for the human race. The basic philosophy of the declaration is expressed in its recognition "of the inherent dignity and of the equal and inalienable rights of all members of the human family." It states that all human beings "are born free and equal in dignity and rights" and "are endowed with reason and conscience." These rights are coupled with corresponding duties to other persons and to the community. The Draft Covenant on Civil and Political Rights offers an extensive list, including among others the right to life, liberty, and security of person; freedom of thought, conscience, religion, and expression; freedom of movement, association, and peaceful assembly; equal status before the law and fair trial; freedom from slavery and inhuman and degrading treatment;

---

[1] The Report of the President's Committee on Civil Rights, *To Secure These Rights* (New York: Simon and Schuster, 1947), groups human rights under four inclusive heads: 1. The Right to Safety and Security of the Person. 2. The Right to Citizenship and Its Privileges. 3. The Right to Freedom of Conscience and Expression. 4. The Right to Equality of Opportunity.

[2] See, e.g., James Frederick Green, *The United Nations and Human Rights* (Washington, D. C.: The Brookings Institution, 1956).

freedom from interference with privacy and home; the right to marry and to found a family; rights of racial, ethnic, and religious minorities; opportunity to participate in public affairs.

The Second Draft Covenant on Economic, Social, and Cultural Rights represents a new departure. It goes far beyond the traditional definitions of civil liberties and reflects the widening preoccupation with human relationships in an increasingly industrialized world. Its postulates include the right to work; favorable working conditions; rest and leisure; participation in trade unions; social security; accordance of special protection to mothers and children; adequate standard of living; health; education; and participation in cultural life.

This realm of human rights and liberties has been receiving wide and increasing attention in recent years, also on the part of the Christian churches. Denominational and interdenominational agencies in various countries are engaged in sustained efforts to develop Christian postulates and to initiate or support measures for their observance wherever threatened.[3] The Commission of the Churches on International Affairs, a joint agency of the World Council of Churches and the International Missionary Council, is performing an outstanding service in this field, notably in relation to the UN and individual governments.

Out of these persistent labors there is emerging a common body of convictions and concerns which deserve to be better known, and acted upon, also by Methodists. They do, in fact, involve The Methodist Church because of its membership in both the National and the World Council of Churches. Even in instances where such pronouncements have no explicit counterpart in statements of The

[3] See, for example, The Reports of the Sections on Church and State, and on the Universal Church and the World of Nations, of the World Conference on "Church, Community and State," at Oxford in 1937; The Report of the Conference on "The World Mission of the Church" convened by the International Missionary Council at Madras in 1938; statements on religious liberty adopted by the Assemblies of the World Council of Churches at Amsterdam in 1948 and Evanston in 1954; statement on *Religious Liberty* adopted by the National Council of Churches and the Foreign Missions Conference of North America in 1954; statement on The Churches and Human Rights adopted by the Federal Council of Churches in 1948; pronouncements by the National Council of Churches on *Religious and Civil Liberties in the United States of America*, 1955, and on *Freedom of Association*, 1957; *Christian Responsibility on a Changing Planet*, Report by the Fifth World Order Study Conference at Cleveland, Ohio, 1958, convened by the Department of International Affairs of the National Council of Churches; statement on *Human Rights and Religious Freedom*, adopted by the British Council of Churches in 1947. For a world-wide study of the subject, see M. Searle Bates, *Religious Liberty: An Inquiry* (New York: Harper Bros., 1945).

Methodist Church, but are consistent with other statements on related issues, it may reasonably be assumed that they express the Methodist stand as well.

There is a larger measure of consensus in world Christianity today with respect to concrete postulates of human rights and civil liberties than with respect to their religious derivation. This is not astonishing if one considers the range of divergent and partly conflicting religious and cultural traditions that constitute the Christian community. It is rather a matter for gratification that, in spite of their diversities, the Christian churches in many respects are able to present a common front in the furtherance of basic human values.

The Christian approach involves several concentric circles of concern which need to be distinguished for the sake of clarity: freedom as a quality of Christian existence; the freedom of the church; religious freedom; and the whole spectrum of human rights, liberties, and duties. These are different areas of concern which, while all are illuminated by the Christian understanding of God, man, and society, nevertheless are linked to differing *specific* aspects of the Christian faith. Much confusion in Christian thinking about the matter is caused by failure to recognize these distinctions. Another cause is to be found in the circumstance that the church has been fairly slow in constructively relating the unique insights of the Gospels to its quickened sense of responsibility for human rights. As a result, the average Protestant attitude is an undigested mixture of Christian beliefs, philosophical and political ideas stemming from beyond the Enlightenment and the French and American revolutions, and, perhaps most potent, prevailing patterns of behavior in the environing culture. It is a tell-tale illustration of the undiscriminating syncretism rampant in much Protestant religion today, which tends to impair the quality and the transforming power of the Christian witness.

It becomes an entirely different matter, however, when Christian groups, as they join with others in the defense of human dignity and freedom, have to translate the demands rooted in their faith into the common language of human rationality and to employ arguments of persuasion which may be accessible and convincing to political authorities and to non-Christian partners. In other words, theology is translated—and legitimately so—into terms of rational philosophy and law. The natural law tradition has itself an ancient heritage. This accounts, at least in part, for the evident fact that church statements in these matters sometimes seem to be indistinguishable from "secular" utterances.

An analysis of the statements issuing from the ecumenical movement reveals characteristic common emphases, and also some notable differences in basic interpretation. The freedom of the church is a primary concern. Oftentimes this claim is argued on the ground that "the Church demands freedom to proclaim the Gospel to all mankind, and in all spheres of life, not for its own sake, but because it has received this commission from God, who is the Lord also of the state." [4] Religious freedom in the broad sense as well as human rights are seen in the perspective of the church and its divine mission to all men. The ultimate justification for claiming religious freedom for all is found in the very heart of the gospel message—a divine love which works by persuasion and not by coercion, and seeks the free response of responsible beings. Some however, holding that their church is the one true church, would draw the inference that it is in duty bound to claim a preferred status in society.

Others, again, adopt a reverse position, starting from the belief in the inherent worth of man and human brotherhood, and view religious freedom and the freedom of the church as specific instances of this general concept.

If the Christian grounds for religious freedom are not easy to define, the proper construction of the Christian bases and criteria for human rights and civil liberties in general presents even greater complexities and is still a matter of controversial discussion. The interrelationship between Christian freedom, general religious freedom, and other human rights, defies easy definition. Hence the explicit references move largely in the realm of general affirmation. The following statements, however, summarize widely held convictions in the ecumenical community.

While the liberty with which Christ has set men free can neither be given nor destroyed by any government, Christians, because of that inner freedom, are both jealous of its outward expression and solicitous that all men should have freedom in religious life. The nature and destiny of man by virtue of his creation, redemption, and calling, and man's activities in family, state, and culture establish limits beyond which the government cannot with impunity go. [5]

[4] *The Oxford Report*, p. 248. It is asserted that the church, as the community where the liberating power of Christ is at work, is the strongest bulwark against forces of tyranny and injustice.

[5] "A Declaration on Religious Liberty," adopted by the Amsterdam Assembly of the World Council of Churches; *The First Assembly of the World Council of Churches*, p. 97. See Augustine, *City of God*, Book XIX.

321

It is affirmed "that all men are equal in the sight of God and that the rights of men derive directly from their status as children of God." [6] The Amsterdam Assembly condemned "any attempt to limit the freedom of the Church to witness to its Lord and His design for mankind and any attempt to impair the freedom of men to obey God and to act according to conscience, for these freedoms are implied in man's responsibility before God." [7] "The Church knows that man has been created in the image of God and has therefore indestructible value, which the state must not impair but rather safeguard." [8]

Methodists have been closely associated with these cumulative efforts of interdenominational and international bodies to establish standards for human rights and liberties and to fight for their observance in legislation and social practice. Similarly, The Methodist Church itself, through its agencies and through dedicated individuals, has been engaged on various fronts of this battle. Because of the inclusive range of human rights, it might be said that this entire volume, in a sense, is a record of it. Certain aspects are treated in other sections, for instance, on race relations, industry, and the family. We shall here merely single out some specific issues on which Methodism has taken an explicit stand.

The section on "Civil Liberties and Civil Rights" in the *Social Creed of The Methodist Church* (1956 edition) is worth citing in full, as it sets forth in compact fashion the official Methodist position in this matter.

We stand for the recognition and maintenance of the rights and responsibilities of free speech, free assembly, and a free press, and for the encouragement of free communication of ideas essential to the discovery of truth.

We stand for the right of all individuals and groups to advocate any peaceful and constitutional method for the solution of problems that may confront society.

We stand upon the principle of testing every such proposal in the light of the teachings of Jesus.

These affirmations, like so many others of a similar kind, may seem innocuous generalities; yet their pointed challenge becomes immediately apparent when they are related to the many flagrant or covert violations of human rights and civil liberties, the instances of fanaticism and witch hunting, in which recent American his-

[6] *Ibid.*, p. 93.
[7] *Ibid.*, p. 78.
[8] *The Oxford Report*, p. 251.

tory abounds.[9] The insidious danger of seeking to defend liberty with incompatible means was tellingly scored by the Council of Bishops in 1948. "In an hour when total totalitarianism threatens freedom, it is imperative that we ourselves do not adopt the practices of the totalitarian state in order to destroy the totalitarian threat. The totalitarian has conquered when the defender of democracy has discarded the civil liberties that are the essence of democracy." [10]

In a *Message on Civil Liberties and Internal Security* in 1955, the Board of Social and Economic Relations voiced its concern over sinister un-American features of certain Congressional hearings on Communist influence in public employment. While affirming the unalterable opposition of Christianity to Communism, it questions the propriety of arbitarily abridging Constitutional liberties expressed in the fair administration of justice and in the protection of the rights of accused persons.[11] "Christians are concerned that false allegations not be made against innocent people, that they be protected from half-truths and biased interpretations of their motives and actions." "To violate civil liberties in order to combat Communism is to use an evil means to try to bring about a good end, and history shows that means and ends are inevitably interrelated."

The statement on civil liberties in the Social Creed is amplified by further references in other sections, which deal with matters often included in declarations of human rights. The claim is made for "equal rights and justice for all men." The sections on working conditions, social benefits for workers, the right to organize for collective bargaining, formulate important standards for the safeguarding of economic rights. Unlike the UN Draft Covenant in its present form, the Social Creed expressly asserts along with Leo XIII's *Rerum Novarum* the right of private ownership of property. Reflecting the deep conflicts of opinion and practice within the church, the section on freedom from discrimination is couched in rather general terms, but it sets forth the basic tenet of civil liberty.

This position has been reiterated and spelled out in numerous utterances by General Conferences and various agencies of the church. Similarly, Methodist spokesmen have over the decades repeatedly raised their voice in denunciation of unchristian and in-

[9] See, for example, G. Bromley Oxnam, *I Protest*, and Martin Luther King, Jr., *Stride Toward Freedom*. Thomas Jefferson went further in his first inaugural than Methodism's Social Creed in 1956.

[10] *General Conference Journal*, 1948, p. 160.

[11] The subsequent quotations are taken from *A Message on Civil Liberties and Internal Security* (1955).

human practices in other fields—lynching, mob violence, denials of equality of opportunity, discriminatory treatment of conscientious objectors, infringements of academic freedom, and so forth.

The Woman's Division of Christian Service on its part has given support to legislative proposals in the field of civil rights: (1) a federal antilynching bill, (2) legislation prescribing procedures of investigating committees of Congress so that accused persons may have rights of defense, (3) anti-poll tax legislation, (4) a permanent fair employment practices commission, and (5) legislation to protect women against discrimination in economic, civil, political, and social life.

The record indicates that Methodism—in its pronouncements and in the activities of many of its leaders, both clerical and lay—on the whole has taken a forthright and courageous stand in this sensitive area of human rights and liberties. This, however, makes all the more glaring the distance between perceived truth and the widespread ignorance and unconcern also among Methodist church members. The deplorable fact that the UN effort to obtain legislative enactment of human rights has virtually come to a standstill, largely because of the resistance of the U.S. government, should cause great concern—and appropriate action. Moreover, there still remain troubled border areas where Methodism, to be consistent with its own witness, must rethink and clarify its stand.

Christian beliefs about religious freedom need to be disentangled from their confusion with befuddled political slogans about separation of church and state. Methodists, along with other Protestants, reject the use of public money and power to support sectarian education and to enforce sectarian beliefs, as incompatible with a pluralistic society. But they may well take heed of the countercriticism that they in turn violate the same principle when exerting political pressure in favor of Prohibition or Sunday-closing laws, when accepting federal funds for the construction of church-related colleges and hospitals, or supporting the military chaplaincy system. These critical questions may be well founded or not; in any case, they call us seriously to re-examine what we mean by rights and liberties in a democratic society, and whether we are consistent in our own beliefs and practices.

CHAPTER TWELVE

Marriage and the Family

METHODISM SHARES WITH CONTEMPORARY CHRISTIAN bodies in general a positive appreciation of the family as intended by God rather than as a concession to human sinfulness.[1] The family serves both social needs (the procreation and rearing of children) and personal needs (the completion of life and the enhancement of mutuality). The loyalty of monogamous family life is viewed as essential to the equality of men and women in marriage (equality of rights and responsibilities alongside differences in functions) and to its task as the basic educational unit in society. The family is not an end in itself, rather it exists for the nurture of persons and so must protect the freedom of all its members.

A basic statement of Methodism on the Christian home was included in the 1940 *Discipline*.

The home is the foundation of society and vital to the stability of both Church and state. Though ordained of God and the source of so much that is dear to us, the home is suffering from open attack by evil forces, competition with business, and sheer neglect. We are faced with such an alarming increase in divorce, juvenile delinquency, broken lives, and disregard of life's sanctities that the very existence of civilization is threatened. It is imperative therefore that the friends of the home be aroused to action and we make the following pronouncements:

1. Recognizing that the overwhelming amount of juvenile delinquency springs from the psychological blocking and thwarting of the child in the inadequate home, we believe that it is the birthright of every child to have the emotional security of a stable home, permanently established with two parents living together and loving each other; we believe that the child should have a safeguard of emotional security and a normal opportunity for self-development in a creative atmosphere, a religious se-

[1] Seward Hiltner, "The Protestant Approach to the Family," in *The Family —A Christian's Concern*, Woman's Division of Christian Service, 1951, p. 1-9.

curity through spiritual nurture of a church-centered home, and a program of education which develops a well-rounded personality.[2]

Family life has been deeply influenced by the revolutionary power of modern technology, industrialization, and urban life. The future of family life cannot, in the circumstances of these powerful social forces, be left to blind chance. Tradition and nature cannot guarantee the stability of the family and the achievement of a Christian home. It is doubtful that it can be nurtured, developed, and preserved as a side line to individualistic interests and the abandonment of essential functions and responsibilities. One social philosopher speaks of the "vast, anonymous, creeping revolution in family functions, with the widespread disintegration of what once was called the home."[3] The MESTA questionnaire responses show that Methodists, while reflecting modern trends, hold to the conservation of important social functions in the family.

33. THE FAMILY

Should seek to reclaim the whole range of
functions once performed by the family

7.1 per cent

May share some functions with other
institutions, but should retain primary
responsibility for moral and religious
education ....60.1 per cent

Should share with other institutions the
responsibility for all of the functions

23.8 per cent

Should accept the more limited range of
functions left to it as other institutions
now care for education, recreation,
moral instruction, security for the
aged, etc. .... 3.8 per cent

Write-in .... 1.0 per cent

No report .... 4.2 per cent

With the high appreciation of the family has gone an early and consistent condemnation of divorce. The Episcopal Address to the 1908 General Conference of the Methodist Episcopal Church stated: "The consecutive polygamy permitted by the divorce laws of some of our states is a disgrace to our country." The 1910 General Conference of the Methodist Episcopal Church, South, called for uniform

[2] ¶ 1713.
[3] Baker Brownell, *The Human Community* (New York: Harper and Brothers, 1950), p. 78.

divorce laws. There has been some relaxation of requirements for the marriage of divorced persons as there has been growing awareness of the problem related to a rising divorce rate. The Social Creed adopted by both churches in 1908 and 1914 respectively called:

2. For the protection of the family, by the single standard of purity, uniform divorce laws, proper regulation of marriage, and proper housing.

3. For the fullest possible development for every child, especially by the provision of proper education and recreation.

4. For the abolition of child labor.

5. For such regulation of the conditions of toil for women as shall safeguard the physical and moral health of the community.[4]

By 1934 the Creed was revised to include the provision of spiritual nurture for every child and educational preparation for marriage, homemaking, and parenthood.[5] In 1956 the Creed read:

We seek equal rights and justice for all men; protection of the individual and the family by high standards of morality; Christian education for marriage, parenthood, and the home; adequate housing; proper regulation of marriage, and uniform divorce laws.

We stand for regulation of working conditions for women, especially mothers, and safeguards for their physical and moral environment; for the abolition of injurious child labor; for the protection, education, spiritual nurture, and wholesome recreation of every child; and for religious and educational programs which will secure these ends.[6]

The 1904 *Discipline* of the Methodist Episcopal Church stated Methodism's position on marriage of divorced persons for much of the next half-century:

No divorce, except for adultery, shall be regarded by the Church as lawful; and no minister shall solemnize marriage in any case where there is a divorced wife or husband living; but this rule shall not be applied to

---

[4] *Discipline*, Methodist Episcopal Church, South, 1918, ¶ 809.

[5] *Discipline*, Methodist Episcopal Church, South, 1934, ¶ 593. In the Episcopal Address to the 1930 General Conference of the Methodist Episcopal Church, South, Bishop E. D. Mouzon said of the family: "In a society like our own where Christianity is the law of the land, we have a right to look to the state for the protection of this fundamental institution of our civilization and of our religion." Then followed the interesting contention that sound law is educative as well as prohibitive. In 1928 the Methodist Episcopal Church had recognized the function of the State in determining the grounds for a valid divorce and in granting a divorce, but it insisted that it was the function of the Church to determine the regulations for the Christian marriage of divorced persons and for the reception of such persons into Church membership. *Discipline* (¶ 70).

[6] *Discipline*, 1956, ¶ 2020.

the innocent party to a divorce for the cause of adultery, nor to divorced parties seeking to be reunited in marriage.[7]

In the 1940 *Discipline* the exception applied "to the innocent person when it is clearly established by competent testimony that the true cause for divorce was adultery or other physical cruelty or physical peril invalidated the marriage vow."[8] By 1956, the restriction was relaxed to include, following "adultery," or other vicious conditions which through mental or physical cruelty or physical peril invalidated the marriage vow."[9] More evidence of awareness of the circumstances which produce divorces, and of the Christian concern for persons and their forgiveness, is found in the 1956 *Discipline:*

Divorce is not the answer to the problems that cause it. It is symptomatic of deeper difficulties. The Church must stand ready to point out these basic problems to couples contemplating divorce, and to help them to discover and, if possible, to overcome such difficulties. In addition, the church must stand ready to depict the unhappy circumstances that are to await the divorced person. As a Christian Church, and as ministers, we are obligated to aid, by counsel, persons who have experienced broken marriages, and to guide them so that they may make more satisfactory adjustments.[10]

On the other hand there has been a gradual stiffening of attitude toward marriage with persons of a different religious affiliation. This is partly due to the increase in the number of marriages across faith lines instead of across denominational lines (as well as in the growth of Roman Catholicism during this half century). In 1904 the Methodist Episcopal Church said:

We do not prohibit our people from marrying persons who are not of our Church, provided such persons have the form, and are seeking the power, of godliness; but we are determined to discourage their marrying persons who do not come up to this description.[11]

[7] ¶ 66. That this was a "Special Advice" rather than a law of the church is evident in the urging in the Episcopal Addresses of 1908, 1912, and 1916 that its mandatory character be so indicated. In 1922 the Episcopal Address to the Methodist Episcopal Church, South, recommended that "a person divorced for any other cause than infidelity, . . . and then marrying another, shall not become or remain a member of our Church; that any minister who shall solemnize the rite of matrimony . . . (in such a case) shall be dealt with as in case of immorality."

[8] ¶ 226.

[9] ¶ 356.

[10] ¶ 2021.

[11] ¶ 65.

In 1956, the General Conference dealt more explicitly with the problem of mixed marriages: [12]

Religious convictions should be a strong tie in marriage. Recent research has emphasized the importance of common cultural and religious backgrounds as the foundations of successful marriage. It is therefore strongly urged that each young person consider carefully before becoming engaged to anyone who does not have a similar religious background. It is important that Protestant youth discuss this problem with their ministers before it is too late. Ministers are urged to discuss with both youth and parents the likelihood of failure in mixed marriages.

Among the duties of a pastor is "to instruct youth in the problems involved in marriage with a member of a church which demands that the children of such a marriage be reared in the faith of that church." [13] The problem of Protestant-Jewish marriages is quite different from those in a Protestant-Catholic marriage. The crux of the problem is that Methodists recognize Catholic sacraments, but Roman Catholics do not fully accept Methodist marriages.

There is some relationship between the Methodist awareness of the problem of mixed marriages and its approval of planned parenthood, "practiced in Christian conscience," as fulfilling rather than violating the will of God.[14] The official approval of birth control by the General Conference of 1956 gave to The Methodist Church a distinctive role in this controversial area. Pastors and laymen had thereafter an authoritative position to which they could refer.

There has been continuing emphasis on parental responsibility for the religious instruction of children presented for baptism.[15] Family prayer and worship are urged and devotional materials for families provided in church-school literature from the 1940's on.[16] Courses of study in preparation for marriage were called for by the General Conference of the Methodist Episcopal Church in 1928, and literature was provided from the 1930's. The 1928 General Conference urged "young people to seek parental, medical, and

[12] ¶ 2021, Sec. 3-b.
[13] *Discipline*, 1956, ¶ 352.
[14] *Discipline*, 1956, ¶ 2021. The recent (Nov. 25, 1959) statements by the Catholic hierarchy makes the issue a political as well as a moral one.
[15] See, for example, *Discipline*, Methodist Episcopal Church, 1924, ¶ 49, and *Discipline*, Methodist Episcopal Church, South, 1938, ¶ 635. In 1940 The Methodist Church affirmed the right of children to learn before adolescence "the facts regarding the origin of life and the nature of their personality as it relates to sex," preferably from qualified parents or from church-school teachers. *Discipline*, 1940, ¶ 1713.
[16] See especially *The Christian Home, Discipline* (1956), ¶ 2021.

pastoral advice" before marriage,[17] and in 1948 ministers were advised to have "an unhurried premarital conference with the parties to be married." [18]

Methodism has continued to press for a waiting period before issuance of a marriage license (and an extended period before granting a divorce), for a medical examination, and for uniform marriage and divorce laws. In 1956, there was recognition of the older adult as needing and deserving a significant place in the family circle.[19]

Probably the central affirmation concerning marriage and the family is found in the 1956 *Discipline:*

Religion and the family naturally belong together. What religion is to accomplish it can do best in the family. What the family must do it cannot do without religion. Religion and the family are natural allies. Religion is inseparable from the family. Family life at its best is a matter of living life at the deepest level, which is a level of relationship to God.

With this as its charter the General Committee on Family Life has been established and its administrating related to the Division of the Local Church of the Board of Education. Under the leadership of Bishop Hazen Werner and the professional staff of the Division a number of significant Conferences on Christian Family Life have been held. In a closely related area the Board of Social and Economic Relations has expressed concern for juvenile delinquency, leading it to publish an important book in this field by Haskell M. Miller.[20]

---

[17] *Discipline*, Methodist Episcopal Church, 1929, ¶ 69.
[18] *Discipline*, 1948, ¶ 355.
[19] *Discipline*, 1956, ¶ 2021.
[20] Haskell M. Miller, *Understanding and Preventing Juvenile Delinquency* (Nashville: Abingdon Press, 1958).

CHAPTER THIRTEEN

Race Relations

TWO GROUPS OF QUESTIONS ON RACE WERE INCLUDED IN THE MESTA questionnaire. The questions and results are as follows:

28. RACE
    1. Members of all races should have the same opportunities, but present patterns must be changed gradually ....52.6 per cent
    2. All discrimination and enforced segregation based on race should be abolished ....18.6 per cent
    3. Some races are inherently inferior, and are not entitled to equal rights and privileges with those of superior capacity .... .6 per cent
    4. Members of all races should have equal opportunities, but segregation is desirable to preserve racial purity .... 2.0 per cent
    5. Write-in .... 2.0 per cent
    6. No report .... 1.9 per cent

Analyzed according to Jurisdictions the percentages are as follows, with special results notable in the Central and Southeastern Jurisdictions:

	1	2	3	4	5	6
Totals	52.6	18.6	.6	24.3	2.0	1.9
C	16.6	80.4	.0	1.5	1.5	.0
NC	56.3	20.2	2.6	17.7	1.8	1.4
NE	55.7	19.7	.7	19.8	1.9	2.2
SC	50.0	18.3	1.2	26.5	1.9	2.1
SE	40.6	8.4	2.9	41.2	4.5	2.4
W	59.4	24.9	.4	12.1	1.4	1.8

29. RACE IN THE ORGANIZATION OF THE METHODIST CHURCH.

1. Racial segregation should be abolished at all levels ....33.2 per cent
2. All jurisdictions, conferences, and churches should follow racial lines ....14.5 per cent
3. The future status of the all-Negro jurisdiction and segregated annual conferences and local churches should be determined under permissive legislation ..19.0 per cent
4. The all-Negro jurisdiction should now be abolished, and segregated annual conferences and local churches should be gradually eliminated by permissive legislation ....20.4 per cent
5. Write-in ....3.6 per cent
6. No report ....9.3 per cent

The responses according to Jurisdictions follow:

	1	2	3	4	5	6
Totals	33.2	14.5	19.0	20.4	3.6	9.3
C	72.7	1.5	7.6	16.6	1.6	.0
NC	39.1	10.2	16.2	22.1	2.2	10.2
NE	39.5	9.1	15.6	23.7	3.4	8.7
SC	28.0	15.5	17.6	23.8	4.7	10.4
SE	10.1	34.1	31.9	9.3	6.5	8.1
W	42.0	6.4	15.2	24.7	3.0	8.7

The differences among the jurisdictions are most marked on the two aspects of racial relations indicated above as compared with any other social question. In the Southeastern Jurisdiction the point of view is clearly that of "separate but equal." There were 41.2 per cent of the respondents who held to equal opportunities with segregation as opposed to 1.5 per cent who hold this view in the Central Jurisdiction and 22.8 per cent in the total sample. As applied to the organization of The Methodist Church, there are significant differences between the Southeastern and the South Central Jurisdictions. These may be noted by viewing questions 1 and 4 together or adding them. The majority of the responses in the South Central Jurisdiction support the abolition of the Central Jurisdiction, though 23.8 per cent hold to gradual elimination of segregated annual conferences and local churches by permissive legislation. Against 51.8 per cent of the South Central Jurisdiction the responses of the Southeastern total 19.4 per cent on abolition of the all-Negro jurisdictional structure. Except for the Southeastern Jurisdiction every jurisdiction holds to abolition. On propositions 1 and 4 together the totals are Central Jurisdiction, 89.3 per cent; North Central, 61.2 per cent, Northeastern, 63.2 per cent; South Central, 51.8 per cent; Southeastern, 19.4 per cent; and Western, 66.7 per cent.

Methodism, like American Christianity as a whole, is divided at the local level on the questions of racial segregation and discrimination. The local churches have largely accommodated themselves to regional mores, customs, habits, and stereotypes, and have condoned, where tensions were high in the secular order, the policy of exclusion of racial minorities, especially with respect to Negroes. The conscience of the church has been increasingly aroused. Frank S. Loescher presented the shocking thesis ten years ago that "Protestantism, by its policies and practices, far from helping to integrate the Negro in American life, is actually contributing to the isolation of Negro Americans." [1] It is at the local level that the crux of the problem exists.

Roman Catholic and Protestant denominations have issued significant statements in recent years recognizing that the heart of the problem is moral and religious, but that ways had to be found to overcome legal segregation and prejudice. In 1958 the Roman Catholic bishops of the United States issued a statement on the question, "Can enforced segregation be reconciled with the Christian view of our fellow man?" They responded that it cannot for two fundamental reasons:

(1) Legal segregation, or any form of compulsory segregation, in itself and by its very nature imposes a stigma of inferiority upon the segregated people. Even if the now obsolete court doctrine of "separate but equal" had been carried out to the fullest extent, so that all public and semipublic facilities were in fact equal, there is nonetheless the judgment that an entire race, by the sole fact of race and regardless of individual qualities, is not fit to associate on equal terms with members of another race. We cannot reconcile such a judgment with the Christian view of man's nature and rights. . . . It is appropriate to cite the language of Pope Pius XII: "God did not create a human family made up of segregated, dissociated, mutually independent members. No! he would have them all

[1] Frank Loescher, *The Protestant Church and the Negro* (New York: Association Press, 1948), p. 106.

united by the bond of total love of Him and consequent self-dedication to assisting each other to maintain that bond intact." (2) It is a matter of historic fact that segregation in our country had led to oppressive conditions and the denial of basic human rights for the Negro. This is evident in the fundamental fields of education, job opportunity, and housing.[2]

The comprehensive and over-all position of The Methodist Church on race is quite clear. Here Methodism's awareness of being a world society is evident: "We join other people of good will around the world in moving toward the day when all races shall share richly without discrimination or segregation in the good things of life. Therefore, we resolutely go forward with the work begun with respect to race relations in the Church and in our world." [3] Because Methodism has a world parish her responsibility for racial brotherhood North and South is especially grave.

Methodism's official position is grounded both theologically and morally. Its attitude is an extension of Christ's teaching that all men are brothers, and its conception of the nature of the church under Christ also requires the rejection of segregation and discrimination on the basis of race.

There must be no place in The Methodist Church for racial discrimination or enforced segregation. Recognizing that we have not yet attained this goal, yet rejoicing in the progress made, we recommend that discrimination or segregation by any method or practice, whether by conference structure or otherwise, in The Methodist Church be abolished with reasonable speed. The growing spirit of brotherhood throughout the church strengthens our confidence that, under the leadership of the Holy Spirit, we will continue to go forward.[4]

As a denomination with a world-wide membership and an inclusive mission, The Methodist Church cannot afford in theory or in practice to take a view less than truly ecumenical. As a member of the World Council of Churches, it participated in drafting and adopting the following resolution in 1954:

The Second Assembly of the World Council of Churches declares its conviction that any form of segregation based on race, color or ethnic origin is contrary to the Gospel, and is incompatible with the Christian doctrine of man and with the nature of the Church of Christ. The Assem-

[2] Quoted in T. F. Pettigrew and E. Q. Campbell, *Christian in Racial Crisis*, pp. 166-67. See Kyle Haselden, *The Racial Problem in Christian Perspective*. Rauschenbusch Lectures. (New York: Harper and Bros., 1959).

[3] *Discipline*, 1956, ¶ 2026.

[4] *Ibid.*, ¶ 2026.

bly urges the churches within its membership to renounce all forms of segregation or discrimination and to work for their abolition within their own life and within society. . . . From its very beginning the ecumenical movement by its very nature has been committed to a form of fellowship in which there is no segregation or discrimination. The Assembly of the World Council of Churches rejoices in this fact and confirms this practice as the established policy of the Council.[5]

When, then, the General Conference speaks to all of Methodism in the same spirit and makes the same resolute demand of all its agencies, schools, hospitals, and churches, this must not be viewed as special pressure from some sections of the nation on others, but as an expression of the profoundest level of fellowship in the body of Christ—the Church universal. The Church's inclusiveness is part of the gospel and no local church or synod is free under Christ to deny this.

The General Conference is solidly with the Supreme Court decision on desegregation in the public schools; it is likewise committed to the elimination of discrimination in all aspects of social life, work, and political activities. A policy of segregation is inherently coercive wherever it is in effect. The Methodist Church has officially repudiated the doctrine of "separate but equal" and does not officially provide for a jurisdictional reservation to the repudiation of all discrimination based on race. The existence of the Central Jurisdiction may be said to be a clear example of "separate but equal." However, the doctrine of equal representation on boards and agencies is actually a polity principle of integration. The General Conference has put the Central Jurisdiction in the line of ultimate extinction by intention and provisional legislation as Amendment IX shows. There is no provision whereby a Jurisdiction may repudiate legislation of the General Conference.

The racial crises in church and society exhibit in a unique way the dilemma of leadership. On the one hand is the demand of Christ; on the other hand is the accommodation of church membership to the standards and ways of the world. The worldliness of the church confronts Christ's law of inclusive brotherhood. As applied to the public-school situation, we may note a number of hypotheses which Pettigrew and Campbell have presented after studying the role of the ministers in Little Rock. These hypotheses rest on two assumptions with respect to the South and the local church. A *Pulpit*

---

[5] *Evanston Speaks. Reports from the Second Assembly of the World Council of Churches:* August 15-31, 1954 (New York: World Council of Churches), p. 57.

Digest poll in 1958 showed that most Southern ministers in the major denominations are willing to accept gradual public school desegregation; and probably most of them believe it to be a Christian imperative.[6] The second assumption of fact is that there is a point at which the minister's defense of desegregation becomes costly to his parish, and to the possibility of his continued leadership within it. At this point the segregationist will pressure him to be silent or withhold financial support or withdraw.

A number of practical dilemmas may arise in varying circumstances.[7]

In times of crisis there is less support of desegregation than in times of non-crisis. Rabid abuse of ministers by segregationists tends to decrease interracial activities. "The more popular the denomination in the local area, the less likely are its ministers to defend positions not accepted by local public opinion." As a consequence the ministers who are often in the position of greatest potential influence are the ones least likely to attempt to lead out. Pastors in popular churches tend to identify with the parish as a going concern. They are under great influence to fulfill the social expectations of their people. This situation holds for churches as social institutions regardless of theology or polity. In many Southern communities and Northern cities the various denominations behave very much like each other.

A hypothesis of singular importance is that "the minister is less likely to support desegregation during a crisis if no ministerial figures of high prestige in his denomination lead the way." [8] When ecclesiastical officials such as bishops and district superintendents default in positive and creative leadership, fail to stand behind men who are expressing the church's official opposition, or even penalize prophetic voices and innovators, parish ministers are not likely to go forward in interracial programs. Pastors expect guidance from the appointed ecclesiastical leadership. Abdication of leadership through silence or inactivity on the part of those in positions of authority has great influence even where there is no formal mandate given. Not only are bishops and district superintendents important, but there are other prestige figures in boards and commissions, in college and university presidencies, and in prominent pulpits that point the direction for the leadership of the local church. The leadership in The Methodist Church has not been unified, decisive,

---

[6] "Southern Ministers Speak Their Mind," *Pulpit Digest*, 39 (Dec. 1958), pp. 13-17, quoted in Pettigrew and Campbell, *op. cit.*, p. 121.

[7] *Ibid.*, pp. 121-26.

[8] *Ibid.*, p. 122.

imaginative, or courageous enough on questions of race relations. Progress in race relations has come primarily through forces in the secular world.

There are many other factors that probably operate in the area of race relations so far as the leadership of the local pastor is concerned. During a crisis older ministers are less likely than younger ministers to support desegregation. A minister's support for desegregation is likely to be less if he and his congregation are involved in major fund-raising projects. A minister who has oriented his pastoral duties to his local parish is less likely to lead during a crisis than is one whose work has been oriented to community-wide responsibilities as well as to the local church. A church with a stable membership is often less likely to follow a minister into new constellations of fellowship than is one whose membership is in flux. Leadership in a crisis is directly related to leadership prior to the crisis and hence to the expectations which the people have of the role of the minister and the church in the issues at stake.

As an institution with marked accommodation to race and class in regional and community patterns, The Methodist Church shares, in the sum, the dilemmas of a "divided America." There is not only a minority who hold to the doctrine of "separate but equal," but there is some deep-lying racism. To what extent the latter entered into the jurisdictional plan of union is hard to determine, but there is evidence that it was not absent. Racism in America was fed not only by biblical arguments, but by interests that influenced the closing of immigration gates, by the impact of world struggles (as witness the internment of the Japanese in World War II) and efforts to confuse anticommunism and anti-Semitism. The response of the churches on the West Coast has been criticized as a feeble and ineffective protest to the relocation of the Japanese. On the other hand the identification in their tragedy on the part of some local ministers and congregations is a glorious chapter. Business and "patriotic" groups made a sorry record. Methodists played a creditable role within the limits laid down by wartime regulations.

But, since the church is profoundly influenced by secular forces, it is well to note some trends that augur well for the future—and the church has played its part in encouraging some of these. On the whole, the minority groups in America have had a good experience. Except in the South, few local prejudices have been translated directly into law; except in the South, no political candidate or party since the Know-Nothings has run successfully on a platform of racism; irrational prejudices, while often acute, have resulted in comparatively little racial violence; the mingling of majority and minority groups during World War II greatly modified the prejudices; laws in several states have considerably alleviated the employment situation; the recent Supreme Court decisions in housing, transportation, and education have indicated a new trend in constitutional law; in many social situations the prejudices against Indians, Negroes, Jews, and Orientals are clearly declining; and the American people responded in marked unity in the war against Nazism.[9]

The struggle for full racial brotherhood promises to be an extended one. Its achievement will depend not only on the massive forces of industrialization, farm to city mobility, the needs of the "cold war," and the bargaining power of the minority groups, but also upon the creative spiritual life that can be released through all channels at all levels of church life. There is ample evidence for the thesis of Pettigrew and Campbell, reiterated by Gordon Allport, that the Protestant ministry is potentially the most effective agent of social change in the South in the decade ahead. If Methodism, over a period of years, would exert in race relations the genius of cumulative and integrated leadership which she exerted in the Crusade for a new World Order, she would achieve much. The problem is one of implementing the official resolutions of the *Discipline* with courage and love.

[9] See Max Lerner, *America as a Civilization*, pp. 501-14.

CHAPTER FOURTEEN

Prohibition and Temperance

26. TEMPERANCE: I, AS A CHRISTIAN,

may drink without reference to religious
scruples 1.2
may drink at social gatherings to avoid offending my host 1.0
may use alcoholic beverages as long as I do so
temperately and within reason 26.5
should totally abstain from alcoholic beverages .56.8
should work for prohibition 8.8
Write-in 3.9
No report 1.8

The above table shows the percentage responses of Methodists
concerning their attitude toward the use of beverage alcohol,
as indicated in the study of "The Beliefs of Methodists" made in
preparation for this study. It is interesting to note that 31.5 per
cent of those responding indicated that they felt free to drink,
either without reference to religious scruples, or to avoid offending
a host, or temperately and within reason, while 56.8 per cent indicated that they should totally abstain, and another 8.8 per cent
added that they should work for prohibition. There is an interesting breakdown by jurisdictions in which the North Central Jurisdiction, the Western Jurisdiction, and the Northeastern Jurisdiction range from 31.4 per cent to 35 per cent answering, "I, as a
Christian, may use alcoholic beverages as long as I do so temperately and within reason," while in the South Central, Southeastern,
and Central Jurisdictions the responses to this question range
from 15.1 per cent to 18.7 per cent. The same kind of response
shows up as the replies from the North Central, Northeastern,
and Western Jurisdictions indicate from 49.5 per cent to 51.8 per
cent saying that they should totally abstain from alcoholic bever-

ages, while this same question brought a 61.1 per cent to a 65.2 per cent response from the South Central, Southeastern, and Central Jurisdictions.[1] These figures indicate a significant change in the attitude of Methodists toward beverage alcohol which is hardly consistent with the traditional Methodist position.[2] At the same time one must note that the majority (54.2 per cent) believe that a Christian should totally abstain from alcoholic beverages.

Since 1792, the Methodist *Discipline* has carried a General Rule forbidding "Drunkenness, or drinking spirituous liquors, unless in cases of necessity." The 1956 *Discipline* adds, "buying and selling spirituous liquors," in addition to drunkenness or drinking of them. In the early 1900's violators of this General Rule were guilty of immorality and faced trial by the church and possible expulsion from the church.

The Methodist churches began the twentieth century on a platform of total abstinence and legal prohibition. "We therefore regard voluntary total abstinence from all intoxicants as the true ground of personal temperance, and complete legal prohibition of the traffic in alcoholic drinks as the duty of civil government." [3] In the early 1900's the Methodist churches changed from routine opposition to drinking alcoholic beverages to a crusade to destroy the alcoholic beverage industry. They sought not only to regulate the behavior of church members through agencies and through literature, but also to influence legislative action and the enforcement of legislation. An increasing number of evils was attributed to beverage alcohol. Increased drinking, anarchism, and the decline of Sabbath observance were all laid at the door of immigrants and of foreign customs, often in a way that bordered on anti-Semitism.[4] In 1909 the Missouri Annual Conference of The Meth-

---

[1] The finding of this survey receives confirmation from a poll of 995 Methodists done by Murray H. Leiffer, reported in "Finding Out What Methodists Think," *The Christian Advocate*, CXXX, Dec. 29, 1955. 12.9 per cent of Leiffer's respondents registered no objection to a Methodist's drinking, 19 per cent thought The Methodist Church should adopt no formal stand on liquor or should advocate moderation, 57.9 per cent stood for total abstinence.

[2] Joseph L. Allen, Jr., suggests: "The movement of temperance away from the center of denominational attention and the relaxation of actual discipline on the drinker may correspond to a movement in The Methodist Church from sect to church attributes." See his dissertation, submitted to the Yale University Graduate School, 1957, "The Methodist Board of Temperance as an Instrument of Church Policy," p. 25.

[3] *Discipline*, Methodist Episcopal Church, 1904, ¶ 63.

[4] See, *Journal of the Texas Annual Conference of the Methodist Episcopal Church, South*, 1909, pp. 64 ff. See also *Journal of the General Conference of 1924 of The Methodist Episcopal Church*, Report of the Standing Committee on Temperance, pp. 683 ff.: "The German Jews got a controlling interest in our liquor trade about sixteen years ago. They introduced the brewery-owned

odist Episcopal Church, South, called the legalized liquor traffic and the open saloon the greatest enemy of the Sabbath, the Church, and Christian civilization. Along with the other denominations in the Federal Council of Churches, the Methodist churches who adopted the Social Creed stood "for the protection of the individual and of society from the social, economic, and moral waste of the liquor traffic."

From the passage of the Prohibition amendment in 1919 until its repeal in 1933, the Methodist churches lived with the law of prohibition, rejoiced in its passage, but somewhat relaxed their efforts in its support. The 1922 General Conference of The Methodist Episcopal Church, South, said of Prohibition: "The fact is daily becoming more evident that the adoption of Prohibition by the United States was the most important far-reaching enactment ever put upon the Statute Books of any nation." [5] There was not only rejoicing. The Episcopal Address to The Methodist Episcopal Church of 1920 stated:

Our further task as a Church of Christ is to provide for the life of those whose house has been swept of those things that were wrong and hurtful. A habit expelled is not a habit slain. An evil prohibited is not an evil wholly destroyed. The old tenants are quick to return to a house left empty. And the Church is tested here as in many other places more by what it provides than by what it forbids. Saloons did furnish meeting places and social centers of an evil sort and political centers of the worst sort for that period. Now it is the function of the Church and of the best society supporting the Church to convert the old agencies, the meeting places, the social fellowship, into instruments for the welfare instead of the destruction of men.[6]

There was, despite this being a time of relative relaxation, a continuing emphasis upon enforcement with support of political officers who themselves were committed to enforcement of the Prohibition laws. There was also from time to time some awareness of the responsibility of the church in the whole matter of enforcement. The Episcopal Address to the 1930 General Conference of The Methodist Episcopal Church, South, was read by Bishop Edwin D. Mouzon. In this address he stated:

---

saloon, the vilest thing that ever saw the sun, with its brothel upstairs, its gambling hall down, operated by an irresponsible, red-nosed bi-ped, often a man who had lived off the earnings of some fallen women and in hundreds of thousands of instances an ex-convict and one who ran it with no obligation to God or man, without respect to any law."

[5] *Journal of the General Conference*, p. 241.

[6] *Ibid.*, pp. 163-64.

Laws for prohibition should be enforced, but we should also observe that this is the church's responsibility as well as the state's. There is equal guilt on the part of those who buy intoxicating beverages as well as on the part of those who sell. So Methodism must renew its educational program. The Church is not affiliated with any political party, but whenever any organization becomes a friend of the liquor traffic, the Methodist Church, South, will oppose it.[7]

The temperance forces of the churches North and South actively opposed Presidential candidate Alfred Smith in 1928. Bishop James Cannon, Jr., of the Southern church was one of the main leaders in the campaign against Governor Smith.

With repeal in 1933 came a period of readjustment, as the temperance forces faced defeat and the temperance movement went on the defensive. It was no longer the main line of Protestant social action. The church was in the midst of a depression along with the rest of American society. It was also facing, during the ten-year period following 1933, increasing problems of race relations in the society, problems incident to the beginning and prosecution of the Second World War, as well as its own concerns with the union of the various branches of Methodism in 1939. The 1930's and the early 1940's had primarily a shift in the temperance movement from political action to education with a much more restrained approach for the attack upon the beverage alcohol industry than previously. There was almost always in the educational approach a looked-for result of political activity at either the local, state, or national level. There was some real recognition that there would have to be both education and legal action at the local and state levels before there could be effective action at the national level again.

The 1940's saw some renewal of temperance concern. This was no longer merely political action or merely education. The 1948 Episcopal Address called alcoholism a disease and urged that the sufferer from alcoholism should be treated as a sick man rather than as a criminal. The bishops, however, said that the church was not blind to the moral responsibility when a man decided to drink or to have alcohol in his home. The church also must see, the bishops noted, such social consequences of drinking as the increase of persons and families going on relief and the increase of automobile accidents due to driving while intoxicated. The address concluded that temperance and beverage alcohol constituted a social as well as an individual question, and should be treated as such

[7] *Journal of the General Conference*, 1930, ¶ 378-79.

by the church. The 1952 General Conference Committee on Temperance asked the schools of theology of The Methodist Church to teach the pastoral care of alcoholics as a part of their concern for the pastoral ministry.

There were two other notes in the late 1940's and in the 1950's in the church's concern with temperance. One of these was a more positive approach to the whole problem in which attention was called to the place of abstinence in the positive Christian life rather than as a negative virtue. The other was the calling of attention to the complexity of the social context of the alcohol problem as one of a whole series of problems involving corrupt politics, dishonest advertising, economic exploitation, divorce and broken homes, mental illness, sexual immorality, judicial corruption, and so forth. Bishop John Wesley Lord, a member of the board since 1948, wrote in *The Voice* for April 1950: "We commit a monstrous hypocrisy when we preach against alcoholism and are unconcerned about the other conditions in society that foster it. This fact alone had led many to be unsympathetic with those who advocate temperance or total abstinence." So evils such as these have been called to the attention of Methodists as the results of drinking, as well as part of the context out of which drinking and alcoholism arise. Bishop Lord also called attention to bad economic conditions, loneliness, and insecurity as producers of alcoholism. The present program of temperance is broad and inclusive, personal and social, educational and redemptive, interprofessional and spiritual.

As outlined in the *Discipline* for 1956 the program of the Board of Temperance now centers around four major emphases:

(1) *Positive education* for a life free from beverage alcohol. It is a broad and comprehensive educational undertaking.
(2) *Commitment to abstinence* is a natural and logical outgrowth of commitment to Christ.
(3) *Rehabilitation* of those who suffer because of beverage alcohol is clearly the obligation of all Christians.
(4) *Legislation* as an effective means to outlaw beverage alcohol is a natural outgrowth of the concern of informed citizens.[8]

The Board is, furthermore, concerned with problems of corruption in politics, narcotic drugs, gambling, and the use of tobacco.

[8] *Discipline*, 1956, ¶ 2022.

The Industrial Order and the Labor Question

METHODISM'S HISTORIC LINK WITH THE ACUTE ISSUES OF the industrial order and the problems of organized labor is through the "Social Creed." This Creed has evolved through several stages and has been modified and enlarged so as to include the whole range of social issues. Its evolution has been closely related to the social ideals of the Federal Council and National Council of Churches. Today the Social Creed is broadly ecumenical in spirit and substance and is an emergent of fifty years of social witness, denominational criticism, and practical experience in the ecumenical movement. Its main thrusts correspond to the idea of the responsible society which has on a world scale developed in such global conferences as Stockholm (1925), Oxford (1937), Madras (1938), Amsterdam (1948), and Evanston (1954). Methodists have participated in, contributed to, and learned from all these conferences as well as from those sponsored by the Federal Council of Churches and the National Council of Churches, especially since the conclusion of World War II.

At Amsterdam the term "the responsible society" was introduced as a conception which might express the cumulative social ethic of the ecumenical movement. The development of the Methodist social ethic throughout fifty years is completely congruent with the following definition by the First Assembly of the World Council of Churches: "A responsible society is one where freedom is the freedom of men who acknowledge responsibility to justice and public order, and where those who hold political authority or economic power are responsible for its exercise to God and the people whose welfare is affected by it." [1]

It was Methodism's sensitivity to the welfare of the people affected by the form and practice of American capitalism at the

[1] *First Assembly of the World Council of Churches, Findings and Decisions* (Geneva: World Council of Churches, 1948), p. 43.

turn of the century that gave birth to the Methodist Federation for Social Service and the Social Creed. Industrial relations have been at the heart of the social question for fifty years because America is so predominantly a business society. Work, health, and labor legislation have been closely related interests in the church's concern.

The MESTA questionnaire posed a group of questions which have the accents of the contemporary period and in themselves indicate the distance which social progress has traveled since 1907. Why should certain occupations be chosen? This presupposes a situation of relatively full employment where options are real. What should be the status of men and women? This question reflects the many new problems which have been precipitated by the social change of two world wars. What is the best form of health insurance? This problem would not have been actual in the days when the idea of social insurance was itself considered revolutionary. What should be the federal government's policy in labor legislation? This question grows out of an era when labor is relatively strong and shares with "big government" and "big business" and "big agriculture" the power structure of the nation.

The responses to the question of occupational choice show a primarily personal or individual, as over against a social and service, term of reference. There is almost equal division between personal satisfaction and stewardship to God.

38. OCCUPATIONS SHOULD BE CHOSEN
    MAINLY IN TERMS OF
    income and social status 7
    security in job and residence 4.8
    personal satisfaction and meaning in work .. 37.0
    use of personal capacities in the service of
        mankind 14.6
    use of personal capacities on the basis of stew-
        ardship to God 36.0
    Write-in 3.2
    No report 3.7

When analyzed by jurisdictions, the Central and the Southeastern jurisdictions show the most marked stress on the use of personal capacities on the basis of stewardship to God and the least accent on the service of mankind as a competing term of reference.

	1	2	3	4	5	6	7
Totals	.7	4.8	37.0	14.6	36.0	3.2	3.7
C	1.5	3.0	27.3	12.1	53.0	3.1	.0
NC	.9	5.1	40.1	16.9	30.1	2.9	4.0
NE	.6	5.9	39.2	13.6	33.3	2.9	4.5
SC	.3	4.4	35.5	14.1	38.8	4.7	2.2
SE	.6	2.8	26.9	9.9	52.9	3.0	3.9
W	.7	5.8	42.9	18.1	25.9	3.4	3.2

The revolution in the relationships of men and women in modern industrial life has occasioned basic changes in their roles in church and community. Albert L. Kraus has pointed out that "if women keep taking jobs at the rate they have for the last five years (1951-56), 17,640,000 married, widowed, or divorced women between 35 and 64, about half the women in this age group will be working by 1975. Based on the same growth rates, the number of working women will reach 32,529,000 of a total working population of 93,385,000. In comparison, of a labor force last year of 68,899,000, women numbered 20,859,000, but only 9,856,000 were married or formerly married women 35 to 64 years old." [2] In the age group of 45 to 54 about 7,153,000 married, widowed, or divorced women—nearly 60 per cent of the total age group— will be working by 1975 if the present rate continues. Not only mothers but many grandmothers will be in the labor force.

What, then, will be the status of men and women? The present Methodist poll reflects fairly common views in all sections of the church. The following national percentages reflect the new place of women in the working world outside the home:

39. STATUS OF MEN AND WOMEN

Woman's place is in the home 6.9

Men and women have complementary but
different roles to play 23.7

The principle of full equality must be modified by woman's responsibility to home
and children 30.6

Men and women should have equal and
identical rights in employment and education in both church and society 34.1

Write-in 2.2

No report 2.5

[2] *New York Times*, Sunday, Nov. 25, 1956. The source is the Bureau of the Census.

Turning to the question of health insurance, the following tables show that some social mode of handling the crises of sickness and accident receives the majority response in every part of The Methodist Church.

42. HEALTH

Socialized medicine would kill the individual initiative of doctors and the self-reliance of their patients 20.4

Health insurance is the best way for people to meet the cost of illness 54.0

The co-operative employment of physicians by voluntary health associations would provide adequate care at lowest cost 15.0

The government should provide free medical and dental care for all the people 1.8

Write-in 3.9

No report 4.8

There is no major difference among the jurisdictions on the model responses, except for the Central Jurisdiction, on socialized medicine.

	1	2	3	4	5	6
Totals	20.4	54.0	15.0	1.8	3.9	4.8
C	7.5	59.1	25.8	.0	4.5	3.1
NC	23.1	52.2	14.9	1.6	3.9	4.3
NE	20.3	53.5	15.3	2.3	4.0	4.6
SC	23.0	53.4	11.8	1.6	3.4	6.8
SE	17.2	56.5	15.1	2.1	3.8	5.3
W	15.6	56.5	17.6	2.1	4.6	3.6

The responses to the question on labor legislation reflect the fact that there is widespread concern over the power of labor unions and the need to control unethical labor practices and racketeering. Considering the fact that "right-to-work" laws have been passed in all the states of the Southeastern Jurisdiction, it is striking that on this question it recorded only 28.3 per cent. Methodism clearly is not opposed to labor as such, though it has developed a program and made an appeal in urban areas that has not attracted workers to it at the same rate as their increase in the population.

43. IN LABOR LEGISLATION THE FEDERAL GOVERNMENT SHOULD

aim primarily at controlling unethical labor
practices and racketeering 44.3
protect labor's right to a union shop but limit
the right to strike in the public interest 14.2
protect labor unions in provision for union
shop, collective bargaining, etc. 3.4
pass "right-to-work" laws and curb the power
of labor unions 29.3
Write-in 2.6
No report 6.2

The several Jurisdictions responded as follows:

	1	2	3	4	5	6
Totals	44.3	14.2	3.4	29.3	2.6	6.2
C	51.5	21.2	6.0	16.7	1.5	3.1
NC	44.0	14.2	4.0	29.6	2.6	5.6
NE	44.4	14.2	3.0	29.3	3.0	6.1
SC	43.2	10.2	1.6	33.5	2.2	9.3
SE	42.5	16.1	3.1	28.3	2.6	7.4
W	49.0	14.6	4.3	26.7	2.4	3.0

The American industrial order is not what it was at the beginning of the present century, not to mention even crueler and crasser periods a hundred years ago or the days of the "great barbecue." No one believes any longer that an "invisible hand" transmutes self-interest into the welfare of mankind. There are still many who think that competition based on profit will be generally beneficial. Although there are small interest groups that would identify the gospel with antisocialism and anticommunism, *laissez-faire* is dead. In one way or another all markets are today managed markets. Competition is not free or perfect. Business leaders recognize more and more that economic life is a network of choices and decisions. And where choices and decisions are presented to men and groups there is a moral situation. By and large the economic life of the United States is not only more productive than it was fifty years ago; it is also more humane.[3] Social responsibility has become an economic category.

[3] Some writers argue that economic life is more humane today because it is more productive. The effect here is probably interactive. The problem of economic justice is both one of distribution and one of producing a large enough "pie" for distributing.

In the first part of this volume we traced the evolving participation of The Methodist Church through five decades of economic life and it is not necessary to repeat here what should now be obvious. Suffice it to say that questions of poverty and unemployment not only lie heavily on the conscience of the church when they occur and persist today in the United States, but they constitute an inescapable goad to social responsibility on a world scale. If poverty and economic depression were gnawing and ugly evils a quarter century ago, prosperity and gross inequality of wealth are still serious dilemmas, as are questions of the investment of church funds and those of other institutions. There is still need to improve working conditions, to assist whole regions of the nation to understand the rights, benefits, and duties of collective bargaining, and to provide adequate security for old age, for insurance against injury, and protection against preventable handicaps to good working conditions. Equally important is the conservation by sound administration of the great social legislation which has given the common man a place and a name in economic and democratic life.

There are deeper and subtler problems that must today be faced in economic life whether in management or labor, in government or agriculture. These are the problems of power, of status-seeking, of conspicuous materialistic display in consumption, of the meaning of work itself, and of the complacency and conformism which blind Americans to the needs of others in today's world. In economic life mankind is the unit of co-operation. Such problems have labels like "the power elite," "the status seekers," "organization man," and "the hidden persuaders." Beneath the "fringe benefits" of a "welfare state" operating in a "mixed economy" there is a drift toward meaninglessness and emptiness.

Organized religion's greatest challenge in economic life today is not primarily to conserve the values of the old social creed, since many of these goals have been written into law and are praised by the very economic groups who initially resisted their passage. The greatest challenge is the meaning of work, productivity, and consumption themselves, the development of values, ideals, and commitments which provide inner meaning to all parties in the industrial order. All alike suffer from bigness, anonymity, impersonality, and loss of personal self-worth. Although it is easy for intellectuals to exaggerate the monotonous and humdrum aspects of work in shops and offices, nevertheless greatly subdivided work and routine production tend to destroy individual pride in work.

In the same way men suffer from the acute failure to relate the enormous energy which has been harnessed in industry to the ultimate ends of life.

Religion must penetrate more deeply the ambivalent and ambiguous entanglements of men and women in the crises of our technological civilization. Science and technology have greatly enhanced man's sense of freedom, power, and creative productivity. At the same time the principles of natural physical law, of secularization, and of human autonomy in modern culture and the processes of interdependent urban life have threatened his personal freedom with a collective fate, his self-worth with depersonalization, his power with powerlessness, and personal creativity with mass production and automation. For many men and women in management, agriculture, the professions, and labor, the effect of these principles and tendencies has been to destroy the biblical and Christian sense of vocation, or calling, and to substitute for it a utilitarian or pragmatic attitude toward work as merely a job. Through recent centuries workers in mine and factory have been caught in a web of new relationships. Work has increasingly become a contractual relationship tied to wages, salary, and other income, displacing work as "a way of life" rooted in an order of creation and a plan of redemption. As a consequence man has become imprisoned in his own finite order of engineering and surfeit of goods and has lost the sense of depth in his own person, his society, and the universe around him.

In the days when labor exploitation was crass, when workers had not won the right of collective bargaining through unions of their own choosing, when there were few laws to protect children and women, when hours were unregulated and social insurance was undeveloped, the Methodist pastor, aided by the Methodist Federation for Social Service, and guided by the courageous leadership of episcopal pioneers, may seem to have had a clearer call to social responsibility than many have today. A well-known Christian labor organizer's testimony illustrates the point.

In my eight years of community relations work for the C.I.O. in the South I always contacted the local Methodist clergyman first when I made an appearance in a strange community because I always found a well informed, friendly, consecrated person. However, some time after the "Pink Fringe" incident I began to find a different attitude and less freedom of Methodist clergymen. In (H), the Methodist minister was president of the Ministerial Association and refused to let me address the Association. He later had a special meeting for the employer to speak to the ministers.

This was the community where we were later denied the right of assembly and freedom of speech by an armed mob.[4]

There are still many such difficult places especially in "right to work" states, but the greatest problem today is not in such rearguard situations but in the quality of economic life in relation to personality, community, and ultimate meaning.

Methodists have helped to write great chapters in the humanizing of economic life. They must now write greater chapters in the conservation of human value and the development of a social order which will provide the environment within which persons can be truly free. Some of the characteristic Protestant insights that contribute to such a complete doctrine of economic life are the following: that no particular form of social or economic organization is ordained by God's will or has any special claim to support on religious ground; that all economic life is accountable to God's intention to have nature serve redemptive ends, not selfish ones; that social institutions are relative to time and space and must therefore constantly be brought under the judgment of God; that forms of social organization which were desirable in one environment or at one stage in social development may be unsuited for the proper service of mankind at another; that leaders of social institutions have an obligation to adapt them to the demands of the kingdom of God; that no form of property ownership is sacrosanct, but that experimentation in varying systems of ownership may not only be allowable but required; that since large power groups are probably here to stay, they must be realistically treated in the light of a just ordering of power responsive to basic human need and personal fulfillment; and that motives and values in economic life be constantly scrutinized, criticized, and directed to proper ends.

In the revision of the Social Creed effected in 1952 any reference to the profit motive was deliberately deleted, lest the church seem to proscribe capitalism in the interest of socialism. But the problem of motivation cannot be avoided either with respect to the system as a whole, the incentives in it, or the motives of persons in labor, management, and the like. Neither business nor the church can ignore motivational issues, for they are of the essence of life,

[4] John G. Ramsey, International Representative, Community Relations, United Steelworkers of America, personal letter, Oct. 20, 1958. Methodists for whom he expresses special appreciation are Bishop L. O. Hartman, Reverend Harold Bosley, Reverend James Chubb, Dean Trimble, Reverend Charles Webber, Dr. Clair Cook, Victor Reuther, Bishop G. B. Oxnam, and Bishop Lloyd C. Wicke. Mr. Ramsey is a Presbyterian.

whether economically or religiously expressed. Says a noted industrialist: "This area of human motivation is an exciting frontier for modern industry, and is perhaps the ultimate challenge of the industrial society." [5] Motivation is an ultimate challenge for industry because it is an ultimate challenge for man, and in this dimension of his being is essentially religious. If a business makes no profit it fails in one essential objective of industry. Unless the profit motive (meaning profit incentives) is subordinated to justice and love, it frustrates the demands of the Christian ethic. To evade the problem of motivation is to evade the Sermon on the Mount and the two-fold commandment which Christ made central.

[5] R. J. Cordiner, *New Frontiers for Professional Managers* (New York: McGraw-Hill Book Co., Inc., 1956), p. 25. Motivation is an ambiguous term. Management and the church may not mean the same thing by it. In the church we learn: "As a man thinketh in his heart, so is he"; whereas in business "motivation research" often refers to work incentives and devices of salesmanship, not to ultimate inner attitudes.

Agriculture

THE METHODIST CHURCH BEGAN AS A RURAL MORE THAN AS an urban church. Due to the high concentration of the population in rural areas until the last half century, it has been largely a rural church and has had a very significant part to play in the development of rural America. Indeed, contrary to popular belief among many Methodists, The Methodist Church is still a rural church. According to recent (unpublished) studies made by Marvin Judy of Perkins School of Theology, 75 per cent of the Methodist congregations are located in town and country areas under 2,500 population. These congregations represent 41.3 per cent of members in the United States. Since Methodism has been in the past and is today a rural church, it would seem that it should have had many significant things to say about agricultural policy in the United States. However, very few official statements were made prior to the merger of the three branches in 1939. We wish to develop briefly the various official statements of agricultural policy in The Methodist Church prior to 1939 and then those since 1939.

The first significant move made by The Methodist Church to recognize a rural way of life and a need for some type of agricultural policy came seven years after President Theodore Roosevelt in 1909 established his Country Life Commission to study rural life. In 1916 the Board of Home Missions of The Methodist Episcopal Church organized two departments, one for rural churches and the other for cities. This was the first official effort toward recognition of the rural church. In the new Social Creed of the Churches in the 1916 *Discipline* of The Methodist Episcopal Church we find the first statement concerning agricultural policy under the heading, "The Community Service Program":

In the general field of social welfare we recommend that during the next four years the Churches concentrate attention, or at least put stress upon Unemployment, Housing, Prison Reform, Recreation. These may well constitute a four years' program of study and action for the federated churches of any city or state. Even the churches in rural communities will find an opportunity to work in one of these fields, each in its own community, while it aids the development of adequate State measures in other communities. We also urge country Churches to consider in this connection their duty regarding "Farm Labor," "Tenancy," and "Rural Cooperation" according to the recommendations of the Country Church Commission of the Federal Council.[1]

The phrase, "even the churches in rural communities," bears witness to the validity of C. M. McConnell's statement: "Anyone who knew The Methodist Church in 1916 and ten years before can bear witness to the fact that the leaders of the Church had gone 'very unwillingly' into any program of ministering to either of the two ways of American life in any distinctive way." [2] The two ways of life were the urban and the rural. The *Discipline* of The Methodist Episcopal Church retained the same brief statement as listed above through the General Conference of 1920 and 1924. However, from the General Conferences of 1928 and 1932 we find the *Discipline* listing within the Social Creed of the church the most significant of all statements concerning agricultural policy prior to 1939:

As in former pronouncements made by General Conferences of the Methodist Episcopal Church, and in addition to them, we believe in making the social and spiritual ideals of Jesus our test for community as well as for individual life; in strengthening and deepening the inner personal relationship of the individual with God, and recognizing his obligation and duty to society. This is crystallized in the two commandments of Jesus: "Love thy God" and "Love thy neighbor." Translating this ideal into agriculture means: (a) That the tiller of the soil shall be encouraged in his efforts to own the land he farms, and society be protected by efficient production and conservation of fertility. (b) That the cost of market distribution from farmer to consumer shall be cut to the lowest possible terms, both farmers and consumers sharing in these economies. (c) That there shall be every encouragement to the organization of farmers for economic ends, particularly for cooperative sales and purchases. (d) That an efficient system of both vocational and general education of youths and adults living on farms shall be available. (e) That special efforts shall be made to insure to the farmer adequate social institutions, including

[1] *Discipline*, Methodist Episcopal Church, 1916, ¶ 586.
[2] Charles M. McConnell, *High Hours of Methodism in Town-Country Communities* (New York: Editorial Department, Board of Missions of The Methodist Church, 1956), p. 42.

the church, the school, the library, means of recreation, good local government, and particularly the best possible farm home. (f) That there shall be a widespread development of organized rural communities, thoroughly democratic, completely cooperative, and possessed with the spirit of the common welfare. (g) That there shall be the fullest measure of friendly reciprocal cooperation between the rural and city workers.[3]

The next official statement concerning agricultural policy came from The Methodist Episcopal Church, South, in 1934. The 1934 *Discipline* had the following brief statement: "We stand for economic and social justice for the farm family and the preservation of the distinctive values of rural life." The southern branch of The Methodist Church has always depended more heavily on agriculture than has the northern branch; and yet, here again, we see the unwillingness of The Methodist Church to launch out into a more effective rural ministry.

In 1936 the Department of Rural Work became a part of the more inclusive Department of Town and Country Work. However in this year all statements concerning agricultural policy which had previously been found in the Social Creed disappeared. No other statement concerning agricultural policy appeared until after the merger in 1939. There seemed to be a certain amount of concern but it was not widespread enough to effect any official statements on agricultural policy.

With merger came the Methodist Rural Fellowship, an organization which had been the concern of many in the area of Town and Country work. The 1939 *Discipline* referred not only to the Annual Conference Commission on Town and Country work, but also to the Methodist Rural Fellowship, which seemed destined to have a great part to play in the rural ministry of the church. The famous "woodshed meeting" of the Methodist Rural Fellowship held during the General Conference of 1940 was a fellowship of those who would be concerned with agricultural policy in Methodism for years to come. The fact that no meeting place was made available for the Methodist Rural Fellowship at General Conference in 1940 is further evidence of the small amount of concern for the rural church.

From 1939 until 1947 very little official notice was given to the rural problem and agricultural policies. During this period there were no episcopal statements; and the *Disciplines* of 1939, 1940, and 1944 carried only the following brief statement: "We stand for the safeguarding of the farmer and his family, and for

[3] *Discipline*, Methodist Episcopal Church, 1932, ¶ 561.

the preservation of all the values of rural life." [4] This was very similar to the brief statement made by The Methodist Episcopal Church, South, in 1934. Does this mean that there was no progress during this ten-year period? By no means.

Several things were beginning to happen. The Methodist Rural Fellowship during this period was becoming established on the annual conference level and was beginning to make certain contributions. The Methodist Rural Fellowship in the Northern New York Conference, for example, took a definite stand for deferment of skilled farm labor in 1942 when the armed services were taking many of the skilled farmers into active service. In 1944 a symposium sponsored by the Methodist Rural Fellowship examined the policies and programs of each Board and Agency of The Methodist Church in connection with service to rural people. Things were just beginning to get started when, in 1947, to use the words of C. M. McConnell, "The Bishops moved in." [5]

The first national conference for Methodism's town and country communities was held at Lincoln, Nebraska, in 1947, with Bishop William C. Martin delivering the keynote address. This conference seemed to be the dawning of a new day in town and country work in The Methodist Church. Nearly all the legislation recommended from the conference received favorable action by the General Conference of 1948. More was done for the rural church at this General Conference than ever before in the history of Methodism. The General Conference adopted the following in the Social Creed:

> We recognize the basic significance of rural areas in relation to population supply, natural resources, community life, and Christian culture. Methodism, because of its large membership and world-wide impact, must accept the responsibility and leadership, not only in the United States but throughout the world, for dignifying and supporting Christian service, and for developing an adequate Christian program in rural areas, pertaining to people in their relationship to God, to soil and all natural resources, and to family, Church, and community welfare. We call upon all leaders of our church, lay and clerical, thus to help establish the Kingdom of God in the countryside. [6]

With a few minor changes the above statement has continued to be an official statement concerning agricultural policy. Legislation was also adopted giving responsibility to the Town and Country Department to help place young people on the land and in the

---

[4] *Discipline*, Methodist Episcopal Church, 1939, ¶ 1695.

[5] McConnell, *op. cit.*, p. 52.

[6] *Methodist Rural Fellowship Bulletin*, VIII, No. 3, Summer, 1948.

local community, "making available information concerning resources for this purpose from private, governmental, and religious agencies, establishing and administering special loan funds," and setting forth the plan of operation of larger parishes and group ministries.[7] The Farm and Home Committee was a part of the legislation adopted to be used on the local church level to help in establishing young people on the land. This all seems to be more significant than anything done previously in that field.

Little official legislation and statements concerning agricultural policy have come since 1948. At the second National Town and Country Conference, Bishop Charles W. Brashares expressed the concern of the bishops, at least in part, when he said: "There is a danger in America that farming may become simply a business of raising crops instead of primarily a way of life for people." [8] He also expressed concern for the family-size farm.

The General Conference of 1952 adopted the following agricultural policy concerning adequate and healthful diets for the world's growing populations:

We believe that economic assistance which "seeks to make the benefits of our scientific advances and industrial progress available for the improvement of underdeveloped areas" is the strongest combatant of the elements of revolution found in our times. There is a tragic shortage of food and other basic necessities in vast areas of our world. Even with present levels of good production maintained, millions of people will starve to death each year.

We urge that government funds and resources be increased for "Point Four" and Technical Assistance programs and that these be channeled through the United Nations' Technical Assistance Program as much as possible. We believe that the original purpose of the "Point Four" and Technical Assistance programs should be carefully guarded against use based primarily on military and/or political expediency.[9]

In 1956 the Social Creed recognized that the farmer should have opportunity to earn a fair income and urged Methodism to lead in developing an adequate Christian program in rural areas everywhere.[10]

[7] Ibid.
[8] Ibid., XI, No. 3, Summer, 1951.
[9] "Representative Actions of Official Church Bodies on Subjects Included in Statement on Ethical Goals for Agricultural Policy," The Department of The Church and Economic Life, Division of Christian Life and Work, National Council of The Churches of Christ in the U.S.A. See also Walter W. Wilcox, Social Responsibility in Farm Leadership (New York: Harper and Brothers, 1956).
[10] Discipline, 1956, ¶ 2020, sec. B, 7.

CHAPTER SEVENTEEN

The State

METHODISTS HAVE ALWAYS ACKNOWLEDGED POLITICAL RE-
sponsibility. The MESTA questionnaire simply confirms the historic
attitude of the denomination.

30. POLITICS

is of no concern to the Christian,
whose citizenship is not of this
world .... .6 per cent
is a necessary evil, and Christians
should be careful not to be contami-
nated by participating in it beyond
necessity .... 2.4 per cent
should call forth the serious and intelligent concern of the conscientious Christian .... 64.4 per cent
is an area which Christians should
regard as a special responsibility .29.4 per cent
Write-in .... 1.5 per cent
No report .... 1.7 per cent

Thus 93 per cent of the respondents take a very positive view of
the political order.

This present volume shows that Methodism, while assuming a
democratic and republican form of government, has had no preconceived or highly organized philosophy of the functions of
the state, but rather has responded pragmatically to social problems as they have arisen in particular historical contexts.[1] As
one surveys the various aspects of social reform and social action,
in each area the function of the state advocated does not seem to

[1] See George B. Taylor, "The Functions of the State in Social Reform as
Found in Some Official Publications of Methodism" (unpublished Th.D. dissertation, Boston University School of Theology, 1955), pp. 256-65.

stem from any preconceived philosophy or doctrine of the state, but rather seems to have been suggested to cope with the particular social problem under consideration, the ends determining the means within certain limits which are expressed when the need for such limitations is indicated.

Because it has been nationally discussed and seems to imply a significant degree of involvement in the economic order, the research team included in its questionnaire an item on the TVA. The over-all totals are given in percentages, and then the breakdown on alternative attitudes by jurisdictions.

34. PUBLIC POWER PROJECTS LIKE TVA

are a threat to our free enterprise
economy .... 9.4 per cent
are questionable because they tax all
all our citizens to provide cheap
electricity for a few............13.5 per cent
greatly improve the total economic
welfare of the nation ....41.0 per cent
provide worthy experiments in the
extension of democracy ....18.7 per cent
Write-in .... 3.0 per cent
No report ....14.4 per cent

Almost 60 per cent of the respondents take a positively favorable view of state action as illustrated in TVA. The distribution by jurisdictions is interesting.

Question 34

	1	2	3	4	5	6
Totals	9.4	13.5	41.0	18.7	3.0	14.4
C	1.5	13.6	48.5	19.7	4.5	12.2
NC	9.9	13.0	41.2	18.6	2.6	14.7
NE	10.4	18.9	35.5	18.5	2.7	14.0
SC	9.2	12.7	39.3	17.1	2.7	19.0
SE	6.8	10.5	48.3	20.2	3.9	10.3
W	11.4	10.9	38.9	19.4	3.9	15.5

The combined scores of the favorable responses, columns 3 and 4, show for the Southeastern Jurisdiction 68.5 per cent and for the Northeastern 54.0 per cent. The Southcentral totals of favorable responses are 56.4 per cent. When one considers that the image which the Southeastern Jurisdiction sometimes has shown of the Northeastern as holding to a strong social gospel implemented by the federal government, this profile is quite significant. It bears out the thesis, perhaps, that the merits of certain projects and proximity to them overweigh any doctrinaire tendencies regarding the role of the state. This response is typically American and Methodist and agrees with the Episcopal Address of 1948 as we shall note below. Nevertheless, the responses are also related to the fact that the TVA is located within the Southeastern Jurisdictional region.

The variety of state practice in Methodist thought and action is striking. When concerned with the particular problems of alcoholic beverages and gambling, Methodism has called upon the state to use every means at its disposal to eradicate these social evils, as witness Prohibition. Constitutional amendments have been proposed to prohibit the production and consumption of alcoholic beverages, to prohibit polygamous marriages, and to prevent the use of public funds for parochial education.

Concern for the victims of war profiteering brought vigorous resolutions on this problem as early as 1924. "We demand the establishment of the principle that the conscription of wealth and labor must be the counterpart of any future conscription of human life. As great odium must be put upon the war profiteer as is put upon the slacker." [1] The point was repeated in 1936. It meant the virtual nationalization of industry in wartime. "We recommend that the federal government assume exclusive responsibility for the manufacture of munitions of all kinds. We further recommend prohibiting the sale of munitions of war to any individual group or nation." [2]

The spirit of this recommendation had, of course, nothing to do with the positive principle of communism. In fact, this was a possible consequence of war to be feared. "Another world war with its terrible trail of debt and its debasing of moral standards would certainly result in reactions leading to communistic experiments and bullying dictatorships. Dean Inge says: 'The most socialistic enterprise in which a nation ever engages is a great war.' In many of its phases war is communistic. Our last (war) proved an introduction for both Fascism and Communism." [3]

In the crucial area of agriculture no direct statement has ever been made concerning the duty and function of the state. No

[1] *Journal, Methodist Episcopal Church, 1924*, p. 721.
[2] *Journal, Methodist Episcopal Church, 1936*, p. 662.
[3] *Ibid.*, p. 141.

systematic statement of the state's relation to property has been officially formulated. The absence of any policy by a state in relation to agriculture is especially singular in the light of the great activity which federal and state governments have initiated in this aspect of the national economy. This may mean an implicit pragmatic approval of policy favorable to the farming industry.[4] We have already noted Methodism's unique role in rural America and its comparative silence on agriculture in the lawmaking bodies of the church. Against the background of this silence the strong praise by the Episcopal Address of 1948 of the Tennessee Valley Authority (TVA) is notable.

Careful and wise administration emphasizing social responsibility had won for TVA high praise and great respect. But by 1948 a combination of jealous politicians, economic reactionaries, and aggressive corporate power interests was lobbying to have the electric power-producing program of the TVA turned over to private corporations. The Episcopal Address defended the government project on the grounds that it was more than an organization to produce electric power, that it was concerned with soil erosion, reforestation, flood control, and the welfare of the whole valley.

Which is wiser when we enter the Tennessee Valley, to call upon a power corporation to develop power efficiently for the benefit of its stockholders or for a public corporation, owned by the people, managed in the Valley itself, charged with developing all the resources of the Valley in the unity with which nature endowed the Valley? . . . Those who have studied carefully, without prejudice, in all probability will come to the conclusion that in this particular situation the use of the public corporation is a better answer in the interests of Christianity.

On the subject of the function of the state in international relations there has been a notable development in Methodist thought during the past half century. Subsequent to World War I and prior to World War II Methodism advocated co-operation among nations and approved the League of Nations; but, while holding that Methodism could not be nationalistic, it assumed that each nation-state would retain its sovereign rights. By 1940 the church was clearly denouncing the absolute demands of nationalism and sovereignty and during World War II conducted the aggressive crusade for a new world order which in the form of the United

---

[4] It should be borne in mind that persons most influential in the State of the Church Committee at the General Conference have been urban rather than rural leaders. Most urban-minded leaders have not thought thoroughly about agricultural issues.

Nations modifies sovereignty at some points. In 1952 the General Conference called for further involvement of the U.S.A. in a revised UN looking toward a world federation of nations.

Methodism's conception of state functions and duties have not only been varied, but they have been stimulated by particular historical situations. The strong pronouncements by the General Conference of The Methodist Episcopal Church in 1932 called upon the Congress to remove the weaknesses and injustices of the prevailing economy and to meet the demands for unemployment insurance, old-age pensions, and public health service, and singled out stock market speculations as the most iniquitous form of gambling—which led to the stock market "crash" of 1929 and the succeeding economic depression. It was not until the scarcity of labor during World War II dramatized the injustices of the limited vocational opportunities open to Negroes that the church spoke out in favor of fair employment practices legislation.

Before the turn of the century, when the federal government sent troops to Utah to enforce monogamy among the Mormons, The Methodist Episcopal Church defended the sanctity of monogamous marriage and urged a constitutional amendment to prohibit polygamy. This incident, along with the rising divorce rate, stimulated a churchly interest in marriage and divorce legislation.[5]

We may conclude, then, that the church's attitude toward the state has been situational and that with respect to the socio-economic order the official pronouncements are complex and embrace no one particular doctrine. Indeed, the endorsement of any one economic system is explicitly repudiated. Apart from brief statements in the Social Creed the Methodist Protestants and The Methodist Episcopal Church, South, said nothing about property rights; but in 1924 and in 1932 and 1936 the utterances of the Northern church indicate a kind of "mixed economy." The 1944 and 1952 General Conferences of the united church tend to confirm this.

In 1924 the General Conference had outlined a significant paragraph on the subject of property rights and the community.

Property rights possess no inherent sacredness which puts them beyond the reach of criticism and revision by the Christian society. We recognize the ethical divergence of property for use and property for power. We maintain the soundness of the principle that a man is entitled only to what

[5] There is a real question whether the civil and religious liberties of the Mormons were properly respected, not to mention due process of law. Emotions raging over polygamy blinded many Protestants and others to some of these constitutional issues.

he has in a real sense earned. Wealth accruing to the holders through monopoly values or special privileges, or through large opportunities for costless saving, is not earned; and wealth created by society should be devoted to development of all the people in ways to be determined by the people themselves.[6]

Thus both private property and the purpose of the state to act in behalf of the community good are affirmed.

This philosophy was reiterated in 1944 with an explicit reference to the Malvern Conference of 1940 with which the name of Archbishop William Temple is so intimately associated. The General Conference said:

We agree with the Malvern Manifesto that: it is a traditional doctrine of Christendom that property is necessary to the fullness of personal life: all citizens should be enabled to hold such property as contributes to moral independence and spiritual freedom without impairing that of others; but where the rights of property conflict with the establishment of social justice or the general social welfare, those rights should be overridden, modified, or if need be, abolished.[7]

That General Conference also recognized the pressing need for a reorganization of the prevailing capitalistic economic system and suggested that the pragmatic approach of experimentation with different forms of ownership was the direction in which society should move. "We believe that a new ordering of economic life is both imminent and imperative. . . . We recognize the need of experimentation with various forms of ownership and control, private, cooperative, and public."[8]

For a number of years the Social Creed had carried the phrase, "the subordination of the profit motive to the creative and cooperative spirit." This phrase was dropped in 1952. It is interesting to note that the deletion of this reference to the profit motive came at the same General Conference that recommended the rebuke of the Methodist Federation for Social Action.

The new phrasing mentions positively the right of private ownership but states as explicitly that Methodism does not espouse any particular economic order. "We stand for the principle of the acquisition of property by Christian processes and the right of private ownership thereof with full acknowledgement of stewardship under God and accountability to him for its use. We espouse

[6] *Journal, Methodist Episcopal Church, 1924,* p. 594.
[7] *Discipline,* 1944, p. 572.
[8] *Loc. cit.*

no particular economic system, and refuse to identify Christianity with any particular economic order." [9] Reformist statements in official Methodist legislation have never been revolutionary in intention.

In the sense that the state is expected to help improve the socio-economic conditions of its citizens, particularly the underprivileged, Methodism can be said to have advocated a "welfare state." It has supported unemployment insurance, old-age pension, public health service, extended social security coverage, Sunday laws, regulations protecting the public interest in films and radio commercials, government soil erosion programs, co-operatives, and low cost marketing facilities. At the same time it has encouraged independent business, free trade, family-sized and privately owned farms. Social guardianship is linked with self-reliance and individual personal fulfillment.

Methodist pronouncements tending toward approval of governmental intervention were strongest in the period from 1924 to 1936 and have on socio-economic questions become more conservative since then.[10] In this Methodist tendencies coincide with those of other denominations and of the major political parties. Continued concern for social reform tends not so clearly to be tied to governmental intervention.

The doctrine of the state needs systematic development in Methodism. Methodism's sense of social responsibility needs clarifying conceptions of governmental operations in relation to civil liberties, the social economic order, international relations, and the relations of church and state. On the whole, Methodism at present holds to principles congruent with those developed by the Evanston Assembly of the World Council of Churches and the National Council of Churches, and has participated in the formulation of both efforts to relate the state to the idea of the responsible society.[11] The idea and power of freedom will be conserved only by those who know the right functions, duties, and limitations of state power and can relate them in a coherent way. This need is highlighted by such problems as the creeping miasma of military domination over society and by the power struggles of privilege on the part of organized business and organized labor for control of government. As new concepts of international political society emerge from the crucible of world conflict and hope, Methodism

[9] *Discipline*, 1952, p. 633.
[10] This is fully demonstrated in both the dissertations by E. E. Brewster, *op. cit.*, and George B. Taylor, *op. cit.*
[11] See W. G. Muelder, *Foundations of The Responsible Society* (Nashville: Abingdon Press, 1959), Ch. 1.

must assume its share of obligations for ecumenical and denominational action.

In their devotion to freedom of religion and to democracy, Methodists have steadfastly affirmed belief in the separation of church and state. The affirmation is linked to a wide variety of interpretations of what it means. Many would agree with Claud Nelson, chairman of the Department of Religious Liberty of the National Council of Churches, and a Methodist, "that separation of the functioning of ecclesiastical and governmental institutions was not intended as necessitating the withdrawal of religious and governmental forces from mutual concern and mutually supporting interaction." [12]

Officially, "The National Council of Churches holds the first clause of the First Amendment to the Constitution of the United States to mean that church and state shall be separate and independent as institutions, but to imply neither that the state is indifferent to religious interests nor that the Church is indifferent to civic and political issues." In this same spirit The Methodist Church holds "that the free democratic way of life ruled by Christian principles can bring mankind to a society in which liberty is preserved, justice established, and brotherhood achieved." [13] But some Methodist leaders would hasten to remind holders of the majority position that separation of church and state is primarily a political matter with theological overtones, and that the doctrine of separation was designed to protect not only freedom of worship but also to protect the state from church aggression. Then, too, there are Methodists who have an almost equal suspicion of the Roman Catholic and of the secularist perspectives.

At the present time the Board of Social and Economic Relations in the New York East Conference is conducting an extended Research Consultation on the church and state. This effort is to be commended and its results should be fruitful to many churches and the ecumenical movement. The outline of study reflects the complexity of the problem which goes beyond the limitations of the present study. Perhaps the chief difficulty which the present study involves is the frequency with which The Methodist Church has spoken directly on social questions from the perspective of church-state relations. Not least is the need to define more sharply the conceptions of state and church, both theologically and institutionally. Volume Three of the present series will make a contribution to these

[12] Claud Nelson, "Church and State," p. 12.
[13] *Discipline*, 1956, ¶ 2020-B.

conceptions and Volume Four will take account of them from the standpoint of strategy.

The areas of study now being explored involve (1) the freedom of the individual in thought, conscience, and communication; (2) the self-determination of the churches in their rites, personnel, property, and support, including such questions as taxation, the courts, and use of public utilities; (3) the efforts of the church to influence the policy of the state on issues which the church designates as "moral," involving both aggressive and defensive social policies; (4) the religious or quasi-religious functions sponsored or supported by the state, such as recognition of days of special piety, symbolic recognition of religion, religious ministration to the armed forces and prisoners, and the payment of college expenses to veterans in church-related schools; (5) the governmental functions performed by, or expected of, the churches either on a contract basis or in some other relationship; (6) the many ways in which church and state impinge upon the family, hospitals and medical practice, education, and the like; and (7) the adjustment of American churches and the government to conditions imposed by international relationships. In these clusters of problems lies a whole panorama of challenges to Methodist education and action.

Although Methodism has not worked out a systematic philosophy on church and state and has probably operated in ways that are not strictly coherent, it has expressed itself on certain values and taken certain actions which may be briefly noted. It has stressed freedom of worship, the rights of conscientious objectors, freedom from military training on Methodist college campuses, and freedom from harassment by congressional investigators. Methodism has emphasized the right to be different, the values of academic freedom and non-conformity, the right for the religious objector to have service alternate to military duty. Methodism has certainly engaged in a manifold demand for social and political action, as we have noted in the discussion of the state. Methodists are not united on such questions as to remunerations and subsidies which they seek or accept from state sources, at home or abroad. The Methodist Board of Hospitals uses federal funds which are available to churches for hospital construction. In the matter of the employment, remuneration, and inevitable restraint of chaplains in the armed forces by government there is probably less concern than there should be.

On one question the General Conference has spoken clearly and relatively extensively, namely on religion and the public schools. The Methodist Church is committed to the public school "as the most effective means of providing common education for all our children." "We call upon our people (1) to acquaint themselves with the program and problems of the public school and to do all they can to encourage and strengthen the work of teachers and administrations, and (2) to present to our ablest youth the spiritual and public-service opportunities of public school teaching as a vocation." This solid commitment to the public schools was followed by an assertion of unalterable opposition "to the diversion of tax funds to the support of private and sectarian schools," lest such a scattering process destroy the public-school system and weaken the foundations of national unity. Religion has a rightful place in the public-school program and it is possible to teach moral principles and spiritual values in such a way as not to violate the principle of separation of church and state.[14]

[14] *Discipline*, 1952, ¶ 2028.

CHAPTER EIGHTEEN

Communism

CHRISTIANITY CANNOT BE IDENTIFIED WITH ANY PARTICU-lar social or economic order. Since it has borne its witness in every part of the world, the institutional structures, and often its mode of existence, have reflected the interaction of the church and its environment. In the present century the issue of communism has been consistently raised because of the vigor of Marxist ideas and the expansive power of the Communist movement. The Communist conspiracy in the United States has been real. Its actual threat to American institutions, however, has never been a major force. Communist imperialism has been a major aspect of world politics and the struggle for men's minds.

In 1944 the General Conference endorsed the Episcopal Address on a point which is close to the heart of the issue which Communism raises today:

Scientific humanism and secular communism speak often of human values and social ideals, but they are prejudiced against the recognition of the supernatural and reject a belief in the future life. This position in itself opens the way for the idolatry of mere physical existence and exercises a devastating effect on the human spirit. . . . Once the Christian doctrine of man is rejected, the way is opened for man's exploitation of man, a merciless attitude on the part of the strong against the weak, savage ruthlessness.[1]

As on many of the deeper social questions Methodism has developed an attitude toward Communism which is a part of the ecumenical witness to the responsible society. The church took an attitude of appreciation toward the utterances of the Oxford Conference of 1937. That gathering rejected the materialism of Communism in deriving all moral and spiritual values from economic needs

[1] *Discipline*, 1944, ¶ 2015.

and economic conditions and in so doing depriving "personal and cultural life of its creative freedom." Oxford also opposed true freedom to the economic autocracy of capitalism and looked with favor on voluntary co-operative enterprises, in which the norms of personal worth of workers, freedom of opportunity, and the ideal of full development of man's capacities were present. Ecumenical discussions of world economic systems have been aware that simple contrasts between capitalism and Communism are fruitless and lead to error. There are dilemmas in the growing power of the state and of giant corporations and cartels. State planning was considered at Whitby in 1947: "The increase of state planning, however necessary to provide security, cannot but threaten individual, and sometimes spiritual liberty; and even often seem ready to purchase security even by the surrender of freedom." [2]

At Amsterdam in 1948 the Assembly of the World Council of Churches condemned both Communism and *laissez-faire* capitalism, but this Assembly, like the one at Whitby, rejected all forms of totalitarianism in the world, whether Fascist, Communist, or religious. The points of conflict between the Christian faith and Marxist ideology and totalitarian practice were reaffirmed at Evanston in 1954 with the comment that the growth of Communism is a judgment upon our modern societies generally for past or present indifference to social injustice in which the church is also involved. These points of conflict are:

(1) The communist promise of what amounts to a complete redemption of man in history; (2) The belief that a particular class by virtue of its role as the bearer of a new order is free from the sins and ambiguities that Christians believe characteristic of all human existence; (3) the materialistic and deterministic teachings, however they may be qualified, that are incompatible with belief in God and with the Christian view of man as a person, made in God's image and responsible to Him; (4) the ruthless methods of communists in dealing with their opponents; (5) the demand of the party on its members for an exclusive and unqualified loyalty which belongs only to God, and the coercive policies of communist dictatorship in controlling every aspect of life. [3]

Like most American documents that have criticized the economic order, Methodist statements have stressed the teachings of Jesus and the worth of personality. Methodists were on the drafting committee of the National Study Conference on the Church and Eco-

[2] "Christian Witness in a Revolutionary World," International Missionary Council (Whitby, Canada, 1947), II, ¶ 3.

[3] *Evanston Speaks*, p. 32n.

nomic Life at Detroit in 1950. Its message was called "An Affirmation of Christian Concern and a Call to Action in Relation to Economic Life," and it said in part:

> Christians judge all economic systems by the imperatives of the Christian faith; Christians must not identify any economic order with the Gospel. The Christian Gospel is not to be found in Adam Smith's "Wealth of Nations" nor in Karl Marx's "Kapital." It is to be found in Matthew, Mark, Luke, and John, in the Acts of the Apostles, the Epistles of the New Testament, and the vision of St. John in the Revelation. It is to be found in the preaching of the Hebrew prophets, in the lives of Saints and Martyrs, in the service of the faithful followers of Christ, and in the continuing revelation of God. That faith affirms the supreme worth of persons. Institutions must be tested finally by their contribution to the enrichment of personality.[4]

The excitement over Communism in The Methodist Church, and in American Protestantism generally, roots in part in the genuine concern over Soviet power and practice and partly in criticism of evils in the social economic order. Those who made an effective judgment of abuses, injustice, or exploitation or showed any concern in behalf of the rights of labor, the protection of women and children, and the enactment of social legislation have been met by accusations of "Communism." The basic issue all along has been social justice which requires social change. Bishop McConnell stated in 1952:

> At present the federation is under attack for its alleged friendliness to communism. I myself do not know a Methodist who is a communist. The Federation is almost always under fire for one thing or another. Still we have to remember that the foes which it fights are those which today are the chief hindrances to making society Christian. Any professing Christian who today serves mammon in the sense that our Lord said "serves mammon" does not know what spirit he is of.[5]

The crises over "Communism" have not only concerned the industrial order, but have been crises in civil liberties as well. Just as the American Civil Liberties Union has been accused of being "Communist" because it defends the civil liberties of all under the

---

[4] This statement was drafted by Bishop G. Bromley Oxnam. See *I Protest*, p. 141. The explicit reference is given here because of the controversies related to him. Generally speaking the authors of reports have been left anonymous. See John C. Bennett, Howard R. Bowen, William Adams Brown, Jr., and G. Bromley Oxnam, *Christian Values and Economic Life* (New York: Harper and Brothers, 1954), pp. 14-15.

[5] Francis J. McConnell, *By the Way* (Nashville: Abingdon Press, 1952), pp. 211-12.

Constitution, so Methodist personalities and unofficial groups have been attacked because they defended the democratic rights of persons who hold to ideas which are under attack. The sincere opponents of those Methodist leaders who have defended the rights of communists or fellow-travelers are often not aware that their own political methods are the sure way to fasten totalitarianism on the nation.

The bishops of The Methodist Church have been very explicit on the real Communist issue. In the Episcopal Address of 1948 they made a definitive statement which was supported by the General Conference.

We reject Communism, its materialism, its method of class war, its use of dictatorship, its fallacious economics, and its false theory of social development; but we know that the only way to defeat it permanently is to use the freedom of our own democracy to establish economic justice and racial brotherhood. It is the man who is not exploited who is deaf to the slogan, "Abolish the exploitation of man by man." It is the man who knows he is treated justly who refuses the sinister suggestion of revolutionary activity to win justice. The most effective anti-toxin to dictatorship abroad is life-giving democracy at home. It is a healthy democracy that is immune to Communist bacteria. . . . The most certain way to destroy dictatorship abroad is to establish democracy at home. Liberty, equality, and fraternity are contagious; and, if present in sufficient vitality, may become epidemic. Let people who suffer dictatorship behold a nation in which man has preserved his liberty, established equality, and practices fraternity, and it is certain as day follows night that such vision will become a revolutionary force that will not rest until freedom is won. Socially controllable inequalities must be removed. Justice and brotherhood within the conditions of freedom are like bells. They sound the death knell of Communism. Communism will never win a democratic and just America. Communism does not grow in the soil of freedom and justice. It takes root in the soil of exploitation. It is democracy—more of it, not less of it—that will win the morrow.

The systematic doctrinal condemnation of the ideology of atheistic Communism is one thing; the development of Christian international relations in the face of the "cold war" is another, especially for a church that recognizes that it cannot be nationalistic. Here, again, the spirit of official Methodist resolutions is like that of the great ecumenical utterances. As to the U.S.S.R. and other areas of international strife, it is imperative to reduce current tensions and to control them so that deeper and more creative influences of reconciliation can be brought to bear. The Evanston Assembly of the World Council of Churches said in 1954:

371

A current political definition of such endeavors is "co-existence." We avoid the use of this term because of its unhappy historical significance and some of its current political implications. "Co-existence" as conceived by Christians cannot imply any willingness to disguise from themselves or others the vast difference which lies between the search for an international order based on belief in Christ and His reconciling work, and the pursuit of aims which repudiate the Christian revelation. There can be no abandonment of the right to assert this fundamental difference and the faith on which it rests.[6]

In 1952 the General Conference was emphatic that Methodism could not condone the ideology or practice of Communism. "It is equally essential," it said, "to avoid fostering hatred. We should not charge the entire Russian people with being Communist. There are still many millions of Christians in Russia. . . . We should make every effort to communicate with these people and send a message of Christian fellowship and goodwill." Even beyond the confines of the Christians in the U.S.S.R. the General Conference registered its conviction that the peoples of neither the Soviet Union nor the United States desire war. "We call upon all of our people promptly to undertake to change the prevailing mood which we believe conducive to war. We urge our respective governments to support a continuing process of negotiations through the United Nations and on other diplomatic high levels, and to keep the door open to any proposal, from whatever source, that holds the possibility of peace." [7]

The best defense against Communism is not military force or the suppression of civil liberties, but the preservation of democratic institutions strengthened by a more thoroughgoing use of them. What is required is more adequate provision for both the physical and spiritual needs of persons of all lands and a recognition of their common aspirations.

[6] *Evanston Speaks*, pp. 41-42.
[7] *Discipline*, 1952, ¶ 2026. At international gatherings some non-Christians from the Soviet Union have shown themselves to be soberly concerned about world order and have expressed international goodwill.

CHAPTER NINETEEN

World Order

FUTURE HISTORIANS, IT HAS BEEN SAID, WILL POINT TO THE emergence of a world community as one of the greatest advances of the twentieth century. With lethal clouds of nuclear destruction hovering above the earth, it can no longer be taken for granted— as prophets glibly assumed only ten to fifteen years ago—that there will be any future historians around to make this judgment. This awesome prospect of annihilation conditions every responsible discussion of world order today and makes the establishment of world community more imperative than ever. On the other hand, if humanity survives, there is another development which makes world order hardly less imperative—the looming population explosion. Yet it is indicative of the hurried pace of events that while the nations are but reluctantly beginning to adjust to the realities of global interdependence, a still larger world of human habitation may possibly be on the threshold of discovery beyond this planet. The ethics of world order may henceforth have to grapple also with the moral, social, and legal problems of outer space.

It goes without saying that these possibilities now impinging upon human society are bound decisively to affect also the Christian attitude to world affairs.

Methodism has an outstanding record of leadership in the witness for world peace. As befits a world-reaching denominational body, its various institutional units, from the General Conference onward, steadily keep the subject in mind in their pronouncements and program activities. Nearly every Annual Conference and many districts have a board or committee on world peace. The Woman's Division of Christian Service is unmatched in its efforts to make the common affairs of mankind a grass-roots concern.

World affairs is an area of responsibility where Methodism to a high degree shares in the range of beliefs and attitudes observable in Protestantism at large. This broad commonality of convictions has been fostered by the interacting participation of Methodist leaders at opinion-forming levels in various interdenominational peace efforts. They have included distinguished figures such as Georgia Harkness, G. Bromley Oxnam, Harold Bosley, Charles F. Boss, Ernest F. Tittle, James C. Baker, Ralph Sockman, Ernest Gross, and John Swomley. The Board of World Peace is intimately associated with numerous peace organizations. From 1925 to 1956 a Methodist, Walter W. Van Kirk, was executive secretary of the Department of International Justice and Goodwill (now the Department of International Affairs) of the National Council of Churches. He played a leading role in the creation of the Church Commission on International Affairs, jointly sponsored by the World Council of Churches and the International Missionary Council. His two successors in the National Council Department of International Affairs belong to the same denomination. Methodists are prominent in the Fellowship of Reconciliation. At the institutional level, agencies of the church are strongly supporting the National and World Councils of Churches and disseminating their pronouncements.

This broad-ranged interpenetration will be exemplified later. But first it would be instructive to take a look at the stance of ecumenical Christianity in international affairs. By a providential coincidence, the nascence of a world community has been accompanied and in part preceded by similar developments within Christianity. The ecumenical movement, with its vision of the one church universal, has incalculably enhanced the Christian sense of world responsibility and provided effective channels for its actualization.[1]

The Commission of the Churches on International Affairs mentioned earlier co-operates with a far-flung network of interdenominational commissions in scores of countries. Among these, the National Council of Churches of Christ in America and its Department of International Affairs hold a place of distinction; their periodical national study conferences on world order, like the most recent one at Cleveland, Ohio, in November 1958, on "Christian Responsibility on a Changing Planet," are significant laboratories of Christian education and action for peace. The availability of this co-operative framework has made it possible for the Protestant and Orthodox churches affiliated with the ecumenical movement to approach international issues from a more universal perspective and to muster vast resources of ethical insight and technical competence,

---

[1] It is suggestive that the ancient Greek word from which the term ecumenical is derived means "the whole inhabited world."

which are making world Christianity a recognized voice in the councils of the nations.

The churches' concern with international affairs in recent decades represents a concerted attempt to develop a more genuine Christian witness, distinct both from irresponsible indifference and from equally irresponsible conformity with government policies or sectional interests. In so doing they have gradually been led far beyond such traditional preoccupations as the question of the Christian's participation in war, to grapple constructively with the inclusive problem of a viable world order. These efforts are admittedly still in the exploratory state, and on many points the Christian mind remains woefully divided and perplexed. Yet some characteristic thrusts may be noted as they are pertinent to our study: the supranationality of the church and its world responsibility; prevention of war and easing of the East-West tension; Christian attitudes to war; furtherance of international law and of organizations for co-operation and exchange; concern for human rights and liberties; [2] aid to underdeveloped peoples.

The recovery of the church in current theological thought, and the experience of ecumenical fellowship, have as a by-product combined in placing the Christian approach to international affairs in a new and larger frame of reference—the supranational church. Here a dynamic insight is being regained which opens wider horizons and offers Christians and churches in every land a reassuring and challenging awareness of being part of a world-wide community beyond nations and ideologies. In reaction to the rabid nationalisms of the day, the Oxford World Conference on Church, Community, and State in 1937 spoke of the task of the supranational church in terms which have set higher standards for Christian loyalty. "We speak as Christians, that is . . . as members of the body of Christ, the universal supranational fellowship." [3] As such, the church carries a special responsibility and possesses peculiar resources for a ministry of international reconciliation. Calling the nations "to order their lives as members of the one family of God," [4] it should itself serve as an exemplar and a leaven of true world community. In the words of a recent American statement: "We believe that Christians are members of the world-wide community of the church, and as such must strive to provide within their own fellowship as well as in their common life as citizens, the kind of community God wills for

[2] See above, Chapter XI.
[3] *The Oxford Conference: Official Report*, p. 65.
[4] *Ibid.*

375

the world." [5] "Christians can witness convincingly for peace only if they and their churches, in their relations with one another across all frontiers, put loyalty to their common Lord above any other loyalty." [6]

This emphasis on the supranationality of the church reaches its climax in the assertion: "If war breaks out, then pre-eminently the church must manifestly be the church, still united as the one body of Christ, though the nations wherein it is planted fight one another." [7] This affirmation showed the real greatness of the Oxford Conference. It is on this basis that the ecumenical community is endeavoring to bring Christian influence to bear on world affairs. The prevailing "cold war" situation has inevitably placed the prevention of a third world war, and the moral requirements of a Christian peace strategy, in the forefront. The Commission of the Churches on International Affairs has indefatigably warned against defeatist acceptance of the inevitability of war, pleaded for sanity and patience and readiness to grasp even the slightest opportunities for negotiation and fair agreement, and outlined concrete steps for a strategy of peaceful change.

The explosive issues of the East-West conflict have been frankly faced. The ecumenical community has repeatedly voiced its unflinching opposition to every form of oppression and aggression and its rejection of Communist atheistic totalitarianism. With equal force it has insisted that the Christian church must not allow itself to be identified with any particular political or ideological system, nor accept the obsessive tendency to judge every event across the globe in terms of the East-West struggle. "We cannot sit complacently and hopefully behind the moral subterfuge which divides the world into 'good' and 'bad' peoples, waiting for the 'bad' ones to be converted to our position." [8] In an interdependent world, where the nations are bound to live together or die together, the churches should support every effort to seek co-operation in social, economic, and cultural matters without compromise of basic convictions, hoping that such steps may gradually lead beyond "cold war" competition to an order of genuine co-operation.

This attitude is evidently inspired by the bold conviction that

[5] Christian Responsibility on a Changing Planet, p. 17. Report of the Fifth National Study Conference on World Order, convened by the Department of International Affairs of the National Council of Churches.

[6] Statement of the Commission of the Churches on International Affairs, August 1951.

[7] The Oxford Conference: Official Report, p. 47.

[8] Christian Responsibility on a Changing Planet, p. 18.

the Soviet system too, however monolithic and solid it may appear, is subject to the changes of history. The following statement, while speaking specifically of the United States, expresses a general conviction in the ecumenical fellowship: "By example and persuasion, by humanitarian measures, and by actions in accord with the purposes of the United Nations, America must do all within its power to assist peoples under Soviet Communist rule to cling to the goals of a free and responsible society, in the hope there may be changes in the Soviet system and policy conducive to freedom and peace." [9]

The churches in the ecumenical fellowship have persistently stood for progressive reduction and international regulation of armaments, and this position is now being advocated with fresh urgency in the atomic age. Thus the World Council of Churches in 1957 reiterated the appeal of the Evanston Assembly "for prohibition of all weapons of mass destruction, including atomic and hydrogen bombs, with provision for international inspection and control." It also urged "that as a first step governments conducting tests should forgo them, at least for a trial period, either together or individually, in the hope that the others would do the same." [10] The General Board of the National Council of Churches, in a pronouncement of June 4, 1958, has expressed itself in favor of "the control and limitation of all nuclear tests by international agreement with a system of international inspection and safeguards under the United Nations as one step toward more fundamental disarmament negotiations."

The commitment of Methodism to world political order and to a global perspective on social and economic questions is unequivocal. Pacifists and nonpacifists are on the whole not divided on these questions. Even during the war they co-operated actively in wrestling with them. The narrative of the response of The Methodist Church to the international crisis has been presented above and need not be repeated here. Responses to the MESTA questionnaire show that the membership are in substantial accord with the official position both on the attitude toward the United Nations and on the matter of economic and technical aid to other countries.[11]

[9] *Christian Faith and International Responsibility*, pp. 11-12. Report of the Fourth National Study Conference on World Order, convened by the National Council of Churches.

[10] Minutes and Reports of the Tenth Meeting of the Central Committee of the World Council of Churches, July-August 1957, p. 53.

[11] *Discipline*, 1956, ¶ 2026, sec. 5 and 12.

35. ECONOMIC AND TECHNICAL AID TO OTHER COUNTRIES SHOULD

await our caring for our own needs and interests .... 3.4 per cent

be granted only if it will advance our military objectives and economic interests .... 1.3 per cent

consider the welfare of the peoples involved as well as American interests .... 45.6 per cent

be allocated on the basis of the needs of humanity as a whole .... 45.1 per cent

Write-in .... 1.1 per cent

No report .... 3.5 per cent

36. UNITED NATIONS

World organization involves dangerous infringement on national sovereignty; hence each nation should pursue its own course, making only such temporary alliances as serve its ends .... 2.7 per cent

The U.N. deserves support as our best political hope for world peace .80.4 per cent

The U.N. deserves full support, but should be superseded as soon as possible by real world government . 8.6 per cent

Full world government, abolishing national sovereignty, is the world's best political hope .... 1.5 per cent

Write-in .... 2.3 per cent

No report .... 4.5 per cent

The above references are illustrative of the board consensus existing in the ecumenical fellowship with respect to world affairs. This consensus extends also to the basic judgment about the evil nature of war. "War is a particular demonstration of the power of sin in this world and a defiance of the righteousness of God as revealed in Jesus Christ and him crucified. No justification of war must be allowed to conceal or minimize this fact." [12]

Within this agreement the pacifist-nonpacifist controversy remains unresolved, however. The prevailing positions are aptly summed up in a report from the Amsterdam Assembly in 1948:

[12] *The Oxford Conference: Official Report*, p. 162.

(1) There are those who hold that, even though entering a war may be a Christian's duty in particular circumstances, modern warfare, with its mass destruction, can never be an act of justice.

(2) In the absence of impartial supranational institutions, there are those who hold that military action is the ultimate sanction of the rule of law, and that citizens must be distinctly taught that it is their duty to defend the law by force if necessary.

(3) Others, again, refuse military service of all kinds, convinced that an absolute witness against war and for peace is for them the will of God and they desire that the Church should speak to the same effect.[18]

Methodism recognizes the divided Christian conscience on the question of participation in war. It holds that government rests upon the support of its conscientious citizens and "holds within its fellowship those who sincerely differ as to the Christian's duty in regard to war." So far as the MESTA questionnaire elicited responses to this question, the present division of the Methodist conscience is as follows:

27. WAR: I, AS A CHRISTIAN CITIZEN,

am obligated to support my country
in war when its continued existence
is at stake, apart from considerations of justice ....47.2 per cent
can support or participate in war
only for the preservation of justice ....41.3 per cent
cannot support or participate in war
in the nuclear age, since war can
no longer serve the interests of
justice .... 3.2 per cent
can under no circumstances support
or participate in war .... 2.5 per cent
Write-in .... 2.6 per cent
No report .... 3.2 per cent

This study shows that the number of absolute pacifists is not large at the present time and is thus probably much smaller than before World War II. The General Conference asks and claims "exemption by legal processes from all forms of military preparation or service for all religious conscientious objectors, as for those of the historic peace churches. We also recognize the right of the individual to answer the call of his government according to the dictates of his Chris-

[18] *The First Assembly of the World Council of Churches: The Official Report*, pp. 88-90.

tian conscience." In both such situations the members of The Methodist Church have the authority and support of their church. This official position of the church has been confirmed by a decision of the Judicial Council, Methodism's supreme court.[14]

It should be added that the invention of nuclear weaponry, with its cataclysmic potentialities, is now stirring a reconsideration of the Christian attitude to war. In the mind of many, its indiscriminate mass destruction radically changes the nature of warfare and challenges traditional arguments of nonpacifists and pacifists alike. The outcome of these searching reflections cannot yet be foreseen, but they may well lead to significant reorientations.[15]

Methodism acknowledges its obligation to help develop a new international ethos. This is related to the conviction that one of the greatest and most pressing challenges facing the world community today is the social and economic advancement of so-called underdeveloped peoples. The International Missionary Council and the World Council of Churches are at present devoting a large part of their program to the task of mobilizing Christian resources and stirring government action in this field.[16] The "haves" among the nations are urged, as a matter of justice and solidarity, to share their resources more generously with the "have nots," to take account of the needs of other nations in determining their own economic policies, and generally, to place the common welfare of mankind above national and group interests. In effective world trade and co-operation the "haves" and "have nots" often exchange positions depending on the type of resources of goods and "know how."

These varied expressions of conviction have a common ground. They exemplify the belief that, in a world order under God, the demands of responsible freedom and social justice are not less imperative in their relations between nations than within each single nation.

---

[14] *Discipline*, 1956, ¶ 2020; Judicial Council Decision, 25.

[15] See, for example, *Christians and the Prevention of War in an Atomic Age —A Theological Discussion*, a provisional study document issued by the Division of Studies of the World Council of Churches in 1958.

[16] See their publications of "The Common Christian Responsibility toward Areas of Rapid Social Change," and also the reports of the World Order Study Conferences convened by the Department of International Relations of the National Council of Churches.

Part Four

Issues for the Future

CHAPTER TWENTY

Emergent Perspectives and Persistent Problems

METHODISM IN THE TWENTIETH CENTURY HAS DEVELOPED an impressive social witness. It has made a significant transition from the individualistic evangelism of the nineteenth century to the inclusive personal and social evangelism of the present. The social concern which was manifested in the organization of the unofficial Methodist Federation of Social Service in 1907 and in the Social Creed adopted in 1908, in the temperance movement of that period, and in only a slight attention to questions of race and world peace, has become a major aspect of the life of The Methodist Church. Almost every phase of the closely knit organization of the church has some direct relationship to social education and action. In a broader and perhaps deeper sense than John Wesley knew, its message today through conferences, boards, agencies, and local churches reflects the historic mark of Methodist preaching: "The gospel of Christ knows no religion but social, no holiness but social holiness."

The church is in the world, but in God's purpose it exists to proclaim his love and righteousness, and to increase the love of God and man in the world. As a historical institution the church has within it the limitations and evils which belong to the human and the finite. Its life participates both in the sin of men and society and in the saving power of Christ and the Holy Spirit. Its mission is ecumenical and its fellowship has the vocation of serving redemptively as an instrument of God's righteous rule on earth.

A. Questions About the Social Gospel Movement

What has been described and interpreted in this book may be called the Methodist participation in the "social gospel" movement in American Christianity. Social Christianity was developed as a dynamic leaven within the major denominations, not as a radical social revolt among the sects. It belongs to the life of the churches,

383

not of the sects. How shall it be understood and evaluated? We have noted that it has had a close relationship to seminaries and theological education. A large literature has been developed by outstanding thinkers and writers. Its work has effected the establishment of social service boards and agencies. Its Social Creed has mobilized purpose and action in denominational bodies and in the Federal (now the National) Council of Churches. Through the ecumenical movement it has expressed a world-wide religious and ethical concern over class divisions and economic conflicts which divide the churches. The movement has embraced consideration of and action on almost every major social question domestic and international. Despite the range of historical and empirical data with which these facets of social Christianity deal, there are some persistent questions about its meaning and significance. These questions take us back to those presented in the first chapter of this book.

Does the social movement represent an intrinsic religious development—a kind of reassertion of "primitive" Christian social ethics stimulated by modern urban crises or problems? [1] Is it the manifestation of the religious power of a few modern prophets? Is it a device or instrument whereby disprivileged groups employ religious beliefs and practices to improve their lot in life? Some, like J. Milton Yinger, ask particularly: "Is it simply a churchlike recognition of new forces in the world, of changes already partly accomplished by secular pressures, to which the churches had to give some recognition or relinquish completely their claim and hope for a universal brotherhood?" [2] This volume shows that Methodism has developed many kinds of response to the multitudinous forces that have operated in its life and environment. Almost every agency within the church acknowledges some obligation to improve the social order.

How shall this widespread growth of social concern be interpreted or explained? It is impossible to isolate one set of circumstances or causes above all others because religion is integrally involved in the whole interactive system of society. Yinger gives an affirmative answer to his own question in interpreting the movement of "social Christianity." This answer has important implications for evaluating the Methodist social response to the challenge of its environment. Yinger holds that the social gospel was primarily a "churchlike accommodation to new forces, and not a

[1] J. Milton Yinger, *Religion, Society and the Individual*, p. 225.
[2] *Loc. cit.*

384

demonstration that churches easily transcended the class lines that limit their appeal and their sphere of action." [3]

The kinds of evidence for this judgment are that the problems which engaged social Christianity in the late nineteenth century had long been in existence. Moreover, he says, the secular movements such as political agitation, labor unions, associations for the advancement of colored people, preceded any extensive protests by religious bodies by about a generation. Then too, business leaders, politicians, editors, and scholars were discovering from a more secular perspective in a mass production economy that the class interests were not injured by the "reforms" advocated. These leaders composed the "progressive conservatives" who rallied round the "new" social standards. Finally, he emphasizes that extensive concern with "social questions" has continued to characterize the work of only a minority of church leaders in schools, commissions, boards, and agencies of the church. Such churchmen, he notes, are "somewhat separated, as national organizations, from continuous contact with most laymen." Here the deviations from the "respectable" religious views are less readily apparent than the views of local pulpits to middle and upper-class congregations.[4]

On this view, contrary to the fears of many lay people and some clergy, the social gospel in the churches "was not the triumph of a radical Christianity, forcing society to justice, but the emergence of new forces to which the churches had to adjust—as they adjusted to the rising commercial classes of the seventeenth century—if they were not to lose what influence they yet maintained over a large group of people and give up the belief in a universally valid Christianity." [5] This latter phrase is significant for "belief in a universally valid Christianity" is a personal and social power which transcends immediate social situations.

In response to an interpretation like that of Yinger's a number of general comments must be made and then some specific analysis must be undertaken.

1. Methodism's responses to the challenges of the twentieth century have steadily grown. The Social Creed and the specific resolutions on major questions provide a comprehensive and systematic body of official social doctrine.

2. This comprehensive expression of social concern is predominantly practical rather than theoretical, but it reflects an important

[3] *Loc. cit.*
[4] *Ibid.*, p. 226.
[5] *Ibid.*, p. 227.

body of theological convictions about social salvation. These issues are treated in Volume Three.

3. It is very difficult, if not impossible, to demonstrate concrete ways in which Methodism apart from social Christianity generally has influenced American social life in a major way. This book has more modestly presented the Methodist response to the events of the twentieth century and has held the question of definitive effect in abeyance.

4. Methodists have not entirely overcome their early tendency to regard an issue as settled after a particular crisis was met or a particular battle was won. In a very real sense "the" social problem has not been solved. There are persistent problems which belong to the very nature of social life. Men and institutions struggle with these problems and in a measure solve certain specific aspects of them. But the problems of family life, government, economic justice, class and status, communication, and the true ends of production and consumption are as perennial as the generations. In recent years the tenor and programs of the work of many agencies of the church show a deepening maturity on the nature and meaning of social Christianity.

5. There is a growing awareness of what Francis G. Peabody once called the correlation of the social problem. Culture is an interacting whole. Almost anything basic which any part of the church undertakes raises the major social questions. Hence there is a tendency for many boards and agencies to tackle a wide range of overlapping social problems. This has made for increased awareness in the church, but it creates some problems which will be noted in what follows.

6. This study has not been able to do justice to the tremendous activity of the Woman's Division of Christian Service, particularly its Department of Christian Social Relations. In the work of the organized women half of the laity of the church are represented. There is at present no comparison between the study program in Christian social ethics conducted among the women and that which takes place among the men. The women have tackled the whole range of problems on which the church has legislated. In some areas its work has been intensive and particularly competent. The work of the women moreover has been written into the legislative history of the United States through the enactment of many good federal, state, and local laws. Perhaps the most important fact is that the Woman's Division reflects the maxim that the real heroes of social action are those who persistently and courageously work for human

rights and welfare after the excitement of dramatic crises is over.

7. In evaluating Methodist responses it is at present impossible to estimate the millions of decisions in daily work that men and women have been led to make as a result of the ministry of the local church or because of some more generally sponsored program or activity. Of necessity, the documentation of this study tends to focus on the life and work of the more visible portions of the church. The real ministry of the laity in daily life largely eludes the organizational patterns of study.

Christianity is both socially immanent and culturally transcendent. In the language of sociology it is at times an independent variable and at times a dependent variable. Sometimes it initiates; sometimes it supports; sometimes it rejects; sometimes it adapts. Like all forces in the interactive whole of a culture it responds to major changes in any basic aspect of culture. Likewise a major movement in religion affects or arouses a response to other segments of culture. Once set in motion, socially sensitive Methodism became part of the causal nexus of American values and movements. Being nationally scattered geographically, American Methodism responded to and helped develop the common socially liberal spirit of the various regions in which it became institutionally significant.

Christianity is much more than a potentially powerful historical force. The sociological perspective tends to reduce religious experience to horizontal dimensions. Moreover, it tends to encourage a spectator's point of view. But for the Christian believer and the Christian church, faith, commitment, and social righteousness are culturally transcendent relationships. The Christian church stands under a divinely ultimate judgment and within a divinely ultimate mercy. Within the worship of the church as the people of God Christians experience a vision of God, they are transformed into a community of love, and they are sent out into the world as a community of service. Methodists have emphasized the centrality of experience and the power of the gospel as the power of God for personal and social salvation. This focus on salvation has made Methodism a denomination that is essentially committed, when fully aware of its basic traditions, to cultural transformation and individual conversion to Christ. It has stressed both the spiritual fellowship of believers and the visible organized institutional character of the church in action. Faith in objective ideal values creates a significant cohesion among the social values of community life which reflects these norms. Methodism's faith requires total social salvation.

Religion's influence can be both direct and indirect. This book has dealt with both sides of this influence. In Prohibition, for example, the institutional power of the church was quite direct. By constantly fostering and openly supporting the democratic ethos, the churches have indirectly influenced secular groups which do not call their social causes and values specifically Christian. Secular groups take up many reform causes in "Christian" America which secular groups do not espouse in certain non-Christian countries. The generalized goals of the American Dream have, as Myrdal and Gabriel have argued, a strong Christian foundation, even when they are not explicitly theological. When, then, a critic like Yinger affirms that the "church cannot change basic secular institutions" but "will sponsor modification of them only when important groups have already moved in that direction," it is important to add that the church releases through indirect action many attitudes, norms, and values which influence the direction that secular action groups take. The integrative function and power of Christianity down through the ages has in this way had a pervasive influence on Western culture, quite apart from its specific crusades, campaigns, and causes. Methodism in America is one major instance of the indirect and direct power of Christianity at work in society. In scope and connectional unity it is the most national of all Protestant denominations in the U. S.A.

B. Conditions of Effective Social Change

In what circumstances does religion exert its greatest force for social change? The theory which we have just been examining gives a threefold answer to this question: Religion will influence the course of social change in the greatest degree (1) when "the strategic decisions of religious individuals are made with the clearest recognition of the 'dilemma of the churches,' (2) when prophetic or charismatic leadership is most abundant, and (3) when religious institutions are most effectively autonomous from the secular institutions of power." [6] We may well measure Methodism by these criteria.

Methodism clearly shares the dilemma of leadership which all responsible churches experience. The dilemma consists of the fact that in order to save the world the church must to a degree identify itself with the world and is therefore to a degree compromised. The social order takes no apocalyptic leaps from injustice into the perfection of the kingdom of God. When the church identifies itself

[6] Yinger, *Ibid.*, p. 307.

388

simply with perfectionist ideals, it is utopian or extremely sectarian. Unless it participates in the world and risks compromise it cannot lead. But if it only participates in the world and loses its mandate and divine commission it cannot lead either. The church to be effective must live in the tension between the social order as it is and the kingdom of God. The dilemma consists of the fact that it participates in both. Being both a theological and a social institution, The Methodist Church, like all churches, needs to understand the dilemma of its historical existence. It must realize what it means to be prophetic within the world in order to manifest the power of Christ in society and to witness to the kingdom in all processes of the social order. To recognize the dilemma of leadership requires that Methodism accept prophetic tension as essential to its life. Its stress on institutional order and peace indicates that Methodism is always in danger of losing its prophetic social power.

The need for abundant charismatic leadership is a second prerequisite for exerting great force for social change. Men like Jesus, Paul, Augustine, Luther, Francis of Assisi, and Wesley had charismatic powers. This means that they exerted great personal power through the spiritual radiance which characterized them. Great social change by religious bodies requires leaders with tremendous faith, integrity, righteous passion, and Christian love. Methodists can build strong denominational structures and institutions by leaders who are skillful bureaucrats and forceful organization men. But Methodism exerts prophetic social power when it has an abundance of charismatic leaders. Such leaders are the fruit of profound religious experience, that is, of evangelical radiance united with great moral and intellectual stature. The best professional programs, produced by routine processes and communicated in the best designed human relations packages, lack the power of authentic expression. One of the institutional dilemmas of contemporary Methodism is what Max Weber called the routinizing of charisma: Wesley become routine is no better than Anglican formalism in the age of the evangelical revival.

The third condition of effecting social change in a major way is maintaining religious autonomy in the church and its institutions. In the language of the Oxford conference of 1937 this means "Let the Church be the Church!" This stress on the authentic character of the church's own nature and witness is compromised whenever the church sacrifices its own goals for worldly success or power or becomes a mere club or a mere mouthpiece for some racial group, special interest, or social class. One reason that Protestant churches are politically and socially as effective in the U.S.A. as they are is the separation of church and state. Not being dependent for their existence on the state and not deriving their economic support from government, they can speak freely and frankly to the political order. Far from making the churches politically ineffective, separation of church and state has made for effectiveness in church social action. Autonomy is a prerequisite of social power.

However, the churches are not so autonomously effective in all phases of their social life as they are in politics. The independence of church life is less evident with respect to economic class and racial composition than in relation to the state. Autonomy resides in part in voluntary association. But as voluntary societies the churches are dependent on carrying the financial supporters along with their own programs. Thus churches may sometimes be politically free, yet economically enslaved by the classes which constitute their membership. It belongs to the dilemma of churches to live in a tension between accommodation and prophetic freedom. This freedom must constantly be renewed spiritually.

Freedom to change the social order depends on a clear awareness of the mission and ministry of the church. There must be, in Reisman's phrase, "inner-directedness." Contrariwise, "other-directedness" in a church is fatal to its spiritual integrity. When the "church is the church" and understands what this means, it increases its power to initiate change. But when leadership and social goals simply reflect the order and disorder outside the churches, the church becomes worldly. The salt has then lost its savor. In many industrial and racial situations today the church has abdicated leadership because its voice is only an echo of the world's noisy contentions.

This study has shown several instances where the church had sold its voice to mill owners and mine operators, to racial prejudice and discriminatory policy, and to wartime patriotism. It has also cited a number of instances in which the church's commitment to the eternal verities has led it to conserve fundamental values and hence to bring change for the better. On the whole the domestic order has become more humane for millions of persons than it was at the turn of the century. Methodism has shared significantly in that social meliorism. Throughout its whole institutional structure it has resources and agencies to develop social responsibility in even more pervasive and significant ways. However, the social structure of Methodist institutional life has moral diseases that tend to injure its social witness.

C. Institutional Moral Diseases

The social witness of The Methodist Church is becoming increasingly typical of Protestant churches as a whole. A century ago one might have noted a marked economic and social gulf between the members of such denominations as the Baptists, Methodists, and Disciples and those like the Episcopalians, Congregationalists, and Presbyterians; but this gulf has almost completely disappeared. Urbanism, industrialism, education, and the domination of middle-class leadership and membership have produced a secular culture which homogenizes the denominations along with American civilization as a whole. This is not an unmixed blessing. The United States is not as pluralistic as it once was. All of the major Protestant bodies have moved toward a common church-type pattern of thought and behavior. The ecumenical consensus is impressive and yet there are signs of danger. Pronouncements on economic matters tend of late to be more informational and less expressive of moral judgment and urgency. The strong concurrence of social opinion among Protestant official bodies in the U.S.A. may show a common lack in sense of direction and moral power. Practical co-operation overlays a shallow wrestle with faith.

Renewal and reconstruction, if there is to be such in Methodism, must come from within the church. Transformation through obedience to Christ and the kingdom of God will not come from the institutional drift of the church. Therefore any stress on institutionalism can mean only a reinforcement of compromise, of accommodation, and complacency. Salvation requires depth in worship.

The Methodist Church is a closely knit organization and its leaders have extensive power. The goals of social justice often tend to be modified or transformed into the success targets of boards and agencies, of local churches, conferences, and jurisdictions. They become self-absorbed and too much preoccupied with their own affairs.

Methodism is afflicted by some serious moral diseases of institutional life that have grave consequences for the prophetic spirit. There is, first of all, the chronic tendency for agencies at all levels to focus on self-preservation as the basic law of institutional life. Institutional leaders and representatives tend to be protective in behalf of their organizations. The result is a failure to develop a realistic, inclusive, synoptic, and co-ordinated program to deal with such complex phenomena as urbanism and the decaying inner city. This failure is evident in the disorganized approach to population mobility, the working classes in the cities, the migration of Negroes, juvenile delinquency, and many other problems which require concerted integration of the total resources of the church locally and nationally.

A second tendency which defeats the prophetic function of the church is competition among its agencies for attention and support in the local church and conferences and the accompanying drive to expand the functions and raise the prestige of a particular board or agency. This institutional disease has become endemic. It involves the further danger that specialized agencies regard themselves as a sort of elite, leading and molding the rank-and-file.

Closely related to rivalry and "empire building" is the stress on quantitative criteria of achievement. Numbers and statistical tables are the bane of Methodist organizations. Pamphlets, tracts, magazines, and the like are measured by the hundred thousand and even by the million. Whether in the field of evangelism or international relations or any cause, the appeal to quantitative measurement often conceals lack of depth and spiritual engagement. Quantitative institutional success is an outward and visible sign, but it does not assure inward and spiritual conversion. The goal of efficiency is easily bought at the price of prophetic self-criticism and zeal.

These tendencies lead to another moral disease, and excessive sensitivity to "public relations" arguments in considering a cause, principle, or program. Instead of transforming society by the renewing of its mind and the conversion of its will, any large institution is tempted to take the view that the customer is always right. The message must be popularized in such a fashion as to "get across." In many local churches temperance is soft-pedaled because so many prominent laymen are drinkers; racial integration is sidestepped because the people are not "ready" for it; lower-class workers are overlooked because churchmen are more sensitive to "leading laymen" in the suburbs; and atomic bomb tests are not repudiated because of the dominance of nationalistic forms of patriotism. The emphasis on the show of pragmatic effectiveness often tempts the church to choose shallow expediency and to sacrifice more basic obligations.

Sensitivity to keeping one's public relations "good" encourages tendencies in the church to copy secular models of the allegedly successful "Madison Avenue" type. Mass communications in the church are especially in danger at this point. Some of the appeal in church periodicals is almost indistinguishable from that of the popular slick magazines. Do the appeals communicate the ultimate perspectives of the Christian ethic which are so desperately needed in the family and in the secular order? It is a tragic commonplace that the symbol of the cross does not rate high in audience perception of radio preaching. Perhaps one reason is that the cross is incongruent with good public relations.

All in all these institutional diseases constitute a grave crisis for Methodism. If quantitative evidence may be given as a protest against quantitative criteria of success, these may be found in examining the major areas of the unchurched. Within the ranks of The Methodist Church the following groups are insufficiently represented as measured by their percentage in the population as a whole: new persons coming into a community; the less well-educated; the divorcees; the victims of alcoholism; juvenile delinquents; nonwhites, especially Negroes, in both the South and the North; unskilled workers, domestics, and the lower classes of the cities. The church which began its life with a militant evangelism and a burning passion for the souls of the masses has drifted away from a fellowship in which people knew each other across class lines and helped each other in matters both spiritual and temporal.

Methodism has many opportunities for prophetic witness, social criticism, and positive example which it neglects. One may be illustrative. The denomination has rendered great service in its program of hospitals and homes. Yet in the larger field of medicine there are serious abuses and lacks. Why does Methodism not take a stronger leadership position in opposition to the materialism that is so pervasive in secular medicine? Fee-gouging by specialists in hospitals; the unwillingness of some young medical students to enter general medicine because there is more money in specialization (specialization has merits on other grounds) ; the growing impersonality of many hospital staffs toward patients; the failure to bring nurse, social worker, pastor, and doctor into an effective team; the unwillingness to expand medical education facilities to meet the expanding population needs, at least partly to protect the profession's favored status; the carelessness with which many observe the Hippocratic oath; and the need for Christian mental hospitals at moderate costs. These problems deserve special attention here because The Methodist Church has largely overlooked them in its social legislation across the years. Other concerns have had the center of the stage. With the increasing longevity of life, responsible health service becomes both a special professional, economic, and social issue.

On a number of other issues also Methodism lacks a well thought-out and clear-cut position. Such issues are the question of nuclear bomb tests, the recognition *de facto* of communist nations, and the seating of Communist China in the United Nations. Methodism's long-time missionary concern in China is unquestionably a strong psychological factor in current attitudes. Another is the fact that Madame Chiang Kai-Shek is "one of our own." Despite the controversial character of these questions, they demand realistic consideration and appraisal. Unless the church can provide leadership which goes deeper to the roots of the problems than personality identifications, the outcome of the issue will by default go to secular forces and the special interests they represent.

In the group of frontier issues for Methodists belongs the major question of the ethics of mass communication. There is little guidance that has come thus far on the complex questions of this field.[7] Nevertheless, Methodism is deeply involved in the use of mass media of communication. The current scandals of the multibillion-dollar private industry that has been allowed to go its own way almost freed of social regulation open up the prospect of many sordid chapters yet to be written. What has the church to say to an industry and an economic order in which the bright new educational potential of television, reaching into fifty million homes, was turned over casually to commercial exploitation with little social responsibility? Left to itself the big, unregulated industry debases and corrupts values, teaches adults and children alike to cheat. The advertiser has become the decadent agent of corruption in American morals and in the American's profile of desires.

The social witness of The Methodist Church owes most to the role played by courageous minorities—often working unofficially for a long period—on questions such as slavery, racial integration, temperance, peace, women's rights, and labor. There is no reason to believe that progress in ethical insight, the overcoming of deadening complacency within today's churches, and the transformation from conformity to renewal, can take place apart from the action of a reawakened and consecrated minority within the church. The saving hope of the church rests upon vigorous and prophetic groups who will speak to the church with ethical and spiritual power so that the church can in turn speak to the world with transforming effectiveness.

Perhaps the greatest spiritual danger of the church is that the rate of complacency and conformity to secular values seem to be increasing more rapidly than dedication to Christian social responsibility. The most calamitous development is the complacency which

[7] See Wilbur Schramm, *Responsibility in Mass Communication* (New York: Harper and Brothers, 1957).

identifies responsibility with conformity to dominant trends in society. With the establishment of special boards and agencies in fields like temperance, social and economic relations, and world peace, instrumentalities are provided to keep great issues effectively before the church; but the danger persists that social concern will be isolated among specialists and that they become an institutional world apart, expressing social conscience *for* the church rather than *in* the church and *through* the church in society.

D. The Vigor of Methodist Social Pronouncements

General Conference pronouncements and resolutions are potentially important instruments of social education and action. How vigorous and significant have they been? E. Eldridge Brewster studied about twelve hundred social pronouncements made by four Protestant denominations (Presbyterian, U.S.A.; Baptist, Northern Conventions; Congregational-Christian; Methodist Episcopal) during the quarter-century between 1924 and 1948.[8] He compared these pronouncements both quantitatively and qualitatively, recognizing that these two types of measurement could not be kept entirely separate. How persistent was the social concern on various issues and what was their prophetic quality? Another study, more limited in scope so far as denominational coverage was concerned, was undertaken by S. Raynor Smith, Jr. He surveyed a hundred years of Methodism's relation to its social environment and its social response in California.[9] The findings of these two studies give important though limited perspectives, in evaluating the church's social witness.

Resolutions vary greatly in prophetic quality. An official pronouncement in a given field may be occasional or infrequently made, passive in tone, very general in scope, summoning no one to concrete action, and directed to the church in quite a moderate manner. On the other hand, a pronouncement may be consistently repeated at each session of the General Conference, be aggressive in its demands, specific in the attitude or action prescribed, requesting action from both the church and the government, and calling for programs which would challenge the foundations of the *status quo*. On the one hand, attention may be directed at piecemeal reform;

[8] E. Eldridge Brewster, "Patterns of Social Concern in Four American Protestant Denominations" (unpublished doctoral dissertation, Boston University, 1952).

[9] S. Raynor Smith, "The Attitudes and Practices of the Methodist Church in California with Reference to certain Significant Social Crises, 1847 through 1949." (Unpublished doctoral dissertation, University of Southern California, 1955).

on the other hand, it may be directed toward basic, though general, social reconstruction. Methodist social legislation has ranged over the whole distance between the poles of prophetic quality.

In evaluating a pronouncement it is important to note the context in which it was developed and the process of its adoption. In some circumstances a mild resolution may have tremendously powerful implications for church and society. Likewise one must note whether a resolution reflected a real consensus of the General Conference, or was put across by some special maneuver, or perhaps reflected the concern of only a few who cared, or even its passage reflected the indifference of those who knew they could evade implementing it. These are difficult variables to study when as many as twelve hundred pronouncements are being analyzed, as in Brewster's study.

Brewster found that Methodism adopted a larger number of social pronouncements per session than the other denominations which he investigated. There was considerable variation in prophetic quality, other churches sometimes exceeding Methodism in this respect on concrete issues. During the years from 1924 to 1948 there was a growing trend in the range and content of issues. Since 1936 the militancy of the economic pronouncements has declined, while there has been a proportionate growth of interest in political issues. Statements on public morals have often been more concrete and aggressive in the action sought than those on world peace, for example.

On many questions Methodist resolutions have paralleled those found in the platforms of the major political parties. Since the Methodist Episcopal Church has convened its General Conference in the same years as the general elections, it is easy to compare church legislation and party platforms. On the whole, the church's pronouncements were closer to the planks of the Democratic Party platforms than to other parties. Much Methodist opinion in the years of the New Deal undergirded its legislation. On matters of world order, the church provided a more advanced position and gave leadership beyond that of the political parties. This has been noted in connection with the discussion of the Crusade for World Order. On world peace Methodism has been an initiator.

What were the areas in which the Methodist Episcopal Church and The Methodist Church expressed sustained interest in the period studied by Brewster? They were: the welfare of agriculture, ethical goals of economic life, wages and living standards, reconstruction of the economic order, unemployment, housing, social security, the rights of labor and management to organize, the profit motive, and equality of opportunity. In the early part of this period Methodists were interested in arbitration and co-operatives and in the forties showed more concern on the conditions effecting unemployment.

From 1936 to 1948 there is evidence of a slackening of concern in questions dealing with property. Correspondingly the agency of action was more the church and less the state. Thus, as the crisis of the great depression declined, the role of government was less emphasized in the economic sphere, though concern for right governmental policy in questions of world order increased. There was a heightened interest from 1936 to 1948 in public questions like gambling, salacious literature, drug addiction, juvenile delinquency, and crime.

In the content of the pronouncements there is evidence of a deepening spirit,[10] a mood of penitence, a desire to share in the experience of sacrifice, more of an expression of human insufficiency, and more explicit recognition of the need for a deep undergirding of spirit.

The Methodist Church, like the other major denominations, was profoundly influenced by the Oxford Conference findings of 1937. Increasingly it has sought to interpret the phrase: "Let the Church be the Church!" But this stress on the church has not always been accompanied by a renewed vigorous affirmation of its witness in the world for total Christian transformation of it. It is probably significant that on economic questions and industrial issues the utterances of the churches since Oxford lack a sharpness and a militant relevance that had developed before that date.

The pattern of response to social issues in the area of world peace follows the historical curve of international crises in the period from 1924 to 1948. In the period from 1924 to 1935 the stress was on the world court, the League of Nations, outlawry of war, disarmament, and church peace action. In the 'thirties there was a mounting affirmation of the rights of conscientious objectors. In the years from 1936 to 1948 one finds condemnation of war, civil liberties, and church peace action emphasized, and after 1940 a renewed interest in the rights of conscientious objectors, peace principles, international world organization, compulsory military training, and war relief. Methodists conformed to the General Protestant pattern in supporting the Kellogg Peace Pact in 1928, in urging disarmament conferences, and in taking an intensive inter-

---

[10] The explicitly theological dimensions of social education and action are dealt with in Volume III of this series.

est in the Munitions Inquiry of 1936. They were perturbed by the revelations of munitions war profits and they supported vigorously American neutrality in the impending struggle.

The international crisis in the late 'thirties, the outbreak of the war in Europe in 1939 and the entrance of the U.S.A. into the conflict in December 1941 were events which challenged the peace testimony of the church which it had developed in the previous two decades.

The majority of Methodists overwhelmingly supported the government in the war effort. Many were convinced that the pacifist tendencies of the previous decade had been mistaken and even lacked full Christian responsibility. They held that the pacifists wrongly appraised human nature and the character of modern tyranny as well as the real nature of coercion within collective security.

Though The Methodist Church adopted resolutions affirming loyalty to the government in the war effort and justified prayers of blessing upon the armed forces for victory, it continued aggressively to condemn war in general and to pass militant moral judgment upon it. It constantly upheld the right of conscience, though it was slow and belated in assuming its share of obligations for maintaining Civilian Public Service Camps.

The contrast between the conduct of the church in the two world wars is significant. The appeal to the world-wide character of Methodism was consistent in orienting the role of the church. Not only was there a greater appreciation for the conscientious objector, but there was a more sober interest in the war and peace aims of the Allied Powers. Pacifist leaders were not basically isolationist, as were many secular opponents to intervention. Methodists in all levels of organization were eager to formulate their own peace aims and to participate in interdenominational efforts having the same goals. They were active and effective in both the Delaware (1942) and Cleveland (1945) Conferences sponsored during the war by the Federal Council of Churches. We have already noted the scope and quality of the Crusade for World Order, which was one of the major contributions of the church. There is no set of questions on which The Methodist Church has expressed more consistent and persistent concern since 1924 than on questions of peace and world order. The persistent and aggressive leadership of the Commission on World Peace is one reason for this, as is the militant leadership given by the youth agencies. As a world church and America's largest Protestant denomination much is demanded of Methodism in support and improvement of the United Nations and in helping create the ethos of a responsible world community.

A church with a universal gospel must expect it to conflict with many policies held by so-called sovereign states. Here the ecumenical movement is invaluable to correct the conformist tendencies of denominations within the various countries. American Methodism needs the corrective criticisms of both world Methodism and the World Council of Churches.

An overview of Methodism's relation to the social environment leads one to agree with certain of S. Raynor Smith, Jr.'s, conclusions. There has been a threefold progression in emphasis from an individual evangelistic concern to a consistently more social outlook, from an individualistic approach to an institutional program, and from social welfare activity to more of a social reform concern. Altogether these trends make for an increased stress on purposeful living and provide opportunities for creative growth for individuals and groups.[11]

Smith's study reinforces in the case of California what Brewster felt in his broader investigation on the following points: (1) Only in limited areas does Methodism bear a witness that is not popular in secular groups. (2) Methodism may be more aware now than formerly of the limitations of the social reform approach to the predicament of society. (3) There is a growing realization of the need for theological and spiritual emphases as well as for social witness. (4) Methodism is experiencing a noticeable tension between the desire to be prophetic and the desire for social prestige.[12]

Beyond these general observations there are also some common specific conclusions in Smith and Brewster. The situation in economic problems is today quite ambiguous. A number of the grosser evils have been generally overcome and the condition of the working man has on the whole greatly improved. Consequently statements on the economic order are less outspoken than in the decade from 1930 to 1940. This is symbolized by the present lack of excitement over the term "profit motive" which in 1932 was a general term for all the dynamic factors of American capitalistic leadership. In 1932 the Methodist Episcopal Church declared the free enterprise system "un-Christian, unethical, and antisocial," but in 1949 an Annual Conference refused to condemn the profit system per se.[13] The basic motivation never was a simple incentive or drive

[11] Smith, *op. cit.*, p. 432.
[12] *Ibid.*, pp. 441-44.
[13] *Journal, Southern California-Arizona Conference,* 1949, p. 166; Smith, *ibid.*, p. 444.

at profit. Then, as now, a whole complex of interests, desires, needs and incentives was at work. Security, status, and power were no less present than the desires for gain and success in enterprise. The General Conference of 1952 revised the Social Creed at this point. Today the church is even more a part of the established social order than formerly, and it is prudent to speak softly and conformably to economic groups well represented in the church.

The vigor of social judgments on race relations has become notable. Following 1940 there has been more development in this field than was previously expected. Wartime manpower demands in industry served to heighten the awareness and general concern over racial tensions and injustice in American life. Totalitarianism and racism in the ideology of Hitler challenged both secular and church groups to declare themselves. Social scientists produced a massive attack on discrimination. Gunnar Myrdal's monumental book, *An American Dilemma,* appeared during World War II. President Roosevelt's Executive Order No. 8802 establishing a code of Fair Employment Practices in war industry, the later comprehensive and challenging report of the President's Committee on Civil Rights, *To Secure These Rights,* and the rising effectiveness of minority-group protests against racial injustice were among the factors which have shaped recent trends of thinking on racial matters. In the denominations studied by Brewster the rate of issuing statements on race problems doubled after 1940 as compared with the previous sixteen years. The official position of The Methodist Church as expressed in 1956 and 1960 is clear and comprehensive, though there is division, as we have seen, at the Annual Conference and local levels of attitude and action.

The crux of segregation and discrimination is in the local community. But the setting of the race problem is regional and national. Church leadership to be effective must take an aggressive and nationally inclusive approach to this as other social problems. While the Negro population of America is still largely Southern, it is shifting at an accelerated rate as Negroes leave the poor rural areas for opportunities in the industrial centers. They are leaving areas where segregation is the established pattern, to go North. From 1940 to 1957 Negroes increased in numbers in nine major Northern cities by over 2,075,000 while in the major cities of the South in the same period the number was 278,000. A striking symbol of the new situation is the fact that in Chicago alone the gain was nearly twice that of all ten Southern cities.[14] By 1960, 40 per cent of the Negroes have come to live in the North.

Most of the Negro population in the North (over 90 per cent) live in large cities. This urban phenomenon creates an inclusive challenge to churches across jurisdictional lines. The increased migration puts great pressure on housing, for example. Negroes have burst the ghetto patterns of the cities in the North, and often the whites have fled to the suburbs, taking their churches with them. In the South the ghetto pattern has increased in the past decade. Many middle-class Negroes are moving from the inner city and buying or renting better housing in previously all-white areas. The demand for housing is enormous and the need for fair patterns of housing is critical. In Detroit, for example, from 1945 to 1955 over ninety-eight thousand new homes were constructed "for whites only" while only two thousand were constructed for Negroes; yet the numerical increase in the Negro population was nearly double that of the white. The new housing developments in the South are following the patterns of the North. Implications for churchmanship are for a strategy that is interracial and oriented in a common city-wide program of evangelism, social justice, and social welfare.

The problem of inclusive church planning extends to education with a focus on economic realities. Many Negroes are still common laborers, but in the North they may, as in Detroit, number only 19 per cent in this class. Indeed, the average Northern Negro may make almost as much income as the average Southern white, although in the North the average Negro income is only one half to two thirds that of whites. Studies of Methodism in the city show that membership gains in the working classes do not keep up with the general population gains. Here class and race problems compound to the detriment of a church which has not come to terms with the basic issues involved and programs required. The predominately middle-class character of present-day Methodism must be modified if the church is to survive in urban America. Meanwhile these middle-class churches must open their doors to the educated middle-class Negro families who are emerging in ever larger numbers and constitute a massive pressure for freedom. Local churches should be barrierless community churches in fellowship and service.

In The Methodist Church unity was bought at the price of racial

[14] See mimeographed "Summary of Interracial Leadership Conferences" issued by the Board of Social and Economic Relations, in 1958. The "Symposium: Christianity and Race," which comprised the Spring number of *The Perkins School of Theology Journal* in 1958 is an excellent contribution to the current discussion in The Methodist Church.

justice and persistent crisis. The crisis of churchmanship for Methodism is particularly acute because the segregated character of the Central Jurisdiction provides low attraction for the Negro today. Along with this weakness we must acknowledge that the Methodist Church has relatively low leadership standing in the Negro community. There is comparatively high leadership status in the African Methodist Episcopal and the African Methodist Episcopal Zion churches. There is an imperative need for a drastically modified posture on the part of Methodism both as a whole and in terms of local performance. In addition, the crisis calls for a large number of well-educated and talented Negro leaders and for adequate economic security for them and their families. Permissive legislation for church integration across jurisdictional lines is a feeble step in the right direction. But permissive stratagems are bound to spell pathetic failure—unless a total program of social responsibility is instituted. The issue is integrate or stultify!

The crux of much social thought and action, we have said repeatedly in this volume, is the local church. There can be no disputing the witness value of inclusive Christian fellowship, service, and action in the congregation at worship and at work. Unless the vision of the Episcopal Addresses, the legislation of the General Conference, and the program of the general boards and agencies are implemented with integrity in local commissions and official boards, much is lost. A further word must, therefore, be said on the make-up and operation of local policy-forming groups. A Negro leader said to a white Annual Conference several decades ago; "You cannot *do* more *for* us than you are willing to *be with* us." What is a local church willing to be?

What has happened to the vigor of our temperance witness? During the years when Prohibition was the law of the land all of the churches maintained a high degree of interest and urged militant action on issues of temperance, prohibition, and law enforcement. The pronouncements which were aggressive in tone were about twice as frequent in the years from 1924 to 1935 as from 1936 to 1947. Since repeal, the emphasis of the churches has tended to stress action within the churches and to focus upon the personal aspects of temperance reform. In the most recent years a new and many-sided approach to alcoholism, alcohol, its victims, and its setting in society and culture, has developed. Evangelism, social welfare, pastoral counseling, rehabilitation, and social action are developing a new constellation of insights and a new strategy. The MESTA questionnaire responses show that 54 per cent of Methodists have a clear conviction on the question of alcohol and deserve better leadership in the local church than they are getting from pastors and leading laity alike. The dilemma of leadership is chronic on this as on other social problems. It confronts the church as a disciplined body within society and it confronts the pastor within the local church. It is the problem of the church within the world and the world within the church. It is the problem of creative, moral, and spiritual conflict and redemptive tension within the individual, within the church and within society. Complacency, conformity, and inner corruption destroy the responsiveness of people and pastor alike.

In dealing with alcohol and alcoholism the church confronts a very special dilemma. An alcoholic is, of course, not a typical drinker. Alcoholics need the saving help of a concerned church. Too many of them feel judged and rejected by total abstainers. Consequently, not enough of them are found within the redemptive fellowship of the body of Christ. It is very difficult to train people into a disciplined abstinence in the use of alcohol and also to train them to have genuine compassion and concern for the alcoholics. The problem is not made easier by the fact that many local congregations are so infiltrated by the cocktail mentality among influential members that pastoral leadership is often stymied by this "fifth column" of drinkers within the family of God. How can we develop personal discipline with compassion and understanding? How can we break through the cocktail mentality to a thoroughgoing educational program for prevention and rehabilitation? The answers lie in the motivations for church membership and the quality of Christian fellowship. In the true ministry of the laity the arguments for individual indulgence are transcended and set aside.

In summary, we may recognize that the evaluation of Methodist pronouncements on various social questions brings us back to the problems of the dilemma of leadership acknowledged earlier in this chapter. The source of so much criticism of the church is a failure to understand this dimension of the problem. It has been clearly grasped by Bishop Francis J. McConnell, a leader in a position to know whereof he spoke. "I have been so placed in fifty-five years of ministry," he writes,

as to hear much criticism of the church. Criticism of the church for its attitude on social questions has seemed to me to be the most serious. This is inevitable, and I sometimes think always will be. . . . Now here is a peril. On the one hand the perfectionist feels that an imperfection must be conquered immediately, and he often blocks progress altogether by demanding the impossible. Even if the perfectionist could just reach out and seize a perfection at once, he could never persuade all men to reach out at the same time, and the perfectionists themselves would vary in their length of reach and firmness of seizure. . . . The danger is even more real in another group—the group of good, ordinary people who are busy with the common tasks, even the drudgeries of life, who are entitled to immense credit for keeping the world going without having much time to look far ahead. So they, without intending to, accept the attitude of those more fortunately placed in the world and acquiesce in admitted imperfection, which is just about the deadliest of all evil social attitudes. This is the chief obstacle to better religious progress in social theory and practice.[15]

E. The Ministry of the Laity

The dilemmas of the church's social witness fundamentally include those of the laity because in the persons of the laity the involvement of the church in the world and with the world becomes actual. The laymen and laywomen are not isolated from the church's corporate reality which includes the clergy. There is little danger that the role of the clergy will be overlooked in the church, but there are many evidences that the ministry of the laity has been little understood in its deeper obligations. It is, therefore, the ministry of the laity with which this volume must conclude its survey of the twentieth century and its evaluation of the Methodist social witness. These comments point to Volume Four which deals with the emergent problems of social strategy.

Salvation must begin at the house of the Lord. We therefore stress the following points: (1) The church has often addressed society without taking upon itself the burden of changing its own form of life and its own policies of operation. These contradictions involve both questions of racial inclusiveness and of business practices in the local church. As a corollary they involve also the class composition of lay control. (2) The church has not yet succeeded in communicating to the laity its basic theological and ethical positions on social questions. Greater attention must in the future be given to the effective adult theological education of the laity. (3) The clergy and the laity both have an inadequate understanding of the meaning of the ministry of the laity. Until this is understood the church will not become truly potent. When it is understood and accepted, there will be a revolution in the educational and action life of the church.

In the first place, Methodism has not everywhere applied its pro-

---

[15] Francis J. McConnell, *op. cit.*, pp. 267-68.

nouncements to its own fellowship. Its verbal witness on race has often been clear, but there is a glaring contrast between its official position and its failure to welcome or assimilate non-Caucasians into predominantly Caucasian local churches. Caste and class are hallmarks of local congregational life in many communities. There is insufficient follow-up of the church's official legislation. Congregations are challenged, in the words of the Amsterdam Assembly of the World Council of Churches, "to make of the church in every place a voice for those who have no voice, and a home where every man will be at home." We must regain the fundamental idea of the people of God as a ministering fellowship. The local congregation cannot manifest the love which makes its members a church unless it does the work of love in the world. In *The Road to Brotherhood* [16] W. B. Selah states that the question whether colored people will become members of white churches will be determined not by any conference but by the attitudes of the people in the local churches. This is probably a fair descriptive statement, but what is erroneous is the further position developed by Selah that local segregation is an appropriate application of the ethics of Jesus. There is no place for segregation or discrimination in The Methodist Church, as the *Discipline* rightly holds, not because it is not Methodist, but because the policy of separation violates the unity of Christian fellowship. Here the true ministry of the church must be by laymen developing inclusive fellowship.

An equally neglected area of salvation in the house of the Lord has to do with its economic life in relation to employees, the raising of money, and the investment of funds.

The response of a local Methodist church to its social environment is bound to be significantly influenced by the composition of membership in its policy-forming boards. In the study by F. Ernest Johnson and J. Emory Ackerman, *The Church as Employer, Money Raiser, and Investor,* [17] the occupational distribution of local Methodist boards is compared with that of others. The following tables show the gross members involved in the studies, the percentage, and the percentage by size of community. It is evident that the class structure of the local church policy-forming boards shows little relationship with the normal distribution of managers, professional people, white-collar workers, and laborers in the population as a whole.

---

[16] Issued by the Board of Social and Economic Relations in 1958.

[17] New York: Harper and Brothers, 1959. These tables were prepared for the study but were not finally published by Harpers.

OCCUPATIONAL DISTRIBUTION OF LOCAL CHURCH POLICY-FORMING BOARDS BY DENOMINATION

DENOMI-NATION	MANAGERIAL PROFESSIONAL	WHITE COLLAR	LABORERS	YOUNG PEOPLE	TOTAL
Methodist	12,244	6,488	6,881	6	25,619
Congregational ...	1,081	497	433		2,011
Presbyterian	2,627	1,219	872		4,718
Lutheran	839	464	464		1,767
Baptist	863	608	693	1	2,165
Brethren	241	90	121		452
Disciples	1,826	1,170	1,517	4	4,517
Evangelical and Reformed	490	240	392		1,122
Episcopal	1,295	528	251		2,074
Federated	278	102	122		502
Total	21,784	11,406	11,746	11	44,947

The above table shows the gross numbers classified in the various denominations in designated categories. The next table shows the same distribution in terms of percentages. The third table shows that there is some difference in these categories when distributed by size of community.

PERCENTAGE OCCUPATIONAL DISTRIBUTION OF LOCAL CHURCH POLICY-FORMING BOARDS BY DENOMINATIONS

DENOMI-NATION	MANAGERIAL PROFESSIONAL	WHITE COLLAR	LABORERS	YOUNG PEOPLE	TOTAL
Methodist	47.79	25.33	26.86	0.02	100.0 %
Congregational ..	53.75	24.72	21.53	0	100.0
Presbyterian	55.68	25.84	18.48	0	100.0
Lutheran	47.48	26.26	26.26	0	100.0
Baptist	39.86	28.08	32.01	0.05	100.0
Brethren	53.32	19.91	26.77	0	100.0
Disciples	40.43	25.90	33.58	0.08	99.99
Evangelical and Reformed	43.67	21.39	34.94	0	100.0
Episcopal	62.44	25.46	12.10	0	100.0
Federated	55.38	20.32	24.30	0	100.0
Total	48.47	25.38	26.13	0.02	100.0 %

PERCENTAGE OCCUPATIONAL DISTRIBUTION OF LOCAL
CHURCH POLICY-FORMING BOARDS BY
SIZE OF COMMUNITY *

POPULATION	MANAGERIAL PROFESSIONAL	WHITE COLLAR	LABORERS	PEOPLE YOUNG	TOTAL
Under 500 ......61.60		11.57	26.83	0	100.00%
500-2,499 ....54.90		17.29	27.81	0	100.0
2,500-9,999 ......51.02		24.43	24.51	0.04	100.0
10,000-24,999 ....48.77		27.34	23.77	0.12	100.0
25,000-99,999 ....44.08		30.24	25.67	0	100.0
100,000 and over .39.12		33.55	27.33	0	100.0
Total 48.47		25.38	26.13	0.02	100.00%

* Note: The total number of board members was 44,947.

Johnson and Ackerman, in studying the church as employer, money raiser, and investor, state as a major finding "that to a disturbing extent the churches and their various agencies take less seriously their corporate responsibilities than their official pronouncements on social and economic problems give the community a right to expect." [18] There is a "marked contrast between the way in which a denominational or an interdenominational assembly addresses itself to economic issues and the indifferent attitude—the lack of sense of involvement—shown by individual churches with respect to such matters in the conduct of their business affairs." [19] Through the years since 1939 The Methodist Church has not only recognized the right of both employers and employees to organize for collective bargaining but also has felt, along with the National Council of Churches, that it is generally desirable to do so. Yet its mind seems to have been on secular employment, not on its own corporate involvement.

Involvement would raise questions along the whole range of employment, investment, and money-raising which the churches have not seriously undertaken as an ethical obligation, not to speak of their being a prophetic witness in society.

Johnson and Ackerman conclude:

The picture we have presented of the economic status of ministers and lay employees, particularly in the smaller churches, is a forceful argument for an ample Protestant strategy directed toward the resources of the Church as a whole in accord with the spiritual needs of the country as a

[18] *Ibid.*, p. 122.
[19] *Ibid.*, p. 122.

whole. This would mean that the areas of greatest need and greatest potential would be regarded, not as mission stations to be "helped," but as essential centers of the Christian movement, having a claim on the resources of the Church at large that transcends—though it does not exclude—considerations which emphasize self-support and local autonomy.[20]

Churches in the "inner city" now stranded and struggling, the marginal churches in the rural areas, and the new ones erected in the highly mobile suburb are parts of an integral enterprise requiring high standards of efficiency and competent leadership in the context of broad community education and action.

Those who work for the church as sextons have wages that are shamefully small. Inadequate also are the wages of office-workers, religious educators, and parish workers, many of whom are women. "Substandard wages and salaries are a social evil." In the field of pensions, there have been notable advances for clergymen in recent years, but these advances would have to be considered distressingly small except for the advent of federal Social Security. The situation with respect to provision for lay employees is relatively much poorer than for the clergy.

Johnson and Ackerman challenge particularly the way major personnel problems are confronted and handled in the various agencies where relatively large staffs, composed of lay workers, are employed, such as publishing houses, denominational headquarters, and board offices. "It is here that the temptation is strongest to assume that since the cause is a holy one the grievances and frustrations that characterize secular mass employment need not be worried about. The personnel people—and many church agencies now have some good ones—know better, for they are trained to recognize the symptoms." [21] Consequently these authors ask whether the organization of the churches' employees on the basis of employee interest is not being mistakenly neglected.

The issue of labor unionism in church agencies is a complicated one, but certain things ought, it seems, to go without argument: (1) The form of organization should be a matter of free choice. (2) If union affiliation is not acceptable to the employees, alternative structures and procedures should be devised on the employees' own initiative, or on joint initiative, that will ensure to the employees the legitimate values that other workers find in union membership.[22]

[20] Ibid., p. 126.
[21] Ibid., p. 127.
[22] Ibid., pp. 127-28.

In all such questions, as well as in money-raising and investment policies, the relation of means and ends is the crucial one. The church is constantly in danger "of assuming that whatever makes for its institutional growth and security is for the glory of God." Not only for the church generally, but Methodism's distinctive reason for existence is threatened when the means it employs cease to be distinctive, i.e., when they become indistinguishable from or inferior to the means employed typically by worldly enterprises. Means and ends must be considered together and the ends must be coherent with the means, as well as the latter be coherent with the former. It is "a responsibility of the Church to make its financial policy an instrument of its institutional program." [23] There must be a "definite, progressive effort to develop and maintain institutional policy in which the sources of the Church's income shall be wholly consistent with the objectives of its program of education and action." [24]

The second question on the role and leadership of the laity in the local church has to do with the communication of the religious beliefs to social attitudes. The MESTA research team was eager to ascertain the social guidance from their religious beliefs which Methodists felt that they received, their reference points for guidance and leadership in areas of social responsibility, and the manner of their participation in social action. In the general fields of temperance, race, technical aid abroad, marriage and divorce, and participation in war, the questionnaire inquired whether Methodists as Christians get (a) direct guidance for their conduct from their religious beliefs, or (b) no direct guidance, but find moral principles to guide their conduct and social policy; or (c) indirect guidance for conduct and social policy; or (d) no guidance, so that decisions are made on the basis of taste and practicality; or (e) made no response. The research team naturally expected a wide range of responses on all these matters. In any case, the subjectivity of the respondents would vary greatly in interpreting questions of this type. No precise validity can therefore be accorded the percentages below.

It is significant that "direct guidance" has the dominant position in the following tables only on matters of temperance and marriage. It may be that this model category shows that Methodism has not been as effective in communicating its religious and moral teachings on segregation, peace, and technical aid to underdeveloped

---

[23] *Ibid.*, p. 131.
[24] *Loc. cit.*

countries as in the above areas of conduct and social attitudes. Indoctrination in past generations has quite clearly been more specific on temperance and family life than on these other questions. In this portion of the questionnaire are to be found the highest proportion of "No Response" reactions. The NR response ranged from 10.4 per cent on temperance up to 15.6 per cent on war.

A consistent one-third feel that religious teachings provide moral principles but no direct guidance—on all issues tested! It is significant that in no case did a majority agree that religious beliefs provide direct guidance for conduct. We may note, again, that Methodists would as Protestants respond with a wide range of difference. Later studies may show whether any correlations can be found between the answers given to specific religious beliefs and the answers on specific items of social attitude. Such correlations might vary widely from what a person subjectively believed his dependence on religious beliefs and moral principles to be.

Guidance from Religious Beliefs

I, AS A CHRISTIAN, GET GUIDANCE FROM MY RELIGIOUS BELIEFS AS FOLLOWS:

	Direct guidance for my own conduct	No direct guidance, but find moral principles to guide my conduct and social policy	Indirect guidance for my conduct and social policy	No guidance but make decisions on basis of taste and practicality.	No Response
21. Whether to drink intoxicants ..	42.9	36.3	6.3	4.9	9.6
22. What to do about segregation .	33.5	38.7	8.1	6.9	12.8
23. Whether to give economic and technical aid to other countries	24.4	36.7	12.2	12.3	14.4
24. What the regulation of marriage and divorce should be	42.2	33.7	7.0	4.1	13.0
25. Whether to participate in war	28.4	37.4	10.2	9.0	15.0

Where do Methodists look for guidance and leadership in areas of social responsibility? To the minister? The local church commission? General church boards and publications? General Conference pronouncements? The National Council of Churches? National publications other than Methodist, such as *Christian Century, Christian Herald?* This group of questions brought forth an amazing proportion of "No Response" omissions. As many as 28.6 per cent indicated no response on these modes of guidance and social expression. The table of replies presented below exposes the weakness of local church commissions, the general agencies of the church, and the General Conference, to communicate with the rank-and-file membership of churches, and thus presents a major challenge in social education. The minister's voice is strong in matters of social guidance. Even he is sought out or heard little, or not at all, or elicits no response much of the time. These statements show his irrelevance in social matters up to 29.7 per cent of the respondents. Although jurisdictional differences were not very important in the over-all pattern on the questions numbered 53 to 58, it is worth noting that nine (9) per cent of all Methodists lean heavily on the National Council of Churches, while 22.7 per cent of the respondents from the Central Jurisdiction do so. Methodists would not expect the laity to follow a local minister blindly. The answers clearly show that the church is not priest-ridden on social questions. Some may regard the indications of guidance as encouragingly high.

Guidance and Leadership in Social Responsibility

DO YOU LOOK FOR GUIDANCE AND LEADERSHIP IN AREAS OF SOCIAL RESPONSIBILITY FROM:

	MUCH	SOME	LITTLE	NONE	NR
53. Your Minister?	33.5	36.8	8.4	6.0	15.3
54. Your local church commission?	10.8	29.7	16.3	18.1	25.1
55. General church boards and publications?	14.6	32.5	15.7	13.9	23.3
56. General Conference pronouncements?	10.1	22.9	19.3	20.1	27.6
57. National Council of Churches?	9.0	20.8	18.7	22.9	28.6
58. National publications other than Methodist, such as *Christian Century, Christian Herald?*	8.1	22.2	14.7	27.0	28.0

Methodists express their social responsibility, according to their own testimony, by voting in national, state, and local elections. However, they do not in large numbers participate in non-church organizations concerned with social problems. Nor do they write many letters expressing their concern. A larger proportion participate in social action as expressed above in order to seek social change than to conserve present traditions. The distribution of responses is shown in the following table:

Social Action
HOW DO YOU EXPRESS YOUR SOCIAL RESPONSIBILITY?

	REGULARLY	FAIRLY OFTEN	SELDOM	NEVER	NR
45. By voting in national elections	83.5	4.1	1.2	2.9	8.3
46. By voting in state elections?	79.6	6.9	1.3	3.3	8.9
47. By voting in local elections?	75.5	10.2	2.1	3.2	9.0

By participation in non-church organizations concerned with social problems.

	REGULARLY	FAIRLY OFTEN	SELDOM	NEVER	NR
48. On the national level	16.7	17.2	21.8	18.0	26.3
49. On the local community level	33.0	27.3	16.1	8.2	15.4

In writing letters expressing your concern:

	REGULARLY	FAIRLY OFTEN	SELDOM	NEVER	NR
50. To members of Congress	3.5	11.3	29.4	41.0	14.8
51. To the editors of newspapers	2.1	5.6	23.3	50.1	18.9

We must conclude from the questionnaire that channels for social action are not clearly Methodist-sanctioned or delineated for the vast majority of Methodists. The implementation of Christian concern and belief in specific areas is often a matter of indecision for the majority of Methodists, even when the denomination as a whole has stated its position or attitude. Methodists do not depend upon the expected channels of information as one might anticipate they would. However, some may feel that the effectiveness of communication is quite commendable. Neither do Methodists consciously implement their beliefs through local or general church agencies. If social action is taken by Methodists, it is mostly in the form of voting. This form of action may be taken in response to pressures outside the church, since voting regularly is a commonly agreed upon mode of good citizenship.

There is a need to develop more effective communication on matters of social education and action between the General Conference, the various boards and agencies of the church, and the local church. Perhaps one way of closing the gap is by the mandatory legislation whereby each local church has a Commission on Christian Social Concerns. But there is no salvation through mandatory commissions as such. This gap must be closed not primarily through an institutional device, but through the "image" or conception which the general church and the local church have of their being or existence. Social education and action must be made an organic part of the Christian definition of salvation.

The third aspect of social salvation in church and community is the reconception of the doctrine of the ministry of the laity. Methodism's social witness has been largely an occupation of the leadership. This leadership is often essentially clerical and in the cases of boards and agencies tends to become a bureaucratic elite. S. Raynor Smith, Jr., concluded in his study that the "social witness of the church was frequently beyond the comprehension or sympathy of the average layman. Out of loyalty to their church, these laymen usually gave assent to Methodism's social pronouncements, but they had little inclination to practice progressive, and sometimes radical, procedures." [25] Such a situation is not likely to change unless the hope of the leaders becomes the purpose of the membership and is translated into practical relevance by the common action of the whole fellowship. This change and translation have basic implications for the redefinition of the role of the laity and for adult education and action procedures in the local church, the Annual Conference, and the community in which the Christian fellowship is at work.

The renewed ministry of the laity was anticipated at the Amsterdam Assembly and became a major emphasis at the Evanston As-

[25] Smith, *op. cit.*, p. 461.

sembly of the World Council of Churches in 1954. Amsterdam said: "We have to learn afresh together what is the duty of the Christian man or woman in industry, in agriculture, in politics, in the professions, and in the home." Evanston emphasized the idea that the people of God are sent into the world to save the world. Spiritual productivity is the layman's vocation and is directed outward in establishing the responsible society. The layman is not primarily a consuming unit of spiritual goods distributed by the clergyman, but is a productive agent of Christian values, and as such he stands in a decisive position in society today.

Layman are front-line ministers at work under God in the social order where daily work takes them. This reconception must not be confused with the view which interprets the new emphasis on the laity as an attempt to secure larger functions or higher status for them in the policy or fellowship of local churches. Neither is it an oblique scheme of recruiting assistants for the clergy, though they are in need of them. Unfortunately many have this image. The MESTA study shows that 59.9 per cent conceive of laymen as non-ordained Christians whose function is to help the clergy to do the work of the church. The more adequate view is that represented by 24.8 per cent of the respondents, who defined laymen as members of the people of God called to a total ministry of witness and service in the world. What is now the minority view must become the majority attitude with appropriate education and discipline to make it effective.

The laity are then not mere fragments of the church scattered about the world who come together for worship, instruction, and specified acts of fellowship on Sundays. On the contrary, as Evanston said, they represent the church wherever they are. It is they who "bridge the gulf between the church and the world, and it is they who manifest in word and action the lordship of Christ over that world which claims so much of their time and energy and labor." The frontiers of God's kingdom are in all those situations where responsible decision-making takes place. When a person becomes a layman in the church he becomes a minister. He ought not to join the church thinking that he is to be ministered unto in exchange for the support he renders the church budget; but he is to minister, not like a clergyman, but like a follower of Jesus Christ amidst the ambiguities of the secular world. The clergy are there to encourage, motivate, council, guide, exhort, admonish, and instruct the laity, though as fellow Christians and not as a separated and self-contained guild. Through worship and the sacraments the clergy minister to fellow ministers who are called to convert the world to the increase of the love of God and man.

A serious charge is made against the clergy that they show too little understanding of the world in which the laity make their decisions. If the clergy are to minister effectively to the laity in their ministry, they must enter deeply into the complexities and dilemmas of modern society. They must grasp the ambiguous character of many social situations and the compromises which power struggles generally entail. To keep the Christian ethic creatively at work as a leaven in the world requires a constant reappraisal of institutions, policies, and programs from the highest perspective, in humble faith, and in relation to the relativities of business and politics.

When the ministry of the laity becomes truly effective, the maintenance function of lay organizations now so prominent becomes secondary and instrumental, and the mission function of church membership becomes primary. Then the social legislation of the General Conference and its subsidiary bodies becomes common platforms for action and compacts of service and witness by clergy and laity together. In this reconception there is a new interpenetration of the ideals and standards of the various professions and occupations, inspired and corrected by the Christian ethic. Social education and action become not so much a crusade of a minority within the church but of action in the world where the church has truly appraised the dilemma of its leadership, has developed a large body of radiant and informed Christian personalities, and has through inner renewal in the worship and sacramental fellowship of the people of God regained a relevant spiritual autonomy within society.

Appendix

Social Characteristics of Methodism, 1959

Sources of Information. TWO TYPES OF SOURCES HAVE been utilized in an analysis of the social characteristics of Methodism. First, there has been a utilization of Methodist resource materials, both from official publications of the church and also from supplementary research studies. Official publications include: *The Methodist Fact Book, 1957,* the most recent issue at the time the study was made; and *The General Minutes of the Methodist Church, 1958.* An additional resource book used was *The Emerging Patterns in Town and Country Methodism, 1959.* Especially helpful have been the MESTA Inquiry on "The Beliefs of Methodists" [1] and the tabulated summaries from the project studies of *Church Surveys* of Boston University School of Theology. The MESTA Inquiry has been based on a representative sample of 5,020 Methodists. The *Church Surveys* studies have provided cumulative data and tabulated summaries from individual survey cards filled out for more than 600,000 Methodists within the past three years.

The second type of reference, the basis for comparison, has been summary data concerning the total U. S. population. The official reference for this has been *The Statistical Abstract, 1958.* Considerable use has been made of the monthly Current Population reports—Series P-20, No. 77, U. S. Bureau of the Census, Department of Commerce.

Sociological Definition of a Methodist. The point of reference will be the Methodist "parishioner" rather than "member" in order to have comparable data. Full *members*[2] of The Methodist Church would include only persons approximately twelve years of age and

---

[1] See Appendix B in S. Paul Schilling, *Methodism and Society in Theological Perspective.*

[2] All persons responding to the MESTA Inquiry were members.

over, for the most part. Most U. S. Census data include reference to persons of all ages. A study based on Methodist parishioners rather than members obviates the difficulty.

A parishioner is defined as any person who is a part of the household of a member family. A member family is a family which has at least one adult member of the church as a part of its household. Parishioners then would include not only all full members of the church in such a family, but also all unbaptized children, all children who have been baptized and who are preparatory members of The Methodist Church if they have been baptized as Methodists, and also any other person in a member household. The members of non-Methodist churches in such a household would be offset statistically by Methodist constituents who have not yet joined the church, and who are part of the non-member households.

Median age of Methodists. The median age of Methodists is approximately 34.5 years, based on cumulative survey reports, with one-half the parishioners above this age and one-half below. A median age of 34.5 years is 15 per cent higher than the total U. S. population which had a median age of 30.2 years in 1950. The median age varies from state to state, with a low of 24 years for New Mexico and a high of 33.7 years for New York State. The median rural farm population age is 26.3 years. The median age has been increasing steadily in the nation from 22.9 years in 1900 to a high of 30.3 years as reported in Current Population Survey reports, 1956, U. S. Bureau of the Census.

Sex Ratio. Eleven out of twenty Methodists are females. There are more females than males in the U. S. population at the present time, according to U. S. Census estimates, but the proportion of females is higher in The Methodist Church than in the total population. There are only 90 males per 100 females in The Methodist Church, as compared to 99.2 males per 100 females in the U. S. population as reported in the 1950 census. The ratio of males per 100 females has been gradually lowering since 1910, at which time there were 106 males per 100 females in the U. S. population. The decline in ratio of males has been attributed to various causes including wars, the employment of men in hazardous industries, and the general improvement in health and longevity for women.

Marital Status. Eight out of ten Methodists 25 years of age and over are married, according to an adjusted report of the MESTA Inquiry, approximately the same ratio as to be found in the total U. S. population. A total of 80.1 per cent of the Methodists 25 years of age and over are married as compared to 78.3 per cent in the same age group for the total population.

418

One in ten Methodists is single, approximately the same ratio as found in the total U. S. population among persons 25 years of age and over. Only one Methodist in one hundred is divorced as compared to more than two per one hundred reported in the total population. However, in view of the opinion of census takers that a large number of divorced persons reported themselves to be "single," there is a possibility that the divorce rate for Methodists is comparatively lower than the given figures would indicate. A greater degree of honesty would be expected for parishioners than for persons not affiliated with a church. Nine Methodists out of one hundred are widows or widowers among those 25 years of age and over.

Family Size. The average size of the Methodist family is 3.6 persons, identical with the U. S. average reported in the 1950 Census. The size of the Methodist family was obtained from the MESTA Inquiry, and compares favorably with the cumulative project studies of *Church Surveys, Boston University.*

The average size of the Methodist household, however, is only 3.1 as obtained from the cumulative reports of *Church Surveys* to date, compared to the average household size of 3.34 as reported in the Bureau of the Census estimate of March 1957. In The Methodist Church a large number of widows, widowers, and single persons have their own household. Many of these are elderly persons, as reflected in the higher median age for Methodists than for non-Methodists.

There is some evidence that Methodists may have a higher longevity record than the total U. S. population, due to a correlation of higher median age with an average family size. The percentage of Methodists 45 years of age and over is 40 per cent higher than the percentage of the total U. S. population in the age grouping, according to cumulative reports from the Church *Surveys* studies.

Education. The average Methodist replying has graduated from high school and has completed one semester of work in college. The median of educational attainment for Methodists is 12.4 years of schooling beyond kindergarten, with one-half of the Methodists having less education, and one-half more. This is somewhat higher than the median educational attainment of 10.8 years for the total population 25 years of age and over, from various reports of the U. S. Bureau of the Census studies as of March 1957. The educational attainment of Methodists has been obtained from the MESTA Inquiry.

The chance of a son or daughter graduating from college is at least three times as high if he or she comes from a Methodist family.

More than one-third of the Methodists 25 years of age and over have graduated from college. As a denomination, Methodists have the highest percentage of students in the State Colleges and Universities of the U. S. in addition to having the largest number of church-related colleges and universities of all the Protestant groups.

Family Income. Methodists have a median family income of $5,329 per year, according to the MESTA studies, with one-half of the families receiving more income and one-half of the families receiving less. This is higher than the median family income of $4,687 for the U. S. total population of males aged 35-54 as reported in Current Population Reports, March 1957, U. S. Bureau of the Census.

This is especially significant in view of the large rural farm population in The Methodist Church. In a bulletin published June 1958, the Census Bureau reported the median money income of urban and rural nonfarm families in the United States to be $5,232 for the preceding year, as compared with the median money income of rural farm families at $2,490 for the preceding year.

Size of Community. Three out of four Methodist congregations are located in communities of less than 2,500 population, according to studies published in *The Emerging Patterns in Town and County Methodism, 1959.* Six out of ten Methodists live in the "town and country," or rural areas of the United States, according to the definition of such areas as places of less than 10,000 population, as defined in the *1956 Discipline of The Methodist Church.* Approximately 33.3 per cent more Methodists live in rural areas than the proportion of the general U. S. population.

More Methodists were reared in small communities than live in them at the present time, according to the MESTA Inquiry. A total of 51.2 per cent more Methodists were reared in communities of less than 2,500 than live in them at the present time. And conversely there are more Methodists living in large cities than were reared in them. There are 66.7 per cent more Methodists living in cities of 10,000 to 99,999 than were reared in them. There are 23.8 per cent more Methodists living in cities of 100,000 and over than were reared in them.

Size of Church. One out of every five Methodists is affiliated with a church of less than 250 members. Nearly one-half of the Methodists are in churches of less than 500 members.

Twice as many Methodists were reared in small churches as are affiliated with the smaller churches at the present time. According to the MESTA Inquiry slightly over one-half of the Methodists were reared in churches of less than 250 members. And conversely the percentage of Methodists who are now affiliated with larger churches is much higher than the percentage reared in them. A total of 76 per cent more Methodists are now in churches of 1,000 or more members than were reared in them.

Denominational Background. Two out of three Methodists were reared in The Methodist Church. Of those reared in other churches, two-thirds came from one or another of these backgrounds: Presbyterian, Congregational, Baptist, Lutheran, or Episcopal. Less than two per cent of all Methodists were reared in a Roman Catholic background. Less than one out of ten Methodists was reared in any background other than those which have been named.

Length of Membership. One out of four Methodists has been affiliated with the church twelve years or less. The percentage of newcomers in The Methodist Church is low, however. A total of 14.5 per cent have been members of the church six years or less. From length of residence studies it has been estimated that a church needs to have 17.5 per cent of its membership composed of newcomers who have lived in the community six years or less, or who have been members of the church six years or less. The median goal of 17.5 per cent has been set for a normal church to keep pace with population growth. The Methodist Church is not keeping pace with total U. S. population growth.

Evangelistic Ratio. During the year 1958 one new member for every twenty-six members was added to the church on profession of faith. The evangelistic ratio is the number of full members of the church required to win one person to Christ and to membership in the church on profession of faith. The Board of Evangelism has estimated that one person should be received on profession of faith for every fourteen members. As a result of hardly more than 50 per cent efficiency in attaining the evangelistic ratio goal, The Methodist Church is growing slightly over half as fast as the total U. S. population. From 1950 to 1958 The Methodist Church has increased in membership from a total of 8,935,647 members in 1950 to a total of 9,691,916 members in 1958, a net gain of 756,269, or 8.5 per cent. From 1950 to 1958 the U. S. population has increased from a total of 150,697,361 persons in 1950 to an estimated total of 174,060,000 on July 1, 1958, according to Robert W. Burgess, Director, Bureau of the Census, Department of Commerce. This represents a gain of 23,362,639, or 15.5 per cent.

Correlation studies on the family size of Methodists and the net gain in membership would indicate that the church is not retaining its own constituency, and is not retaining its share of the total population. Most of the net losses are due to Methodists on the move, whose church membership has not moved to the new places of residence. One out of five Americans aged one year and over changes his place of residence each year, according to the results of a sample survey conducted by the Bureau of the Census from April 1956 to April 1957. The average American would be moving once every five years.

Church School. For every hundred members of The Methodist Church, there are seventy-four members of a Methodist Church School. Approximately one out of five members of a Methodist Church School is not a parishioner of the church, and is not affiliated with the church in any other way than through a relationship to the church school. They are not in church member families or households.

Methodist Church Schools are becoming expanding frontiers of evangelistic opportunity. Some are located in areas not now served by a Methodist Church. Some church schools, formerly closed, have been reopened. From 1956 to 1958 Methodist Church Schools have increased from 37,923 to 38,350, a net gain of 427. During the same period of time Methodist Churches, or "preaching places," have decreased from 39,845 to 39,317, a net loss of 528.

Race. Less than one out of twenty members of The Methodist Church is nonwhite, but more than one out of ten persons in the total U. S. population is nonwhite. The Bureau of the Census reported a total of 11.5 per cent of the U. S. population as nonwhite in 1950. One out of twenty-five Methodists (3.9 per cent of the total) is a member of the Central Jurisdiction which consists almost entirely of Negroes. An estimated 7 per cent of the members of the other Jurisdictions are American Indian, Japanese, Chinese, or Negro, mostly the latter.

Nearly one fourth of the members of all Methodist bodies are Negroes, however, and are members of the following four more or less *segregated* groups: African Methodist Episcopal Church, African Methodist Episcopal Zion Church, the Colored Methodist Episcopal Church, and the Central Jurisdiction of The Methodist Church.

More than four out of ten Negroes will be living outside the South in 1960, according to estimate reported in *The Methodist Fact Book, 1957.* The evangelistic ratio of the Central Jurisdiction is low at the present time. There has been an assimilation of six congregations over scattered areas from the Conferences of the Central Jurisdiction to the Conferences in various other Jurisdictions of The Methodist Church. In 1958 one person was received on profession of faith for every thirty-one members of the Central Jurisdiction. For the most part, Negroes are not being reached efficiently by the Central Jurisdiction.

Occupation. The occupational profile of Methodists shows a preponderance of professional men and women and managers, as compared to the total U. S. population, 1958 estimate from the Bureau of the Census. Conversely, the proportion of operatives, service workers, and laborers is very low compared to the total population.

Generally speaking, Methodists have a much higher percentage of persons in the professional, managerial, and so-called "white collar" occupations in urban life. Methodists have about the same percentage in the so-called "blue collar" occupations, meaning primarily the craftsmen.

The percentage of professional men and women in The Methodist Church is over three times as high as the percentage of professional men and women in the total population. This is correlated with the fact that the percentage of college graduates in The Methodist Church is three times as high as the percentage of college graduates in the total population.

The percentage of farm operators and various types of managers is approximately 6 per cent higher than the percentage of managers and farm operators in the total population.

The percentage of sales workers in The Methodist Church is less than one per cent higher than the percentage of sales workers in the total population.

The percentage of clerical workers in The Methodist Church is approximately 2 per cent higher than the percentage of sales workers in the total U. S. population.

The percentage of craftsmen in The Methodist Church is approximately 3 per cent lower than the percentage of craftsmen in the total population.

The percentage of operatives in The Methodist Church is 12.6 per cent lower than the percentage of operatives in the total U. S. population.

The percentage of service workers and laborers is 14.3 per cent lower than the percentage of service workers and laborers in the total U. S. population.

The percentage of private household workers in The Methodist Church is 2.9 per cent lower than the percentage of private household workers and domestic service employees in the total U. S. population.

Summary. In general it can be said that Methodists have characteristics similar to the total population in respect to family size. The median age is slightly higher than for the total population. The sex ratio of males per 100 females is slightly lower for Methodists than for the total population.

Characteristics which pertain to attainment find the Methodists far ahead. Methodism, then, reflects socially the configuration of the total population of the United States. In family stability, educational attainment, longevity, and occupational status, Methodism is exceptional. Its families stay together, its members are well educated and long-lived. In all other ways studied, the Methodists of the various census regions are truly representative of the general populace.

The Methodist Church is of service to persons in all occupational groupings, though not wholly adequate in serving the manually employed. There is sparse evidence that other denominations have been more effective here, but there is little comfort in this.

Perhaps the most dramatic social trend noted here is the migration of Methodists from rural to urban areas. The sample clearly evidenced the earlier rural training of members who are now urban residents. The large number of urban Methodists in the next generation will constitute a major challenge.[3]

[3] This survey reveals the paucity of presently available information about the social characteristics of Methodists. Thus, for example, there are no data in Conference Journals which are comparable with Federal Census data classifications. Similarly, the Conference Minutes fail to indicate the physical location of Methodist properties, churches, and so forth. If such geographical (township, county, etc.) identification could be obtained, it would be possible to establish far more profitable correlations between census data and Methodist data.

Bibliography

Bates, Ernest Sutherland. *American Faith.* New York: W. W. Norton and Company, Inc., 1957.

Beach, Waldo and Niebuhr, H. Richard. *Christian Ethics: Sources of the Living Tradition.* New York: The Ronald Press Company, 1955.

Becker, Carl L. *Freedom and Responsibility in the American Way of Life.* New York: Vintage Books, Inc., 1945.

Bosley, Harold A. *What Did the World Council Say to You?* Nashville: Abingdon Press, 1955.

Brewster, E. Eldridge. "Patterns of Social Concern in Four American Protestant Denominations." Unpublished doctoral dissertation, Boston University, 1952.

Brown, Charles R. *The Gospel for Main Street.* New York and London: Harper and Brothers, 1930.

Brownell, Baker. *The Human Community.* New York: Harper and Brothers, 1950.

Cantril, Hadley (ed.). *Public Opinion, 1935-1946.* New Jersey: Princeton University Press, 1951.

Carter, Paul A. *The Decline and Revival of the Social Gospel.* Ithaca: Cornell University Press, 1954.

Chalmers, Allan Knight. *They Shall Be Free.* New York: Doubleday and Company, 1951.

Corey, Lewis. *The Decline of American Capitalism.* New York: Covici-Friede, 1934.

Cross, Robert D. *The Emergence of Liberal Catholicism in America.* Cambridge: Harvard University Press, 1958.

Curti, Merle. *The Growth of American Thought.* New York: Harper and Brothers, 2nd ed., 1951.

Doctrines and Discipline of The Methodist Church.

Dombrowski, James. *The Early Days of Christian Socialism in America.* New York: Columbia University Press, 1936.

Douglass, Paul F. *The Story of German Methodism: Biography of an Immigrant Soul.* New York: The Methodist Book Concern, 1939.

Gabriel, Ralph Henry. *The Course of American Democratic Thought.* New York: The Ronald Press, 2nd ed., 1956.

Harmon, Nolan B. *The Organization of the Methodist Church.* Nashville: Methodist Publishing House, revised ed., 1953.

Herberg, Will. *Protestant-Catholic-Jew. An Essay in American Religious Sociology.* Garden City, New York: Doubleday and Company, Inc., 1955.

Hofstadter, Richard. *The American Political Tradition.* New York: A. A. Knopf, 1951.

_____. *Social Darwinism in American Thought, 1860-1915.* Revised Edition. Boston: Beacon Press, 1955.

Hopkins, Charles Howard. *The Rise of the Social Gospel in American Protestantism 1865-1915.* New Haven: Yale University Press. London: H. Milford, Oxford University Press, 1940.

Johnson, F. Ernest. *The Church and Society.* Nashville: Abingdon Press, 1935.

_____. *Well-springs of the American Spirit.* New York: Harper and Brothers, 1948.

McConnell, Francis John. *By the Way.* Nashville: Abingdon Press, 1952.

Martin, Isaac Patton. *History of Methodism in the Holston Conference.* Knoxville: Methodist Historical Society, 1944.

Merton, Robert E. (ed.). *Reader in Democracy.* Glencoe, Illinois: The Free Press, 1952.

Miller, Robert Moats. *American Protestantism and Social Issues.* Chapel Hill: University of North Carolina Press, 1958.

Moore, John M. *The Long Road to Methodist Union.* Nashville: Abingdon Press, 1943.

Muelder, Walter George. *Foundations of the Responsible Society.* Nashville: Abingdon Press, 1959.

Oxnam, G. Bromley. *I Protest.* New York: Harper and Brothers, 1954.

Shelton, Arthur E. "The Methodist Church and Industrial Workers in the Southern Soft Coal Fields." Unpublished doctoral dissertation, Boston University, 1950.

Simon, Herbert A. *Administrative Behavior.* Second Edition Revised. New York: The Macmillan Company, 1957.

Smith, S. Raynor, Jr. "The Attitudes and Practices of the Methodist Church in California with Reference to Certain Significant Social Crises, 1847 through 1949." Unpublished dissertation, University of Southern California, 1955.

Smith, Timothy. *Revivalism and Social Reform.* Nashville: Abingdon Press, 1958.

Spann, J. Richard (ed.). *The Church and Social Responsibility.* Nashville: Abingdon Press, 1953.

Sweet, William Warren. *Methodism in American History.* Nashville: Abingdon Press, 1933.

Thacker, Ernest W. "The Methodist Church in Southern California in Relation to the Social Gospel 1928 through 1941." Unpublished doctoral dissertation, University of Southern California, 1952.

Tippy, Worth M. (ed.). *The Socialized Church.* New York: Eaton and Mains, 1909.

Troeltsch, Ernst. *The Social Teaching of the Christian Churches.* 2 vols. Translated by Olive Wyon. New York: The Macmillan Company, 1931.

Ward, Harry F. (ed.). *Social Ministry.* New York: Eaton and Mains, 1910.

Yinger, J. Milton. *Religion in the Struggle for Power.* Durham; North Carolina: Duke University Press, 1946.

_____. *Religion, Society, and the Individual*. New York: The Macmillan Co., 1957.

Rights and Liberties

Barth, Alan. *The Loyalty of Free Men*. New York: Pocket Books, 1952.

Bates, M. Searle. *Religious Liberty: An Inquiry*. New York: Harper and Brothers, 1945.

Chafee, Zechariah, Jr. *The Blessings of Liberty*. Philadelphia: J. B. Lippincott Company, 1956.

Cushman, Robert E. *Civil Liberties in the United States*. Ithaca, New York: Cornell University Press, 1956.

Green, James F. *The United Nations and Human Rights*. Washington, D. C.: The Brookings Institution, 1956.

Macarthur, Kathleen W. *The Bible and Human Rights*. New York: Whiteside, Inc., 1948.

Oxnam, G. Bromley. *I Protest*. New York: Harper and Brothers, 1954.

President's Committee on Civil Rights. *To Secure These Rights*. New York: Simon and Schuster, 1947.

Rall, Harris Franklin, et al. *Religion and Public Affairs*. New York: Macmillan Company, 1937.

Marriage and the Family

Anshen, Ruth Nanda (ed.). *The Family: Its Function and Destiny*. New York: Harper and Brothers, 1957.

Bertocci, Peter. *The Human Venture in Sex, Love, and Marriage*. New York: Association Press, 1951.

Bowman, Henry A. *Marriage for Moderns*. New York: McGraw-Hill Book Company, 1954.

Duvall, Evelyn M. *Family Living*. New York: Macmillan Company, 1955.

Groves, Ernest R. and Groves, Gladys H. *The Contemporary American Family*. Philadelphia: J. B. Lippincott Company, 1947.

Hess, Robert D. and Handel, Gerald. *Family Worlds: A Psychosocial Approach to Family Life*. Chicago: University of Chicago Press, 1959.

In Holy Matrimony. Nashville: The Methodist Publishing House, 1958.

Jacobson, Paul. *American Marriage and Divorce*. New York: Rinehart and Company, 1959.

Johnson, Paul E. *Christian Love*. New York: Abingdon-Cokesbury Press, 1946.

Lewinsohn, Richard, M.D. *A History of Sexual Customs*. New York: Harper and Brothers, 1958.

Maynard, Donald M. *Looking Toward Christian Marriage*. Nashville: Abingdon Press, 1958.

_____. *Your Home Can Be Christian*. Nashville: Abingdon Press, 1952.

Merrill, Francis E. *Courtship and Marriage*. Revised Edition. New York: Henry Holt and Company, 1959.

Miller, Haskell M. *Understanding and Preventing Juvenile Delinquency*. Nashville: Abingdon Press, 1959.

Mudd, Emily H., et. al. *Marriage Counseling: A Casebook*. New York: Association Press, 1958.

Nimkoff, Myer F. *Marriage and the Family*. Boston: Houghton Mifflin Company, 1947.

Parsons, Talcott and Bales, Robert F. *Family, Socialization and Inter-action Process.* Glencoe, Illinois: Free Press, 1955.

The Pastor's Manual for Premarital Counseling. Nashville: The Methodist Publishing House, 1958.

Werner, Hazen G. *Christian Family Living.* Nashville: Abingdon Press. Copyright 1958, The Graded Press.

Zietz, Dorothy: *Child Welfare, Principles and Methods.* New York: John Wiley and Sons, Inc., 1959.

Race Relations

Alexander, W. W. *Racial Segregation in the American Protestant Church.* New York: Friendship Press, 1946.

Ashmore, Harry S. *An Epitaph for Dixie.* New York: W. W. Norton, 1958.

Brown, Robert R. *Bigger Than Little Rock.* Greenwich, Conn.: Seabury Press, 1958.

Campbell, Ernest Q. and Pettigrew, Thomas F. *Christians in Racial Crisis: A Study of Little Rock's Ministry.* Washington, D. C.: Public Affairs Press, 1959.

Coleman, James S. *Community Conflict.* Glencoe, Illinois: Free Press, 1957.

Culver, Dwight W. *Negro Segregation in the Methodist Church.* New Haven: Yale University Press, 1953.

Davis, Allison W., Gardner, B. B., and Gardner, M. R. *Deep South.* Chicago: University of Chicago Press, 1941.

Dollard, John. *Caste and Class in a Southern Town.* New Haven: Yale University Press, 1957.

Gallagher, Buell G. *Color and Conscience: The Irrepressible Conflict.* New York: Harper and Brothers, 1946.

Haselden, Kyle. *The Racial Problem in Christian Perspective.* New York: Harper and Brothers, 1959.

Hill, Herbert and Greenberg, Jack. *Citizen's Guide to De-segregation.* Boston: Beacon Press, 1955.

King, Martin Luther, Jr. *Stride Toward Freedom.* New York: Harper and Brothers, 1958.

Loescher, Frank. *The Protestant Church and the Negro.* New York: Association Press, 1948.

Myrdal, Gunnar. *An American Dilemma.* New York: Harper and Brothers, 1944.

Pettigrew, T. F. and Campbell, Ernest Q. *Christians in Racial Crisis.* Washington, D. C.: Public Affairs Press, 1959.

Pope, Liston. *The Kingdom Beyond Caste.* New York: Friendship Press, 1957.

Richardson, Harry V. *Dark Glory.* New York: Friendship Press, 1947.

Simpson, G. E. and Yinger, J. Milton. *Racial and Cultural Minorities.* New York: Harper and Brothers, 1953.

Soper, Edmund D. *Racism: A World Issue.* New York: Abingdon-Cokesbury Press, 1947.

Wogaman, Philip. *Methodism's Challenge in Race Relations.* Washington, D. C.: Public Affairs Press, 1960.

Woofter, Thomas J. *Southern Race Progress.* Washington, D. C.: Public Affairs Press, 1959.

Prohibition—Temperance

Alcohol, Science, and Society. Twenty-nine lectures with discussion as given at the Yale Summer School of Alcohol Studies. New Haven: *Quarterly Journal of Studies on Alcohol,* 1945.

Alcoholics Anonymous, The Story of How Many Thousands of Men and Women Have Recovered from Alcoholism. New York: Works Publishing, Inc., 1950.

Allen, Joseph Land. "The Methodist Board of Temperance as an Instrument of Church Policy." Unpublished doctoral dissertation, Yale University, 1957.

Clinebell, Howard J., Jr. *Understanding and Counseling the Alcoholic.* Nashville: Abingdon Press, 1956.

Earle, Clifford. *Alcohol and Christian Responsibility.* Philadelphia: Department of Social Education and Action, Board of Christian Education, Presbyterian Church in the U. S. A., n.d.

Dabney, Virginia. *Dry Messiah.* New York: Knopf, 1949.

Dahl, Robert A. and Lindblom, Charles E. *Politics, Economics, and Welfare.* New York: Harper and Brothers, 1953.

Gordon, Ernest. *The Wrecking of the Eighteenth Amendment.* Francestown, N. H.: The Alcohol Information Press, 1943.

Haggard, H. W. and Jellinek, E. M. *Alcohol Explored.* Garden City, New York: Doubleday & Company, Inc., 1942.

Hirsch, Joseph. *The Problem Drinker.* New York: Duell, Sloan and Pearce, 1949.

Hammaker, Wilbur E. *Drinking—Right or Wrong?* Columbus, Ohio: School and College Service, 1949.

King, Albion Roy. *Basic Information on Alcohol.* Mount Vernon, Iowa: Cornell College Press, 1953.

McCarthy, Raymond G. *Alcohol and Social Responsibility.* New York: Thomas Y. Crowell Company, 1949.

The Methodist Church in Action Against Alcohol. Washington, D. C.: The Board of Temperance, 1950.

Pickett, Deets. *Some Notes on the Alcohol Problem.* New York: Abingdon-Cokesbury Press, 1947.

Pickett, Deets. *Temperance and the Changing Liquor Situation.* New York: The Methodist Book Concern, 1934.

Powdermaker, Hortense. *After Freedom: A Cultural Study of the Deep South.* New York: The Viking Press, 1937.

Prohibition: A National Experiment. Edited by James H. S. Bossard and Thorsten Sellin. Vol. 163, September 1932, of the *Annuals of the American Academy of Political and Social Science.* Philadelphia: The American Academy of Political and Social Science, 1932.

Straus, Robert and Bacon, Selden D. *Drinking in College.* New Haven: Yale University Press, 1953.

Tilson, Everett. *Should Christians Drink?* Nashville: Abingdon Press, 1957.

Wilson, Clarence True. *Dry or Die: The Anglo-Saxon Dilemma.* Topeka, Kansas: The Temperance Society of the Methodist Episcopal Church, 1913.

Young, Pauline. *Scientific Social Surveys and Research.* Second Edition. New York: Prentice-Hall, Inc., 1949.

Industry and Labor

Bennett, John C., *et al. Christian Values and Economic Life.* New York: Harper and Brothers, 1954.

Bowen, Howard R. *Social Responsibilities of the Business Man.* New York: Harper and Brothers, 1953.

Cordiner, Ralph Jarron. *New Frontiers for Professional Managers.* New York: McGraw-Hill Book Company, Inc., 1956.

Donham, W. B. *Business Adrift.* Washington, D. C.: Brookings Institution, 1931.

Federal Council of Churches. *Pronouncements on Religion and Economic Life.* New York: Federal Council of Churches, 1947.

Fitch, John A. *Social Responsibilities of Organized Labor.* New York: Harper and Brothers, 1957.

Hacker, Louis Morton. *American Problems of Today.* Washington, D. C.: Brookings Institution, 1938.

————— and Kendrick, B. B. *The United States Since 1865.* Washington, D. C.: Brookings Institution, 1932.

Hardin, E. W. *The Attitude of the Methodist Episcopal Church, South, in North Carolina toward the Textile Industry in North Carolina.* B. D. thesis, Duke University, 1938.

Johnson, F. Ernest. *The Social Gospel Re-examined.* New York: Harper and Brothers, 1940.

Johnson, F. Ernest and Ackerman, J. Emory. *The Church as Employer, Money-Raiser, and Investor.* New York: Harper and Brothers, 1959.

May, Henry F. *Protestant Churches and Industrial America.* New York: Harper and Brothers, 1949.

Muelder, Walter G. *Religion and Economic Responsibility.* New York: Charles Scribner's Sons, 1953.

Oxnam, G. Bromley. *Labor and Tomorrow's World.* Nashville: Abingdon Press 1945.

Perlman, S. and Taft, P. *History of Labor in the United States, 1896-1932.* New York: The Macmillan Company, 1935.

Peterson, Florence. *American Labor Unions.* New York: Harper and Brothers, 1945.

Pope, Liston, *Millhands and Preachers.* New Haven: Yale University Press, 1942.

Root, Edward T. *The Bible Economy of Plenty.* New York: Harper and Brothers, 1939.

Shannon, F. A. *America's Economic Growth.* New York: The Macmillan Company, 1951.

United Steel Workers of America. *Work for Rights.* Pittsburgh, Pennsylvania, 1958.

Ward, A. Dudley (ed.). *Goals of Economic Life.* New York: Harper and Brothers, 1953.

Agriculture

Loomis, C. P. and Beagle, J. A. *Rural Social Systems.* New York: Prentice-Hall, 1950.

McConnell, Grant. *The Decline of Agrarian Democracy.* Berkeley: University of California Press, 1953.

Rich, M. *The Rural Church Movement.* Columbia, Missouri: Juniper Knoll Press, 1937.

Schmucker, Calvin. *How to Plan the Rural Church Program.* Philadelphia: The Westminster Press, 1954.

Seifert, Harvey. *The Church in Community Action.* Nashville: Abingdon Press, 1952.

Smith, Rockwell C. *People, Land, and Churches.* New York: Friendship Press, 1959.

Vidich, A. J. and Bensman, Joseph. *Small Town in Mass Society.* Princeton: Princeton University Press, 1958.

Warren, R. *Studying Your Community.* New York: Russell Sage Foundation, 1955.

Wilcox, W. W. *Social Responsibility in Farm Leadership: An Analysis of Farm Problems and Farm Leadership in Action.* New York: Harper and Brothers, 1956.

The State

Bennett, John C. *The Christian as Citizen.* New York: Association Press, 1955.

————. *Christians and the State.* New York: Charles Scribner's Sons, 1958.

Cullmann, Oscar. *The State in the New Testament.* New York: Charles Scribner's Sons, 1956.

Ebersole, Luke. *Church Lobbying in the Nation's Capitol.* New York: The Macmillan Company, 1951.

Ehrenstrom, Nils. *Christian Faith and the Modern State.* Chicago: Willett, Clark and Company, 1937.

Hutchinson, Paul. *The New Leviathan.* Chicago: Willett, Clark and Company, 1946.

Johnson, F. Ernest (ed.). *American Education and Religion: The Problem of Religion in the Schools.* New York: Harper and Brothers, 1952.

High, Stanley. *The Church in Politics.* New York and London: Harper and Brothers, 1930.

Methodist Pronouncements Compared with Political Platforms. New York: Methodist Federation for Social Action, 1948.

Miller, Randolph C. (ed.). *The Church and Organized Movements.* The Interseminary Series, Vol. II. New York: Harper and Brothers, 1946.

Nelson, Claud D. *Church and State.* New York: National Council of Churches of Christ in the U.S.A., 1953.

Pfeffer, Leo. *Church, State and Freedom.* Boston: Beacon Press, 1953.

Stokes, Anson Phelps. *Church and State in the United States.* 3 vols. New York: Harper and Brothers, 1950.

Communism

Adamic, Louis. *Dynamite: the Story of Class Violence in America.* New York: Viking Press, 1934.

Corey, Lewis. *The Decline of American Capitalism.* New York: Covici-Friede, 1924.

Hordern, William. *Christianity, Communism, and History.* Nashville: Abingdon Press, 1954.

Hunt, R. N. Carew. *The Theory and Practice of Communism*. New York: Macmillan Company, 1951, revised.

Jones, E. Stanley. *Christ's Alternative to Communism*. Nashville: Abingdon Press, 1935.

MacKinnon, O. M. (ed.). *Christian Faith and Communist Faith*. New York: St. Martin's Press, 1953.

Rogers, Edward A. *A Commentary on Communism*. New York: Frederick A. Praeger, Inc., 1951.

Stouffer, Samuel A. *Communism, Conformity, and Civil Liberties*. Garden City, New York: Doubleday and Company, 1955.

World Order

Abrams, Ray H. *Preachers Present Arms*. Philadelphia: Round Table Press, Inc., 1933.

Boss, Charles F., Jr. *Conscription and the Christian Testimony*. Chicago: Commission on World Peace, 1946.

Butterfield, Herbert. *Christianity, Diplomacy, and War*. Nashville: Abingdon Press, n.d.

Cadoux, C. J. *Christian Pacifism Re-examined*. Oxford: Basil Blackwell and Mott, 1940.

Commission of the Churches in International Affairs, August, 1951.

Conscience and the War. A Report on the Treatment of Conscientious Objectors in World War II. New York: American Civil Liberties Union, 1943.

Cranston, Earl. *Swords or Ploughshares*. New York: The Abingdon Press, 1937.

Gladden, James W. *The Methodist Church and the Problem of War and Peace: An Analysis in Social Understanding*. A reprint of an abstract of a doctoral dissertation, *University of Pittsburgh Bulletin*.

Grant, Robert M. *The Sword and the Cross*. New York: The Macmillan Company, 1955.

Hamilton, A. I. *Students Against War*. Published by the National Council of the Methodist Youth and the World Peace Commission, 1937.

Hutchison, John A. *We Are Not Divided*. New York: Round Table Press, Inc., 1941.

Jones, Rufus M. (ed.). *The Church, the Gospel, and War*. New York: Harper and Brothers, 1948.

Knudson, A. C. *The Philosophy of War and Peace*. Nashville: Abingdon Press, 1947.

Lee, Umphrey. *The Historic Church and Modern Pacifism*. Nashville: Abingdon-Cokesbury Press, 1943.

Niebuhr, Reinhold. *Christianity and Power Politics*. New York: Charles Scribner's Sons, 1940.

————. *Why the Christian Church Is Not Pacifist*. London: Student Christian Movement Press, 1940.

Nuelson, John L. *Der Methodismus in Deutschland nach dem Krieg*. Bremen: Buchhandlung und Verlag der Traktathauses, n.d.

Oxnam, G. Bromley and Boss, Charles F., Jr. *When Hostilities Cease*. Chicago: Commission on World Peace, 1941.

Raven, Charles E. *The Theological Basis of Christian Pacifism*. New York: Fellowship of Reconciliation, 1951.

Rutenber, Culbert G. *The Dagger and the Cross.* New York: Fellowship of Reconciliation, 1950.

Smith, S. Raynor, Jr. "The Attitudes and Practices of the Methodist Church in California with Reference to Certain Significant Social Crises." Unpublished dissertation, University of Southern California, 1955.

World Council of Churches. *Evanston Speaks: Reports of the Second Assembly of the World Council of Churches:* August 15-31, 1954. New York: World Council of Churches, 1954.

World Council of Churches. *The First Assembly of the World Council of Churches: The Official Report.* New York: Harper and Brothers, 1949.

World Council of Churches. *Minutes and Reports of the Tenth Meeting of the Central Committee of the World Council of Churches,* July-August, 1957.

General Index

Acceptance of Christian concern, 5-15
Action, social, 5-10, 13, 23-37, 45, 49, 51, 130-35, 137, 213-28, 369, 370-72, 411-13
Agricultural problems, 130-31, 134, 317, 349, 353-57
Alcoholism, 24, 31, 72-73, 116-21, 297-300, 339-43, 402-3, 250
Anti-saloon League, 64-69, 299-300
Atomic energy, use of, 205
Attitudes under prohibition, 339-43

Birth control, 54, 175
Board of Education, 295
Board of Hospitals and Homes, 308-11
Board of Lay Activities, 296
Board of Publications, 292-93
Board of Social and Economic Relations, 13, 24, 216, 223-27, 323, 330, 365
Board of Temperance, 297-300
Business ethics, 41, 44-45

Canadian co-operation, 188
Capitalism, growth, 44-46; threatened, 33, 60, 139, 369
Chamber of Commerce, U.S., 229
Change, social, 5-7, 10, 388-91
Chaplains, 152
Charities council, 58
Child labor, 55, 60-64, 74
Chinese Exclusion Act, 39
Christian Citizenship, Department of, 25
Church in economic relations, 405-9
Church of God, 110
Church Peace Union, 80-81
Commission on World Peace, 157

435

438

Index of Persons

Abrams, R. H., 80
Ackerman, J. E., 405
Adamic, Louis, 97
Allen, Frederick L., 26, 138
Andrews, Bishop, 40
Arnold, Thurman, 117
Ashmore, Harry S., 254
Atkins, Gaius G., 28

Baer, George F., 46
Baker, James C., 164, 170, 207
Baker, R. S., 45, 207
Barnett, Albert, 226
Barth, Alan, 205
Bartlett, Dorothy, 288
Barton, Bruce, 94
Baruch, Bernard, 95
Bates, E. S., 27
Becker, Carl L., 26
Bender, Mrs. C. A., 288
Bennett, John C., 180, 214
Billings, Warren, 84
Blake, Edgar, 168
Bosley, Harold, 187
Boss, Charles F., Jr., 157
Bourne, R. S., 80, 93
Bowie, W. R., 148
Brashares, C. W., 357
Bryan, William J., 46, 47
Bryce, Lord, 59
Brown, Charles F., Jr., 157
Bucke, Emory S., 221

Cadman, S. Parks, 148
Callen, E. Glenn, 274